Nathalie Sarraute
and the Feminist Reader

Nathalie Sarraute and the Feminist Reader

Identities in Process

Sarah Barbour

Lewisburg
Bucknell University Press
London and Toronto: Associated University Presses

Associated University Presses
440 Forsgate Drive
Cranbury, NJ 08512

Associated University Presses
25 Sicilian Avenue
London WC1A 2QH, England

Associated University Presses
P.O. Box 338, Port Credit
Mississauga, Ontario,
Canada L5G 4L8

The paper used in this publication meets the requirements
of the American National Standard for Permanence of Paper
for Printed Library Materials Z39.48-1984.

*PQ
2637
.A783
Z57
1993*

Library of Congress Cataloging-in-Publication Data

Barbour, Sarah.
  Nathalie Sarraute and the feminist reader : identities in process
/ Sarah Barbour.
    p. cm.
  ISBN 0-8387-5235-7
    1. Sarraute, Nathalie—Criticism and interpretation.   2. Feminism
and literature—France—History—20th century.   3. Authors and
readers—France—History—20th century.   4. Identity (Psychology) in
literature.   5. Reader-response criticism.   6. Sex role in
literature.   I. Title.
PQ2637.A783Z57   1993
843'.914—dc20   92-52716
                                                        CIP

106-93

for my parents

Contents

Acknowledgments

Nathalie Sarraute and the Feminist Reader is a work that took shape over time: the time of graduate school, professors and friends in Ithaca, New York, and the time of teaching, colleagues and friends in Winston-Salem, North Carolina. My thanks go to Nelly Furman for introducing me to the works of Nathalie Sarraute in the early 1980s and for extending her support and encouragement during the writing of the dissertation. David Grossvogel has also sustained me over the years, offering a model for the way in which literary criticism and creativity are part of the same process. The completion of the manuscript would have taken much longer without Elizabeth Phillips's scrupulous reading and insightful comments, and Eva Rodtwitt provided an equally rigorous critique of my English translations of French passages; both of these friends were especially steadfast during the final stages. I am also endebted to Kari Weil and Mary DeShazer for, among other things, their comments on the introduction, and to the participants of the "Feminism and/in French Literature" conference at the University of South Carolina for their feedback on a version of Chapter 2. I was bound to write this book because it had been on my mind for a long time, but I am grateful to Germaine Brée for offering me the encouragement to write it the way I wanted to.

Other friends also joined directly and indirectly in the conversations necessary to bring these thoughts to life; among them, I would like to thank Susan Henderson, Jane Dickinson, Rachel Dickinson, Lucrecia Freebairn, Nancy Sokol, Julian Euell, Tama Engelking, Barbara Clark, Victoria Bridges, Pam Olano, Gillian Overing, Mary Friedman, Anna Krauth, Byron Wells, Teri Marsh, Susan Leonard, and Sarah Watts. My thanks to Tom Mullen and Ed Wilson for their support of my leave request, and to Wake Forest University for granting me the time necessary to prepare the manuscript. Cathy Harris deserves a special thanks for enduring my frantic moments during the final printing, as do the editors at Associated University Presses for doing so well the work that editors do. I would like to thank Sarraute's publishers, Editions de Minuit and Gallimard, for their kind permission to reprint passages from her works. And finally, this book could have been written without the encouragement and support of my longtime friend, Michael Rambo, I just would not have enjoyed it as much.

Nathalie Sarraute
and the Feminist Reader

Introduction

Nathalie Sarraute situates her work within a tradition of psychological realism at the same time that she proposes radical innovations of that tradition. She maintains these two positions simultaneously because she conceives of the evolution of the novel as a movement through history. Thus her novels do not discard or revise past works but rather they internalize them in an effort to expand the notion of what is possible for psychological realism. In addition, as one of her latest critics observes, her novels also set up a system for making meaning which relies on simultaneous references to a variety of socio-cultural registers.[1]

The following study of seven of Sarraute's novels aspires to a similar simultaneity in relation to the resonances which they provoke for a feminist reader reading through time. It takes as its model Sarraute's concept of simultaneity, which invites an understanding of time both as a diachronic movement through "phases," from the psychological realism of Dostoyevski to that of Kafka to her own; and as a synchronic encounter, which elicits simultaneous relationships to different "phases."

When Sarraute compiled the prose pieces she had been writing since 1932 into a volume entitled *Tropismes*, publishers did not have such a generous concept of the evolution of literature. "Ce qui m'étonnait," Sarraute later notes, "c'est qu'à une ou deux exceptions près, personne ne voyait ce qui me paraissait évident. Le livre s'est promené d'éditeur en éditeur de 1937 à 1939 avant d'être publié par Robert Denoël" [What surprised me was that with one or two exceptions, no one saw what appeared to me to be obvious. The book was dragged around from publisher to publisher from 1937 to 1939 before being published by Robert Denoël].[2] What seemed "évident" to Sarraute was the psychological reality of "tropisms," the term she borrows from biology to describe "certaines actions intérieures" [certain interior actions], "des mouvement indéfinissables qui glissent très rapidement aux limites de notre conscience [et qui] sont à l'origine de nos gestes, de nos paroles" [the indefinable movements that slip by very rapidly at the limits of our consciousness (and which) are at the origin of our gestures, of our words].[3]

Sarraute soon decided to represent tropistic reality in the longer form of the novel, showing "someone who seeks out these tropisms through two semblances, characters externally resembling traditional ones [. . .]." The result was *Portrait d'un inconnu*, written during and after World War II, and its "continuation," *Martereau*. Both novels present narrators who serve as the "center" from which tropisms radiate, and both received the same reception as her first work. Sarraute continues:

> During that time, I lived in almost complete solitude from a literary point of view, and I thought that it would be interesting to find out why these novels didn't awaken even a slight echo since no editor had accepted *Le Portrait d'un inconnu* even with a preface by Sartre. With a good deal of difficulty, one was found who sold the novel for the price of the paper. After getting rid of 400 copies, I didn't have a cent, and I said to myself, "Why do I feel that I'm going in the right direction and that it is not possible to give in and write in the traditional manner?"[4]

Sarraute published two articles in *Les Temps Modernes* in 1947 and 1950, in an effort to explain the necessity for radical changes in the form of the novel, but "it all fell on deaf ears": "The word 'traditional' didn't mean a thing to anybody. There was the novel, that's all." In her collection of essays published in 1956, *L'Ere du soupçon*, Sarraute presented not only the particular innovations of form necessary for a literary re-presentation of tropistic reality, but through a re-reading of certain of her predecessors she also showed how her novels were the next step in the evolution of that genre. "*L'Ere du soupçon* received rather wide acclaim," Sarraute reports, "probably, the situation having changed, the time was ripe, [. . .] it interested the critics and the readers much more than my other books."[5]

In his preface to *Portrait d'un inconnu*, Sartre labels it an "anti-roman" and compares it to *Les Faux monnayeurs* by André Gide, as well as to the works of Vladimir Nabokov and Evelyn Waugh: "[Il] s'agit de contester le roman par lui-même, de le détruire sous nos yeux dans le temps qu'on semble l'édifier, d'écrire le roman d'un roman qui ne se fait pas, qui ne peut pas se faire. Ces oeuvres étranges et difficilement classables ne témoignent pas de la faiblesse du genre romanesque, elles marquent seulement que nous vivons à une époque de réflexion et que le roman est en train de se réfléchir" [(It) has to do with the novel contesting itself, with destroying itself before our eyes at the very moment that it seems to be constructing itself, with writing the novel about a novel that is not there, that cannot be there. These strange and difficultly classifiable works do not demonstrate the weakness of the genre, they merely demonstrate that we are living in an age of reflexion and that the novel is in the process of reflecting on itself].[6]

The self-reflection and self-consciousness that Sartre identified were among the fundamental characteristics that critics attributed to what was soon called the *nouveau roman* [new novel] group. In 1957 Sarraute's first two novels were reissued. Their self-questioning narrators, as well as the diverse narrative voices in her third novel, *Le Planétarium* (1959), established Sarraute's work as emblematic of this unconventional form. When the first book-length critical work on Sarraute appeared in France in 1965, she had already won the *Prix International Littéraire* in 1963 for her fourth novel, *Les Fruits d'Or*.[7] With Alain Robbe-Grillet, Michel Butor, Claude Simon, and others, Nathalie Sarraute had become established as the "pionnière du nouveau roman," the founding member of a new group of novelists.[8]

This "story" of Sarraute's early years as a writer (1932–1965), linear in its approach, underlines the interest in time that lies at the heart of the following study of her novels. This interest is taken not to trace Sarraute's "evolution" as a writer—other studies do that well enough— but rather as a way to discuss sarrautien criticism as its evolution parallels the innovations in form found in her novels, and feminist literary criticism in the United States as it has developed over time.

The terms *develop* and *evolution* suggest a notion of time as "project, teleology, departure, progression and arrival," "the time of history,"[9] and a movement toward a "fuller, greater, or better state," "a gradual process by which something changes in a significantly different, especially more sophisticated, form."[10] This is the sense in which Sarraute and her fellow *nouveaux romanciers* used these terms, but their sense of the "telos" of the novel's evolution is not as fixed as the above denotations suggest.

Read, for example, Sarraute's comments in *L'Ere du soupçon* on the innovations in style found in the work of Ivy Compton Burnett: "[. . .] il est évident que cette technique, comme aussi toutes les autres, paraîtra un jour prochain ne pouvoir plus décrire que l'apparence. Et rien n'est plus reconfortant et plus stimulant que cette pensée. Ce sera le signe que tout est pour le mieux, que la vie continue et qu'il faut non pas revenir en arrière, mais s'efforcer d'aller plus avant" [[. . .] it is obvious that this technique, like all the others, will seem one fine day to describe nothing other than appearances. And nothing is more comforting and more stimulating than that thought. That will be the sign that all is for the best, that life continues and that we must not retrace our steps, but force ourselves to go even further forward].[11]

Robbe-Grillet's reflection on his "predecessors" in his own collection of essays, *Pour un Nouveau Roman*, articulates the same idea from the opposite direction: "Flaubert écrivait le nouveau roman de 1860, Proust le nouveau roman de 1910. L'écrivain doit accepter avec orgueil de porter sa propre date, sachant qu'il n'y a pas de chef-d'oeuvre dans l'éternité, mais seulement des oeuvres dans l'histoire; et qu'elles ne se survivent que dans la mesure où elles ont laissé derrière elles le passé, et annoncé l'avenir" [Flaubert wrote the new novel of 1860, Proust the new novel of 1910. The writer must accept with pride to carry his own date with him, knowing that there is not a *chef d'oeuvre* for eternity, but only works in history; and that they only survive because they have left the past behind them and announce the future].[12]

These remarks represent a call for change, but rather than proposing an image of "departure and arrival," both suggest a spiral that ascends with the age of the world. The "telos" is not considered a final point of completion; it is merely a proposed end, in the case of the novelist to represent reality as it is perceived at a point in time. "As for me," Sarraute tells Germaine Brée in an interview in 1973, "after reading Proust and Joyce, which I did between 1922 and 1924, and then reading Virginia Woolf, I felt that it was no longer possible to write as people had done previously [. . .]."[13] This recognition envisions a line which connects her novels to those of the past and moves ever onward in a constant re-evaluation of the form the novel takes at continually changing points in time. Thus when asked if she agreed that Sartre's term "anti-roman" applied to her novels, Sarraute responded, "Non, parce qu'elle vient de l'idée que Sartre se faisait de ce que doit être un roman" [No, because it comes from the idea that Sartre had about what a novel must be].[14]

This evolutionary notion of the novel necessarily rubs off on the work of the critic, as seen in A. S. Newman's remarks in an article about *Le Planétarium*: "I do not have [. . .] a shining new 1973 critical model for which you should trade in your old. I simply wish to propose that evolving attitudes in literary production call for, may require, matching attitudes in literary reception."[15] Newman proposes a "new criticism" for reading Sarraute's novels which is a strictly formalist analysis of the levels and variety of "discours" found there. His approach shows how her novels evolve from a relatively descriptive style to a more performative one.

The problematization of linearity found in the works of the *nouveau romanciers* issues from a changing notion of the literary text itself, which represents an investigation of what has been considered literature's mimetic relationship to lived reality. The innovations in form enacted by these works constitute a reflection on the act of creation and of making meaning as it effects a more reciprocal perception of the relationship between art and reality. Some of Sarraute's critics read the attention to literary creation in her novels as an invitation to look for her own evolution as a writer through an analysis of her narrators or narrating voices.[16] As Newman also notes, however, the self-reflection in Sarraute's novels implicates the reader, as is perhaps best described in the quote he cites from Roland Barthes's early writings: "En effet, le problème n'est pas d'introspecter les motifs du narrateur ni les effets que la narration produit sur le lecteur: il est de décrire le code à travers lequel narrateur et lecteur sont signifiés le long du récit lui-même" [In effect, the problem is not to second guess the motives of the narrator or the effects that the narration produces in the reader: it is to describe the code by which narrator and reader are signified through the story itself].[17]

In a more recent study, *Sarraute Romancière: Espaces intimes*, Sabine Raffy further illuminates the concept of the subject found in Sarraute's work. This critic questions the validity of any "linear" approach that suggests an evolution in Sarraute's style or in her "personnages," because her work presents "une verticalité de l'être, que la chronologie oblitère" [a verticality of being that a chronology obliterates].[18] Raffy proposes to tell "quelque chose comme une histoire synchronique" [something like a synchronic story]. By means of "une superposition d'approches critiques tirées de disciplines différentes" [a superimposition of critical approaches drawn from different disciplines], Raffy hopes to remain true to what she calls the "épaisseur subjective" [subjective thickness] of Sarraute's characters as they are constituted by similarly synchronic references to different systems of meaning.

From our point in time, we can recognize the difficulties Sarraute's work presented to the early critics as a failure to acknowledge the dilemma created by the shift which Barthes discerns and the "verticalité de l'être" noted by Raffy. This shift results from a blurring of the line between art as *that* and reality as *this*, because attention turns not to the (personal, sexual, literary) identity of the author of *those* lines but to the author of *these* lines that we as critics produce in relation and in reaction to reading. Sarraute's novels made critics self-conscious about their objectivity, while the studies by Newman, Raffy, and others of Sarraute's novels invite an investigation of the critic's own subjectivity. As Raffy's study suggests, the impersonal quality of Sarraute's "characters" and the overall absence of plot in the novels allow her readers to take stock of the synchronic nature of "l'épaisseur subjective" which creates our own "verticalité de l'être." The above narration of Sarraute's publishing career also highlights, however, that although the form of her novels forces our attention to the synchronic side of making meaning, the writing and reading of these novels is necessarily a diachronic activity, taking place in time and passing through time to create a "horizontal thickness" by which a reader's critical and personal subjectivity is likewise continually constituted.

The horizontal thickness of feminist literary criticism in the United States has contributed to my own critical "épaisseur subjective" since my first reading of Sarraute. Feminist literary criticism is founded in and maintained as a movement, both in the sense of a political activity and of a process. Following the movement of this criticism I, like other feminist critics, have been uncomfortable with the notion of an "evolution" "toward" some perfect end. The use of the word *toward* in the titles of articles since the 1970s marks both the desire for a theory and the firm belief that feminism moves more like a spiral, an image that parallels the one inspired by the *nouveau roman*. At a certain moment in feminist scholarship in the United States, for example, French feminist thought seemed to be "too theoretical" when it came to the conclusion that because language is patriarchal, women can only either speak men's language or remain silent. And while feminists in this country were reviving "lost" texts and searching for what was "different" about women's writing in order to create a "tradition of our own," French feminists could only repeat that we were reinscribing patriarchal notions.[19]

Feminist literary criticism in this country has more recently entered into a dialogue with French feminist theory, but as the feminist critic moves through time, often there is a strong desire to subscribe to a kind of linear thinking that says the most recent is the best or the "truest." Such a conclusion, like Sartre's term "l'anti-roman," presumes a fixed notion and obscures the fluidity inherent in the constitution of "l'épaisseur subjective" of a critic or a movement, in synchronic and diachronic, vertical and horizontal, terms. One way to rephrase the discussion is to consider Julia Kristeva's term *generations* of feminism. In her 1979 essay "Le Temps des Femmes," translated into English in 1981 as "Women's Time," Kristeva qualifies "generation" as a term which "implies less a chronology than a *signifying space*, a both corporeal and desiring mental space."[20]

Toril Moi observes in her introduction to an English translation of this essay that Kristeva distinguishes between the first wave of egalitarian feminists who demanded equal rights with men, that is, their right to a place in linear time, and the second generation's emphasis on "women's radical difference from men," which demanded women's right to remain outside the linear time of history and politics.[21] Kristeva and others argue, however, that second-generation feminism's valorization of what is named "the feminine" against "the masculine" tends to establish a "counter ideology" and risks reinscribing patriarchal dichotomies, linear/cyclical, analytical/intuitive, cultural/natural, which threaten women's access to subjecthood in the realm of the symbolic and in society as it exists today. For Kristeva, a third "attitude is possible, thus a third generation, which does not exclude [. . .] the *parallel* existence of all three in the same historical time, or even that they be interwoven one with the other."[22]

Sarraute has always disassociated herself from the feminist movement in France as it has been defined, and the feminists writing in France in the 1970s left Sarraute's works alone.[23] Among the studies in English, Gretchen Rous-Besser's identification of Sarraute as a "pioneer for feminine equality"[24] represents a moment in feminist criticism in this country that corresponds to Kristeva's "first generation," and Helen Watson-Williams's identification of "the unnameable vital force" in Sarraute's works that is "consistently expressed in the feminine gender"[25] invites a "second-generation" reading of elements of Sarraute's style as specifically feminine. Another critic, Valerie Minogue, prefers to dismiss any critique of women's roles in Sarraute's novels and returns the discussion of Sarraute's gender to a more "neutral" terrain, stating that "specific issues, such as sexual equality, are subsumed in a far more general concern with human truth—a concern characteristic of the French 'moraliste' tradition."[26] The critical desires reflected in the approach taken by Rous-Besser or in an analysis that addresses the feminine specificity of Sarraute's style are, however, (specific) desires that the "far more general concern with human truth" has systematically ignored. It is precisely that repression which makes these desires part of the feminist reader's "épaisseur subjective."

As feminists in the United States have begun to investigate the problematics of a position founded on either "women's radical difference from men" or on a valorization of the "feminine," there is often a tendency to repress the desires of the first and second generations which are represented by these positions. Those desires, however, will not go away as long as we are each following a personal chronology in an effort to understand ourselves as subjects within patriarchy. Sarraute's work offers the feminist reader not only a recognition of her own personal and critical "épaisseur subjective," which may maintain simultaneously positions of Kristeva's first and second generations, but also a reading experience in which Kristeva's "third attitude" is possible. Sarraute's style, especially her use of personal pronouns in the later novels, forces the reader out of the first two positions and breaks down "the dichotomy man/woman as an opposition of two rival entities." "The implacable difference," as Kristeva calls it, between these entities is thus experienced "in the very place where it operates with the maximum intransigence, in other words, in personal and sexual identity itself, so as to make it disintegrate in its very nucleus."[27]

The following study is linear, in part in relation to Sarraute's works, but also in relation to itself, and this is for two reasons. The first reason is because a recognition of my own critical "épaisseur subjective" took place over time; that is, from the late 70s through the 80s, when feminist literary critics in the United States started at each of the first two generations, staying at times and stopping at times, in an attempt to redefine women in patriarchy. Sometimes we can only recognize where we are when we look at where we have been. The second reason is that the manifestation of Kristeva's "third approach" in Sarraute's works is most fully appreciated when her earlier novels are read before her later ones.

The first chapter presents a review of the book-length critical studies on Sarraute in this country and in France from 1965 to 1988, or rather, it presents a "reading" of these studies in an effort to see where they suggest limits or points of entry for yet another reading of Nathalie Sarraute. The limits are given in part because of a critic's desire to lay fixed notions onto a very dynamic work. These are the same limits that a feminist reader encounters when she attempts to present Sarraute's (or any woman writer's) work as a model for what has been called "écriture féminine." I would like to leave this term oscillating between two translations for the moment, that is, "feminine writing" and "writing in the feminine," because each of these implies a different concept to be discussed later.[28] Points of entry are offered by critical studies which address Sarraute's novels in terms of the dynamic they enact between form and content. An attention to this aesthetic interrelationship opens onto the relationship of the reader to a text which feminist writers have made a political one.[29] The autobiographical narrative analysis in Chapter 2, of one of the prose pieces from Sarraute's first publication, *Tropismes*, dramatizes the issue of reading at the intersection of feminist critical practice in the United States and feminist culture theory in France.

Chapter 3 breaks with Sarraute's publishing chronology to investigate her fourth novel, *Les Fruits d'Or*, in which there are no characters, only voices discussing a novel in its rise and fall in popularity. The discourse of these voices ultimately reveals more about the tropistic movement of the narrative figures than about the object of their discussion. The problematics represented in this novel of the subject's relation to discourse characterizes my own investigation of the presence of gender in the other novels discussed. *Les Fruits d'Or* ends with the voice of one who has been called "an ideal reader." The voice speaks in the first person, but the few adjectives referring to this subject identify it as masculine. The qualities characterizing the ideal reader are represented throughout the novel by voices identified as feminine, but these figures have been repressed by other (usually masculine) voices.

The repression of what is identified as "feminine" in *Les Fruits d'Or* thus frames the discussion of Sarraute's first two novels in Chapter 4. *Portrait d'un inconnu* and *Martereau* are both narrated in the first person by young masculine figures who seek union with older masculine ones. This union depends upon the repression of feminine figures who alternately represent a feminine "lieu commun" [common place/commonplace] and one kind of tropistic perception. The narrator at the end of *Portrait* rises from tropistic depths to reside in "le lieu commun" where gender differences are represented by well-delineated roles. At the end of *Martereau*, however, the narrator recognizes that the single-dimensional mythic role he has drawn for Martereau cannot contain his "épaisseur subjective" because masculine and feminine traits as they are constructed in the novel can be arbitrarily assigned to either masculine or feminine figures.

Chapter 5 presents a discussion of gender difference as it is represented by the play of socio-sexual constructs which a variety of figures enact in Sarraute's third novel, *Le Planétarium*, and by the play of pronouns in her fifth, *Entre la vie et la mort*, where attention to gender constructs is displaced by a more active experience of difference in relation to discourse. An investigation of difference continues in Chapter 6 with a discussion of Sarraute's sixth and seventh novels, *Vous les entendez?* and *"disent les imbéciles,"* in which the dichotomy self-other, like the dichotomy masculine-feminine in the earlier novels, is ultimately broken apart.

Sarraute explains in the Preface to *L'Ere du soupçon* that her style came about as she sought to give the reader sensations analogous to the tropistic reality she perceived, but in the process, this style gives the feminist reader a place beneath or beyond the dichotomies that have never ceased to particularize her. The critical reflections in the final chapter focus on a comparison of Virginia Woolf and Nathalie Sarraute as a way of conceptualizing both the parallel existence of second and third generations of feminism and the critical/personal possibilities offered by the space Sarraute's style creates beyond gender. Like Virginia Woolf, Nathalie Sarraute can be criticized from a variety of feminist positions, but the juxtaposition of these two writers' works allows us to consider reception and reading, of ourselves and of others.

Following the lead that Sarraute's novels offer, I engage them as a reader who is also a feminist reader. By virtue of my background as a feminist critic and my investigation of my own subjectivity, I focus on the role that gender plays in her first seven novels. This is perilous territory for a reader of Sarraute because of the irony of her writing. Newman warns that nothing can be taken at "face value" in her work, "and this most importantly as regards the factors of *énonciation*: to whom can opinions expressed be attributed—author, character (which one?), or neither?" "There is no lack of examples of misreadings," he concludes, "arising from this irony."[30]

By virtue of the very impersonal quality of the narrative figures in these novels, the discourses represented there resonate within different systems of thought such that a concern with the origin of énonciation is displaced by the reader's own problematized process of making meaning. It is precisely this indeterminate quality which opens her novels up to so many readings, and if misreadings there are, I suspect they arise not only from the ambiguity of the origins of énonciation in the narration but also from a critic's unacknowledged attempt to attribute to the author that which the irony there elicits in the critic's very personal, tropistic experience of reading. If her novels reveal nothing else to any reader with an "agenda," however, psychoanalytic, existentialist, feminist or otherwise, they reveal, in their irony, the deadening "carapace" of critical grids.

It is thus within an investigation of the construction of gender that the following study is situated, for although Sarraute's work discourages an analysis based strictly on gender or strictly on anything, there are at the same time certain images and relationships which provoke and eventually problematize such a reading for the feminist reader. This reading of Sarraute's novels through the "time of feminism" is not made, however, in an effort to proclaim her work an example of "écriture féminine," nor do I wish to claim her as a "feminist" or a "woman writer." Reading Sarraute's novels in their "evolution," I have found that they forced my own reading to evolve. I therefore propose that they open up a space *beyond* the frozen shells of gender that continue to bind women and men personally and critically; this is a space in which we as readers are moved *toward* a more personal understanding of our use of narrative and of socio-sexual constructs in the continual, day-to-day constitution and reconstitution of subjectivity. The power of Sarraute's works lies in the solitary experience of our encounter with her presentation and perception of reality. In this encounter we are forced to experience the fluid nature of subjectivity—to internalize and explore the dimensions within personal and sexual identity which, by extension, affect the identity of larger political movements.

1

Critics Read Sarraute

During the 1960s in France, the *nouveaux romanciers* presented a univocal cry for a renewal of the novel's form; within their own circle, however, it was clear from the beginning that each was responding to a particular set of motivations. Sarraute's call for innovation grew out of her earliest efforts to express tropistic reality, which she identifies as "le psychologique" [the psychological]. The connotations of this term led her contemporaries and her critics to misunderstand her intentions.

Sarraute describes her first article, "De Dostoïevski à Kafka," as "a defense of psychology" which was misinterpreted as a defense of a traditional "analysis of feelings." She explains that she "wanted rather to state that there was a kind of psychology in movement, an inner world in movement, which should be brought to light—that people were wrong always to oppose Dostoevsky to Kafka because Kafka himself certainly had not been able to do without the inner world of the psyche."[1] "Qu'entendez-vous par psychologie?" she asked in 1962. "Si vous entendez par là, l'analyse des sentiments, la recherche des mobiles de nos actes, l'étude des 'caractères,' alors je crois qu'aujourd'hui une oeuvre romanesque non seulement ne peut pas être psychologique, mais encore qu'elle ne *doit* pas l'être. Mais si vous entendez par là, la création d'un univers mental, alors je ne connais aucune oeuvre littéraire et je n'en conçois aucune qui ne *soit* psychologique"[2] [What do you mean by psychology? If you mean an analysis of sentiments, a search for the motives behind our actions, the study of "character," then I think that a novelistic work not only can not be psychological, but that it *must* not be. But if you mean the creation of a mental universe, then I do not know of, nor can I conceive of, any literary work which is *not* psychological]. Sarraute believes that the novel represents an attempt to reveal a reality which she feels exists but that is as yet unknown, "le psychologique," and she clarifies her mimetic intention with a statement from Paul Klée: "L'art ne restitue pas le visible, il rend visible" [Art does not reconstitute the visible, it makes visible].[3] The dichotomy implied by her use of the term "le psychologique" was antithetical to the project of her fellow *nouveaux romanciers.*[4] For Robbe-Grillet, often cited as the theoretician of the *nouveau roman*, literature cannot be mimetic, it can only show surface reality "in the making."

Both Sarraute and Robbe-Grillet situate their projects against writing that seeks to "restituer le visible," but they differ in what they want to "rendre visible." The "univers mental" that Sarraute's writing presents lies between an imitation of a "known reality"—what she calls "le domaine de journalism," "la réalité dans laquelle [l'écrivain] vit, celle que tout le monde voit"[5] [the domain of journalism, (. . .) the reality in which [the writer] lives, the one which everyone sees]—and an invention of reality as Robbe-Grillet envisions it: "L'écriture romanesque ne vise pas à informer, comme le fait la chronique, [. . .] elle *constitue* la réalité. Elle ne sait jamais ce qu'elle cherche, [. . .] elle est invention, invention du monde et de l'homme, invention constante et perpétuelle remise en question" [Writing in the novel does not try to inform, like the chronicle does, (. . .) it *constitutes* reality. It never knows what it is looking for, (. . .) it is invention, invention of the world and of man, a constant invention and a perpetual putting into question].[6]

Thus Sarraute subscribes to a mimetic tradition, but she also recognizes that radical changes must be made in that tradition in order to represent this existing reality, "le psychologique." There is a "lien indissoluble entre la réalité inconnue et la forme neuve qui la crée" [indissoluble link between the unknown reality and the new form which creates it], she writes, and "toute exploration de cette réalité constitue une exploration du langage" [any exploration of that reality constitutes an exploration of language]. This exploration lies beyond the recognition that we invent reality through language; it moves instead toward the unknown reality of tropisms where the very need for that invention is expressed. Sarraute finds that when "l'écriture romanesque" deviates from this exploration, it risks being limited by its own "esthétisme" or "académisme" [aestheticism, academicism].[7]

The traditional qualities perceived in Sarraute's mimetic intentions often obscured the displacement of the process of signification put into play by her search for new forms. In Stephen Heath's study, *The Nouveau Roman: A Study in the Practice of Writing*, he describes Sarraute's unique position in relation to the other *nouveau romanciers* as an "ambiguity of approach" which led to numerous "misreadings." He explains, for example, that if he had written his study of the *nouveau roman* before Sarraute's fifth novel, *Entre la vie et la mort*, appeared in 1968, he would have come to the same conclusion as Lucien Goldmann in 1964, that Nathalie Sarraute is "at the close of an established tradition rather than at the start of a new one."[8] "Traditionnelle elle le reste" [She remains traditional], A. S. Newman wrote in the introduction to his study, but, he concludes, "le déplacement opéré par Nathalie Sarraute l'a conduite à exploiter certaines potentialités du langage qui nourissent le courant 'révolutionnaire' [. . .]" [the displacement operated by Nathalie Sarraute led her to exploit certain potentialities of language which nourish the "revolutionary" current (. . .)].[9]

The re-viewing of the novel's conventions and its language by Sarraute and the other *nouveaux romanciers* affects the role of the critic, because it also challenges the innocence of critical terms. The new criticism that the *nouveau roman* provoked posed a new question, how to read. This question not only responds to the collaboration of the reader insisted upon by the *nouveaux romans*, but it also allows these novels to exist on their own terms without reference to other criteria. Interpretation, judgment, and evaluation are necessarily a part of the act of reading, and the enduring presence of past works comes into play as one reads.

Sarraute's mimetic intention led traditionally oriented critics to interpret or evaluate the relationship between the sociological details of the setting where tropistic movement takes place in her novels and a known reality, her own personal history, for example, or the post-war Parisian bourgeoisie. Her discussion of certain predecessors led others to make static analogies between her work and that of the earlier writers she names in *L'Ere du soupçon*, thus ignoring the dynamic, evolutionary relationship she has with them. In addition, Sarraute's use of the term *le psychologique* to describe the world of tropisms invited thematic studies which interpreted the novels purely at the level of content and took little account of the radical form which accompanies her notion of that term. Other thematic studies address the relationship of form to content at the same time that they discuss Sarraute's style as it interacts with Sartre's existential terminology or Freudian vocabulary. Sarraute's use of poetic language and of several narrative voices, in an effort to prevent the reader from simply observing tropisms from afar, frustrated some critics at the same time that it inspired others to examine her work in terms of linguistics, narrativity, and the reader.

Even though the first four critical studies, three in French and one in English, were written before the publication of *Entre la vie et la mort* in 1968, each reveals a certain self-consciousness about the role of the critic in relation to Sarraute's novels. In the introductory comments of the first book-length critical study in French (1965), Mimica Cranaki and Yvon Belaval ask the question, "Que faire avec Nathalie Sarraute?" [What to do with Nathalie Sarraute?]—

L'homme et l'oeuvre. Pourquoi pas l'oeuvre seulement? Si l'on écoute les critiques, pour les uns l'homme éclaire l'oeuvre, pour les autres cette

supposée lumière est inutile, et ni les uns ni les autres ne viennent à bout
de leur problème. Quant aux auteurs, on les voit de plus en plus nombreux,
depuis Rousseau, à se camper en personnages, à ce point qu'aujourd'hui on
n'écrit plus que des Mémoires. On peut les suivre dans leur jeu. Mais que
faire avec un auteur qui refuse le jeu, pour qui tout personnage, littéraire ou
réel, n'est qu'un masque, une convention, une poupée pour musée Grévin?[10]

[The man and the work. Why not just the work? If one listens to the critics,
for some the man illuminates the work, for others that supposed illumination
is useless, and neither resolves their problem. As for the authors, we see
them, since Rousseau more and more numerous, planting themselves firmly
in their characters, to the point that today they write scarcely more than
Mémoires. We can follow them in their game. But what to do with an author
who refuses the game, for whom any character, literary or real, is only a
mask, a convention, a wax figure for the musée Grévin?]

Sarraute's treatment of the novel's most basic convention, the fictional
character, as merely a convenient mask hiding the more problematic
reality of tropistic movement undermines for some critics what Heath
calls the traditional "task of criticism," "precisely the construction of
an author."[11]
    Heath articulates Cranaki and Belaval's question in different terms.
"The radical shift in emphasis" of modern French writing from "mono-
logistic realism" to "the practice of writing" deconstructs the "innocence of realism" and poses the "problem of reading": "Its 'realism' is
not the mirroring of some 'Reality' but an attention to the forms of
the intelligibility in which the real is produced, a dramatization of
possibilities of language, forms of articulation, limitations, of its own
horizons."[12] Only A. S. Newman and Sabine Raffy offer an investigation
of the formalist function of "les discours" in Sarraute's novels, but most
of her critics recognize the implications that the "deconstruction of the
innocence of realism" had for their own project. That recognition begins with Cranaki and Belaval's question about the critic's search for
the author; it leads to questions about how to treat a work's content
when it is so inextricably tied to its form and how to bear witness to
this author's "chronology" when her works mock linearity; and it ends
up as a reflection on the value of a "traditional" and/or "formalist"
approach.
    The terms traditionalist and modernist will mean different things to
different critics as they review the studies that precede their own. Noting that many critics reviewing Sarraute's novels in journals or news-
papers discuss them in terms of plot, characters, or setting, Cranaki and
Belaval observe that "il n'y a pas d'anti-critique pour répondre à l'anti-
roman" [there is no anti-criticism to respond to the anti-novel].[13] In
Sarraute Romancière: Espaces intimes, Sabine Raffy describes her ap-

proach as a nonlinear one because the linearity constructed by all of Sarraute's critics "manquent ce qui fait la modernité et la particularité de l'oeuvre sarrautienne: l'éclatement du sujet, la superposition des masques, la décomposition de l'être" [miss what is modern and particular to the sarrautien oeuvre: the explosion of the subject, the superimposition of masks, the decomposition of being].[14]

In the discussion that follows, traditional refers to thematic studies, that is, the three thematic narratives which separate content from form, or to studies that appear to be static, that is, the two which evaluate or interpret Sarraute's relationship to her predecessors without considering Sarraute's own repeated belief in the dynamic nature of the novel's evolution.

In the early critical studies, the term formalist represents an attention to Sarraute's style—how it works, its effects on the reader, and her use of narrators or multiple points of view. In some cases, themes that are discussed statically in one work are picked up in a following study to be treated in formalist terms, that is, in terms of the dynamic presentation of a theme as it affects the reader, or in terms that are more theoretical and less impressionistic. Newman, like Raffy, gives an added dimension to the term formalist, because for these critics, a formal analysis is not simply a study of Sarraute's style and its effect on the reader, it gives attention to how Sarraute's texts open onto a discussion of the making of meaning in a novel.

"What to do with Nathalie Sarraute?"

The traditional task of the critic has been perceived as a reconstruction of the author through that author's work. As seen in the question which introduces the study by Cranaki and Belaval, "Que faire avec Nathalie Sarraute," these critics are self-conscious about this approach. Nevertheless, they begin their study with an account of Sarraute's childhood. They explain that they use her biography to show that Sarraute's art did not rise up "ex nihilo," because "il répond à une expérience personnelle de l'enfance et de l'adolescence" [it responds to a personal experience of childhood and adolescence].[15] That experience was her childhood reading of the classics; for what she found missing was the "véritable réalisme" [true realism] she perceived in tropistic movement. This experience is the source of the "nouvelle analyse" [new analysis] which is the source of Sarraute's originality.[16] These critics' study thus begins as a defense against the current charge that Sarraute's novels, like the other nouveaux romans, were simply cold, literary experiments.

Cranaki and Belaval also defend Sarraute against critics who read her articles as a call to break with the past, and this defense is similarly placed in terms of her personal response to literature. She takes a stand in relation to her predecessors, they observe, not to "juger objectivement" [judge objectively], but "au contraire pour se découvrir elle-même" [on the contrary, to discover herself]: "C'est elle qu'elle met à l'épreuve. Ses lectures deviennent des histoires d'amour. Pour ne pas être dévorée, il lui arrive d'avoir à se défendre contre ce qu'elle aime" [It is herself she puts to the test. Her readings become love stories. In order not to be devoured, she has had to defend herself against what she loves].[17] Sarraute's innovations in the novel's form are thus explained as an effort to prevent the reader from being seduced, as she was seduced, into thinking that the "reality" presented in the novels by the classics is "true" reality.

The phrase Cranaki and Belaval use to describe Sarraute's novels can be seen as the model for their own study: "l'importance n'est pas ce qu'on voit, mais ce qu'on voit par transparence; n'est pas ce qui tombait sous l'analyse traditionnelle, mais ce qui implique tout instant dans l'instant où il est reçu, et non quand il est conçu après coup" [the importance is not in what one sees, but in what one sees showing through; it is not what falls under traditional analysis, but what each instance implies in the instant that it is received and not when it is conceived after the fact].[18] Sarraute thus does not deny the novel's "realist" capabilities; she redefines realism, just as Cranaki and Belaval attempt to redefine their own critical approach. They diminish the distance between critic and author by culling from Sarraute's interviews and articles her own description of writing, interlacing her words with their own.

In the second work to appear in French, *Nathalie Sarraute* (1966), René Micha looks for a beginning to the beginning, the origin of tropisms, because he finds that already in her first publication "ils indiquent une méthode" [they indicate a method]. "Plusieurs fois," Micha remarks, "j'ai interrogé Nathalie Sarraute sur l'origine des tropismes" [several times I asked Nathalie Sarraute about the origin of tropisms], but Sarraute affirmed that "rien d'elle" [nothing of herself] is found in her novels. Micha thus does not establish the origin of "le psychologique" in Sarraute's childhood; he locates it instead in what he calls "une sorte de connaissance intuitive et un effort de re-création" [a kind of intuitive knowledge and an effort of re-creation].[19]

The critic traces this "connaissance intuitive" to "une certitude que les autres vous ressemblent" [a certainty that others resemble you]: "Cette certitude, Nathalie Sarraute la possède au plus haut point. Elle part toujours: ou bien de ses propres sensations, étant sûre que les autres les éprouvent, ou bien des sensations qu'elle voit en elle comme des virtualités" [That certainty is one which Nathalie Sarraute possesses to the highest degree. She always sets out: either from her own feelings, being sure that others feel them as well, or from feelings that she sees in herself as virtualities]. By describing the world from a place which is not "dehors" [outside] but is at "les bas-fonds de l'âme" [the very depths of the soul], her work allows her readers to experience "l'instinct commun" [the instinct we have in common].[20] That depth is created by the image of tropisms, drawn not from psychology but from botany, which represents for Micha her unique approach to the world.

Micha situates Sarraute's work in the larger evolution of aesthetics and stresses what she says about her connection to the past, quoting from something she wrote to him: "'Les tropismes, elle m'a écrit un jour, voudraient être non pas, bien sûr, un progrès dans la qualité, mais un petit pas plus avant dans l'exploration de l'âme où les autres ont fait un pas de géant'" ["Tropisms," she wrote to me one day, "would like to be not a progress in quality, of course not, but a little step forward in the exploration of the soul where others have taken giant steps"].[21]

Gretchen Rous-Besser published one of the first studies on Sarraute in English, Nathalie Sarraute (1979), and like Cranaki and Belaval and Micha, she too introduces her study with a comment on this writer's "originality" but for different reasons. Instead of locating Sarraute's inspiration in her childhood reading, Rous-Besser points to her "interesting" personal history that is "so out of the ordinary": "Thanks to her father's encouragement and to the extraordinary milieu of Russian intellectuals among whom she grew up, Nathalie Sarraute never faltered in her ambition to make a career for herself and in her confidence that a woman could achieve success on the same level as a man."[22] Although Rous-Besser acknowledges that Sarraute's 1968 novel, Entre la vie et la mort, is a satire of the public's desire to create a "cult of personality" around a writer, this critic cannot help but make a gesture of "veneration." The closing lines of the preface to her study describe how she was first inspired by Sarraute the person, the woman writer, during a personal appearance at Columbia in 1964: "Sarraute herself is a pioneer, a pathfinder, an adventurer into the unknown—the unknown realms of the mind [. . .] and the untracked paths of feminine equality. A remarkable person [. . .]."[23]

Rous-Besser's description of Sarraute implies a particular feminist moment in which women are encouraged to take their place among men in a man's world, as revealed by the analogy she draws to describe Sarraute's work habits: "[she] sets out from home each morning—like a businessman commuting to his office—and sits down [to write] at a neighborhood café." Sarraute has succeeded in a "man's world," in Rous-Besser's estimation, and it is thus that she reads certain of Sarraute's portrayals of women as satirical: "In light of what Sarraute has herself accomplished, it is understandable that she should have slight patience with many of her compatriots who conform, so easily and unthinkingly, to the stereotypes that have been offered to them for emulation. No wonder she satirizes the women who remain enshrouded in the cocoons of their women's lives."[24] The implications of distinguishing Sarraute as a woman writer remain on a personal rather than a theoretical level as Rous-Besser's discussion continues; these issues are never raised again after the preface and first chapter. This critic presents instead Sarraute's novels chronologically and thematically, "to let the works speak for themselves," and contributes to the discussion of style and evolution that Cranaki and Belaval began.[25]

Rous-Besser's tendency to create a cult of personality around Sarraute is more important in our discussion for the desire it reveals than for the critical awkwardness it represents. Gender was not an issue for the male critics, because their gender had traditionally been considered universal. Sarraute was a woman writer, but her writing made no reference to that fact and differed considerably from what has been considered "feminine writing."[26] Although Sarraute differed from her male contemporaries in the *nouveau roman* group, her writing made the same challenges to convention as theirs did, so Cranaki/Belaval and Micha address *those* similarities and differences. Rous-Besser's desire to celebrate Sarraute as a *woman* writer and to read her portrayal of women as a satire of women's position in society is similarly a response to a challenge to be discussed later. That challenge, briefly stated, is represented by the ongoing discussion among feminist critics about the nature of their enterprise, about what part gender plays in writing and in reading, and about the need to establish not only a tradition (a canon?) of women writers but also a theory of their writing.

In the first critical study to appear in English, *Nathalie Sarraute* (1968), Ruth Temple does not look for the woman or the writer in Sarraute's work, nor is she interested in Sarraute's notion of evolution. Temple chooses instead to discuss Sarraute's novels in the context of the *nouveau roman*, "the movement to which it owes, if not its form, something of its reputation, and of which she is now regarded as the *chef de file*."[27] More than any of the critics discussed above, Temple holds tightly to her tradition of criticism, finding the French New Novel in general to present difficulties for the American reviewer who wishes to know what the works are *about*. When the subject of the novel "approaches nothing," she writes, "the reviewer of that novel has no easy task." Temple hopes to solve this problem by discussing Sarraute's novels and critical essays in "chronological order, theory illuminating practice and practice theory" as a way of revealing the "dialectic" between them.[28] Temple's use of this term suggests that she does not intend to subordinate Sarraute's practice to her theories, but the critic proceeds to read Sarraute's articles on literature as if they held the key to the enigma of the "revolutionary form" found in *Tropismes*. In seeking to explain this French New Novelist to the American public, that is, an author who uses "traditional novel technique for enigmatic ends," Temple focuses more on the content of the novels—themes represented, "characters," and methods used—than on the interaction of form and content characteristic of the very context she has chosen. Temple admits that her reading of these novels may serve to "normalize" Sarraute's work, but the "effect" she explains is "intentional: to redress the balance. In their concern for novelty, critics have obscured the traditional elements, which are no less there and no less commendable."[29]

Cranaki and Belaval gave Sarraute eighteenth-century predecessors and Temple reaches even farther into the past, describing as "classical" the "symmetry," "precision," and "control" in the novelist's style. Temple further notes that Sarraute's narrator is similarly reminiscent of France's classical age, "by his use of 'I' he gives the story verisimilitude." Among modern writers, Temple finds that Sarraute's narrator resembles those of Woolf, James, Gide, and Huxley, in which a "privileged observer and participant" is seen as a "stand-in for the author."[30] By extension, Proust's work serves as an analogy for Temple, in terms of the "theme of creating a book," and she finds that Proust's "analysis of art as instrument" provides a useful analogy for Sarraute's effort to make sensations live in a reader. Temple bases her comparison of Sarraute and Woolf on the fact that they both began to read Proust at about the same time in their lives, which helps explain that though their metaphors are "dissimilar in their effect," they both share an effort to convey "the ineffable through metaphor."[31] She also notes that D. H. Lawrence "was equally preoccupied with the substance below consciousness" and cites from a letter in which he describes the "allotropic states of the ego."[32] Temple's search for specific analogies in the work of other writers best exemplifies a static, ahistorical notion of literary tradition rather than the more dynamic one represented in the studies by Cranaki and Belaval, Micha, and Rous-Besser.[33]

Nathalie Sarraute and Fedor Dostoevsky (1973) also presents a more static reading of Sarraute's novels. Ruth Levinsky's stated intention in her comparative study is to achieve a dialectical understanding of these two writers in order to gain "greater insight into Sarraute's novels and also possibly into Dostoevsky's novels." Noting that they share "a mutual distrust of logical reality," Levinsky details how Dostoevsky influences Sarraute in "subject matter, characterization and technique."[34] Levinsky is troubled as a reader, however, to find a "constantly changing reality" in Sarraute's work which "poses a problem for a novelist dedicated to truth, as truth seems to have many faces."[35]

What Levinsky finds to be "somewhat contradictory" is that the reality Sarraute discovers beneath the surface is not an individuated subjectivity but instead an "anonymous subterranean world [. . .], alienated, tortured, full of doubts, anxieties, fears, hates, and conflicts." Unlike Dostoevsky's characters, who are "vividly lifelike" and represent "an essentially optimistic view of life," Sarraute's novels present characters by means of insect, plant, and animal imagery to create a "pessimistic" representation of human nature and relationships "similar to those of a lower species of life"; thus her work does not "envisage a change or development in this situation."[36] This pessimism, Levinsky concedes, could be a product of Sarraute's "particular historical moment [. . .], a Post-Freudian, Post Existential-Absurdist twentieth century period, of which Dostoevsky can be considered a precursor."[37]

Another troubling aspect that Levinsky finds in Sarraute's work is her use of fantasy and myth. Where Dostoevsky uses fantasy and dream to "enhance the contrast" between subjective and "objective" reality, Sarraute's work confuses realities. She "seems to consider fantasy, and particularly literature, an essential ingredient of reality," Levinsky writes, explaining that Sarraute's characters "transform reality through the media of literature, art, fairy tale and myth." Levinsky resolves what she considers to be Sarraute's problematic use of myth by cataloguing the myths she shares with Dostoevsky.[38]

The difference Levinsky finds between Sarraute and Dostoevsky is their representation of "the complexity of human personality." Frustrated by Sarraute's psychological realism which "reduces to zero" that complexity, Levinsky praises Dostoevsky for his investigation of "man's inner world" and of "the agonized world of alienated persons": "His psychological exploration reveals that extreme loneliness and isolation create a distorted, angry person who is both masochistic and sadistic and who for purposes of general description can be called neurotic."[39]

Sarraute's critique of André Gide's psychological interpretation of Dostoevsky reveals the extent to which Levinsky's terminology also represents a misunderstanding of "le psychologique": "'Tous ses personnages, écrit Gide, sont taillés de la même étoffe. L'orgueil et l'humilité restent les secrets ressorts de leurs actes, encore qu'en raison des dosages divers, les réactions en soient diaprées.' Mais il semble que l'humilité et l'orgueil ne sont, à leur tour, que des modalités, des diaprures. Derrière eux, il y a un autre ressort plus secret encore, un mouvement dont l'orgueil et l'humilité ne sont que des repercussions"

["All his characters," Gide writes, "are cut out of the same cloth. Pride and humility remain the secret motives of their acts, even though their reactions might have different shades because of the variety of dosages." But it seems that humility and pride are, in turn, only modalities, only shadings. Behind them, there is a motive which is even more secret, a movement of which pride and humility are only the repercussions].[40] In Sarraute's analysis, Gide's use of psychological terms masks a more fundamental movement in Dostoevsky's characters. At the end of this passage, Sarraute suggests that we might use Katherine Mansfield's term as a way to describe this movement as a "terrible desire to establish contact."

In the title essay of L'Ere du soupçon, Sarraute explains that the novelist should leave the creation of flesh and blood characters to the cinema or the theater and "le priver le plus possible de tous les indices dont, malgré lui, par un penchant naturel, il s'empare pour fabriquer des trompe-l'oeil" [deprive the reader as much as possible of all details which, in spite of himself and because of a natural tendency, he latches onto in order to manufacture such illusions].[41] It is "ces 'types' humains en chair et en os" [these human "types" in flesh and blood], the "life-like" characters with whom Levinsky wishes to identify, who reduce the presentation of human complexity in a novel. Both Temple and Levinsky appear to be frustrated as readers of Sarraute, because they are readers who attempt to create a character (out of her novels or out of Sarraute herself) with whom or against whom they can identify. As Sarraute says, left on our own, we all seem to exercise that tendency. If Temple and Levinsky identify, in a sense, against Sarraute, Cranaki and Belaval tend to identify with her. This tendency leads them to have a more dynamic, less static approach to her work and to read particular aspects which the traditional reader finds problematic in relation to the work as a whole.

Levinsky focuses on the "anonymous" quality of Sarraute's characters and interprets it as pessimistic because it erases "individuality." Cranaki and Belaval, on the other hand, admit that this quality exists, but they interpret it in the context of another aspect of Sarraute's novel, the importance of dialogue. This constant interaction between Sarraute's "unindividuated characters" leads Cranaki and Belaval to align Sarraute with Freud's "schopenhaurien pessimism." Dialogue is conversation, they explain, which is "sous-conversation," and it demands a partner: "Si jamais les hèros n'y existent que par relation à quelqu'un, c'est que le fond de l'homme est, en définitive, cet intérêt passionné pour l'homme" [If the heroes only exist (in her novels) in relation to someone, it is because the basis of humanity is, definitively, that passionate interest in the other]. "Le mal, c'est peut-être les autres," they conclude, "mais l'amour aussi, c'est les autres" [Perhaps evil is others, but love is also, others].[42] This dialogue is not between individuated subjects, Cranaki and Belaval explain, because the particular has been generalized. This is Sarraute's technique for making the reader experience tropistic reality, that is, "le véritable réalisme" that she saw missing in works by earlier writers, "le même fond commun" [the common foundation] that we all share.

Temple and Rous-Besser also identify "le même fond commun" in Sarraute's novels as characterized by certain classical elements, but while Temple lists the stylistic traits which Sarraute shares with classical writers, Rous-Besser discusses Sarraute's style as it relates to content to produce a classical "effect." She parallels the anonymity of the characters to the "disintegration of plot" in the novels which is a "paring down to essentials," "concision and distillation": "What remains [. . .] are the common feelings and experiences that are not dependent on any particular moment of history, of cultural acclimatization, but belong to the common heritage of humankind [. . .]; she depicts the world as she sees it and human nature as it is."[43] "But this," Rous-Besser concludes, "has always been the way of the classical moralists, whose portrayal of human frailties contains no overt message but rather an implicit ethic."

Although Rous-Besser is more sensitive than Temple to the relation of form to content, she cannot resist identifying Sarraute as "moraliste," in spite of an interview she had with the writer in which she denies such a perspective: "[The] only morality for the novelist consists in trying to preserve for the novel its quality of a work of art. [. . .] I must insist that at no moment have I sought to deliver a message, to give the slightest moral instruction."[44] Rous-Besser's personal investment in the personality she has woven around Sarraute as a "pioneer into the unknown paths of feminine equality" leads her to interpret Sarraute's statement as an effort to transcend "the limitations of political or social boundaries" in order to present a view of men and women as all sharing the same humanity.[45] This critic's image of Sarraute also leads her away from Sarraute's notion of evolution in terms of the novel, that is, toward a description of Sarraute's innovations as "revolutionary," part of "the ever-renewed opposition between the champions of tradition, reverently turned toward the past, and the revolutionary innovators, resolutely facing the future."[46]

Just as Sarraute has stated that she is not a "moraliste," she also has refused to be identified as a "woman writer." Valerie Minogue cites an interview Sarraute had with John Ardagh in which she "decisively rejected any classification as a specifically 'woman writer,' stressing that 'Any good writer is androgynous, he or she has to be, so as to be

able to write equally about men and women. . . .'"[47] Another inter-
viewer recently asked her a similar question, "What about your own
feminism?" Sarraute responds: "I militated for the women's vote in
1935. I have always been a feminist in so far as I want equal rights for
women. But the idea of 'women's writing' shocks me. I think that in
art we are androgynous. Our brains are not different, but until now
women were less educated, so they produced fewer works of art. People
always compare women to each other."[48] The feminist reader is tempted
to read this claim through her own subjectivity and desires, as Rous-
Besser did, that is, ignoring it and calling Sarraute a "woman writer."
New Criticism has taught us that the "intentions" of the author may
(should) be read separately from the "production" of a text. As this
account of the early critics of Sarraute shows, however, when a critic
engages a work through the author, the act of ignoring or citing an
author's intentions indicates more about a critic's desires than about
the question of an author's intentions.

"L'Etre sarrautien"

In his study of Sarraute published in the late 1960s, Jean-Luc Jaccard's intentions are primarily thematic.[49] It is a narrative interpretation which addresses neither the problematics of form and content that
earlier and later critics found there, nor Sarraute's original contribution
to an evolution of "la substance romanesque." Two other studies published a few years later are similar in approach: that of Christine B.
Wunderli-Muller, *Le Thème du masque et des banalités dans l'oeuvre
de Nathalie Sarraute*, and of Elisabeth Eliez-Ruegg, *La Conscience
d'autrui et la conscience des objects dans l'oeuvre de Nathalie Sarraute*.[50] All three critics rearrange the elements in Sarraute's novels to
construct a composite "être sarrautien" [sarrautien being] on an existential journey through an inauthentic world.

These thematic works borrow Sartre's terminology found in his preface to *Portrait d'un inconnu*, where the self that emerges from Sarraute's work is described in terms of "inside" and "outside." Nathalie
Sarraute, he writes, "ne veut prendre ses personnages ni par le dedans
ni par le dehors parce que nous sommes, pour nous-mêmes et pour les
autres, tout entier dehors et dedans à la fois. Le dehors, c'est un terrain
neutre, c'est ce dedans de nous-mêmes que nous voulons être pour les
autres et que les autres nous encouragent à être pour nous-mêmes. C'est
le règne du lieu commun" [does not want to take her characters from
either the inside or the outside because we are, for ourselves and for
others, completely outside and inside at the same time. The outside is

a neutral terrain, it is the inside of ourselves that we want to be for others and that others encourage us to be for ourselves. It is the reign of the commonplace]. An autonomous subjectivity that is different from the others poses a threat to the stability of the "terrain neutre." By assuming a character and a social moral judgment recognizable to others, the individual can enter this zone, which is "à la fois subjectivité de l'objectif et objectivité du subjectif, [. . .] le loisir d'être subjectif dans les limites d'objectivité" [both a subjectivity of the objective and objectivity of the subjective, (. . .) the freedom to be subjective within the limits of objectivity].[51]

At the same time, however, as the individual listens to the conversation in this "lieu commun" [common place/commonplace], described by Heidegger as the "parlerie du ON" [what THEY say], the individual senses an "inauthenticity" which creates the anxiety that the fixed character of the commonplace is only a mask. Sartre notes that beneath the "normal" daily conversation there lies a desire to flee from "authenticity," that is, from "le vrai rapport avec les autres, avec soi-même, avec la mort [qui] est partout suggérée mais invisible. On la pressent parce qu'on la fuit [. . .]" [a true relationship with others, with oneself, with death (which) is everywhere suggested but invisible. We feel it because we flee it (. . .)]. Thus it is that conversation is a "échange rituel de lieux communs" [ritual exchange of commonplaces] which hides "sous-conversation" [sub-conversation]. An individual for Sarraute is not a classifiable character, "c'est le va-et-vient incessant et mou entre le particular et le général" [it is an incessant and feeble movement between the particular and the general].[52] Sartre classifies *Portrait* as an "anti-roman" because Sarraute has made "le mur d'inauthenticité" [the wall of inauthenticity] the subject matter of her novel.

The studies of Jaccard, Wunderli-Muller, and Eliez-Ruegg offer an interpretation and elaboration of Sartre's terms. All three critics view the refusal of traditional literary conventions represented by the *nouveau roman* group and Sarraute's particular representation of the "lieu commun" as a critique of bourgeois values that conventional literature had represented as "real." The "être sarrautien" in these studies finds himself in a state of "angoisse" [fear]: for Jaccard, it is an existential anguish, a fear that there is no meaning for existence; for Wunderli-Muller, it is a fear of "le regard" [the look] of the other because "être différent signifie être regardé, jugé par eux" [to be different means to be looked at, judged by them]; and for Eliez-Ruegg, it is a fear of tropistic movement itself.[53] In response to this situation, the "être sarrautien" seeks to escape, either by objectifying himself as an "être-en-soi" [being-in-itself], that is, by putting on the mask of a "personnage" [character] or a buffoon, or by appropriating the object-world around him, to internalize the threatening exterior.[54] As in Sartre's analysis, these escapes represent "inauthenticity," and for all three critics literary creation offers the possibility of a more "authentic" life.

For Jaccard, the inauthenticity of the individual in Sarraute's work is specifically related to the work of the writer, who, like the "être sarrautien" in relation to others, risks having an inauthentic relationship to characters. Jaccard's writer recognizes his own "angoisse existentielle" when he breaks through the protective wall of the conventional character and demystifies the character's truth and unity. The "être-romancier" [novelist-being] is fated to remain within the confines of society, language, tradition, and in the end, resorts to living in "bad faith": "On s'ennuie, on trouve la 'vie' monotone, mais on préfère cette monotonie au chaos qui résulterait de la rupture de cet ordre" [We get bored, we find "life" to be monotonous, but we prefer that monotony to the chaos that a rupture in that order would bring].[55]

In Wunderli-Muller's study, the "être sarrautien" is also conscious of the inauthentic quality of the world, even though he is not a writer. "Par mauvaise foi" [By an act of bad faith], he hopes to lose that consciousness by killing everything in him that distinguishes him from the others and by believing that "le bonheur" [happiness] is possible.[56] Wunderli-Muller identifies a sociological concern in Sarraute's novels, the relationship of the individual to society. This critic has chosen to follow the "être sarrautien" "dans sa dissolution et sa transformation" [in his dissolution and his transformation] within society, "représentée chez Nathalie Sarraute par la bourgeoisie" [represented in Sarraute's work by the bourgeoisie]. Wunderli-Muller concludes that although we may wish for there to be "un noyau indestructible, une essence qui n'est nullement influencée par ce que nous vivons" [an indestructible core, an essence which is in no way influenced by the lives we live], it does not exist: "Nous sommes essentiellement influençables, et c'est ce qui nous fait redouter le contact des autres bien que ce contact nous soit indispensable" [We are essentially able to be influenced, and that is what makes us fear contact with others even though this contact is indispensable to us].[57]

Although Eliez-Ruegg identifies the material world represented in Sarraute's work as bourgeois, her interpretation is not sociological. In her investigation of the characters' relationship to the objects in this world and to others as objects, Eliez-Ruegg finds a dialectic in these novels between "consistance et inconsistance" [consistency and inconsistency]. That is, responding to the threat of tropistic movement, Sarraute's characters either stick a mask on the other to stop the movement or attach themselves to the other to become part of the movement. By tracing the changing relationship of Sarraute's narrators to the world of tropisms, Eliez-Ruegg reveals that this dialectic dissolves into "un anéantissement quasi complet des distinctions entre êtres et objets" [an almost complete annihilation of the distinction between beings and objects].[58] Without the distinction there is freer movement, a liberation of a psychological element which "faire vivre le flux tropistique à l'état pur" [makes the tropistic flux live in its pure state]. Eliez-Ruegg finds that in *Portrait d'un inconnu* and *Martereau* tropisms are discovered by the narrator who acts as a mediator and consequently prevents in others "la libre circulation des tropismes" [the free circulation of tropisms]. "Hypersensibilité" [hypersensitivity] is no longer limited to one character in the next novel, *Le Planétarium*, as each character can be the "corps conducteur" [conducting body] for tropisms. The psychic element is in a greater state of flux, and personal identity vanishes in the fourth novel, *Les Fruits d'Or*. In *Entre la vie et la mort* neither characters nor objects are identifiable; the theme itself is the catalyst, "le conflit de la création artistique" [the conflict of artistic creation].[59]

All three critics recognize this theme. For Wunderli-Muller it is represented more statically as Sarraute's general style, marked by a "sensibilité extrêmement fine" [extremely fine sensibility] which invites the reader to "deviner" [guess] that authenticity is "une valeur qui nous hante et à laquelle nous aspirons autant que possible" [a value which haunts us and toward which we aspire as much as possible].[60] The theme of artistic creation for Eliez-Ruegg is identified as a movement toward freer expression by means of a less inauthentic relationship to objects: "L'acte créateur est le mouvement par lequel l'être, brisant la gangue du lieu commun, fait jaillir ses éléments intacts et neufs—dégagé par le contact avec l'objet—leur donner une cohésion, les construit en un modèle: l'oeuvre d'art elle-même" [The creative act is the movement by which the being, by breaking the grip of the commonplace, makes its new elements spew forth intact—put into motion by contact with the object—to give them a cohesion, to construct them into a model: the work of art itself].[61]

Jaccard also concludes his analysis with the interpretation that art allows the individual to escape the "angoisse" of the human condition. That individual, however, is not the writer. The writer may live on through the novel, Jaccard explains, but its life depends on others to make it live. If the novel's readers are not authentic, that is, if their taste is dictated by "le lieu commun," the novel could be left for dead. This is the theme Jaccard sees emerging in *Les Fruits d'Or* because the novel ends with an authentic reader, the only hope left for the writer: "Ce lecteur idéal existe, il y en aura toujours, mais il ne se sent pas sûr de son goût face à l'assurance des autres qui jugent de tout avec sûreté. Il doute toujours de lui, mais dans la lecture (ou par l'écriture) il se dépasse" [This ideal reader exists, there will always be one, but he is not sure of his taste when faced with the assurance of the others who judge everything with certainty. He always doubts himself, but in reading, by reading (or by writing) he goes beyond himself].[62]

Jaccard wrote his study before the publication in 1968 of *Entre la vie et la mort*, a novel whose "central character" is a writer, so the chronology of Sarraute's publishing probably accounts for his emphasis on the reader. This reader, like the "être sarrautien" that these thematic critics construct, is *characterized* as moving between the general (bourgeois society, "le lieu commun") and the particular (the individual). The problem of a reader (or of an "être") as a subject *constituted by* that movement remains to be formulated by critics who address more specifically Sarraute's notion of "le psychologique" in its constant relationship to language.

This is a relationship that the thematic critics ignore, but it is one which Cranaki and Belaval address when they discuss the ambiguous relationship of the author to the narrator(s) and, by extension, of the reader to the text. "L'observateur suprême qui ne se manifeste dans le roman que par son expression sans se révéler en personne," they ask, "est-il l'auteur lui-même?" [The supreme observer who only shows himself in the novel by his expression without revealing himself in person, is it the author himself?][63] How can Sarraute use the first-person narration to present such intensely complex emotional states, they ask, without this observer becoming a stand-in for the author? Cranaki and Belaval answer their own question: "Alors, le *je* adopté par Nathalie Sarraute n'est le sien que dans la mesure où il exprime la vision, le style, l'originalité de Nathalie Sarraute. Sinon, il est le *je* que chacun d'entre nous peut retrouver en soi: non pas le *je* moral ou social qui se compose en une personne dont le masque tient plus ou moins mal, mais cet observateur secret, tenace, impitoyable, posté centre le Ça et le On"[64] [Well, the *I* adopted by Nathalie Sarraute is her own only to the extent that it expresses her vision, style and originality. Otherwise, it is the *I* that each of us can find in ourselves: not the moral or social *I* which composes itself into a person whose mask fits more or less badly, but that tenacious, impitiable, secret observer posted between the *id* and the *they*]. In Cranaki and Belaval's analysis, Sarraute's "je" does not run the risk of becoming either a fixed character or a stand-in for the author, because this pronoun's antecedent is *not* a character; rather it represents a state of being in interaction with others.

In addition, the narrating "je" does not become fixed because, as most critics note, this observer is in turn observed. When the narrator's position as observer is taken away, the reader's is forced to shift as well.[65] Cranaki and Belaval note that "je" as the observing eye/I moves

from one character to another. The variety of subjects turning around
an object becomes not a means of knowing the object more fully, but
of presenting the "inauthentic" terms by which a subject perceives an
object. This excess of the "inauthentic" creates the true reality of "le
lieu commun," that is, the fearful scramble for terms, words, and clichés which takes place as the various subjects identify with or differen-
tiate themselves from others in relation to an object.[66]

The constantly shifting position of the observer puts the "truth" or
value of the observations into question at the same time that the observer often shifts within himself or herself. Cranaki and Belaval's
analysis of the oscillation between "je sais" [I know] and "peut-être"
[perhaps] in one of Sarraute's passages gives an emblem to this shift,
which is also marked by verbs moving between indicative and conditional modes. These critics find that the very basis of knowing is rendered in its complexity, such that the terms, "je sais . . . je le sais . . .
sûrement" [I know . . . I know it . . . surely], vary in the quality of their
certitude. "Savoir, sentir sont synonymes," they write. "Je connais bien
mieux les gens avec qui je vis que je ne les définerais, [. . .] ce sont des
objets de sentiments" [To know and to feel are synonymous. I know
the people I live with much better than I can define them, (. . .) they
are objects of feelings]. This knowledge by feeling is shared by all. The
observer is always aware that the observed is "human," recognizable,
that the knowledge of the other becomes the knowledge of the self. The
dominant emotion of this "lieu commun" is then fear, fear of being
unmasked by observation, and it is "le regard des autres" [the look of
others] that establishes presence in this subjective universe; "on se
sent regardé" [one feels looked at], Cranaki and Belaval write. Vision
becomes touching, as "le regard" goes beyond simply looking.[67]

In linguistic analyses of chosen passages, Cranaki and Belaval allow
the complexity of that bond to be fully realized. They note, for example,
a predominance of verbs over nouns, and the use of the present tense
characteristic of the *nouveaux romanciers*. In addition, Sarraute uses
"cela" to introduce many verbal constructions: "A la place de 'ces
paroles lui font mal'; on aura: 'Cela lui fait mal ce qu'elles lui disent
là' [. . .]. Le 'cela' toujours en tête de la phrase, immobilise et transforme
en objet de vision la mouvance psychologique portée par le verbe"
[Instead of "these words that they say hurt him"; we will have: "That
hurts him what they say to him" (. . .). The "that" always at the head of
the sentence, immobilizes and transforms the psychological movement
carried by the verb into an object].

Similarly, the use of "c'est" [it is] plus an adjective or noun at the
beginning of a sentence serves to express a "coagulation objectale"
[objectal coagulation] of all the details that follow, as seen in this exam-

ple: "C'est curieux, cette sensation qu'elle avait souvent que sans lui, autrefois, le monde était un peu inerte, gris, uniforme [. . .]" [It's curious, that sensation she often had that without him, before, the world was a little inert, grey, uniform (. . .)].[68] Cranaki and Belaval also note that Sarraute's frequent use of indefinite expressions such as "quelque chose" [something], "une sorte de" [a kind of], "on dirait que" [one would say that], and "comme si" [as if], all contribute to the indecision and uncertainty of the observing I/eye.

These critics trace the evolution of Sarraute's style from long, sinuous Proustian phrases in the earlier novels to the use of more ellipses and shorter sentences in later ones, which corresponds to the "amorcelle-ment" [piecelike] treatment of scenes and tableaux, as well as fewer metaphysical expressions because the use of "comme" [like/as] seems to disappear: "La signification éclate d'elle-même, sans être provoquée par la comparaison" [The meaning explodes on its own, without being provoked by the comparison].[69] The "action" of her "characters" always reveals a psychic reality. Dialogue becomes more and more the center of later novels, as the excess of conversation replaces the complex of images seen earlier.

Their discussion of form in its relationship to content reflects Cra-naki and Belaval's approach to Sarraute's novels as a study of the inter-relationship between the author and her work, similar to that between the narrator(s) and their texts. Overall, these critics find a unity of theme and structure in Sarraute's work and conclude that from *Tropi-smes* to *Les Fruits d'Or*, she has turned from the past "auquel elle demeurait infantilement attachée" [to which she was remaining child-ishly attached], liberating herself with each work "pour observer ceux qui l'entournent, les saisir sur le vif, et avancer vers une vérité qui dépasse, de quelque manière qu'on le définisse, le psychologique" [in order to observe those around her, to seize them on the spot, and ad-vance toward a truth which surpasses the psychological as it is de-fined].[70] Their consideration of this psychological reality in terms of the formal aspects of its presentation serves to illustrate the limitation of the more strictly thematic analyses which, though frequently allud-ing to the critical implications of this relationship, neglect the ques-tions it raises for the activity of reading itself.

The Dichotomous Self and the Act of Creation

As seen in the summary of Sartre's preface to *Portrait d'un inconnu*, and as Sarraute herself describes it, "le psychologique," which makes up the "fond commun," is identified as a movement between two

points, a pre-verbal, unformed, non-differentiated reality of "profondeurs" [depths] and the surface reality represented in traditional "realist" fiction. This opposition led critics to adopt a vocabulary of
dichotomies in their discussions—objective-subjective, interior-exte-
rior, adult-child, inauthentic-authentic, culture-nature—and to find
corresponding images in the texts themselves. For example, Rous-Besser observes that "whatever is solid, concrete, well-defined, impene-
trable belongs to the domain of objective reality; in contrast, whatever
is soft and spongy, blurred, nebulous, suggests those disquieting re-
gions of the psyche."[71]

Cranaki and Belaval clarify the psychological reality of tropisms as
an interaction between Heidegger's "'on' inauthentique de la parlerie
quotidienne" [inauthentic "they" of daily speech] and the "ça" [id],
which they understand in Freudian terms as "quelque chose d'insolite
et violent" [something strange and violent]: the on is "le mensonge, la
grimace de convention, par opposition à la vérité de l'instinct. D'un
côté, donc, le social, de l'autre, la nature [. . .]" [the lie, the frown of
convention, in opposition to the truth of instinct. On one side, then,
the social, and on the other, nature (. . .)].[72] The dichotomy they see at
work in these novels is described in terms of nature-culture which
usually parallels the traditional dichotomy female-male, but in their
analysis it represents that of child-adult. The "vérité d'instinct" originates for these critics in Sarraute's childhood and is the source of her
authenticity.

Micheline Tison Braun's study of Sarraute's novels, *Nathalie Sarraute ou la recherche de l'authenticité [Nathalie Sarraute, or the
Search for Authenticity]*, was published in 1971 and articulates an
interpretation of "le psychologique" which resembles that of Rous-Besser and Cranaki and Belaval, but with a different attention to Sarraute's
style. Tison Braun distinguishes "le psychologique" from a traditional
analysis of feelings and characters by describing it in Sarraute's terms
as a movement between the "mécanique" [mechanical] and the "vivant"
[living], that is, between inauthentic and authentic reality. In a discussion of the philosophical implications of Sarraute's "micro-psycho-
logique" as it is represented in "des moments romanesques" [novelistic
moments], Tison Braun, like Micha and Cranaki and Belaval, shows
how this concept of reality enriches the "substance romanesque."[73] Her
thematic analysis as it figures in the title of her work is based upon
an interpretation of Sarraute's use of images, which introduces Tison
Braun's own dichotomy between intellection and sensation.

The critic establishes this dichotomy in her analysis of Sarraute's
style. Whereas the traditional novel uses "explication" to present the
unconscious, Tison Braun explains that Sarraute presents it "autour

d'une image" [around an image]. The image gives the reader access to personal desires and fears, nostalgia and dreams, but it is not used as metaphor or allegory, "destinée à faciliter la compréhension" [destined to facilitate comprehension (. . .)]; it is instead, "la pensée même en train d'éclore, la matière mentale avant son élaboration—et sa déformation—par l'intelligence" [thought itself in the process of blossoming, mental matter before its elaboration—and its deformation—by intelligence].[74] Sarraute thus does not create a new, subjective language to express this mental matter; she revives a forgotten language, what Tison Braun calls a "langage primordial" [primordial language]. The reader must "réapprendre" [relearn] this language, "le repenser avec la conscience développée" [rethink it with a developed consciousness], "non pour le traduire en concepts mais pour l'approfondir et l'éclairer dans son essence" [not to translate it into concepts but to deepen and illuminate it in its essence].[75]

This analysis recalls the theme of creation that earlier critics found in Sarraute's novels. Cranaki and Belaval discuss "le thème de l'art, de la littérature, de la création" [the theme of art, of literature, of creation], but more in terms of the narrator than of the reader.[76] Temple describes the central character in the first two novels as "woven into the story as a double (. . .). It is as if the artist were reporting a phase of the creative process."[77] Rous-Besser discerned a "central consciousness" in the early novels, one voice among many, a self-conscious, self-reflecting voice which leads her to accept Pingaud's opinion that this is a "novelist in search of a subject, never arriving at a finished product."[78]

Tison Braun's interpretation is unique among the early critical studies because it links the central narrative figure more directly to the reader. Sarraute's "réflexion presque obsédante sur l'art du roman" [almost obsessive reflection on the art of the novel], Tison Braun explains, cannot be separated from the psychological material that the reader experiences.[79] This "réflexion" represents the formation of personality, and the personality of the artist echoes that of the reader as the narrative voice is concentrated in one character in the first two novels and divides in the novels that follow. Sarraute presents the "quest for authenticity" in a style that not only invites a parallel to the artist's search for a representation of the novelistic substance, but more importantly, puts the reader at the very center of that quest.

Basic to this style, and to Tison Braun's dichotomy between intellection and sensation, is Sarraute's irony, which discourages intellection both inside and outside the text. Sarraute's works may seem to resemble the "regular" novel, this critic writes, but "une indéfinissable ironie décompose le personnage si bien construit, les intrigues amorcées restent en plan, les sentiments s'étirent, se tordent et se retournent en leur contraire, les peintures en trompe-l'oeil révèlent leur surface plane, les décors remontent vers les cintres" [an indefinable irony decomposes the character who has been so well constructed, the pieced together plots remain in place, the sentiments expand, twist and turn around to become their opposite, paintings in *trompe-l'oeil* reveal their flat surface, the decor retreats to the wings].[80] Intellection in Tison-Braun's interpretation is a form of inauthenticity, "la stylisation mensongère du *on*" [the lying stylization of the *on*].[81]

As seen earlier, Cranaki and Belaval describe the sarrautien subject as a "secret observer posted between the *ça* and the *on*," that is, between nature and culture, instinct and intelligence. For Tison Braun these two components of "le psychologique" have been internalized by the subject such that the split exists within the subject itself. Tison Braun describes the *je* in Sarraute's novels as a combination of "la conscience réfléchie et donneuse des formes" [the consciousness that reflects upon itself and gives forms] and the *ça*, "substance informe à la fois de nous-même et du monde" [the unformed substance of both ourselves and of the world]. The figure of *je* must decide whether it will remain in the domain of the *ça*, "informe, inexistant" [unformed and inexistent], or whether it "se redressera dans la liberté créatrice" [will stand up tall in creative freedom]: "C'est ce choix initial entre la vie et la torpeur, c'est de cette réponse à l'appel qui naît la personnalité" [It is this initial choice between life and the torpor, it is from this response to the call that the personality is born].[82]

Tison Braun notes a gradual constitution of the artistic personality "entre *Tropismes*, où le dissident prend conscience de son malaise, et *Entre la Vie et la Mort*, où il entrevoit la possibilité d'une solution par la création d'une oeuvre" [between *Tropismes*, where the dissident becomes conscious of his malaise, and *Entre la vie et la mort*, where he sees the possibility of a solution in the creation of a work of art].[83] The "dissident" perspective in *Tropismes* emerges in the narrators of *Portrait d'un inconnu* and *Martereau*, then divides into several narrative voices in *Le Planétarium*. In the fourth novel, *Les Fruits d'Or*, the reputation of a book bearing the same title as Sarraute's is discussed. For Tison Braun the subject of this novel dramatizes the parallel of the creation of art and the self in a fickle world of taste which expresses itself with clichés and platitudes. In the last novel discussed, *Entre la vie et la mort*, Tison Braun finds that this parallel is made more specific because a writer figures as the central character, an accumulation, as it were, of all Sarraute's narrating voices.

Sarraute's exploration of the process of artistic creation becomes an investigation of the "la nature de ce moi dont tout le monde parle sans le connaître" [nature of this self which everyone talks about without knowing about]. Tison Braun explains that the self emerging from Sarraute's novels cannot be defined as "l'être-en-soi" [being-in-itself], and, she adds, "il n'a pas non plus pour essence cette liberté vide, entièrement contingente, de Sartre" [neither does it have as its essence that empty, entirely contingent liberty of Sartre]. It is rather "un être incertain, qui s'attend ou se cherche ou s'égare ou se cache, incompréhensible à lui-même, tantôt force, tantôt forme, tantôt aspiration ou absence douloureuse" [an uncertain being, who expects or looks for itself or loses itself or hides itself, incomprehensible to itself, at times a force, at times a form, sometimes aspiration or miserable absence]. This divided self is unified by two contrary feelings, "l'horreur qui nie et menace sa liberté et son intégrité" [the horror of what denies and threatens its freedom and its integrity] and "l'amour d'une voix inconnue qui l'appelle" [the love of an unknown voice which calls it].[84]

The unknown voice is the call to a vocation, to creation in any form, and it is through creation that the self is constituted: "Car toute activité créatrice, qu'il s'agisse d'art, de sentiment ou de la plus humble création matérielle, pose la question de la nature du Je, puisqu'elle implique une prise de position de ce Je à l'égard de ce qui n'est pas lui" [For any creative activity, whether it has to do with art, feeling or with the more humble material creation, poses the question of the nature of the I, because creation implies that this I take a position in relation to what is not I].[85]

Although Sarraute's works do not presume to present a formula for authentic art, Tison Braun sees an aesthetic emerging in negative terms: "pas d'art réaliste, [. . .] pas d'art subjectif et informe, [. . .] pas de fausses cathédrales de mots. L'art, c'est la sensation absolument originale, décantée et élaborée, suffisamment variée et puissante pour créer une structure vivante" [not realist art, (. . .) not subjective, unformed art, (. . .) not fake cathedrals of words. Art is the absolutely original feeling, decanted and elaborated, varied and powerful enough to create a living structure].[86]

In her 1981 study, The Novels of Nathalie Sarraute: Toward an Aesthetic, Helen Watson-Williams continues Tison Braun's analysis of the reader's role in Sarraute's novels, but here the reader occupies a position in relation to an aesthetics rather than to the broader process of personality formation. Watson-Williams describes Sarraute's work as a "highly personal fragment of experience [which] amounts to an artistic autobiography." This critic's investigation of the "personal aesthetic" that takes shape from the publication of Tropismes (1939) to that of 'disent les imbéciles' (1976) privileges the artist; that is, Watson-Williams's analysis is limited by her feeling that although Sarraute's subject matter is "the raw stuff of living in which she moves like us all," it is only the writer who "can explore and express it."[87]

In an interpretation very similar to that of Tison Braun and of Eliez-Ruegg, Watson-Williams analyzes what she finds to be a progression in Sarraute's novels which moves the reader increasingly into the author's position, but it is "between consciousness and subconsciousness."[88] Watson-Williams notes that in the first novel, *Portrait d'un inconnu*, the work of art is "communication, an active encounter, between observer and observed." This encounter is dramatized at the end of the fourth novel, *Les Fruits d'Or*, because, as Jaccard has noted, there remains one reader who continues to have his own opinion of the book; the artistic experience frees the observer from the others.[89] Sarraute's third novel holds a key position for Watson-Williams in relation to the others because *Le Planétarium* presents the character of Alain, "a critic, lover and potential creator of art" who "enters into a solitary, alienated world characteristic of the reader at the end of [the following novel] *Les Fruits d'Or* and [eventually] the writer in *Entre la vie et la mort*."[90]

Although Watson-Williams admits that Sarraute could be accused of writing a "thematic" novel with *Entre la vie et la mort*, the tale of a writer struggling to survive, the creative act this critic sees emerging from the novel is a "self-subordinating act." In her analysis, the approach to the work of art is more important than the subject matter or the artist because the word is the dominant sense impression. The reader enters into the creative process because Sarraute's style presents words as if they were overheard by an "anonymous but active" narrative voice who does not intrude. Watson-Williams explains that Sarraute's technique is marked by the "absence of attributions of speech to speaker, of description and setting, the minimum details of personal appearances [. . .] together with flexible and free syntax: all these aspects of an individual method and style become unmistakably 'Sarrautien.'"[91] Sarraute's sixth novel carries this freedom even further, because it represents a "total rejection of traditional narrative method in treating speakers, settings and sequence of action," Watson-Williams writes, noting that "*disent les imbéciles*" is an "extreme illustration of the narrative principle Nathalie Sarraute formulated in 1950," that is, "the primacy of psychological matter over all other fictional considerations."[92] This critic concludes that the substance of Sarraute's work combines with its form to present her "personal 'parcelle de réalité' with an honesty and imaginative power in her unifying and self-sustaining vision which transforms it ultimately into a poetic expression of compassion."[93]

As the title of her work describes, Watson-Williams's reading of Sarraute's novels moves "toward an aesthetic," that is, toward an abstraction of *principles* in a work which privileges the experience of *sensation* over that of intellection. What is awkward about this discussion is this critic's unacknowledged move between the general and the particular as she traces the way in which Sarraute brings the reader into the author's territory in general terms, then returns to praise Sarraute's particular view of reality. This is especially problematic for the feminist reader when both the general and the particular in this analysis are subsumed under masculine terms.

The most provocative example of this problem is Watson-Williams's observation that "the feminine nouns in Sarraute's novels express the quality that brings the written words to life," "cette petite chose impalpable, timide, tremblante" [that little impalpable, timid, trembling thing]. Instead of investigating the implications of an alignment of feminine nouns with what has been called by earlier critics "la vérité d'instinct" or identified as a "langage primordial" when she describes these qualities, Watson-Williams reinscribes a paradigm whereby the artist is masculine and the muse is an internalized feminine element: "Inspiration, a personification in the conventional, Romantic sense, almost a Muse. It seems external to the writer, a stimulating self-contained entity with which he maintains a delicate relationship." Watson-Williams's description of the creative process as it is enacted by Alain Guimier in *Le Planétarium* continues to be marked by a male orientation to desire, and, she continues, "[when] the writer of *Entre la vie et la mort* is well-launched in the public account of his creative method, he suddenly becomes aware of his misconduct in this precious intimacy. Without realizing it, he has taken liberties, used force and domination where he was formerly cautious, respectful, patiently attentive [. . .]"

Not only is the artist male in this description, even though Sarraute is female, but the relationship between (male) artist and (female) Muse is marked by courtly language in a modern setting: "But he has forced where he should have wooed; he has disciplined where he should have obeyed. To please his stylistic pretentions he has groomed her until all individuality and life have been eliminated and she has acquired the anonymous and frail grace of a fashion model, with all the mannequin's detachment. He will redeem his errors and start again, if only she, his personal inspiration, will return to breathe life into the inert and mechanical state of mind he now endures [. . .]."[94]

For a feminist reader who is also anglophone, the gender of nouns in French rarely passes unnoticed. Watson-Williams's reading enacts the dilemma of what Tison Braun described as the divided self, but here it is in terms of the female self. It seems that Helen Watson-Williams's *ça* notices that "the quality that brings written words to life" is represented in Sarraute's work by feminine nouns, but the "parlerie du *on*" stepped into her analysis and appropriated that experience in masculine terms. As A. S. Newman's comments on the irony in Sarraute's writing remind us, the source of the discourse in her novels which aligns feminine nouns with the "vérité d'instinct" remains so determinately ambiguous that a critic can only be self-conscious about attributing this gesture to the female author.

On the other hand, Nathalie Sarraute does have something to say about her use of masculine and feminine pronouns which remains above Watson-Williams's imagery and raises instead a more problematic notion for the feminist reader: "But I hardly ever think of gender when I write about my characters. I often prefer *he* to *she* because *he* is neutral but *she* is only female."[95] As Monique Wittig comments in her essay "The Mark of Gender," however, there is "nothing natural," or neutral, about gender for anglophone feminists: "They have extrapolated the term *gender* from grammar and they tend to superpose it on the notion of sex. And they are right insofar as gender is the linguistic index of the political opposition between the sexes and of the domination of women. In the same way as sex, man and woman, gender, as a concept, is instrumental in the political discourse of the social contract as heterosexual."[96] As will be discussed in Chapter 3 of this study, the dichotomies that Sarraute's critics identify in *Portrait d'un inconnu* and *Martereau* can be read in terms of gender at precisely the point where Watson-Williams finds it, in the use of feminine nouns.

Sarraute's later novels move away from an opposition of male and female and toward what Françoise Calin calls in her 1976 study the erotic undertone of Sarraute's writing. Calin's observations are similarly marked by gendered (courtly) imagery, but it is an acknowledged metaphor and is used to defend Sarraute against critics who charge that she ignores "les passions amoureuses ou sexuelles des personnages" [amorous or sexual passions of characters]. Calin notes on the contrary that a character's desire for the Other is a *passion* inspired by discourse: "L'éroticisme y imprègne l'anodin de la vie quotidienne métamorphosant—par la vertu magique du verbe—en amant et maîtresse deux êtres qui se croisent dans un couloir [. . .]. L'éroticisme chez N. Sarraute exprime, sans la trahir, la violence du désir d'union totale avec l'Autre qui hante tous les personnages" [Eroticism impregnates the banality of daily life metamorphizing—the magic virtue of the verb—into lover and mistress two beings who pass in a hallway (. . .). Eroticism in Sarraute expresses, without betraying it, the violence of the desire for total union with the Other which haunts all the characters].[97]

Calin goes on to call the interaction between narrative figures "des ballets de séduction" [dances of seduction], which gives our discussion of Sarraute's later novels an image for the relationship of the reader to the text. In that relationship the reader is forced out of the dichotomies that characterize gender and into a fluid identity marked by the subject's movement between various positions of discourse and among contextualized images of gender.

Sarraute's Reader as "acteur" and "témoin"

Calin's study, La Vie retrouvée: l'étude de l'oeuvre romanesque de Nathalie Sarraute, is both thematic and formalist in its approach. She devotes the first part of her analysis to a thematic discussion which looks at the works "simultanément" [simultaneously] in order to give cohesion to the individual interpretation of Sarraute's novels that follows in part two. Calin's overall concern is with the thematic and stylistic unity of the work as a whole, "ce tout indivisible" [this indivisible whole] which presents Sarraute's notion of "le psychologique." Part one is subdivided into two parts, "la recherche psychologique" [the psychological search] and "la recherche technique" [the technical search], but Calin emphasizes that this division does not represent a "dissociation" between form and content at the level of the texts themselves, but rather "au niveau de la perception de l'oeuvre" [at the level of the perception of the work as a whole].[98]

This critic's opening discussion reveals how her approach differs from more static, thematic interpretations. Instead of identifying Sarraute's novels as a satire of the bourgeoisie, she looks at the novels' "sociological details" of bourgeois life in an effort to understand why they appear in a work which proposes to "plonger le lecteur 'dans une matière anonyme'" [plunge the reader "into an anonymous matter"].[99] Sarraute's characters "s'incrivent dans un cadre social" [are inscribed in a social cadre], but instead of reading that setting as the reflection of a reality outside the text, Calin reads the contexts in which the word "bourgeois" is pronounced in the novels, specifically in Portrait d'un inconnu and Le Planétarium. The examples she analyzes show that although these characters' world is bourgeois, the interpretation of that qualification, as well as any judgment of the world described by the word "bourgeois," fluctuate according to who is narrating a particular scene and for what purposes. Calin's analysis is guided by questions, such that it becomes a demonstration of how the "sociological details" that are used figure in the novels and are then rendered suspect from within—"Comment sont-ils présentés? En quels termes l'auteur les décrit-elle? Comment choisissent-ils leurs masques?" [How are they presented? What terms does the author use? How do the characters choose their masks?].[100]

In the second part of the thematic discussion, Calin investigates the "technical" elements which allow Sarraute to present tropistic movement without destroying it, specifically the narrators and the "multiplicitiés de points de vue" [multiplicities of points of view]. The distinguishing characteristic of Sarraute's narrators in Calin's analysis is that they are both "des acteurs" [actors], limited to one point of view, and "des témoins" [witnesses] who doubt the "truth" of that perspective, that is, both "conscience réfléchie" [a reflected consciousness] and "conscience réfléchissante" [a reflecting consciousness]. Calin finds that these narrators are the most self-reflective when they are searching for proof that "les autres et eux-mêmes sont faits de la 'même substance'" [others and themselves are made of the "same substance"].[101]

Calin's investigation of the relationship of the narrator's telling to the event related leads her to a discussion of the notion of time as it is represented in these novels and to a parallel with Proust's work that earlier critics failed to notice. She notes that both authors present "une superposition totale de deux couches de temps" [a total superimposition of two levels of time] which occurs as a past event and melts into a present moment through the experience of a sensation, not through words. In the account of such an experience, the narrator brings the past into the present by shifting verb tense, from imperfect to present, such that the "singularité isolatrice" [isolating singularity] of the imperfect becomes an exemplary truth of the present.[102] Calin's terminology in this discussion is rarely overdetermined by other philosophical or psychological contexts. In her analysis of the effect of this generalizing, for example, she spares her analysis the category of "moraliste" that so many other critics have used, choosing instead the distinction between "l'événement" [the event] and "l'éventualité" [the eventuality], between a particular, finite past moment and a general, more eternal possibility.

Calin begins her discussion with "une idée reçue" [a generally accepted idea]—Sarraute's work is often read as a satire of the bourgeoisie—and then presents an interpretive reading which questions this assumption. Like tropistic movement itself, Calin's conclusions remain unarticulated beneath her discussion because she is more interested in describing the impressions created by Sarraute's writing than in coming to any definitive conclusions. Rhetorical questions lead the reader through a series of masks, themes, and words to the idea that tropisms "constituent notre vie psychologique à l'état naissant" [constitute our psychological life at the nascent state]. This critic's approach is that of a critical reader, perhaps of Jaccard's "ideal reader." One of the images Calin uses to describe Sarraute's work characterizes her own study as well: Nathalie Sarraute "saisit [. . .] l'être avant qu'il ne se pétrifie en personnage, l'existence avant qu'elle ne meure dans l'inauthentique" [seizes (. . .) the being before it petrifies into a character, existence before it dies in the inauthentic].[103]

Une Poésie des discours by A. S. Newman appeared the same year as the study by Calin and takes up where she leaves off. Newman moves his critical emphasis away from a reader's impression and toward the act of reading itself. He delineates his study as an investigation of the "poétique du roman" [poetics of the novel] that Sarraute's work proposes and orients his discussion with Pouillon's description of the novel: "'Le but d'un roman [. . .] est d'exprimer une expérience à l'aide d'une histoire (traiter un sujet à travers une intrigue)'" ["The object of a novel (. . .) is to express an experience with the help of a story (treat a subject through a plot)"]. Newman explains that Sarraute's works displace the object of the novel's exploration: "le but du roman de Nathalie Sarraute est d'exprimer une expérience à l'aide d'un être (traiter une matière psychique à travers un sujet)" [the object of the novel for Nathalie Sarraute is to express an experience with the help of a being (treat psychological material through a subject)].[104] Similar "matière psychique" can be found in earlier novels, and one can discern "plots" and "characters" in Sarraute's work, but Newman finds these conventions to be secondary, even "parasitaire" [parasitic] to this novelist's material. Newman discerns a "poétique du roman" emerging from Sarraute's work because of "une exploitation de la spécificité du roman—ses discours" [an exploitation of what is specifically novelistic—its discourses]. The "nature obsessivement discursive" [obsessively discursive nature] of Sarraute's novels re-presents an experience of reality by means of conversation in relation to "sous-conversation" and leads Newman to read her works in light of theories of discourse, most specifically those of Emile Benveniste and Mikhail Bakhtin.[105]

The purpose of Newman's study, however, is not to identify the displacement that operates in Sarraute's novels in order to "voir comment ce déplacement se traduit dans les romans" [see how it is translated into the novels]; it is rather to discern from her texts "comment leur spécificité productive *impose* cette vision au lecteur" [how their productive specificity *imposes* that vision on the reader].[106] This occurs through Sarraute's use of the fundamental ambiguity of the novel's language. Newman formulates in more critical terms Calin's description of the narrators as "témoins" and "acteurs" when he proposes that the ambiguity in the novels arises most profoundly where there appears to be an opposition between narration, that is, the words of the author

spoken through a narrator—be it in first or third person—and representation, that is, when the author seems to disappear and the characters
represent themselves as in drama: "Roman par sa forme extérieure,
tenant du drame par l'effacement de la voix narrative au profit de celles
des personnages, le texte de Sarraute est poétique dans son inspiration
et dans sa réalisation. Il existe une poésie des *mots:* le poète assemble
des mots afin de créer des sens qui les dépassent. De la même façon,
il y a une poésie des *images*" [Novel by its exterior form, tending toward
drama by the effacement of the narrative voice in the service of those
of the characters, Sarraute's text is poetic in its inspiration and in its
realization. There exists a poetry of *words:* the poet assembles words
in order to create a sense that surpasses them. There is similarly a
poetry of *images*]. Newman's study traces how Sarraute arranges what
is specific to the novel, described as "un discours qui en contient d'autres" [a discourse which contains others], into "un jeu des Registres et
des Optiques" [play of Registers and of Perspectives] to create "non pas
un roman poétique, mais une poésie romanesque" [not a poetic novel,
but a novelistic poetry].[107]

Consequently, Sarraute's work poses for Newman the problem of
reading which arises immediately because "l'ironie irréductible est que
la signification est *autre*" [the irreducible irony is that meaning is
other]. As the narration becomes more and more an indistinguishable
mixture of conversation and "sous-conversation" there is a displacement of the process of signification. Instead of reading by means of a
code in which words point away from themselves to signify transparently a concept or object, the reader must discover the code created by
words as they are spoken within the text. Newman reads the language
of Sarraute's novels as it is spoken rather than as it is written in much
the same way that Calin analyzed the use of the term *bourgeois.*

This displacement of the process of signification is related to the
second aspect of Sarraute's work which poses the problem of reading,
that is, narrative perspective, the means by which the traditional reader
is oriented and by which information is given. Newman organizes the
question of narrative perspective as it is posed in Sarraute's novels into
two questions: that is, not simply, "quel est le personnage dont le point
de vue oriente la perspective narrative?" [who is the character whose
point of view orients the narrative perspective?]—but also, "qui est le
narrateur?" [who is the narrator?]. These two terms are represented in
Newman's interpretation by the terms *point de vue* and *optique. Point
de vue* is a relationship of the author to the characters. *L'optique* is
described as that of the characters within the fictive universe. Sarraute's
novels impose on the reader "la réalité de cette distinction entre ces
deux phénomènes différents, quoique liés [. . .]" [the reality of this

distinction between these two different though related phenomena
(. . .)].[108]

Newman finds that the source of "énonciation," that is, the play between "le point de vue" and "l'optique," becomes more and more obscured in the course of Sarraute's six novels published at the time of
his writing. There is no "real referent" in the novel and the author
is the creator of all discourse found there, Newman explains, so the
opposition itself is shown to be false.[109] Sarraute's use of "style indirect
libre" [free indirect discourse] ultimately problematizes the origin of
discourse as that of an omniscient narrative voice or of a character.
"Ni l'un ni l'autre ne s'expriment," Newman writes, "tous deux sont
exprimés" [Neither one nor the other expresses itself, both of them are
expressed], or, he adds, citing G. Picon: "A la place d'une parole sur la
vie, nous entendons la vie même qui parle" [In place of a word about
life, we hear life itself speaking].[110]

The identification of the narrative voice is gradually effaced and the
reader becomes more immersed in the world of tropisms (Sarraute's
"point de vue") where there is no mediating voice. Newman summarizes this effacement with his own play of prepositions. In Tropismes
the "discours" is situated "devant" [in front of] tropistic movement and
the "scripteur" is the writer; the narrators are the "scripteurs" in the
first two novels and the "discours" is "sur" [about] the tropistic movement of others. The novels that follow become more performative in
nature, the "scripteur" disappears altogether to allow for the "discourse
des tropismes" [discourse of tropisms] to take place. The "spécificité
productive" [productive specificity] of these displacements imposes
Sarraute's particular vision on the reader.

As seen most specifically in the studies by Temple and Levinsky, as
well as in the thematic interpretations, these readings seek to resolve
the "irreducible irony" that Newman speaks of by taking Sarraute's
language at face value. These analyses act as intermediaries between
reader and text by describing Sarraute's point of view in terms of "le
psychologique," a philosophy of "l'autre," an aesthetic of the novel, or
in terms of the presence or lack of social or historical realities. As
Cranaki and Belaval conclude in relation to their remark that there is
not an anti-criticism to respond to the anti-novel: "Ce sont bien des
romans. Mais le point de vue a changé" [These are certainly novels. But
the point of view has changed].[111] Newman's investigation of Sarraute's
novels responds to the "new habits of reading" that her works propose
by shifting the emphasis from *what* her novels signify to *how* signification takes place, and by extension, how that shift in the process of
signification imposes a new reading identity on the reader. Newman is
sensitive to the subjectivity of any reading. His subjectivity is expressed

in this study as that of a critic who explores the constitution of the reading subject enacted in Sarraute's novels. Three later critics, Valerie Minogue, André Allemand, and Sabine Raffy, also address the act of reading Sarraute's novels. Unlike Newman, however, their subjectivity is represented by the humanist or existentialist implications of the creative nature of reading that Sarraute's novels invite.

The Critic's "Pursuit of the Universal"

Nathalie Sarraute and the War of the Words: A Study of Five Novels by Valerie Minogue, published in 1981, is formalist in the sense that Minogue studies Sarraute's first five novels chronologically "to show the nature and effects of the literary strategies adopted by Nathalie Sarraute in her pursuit of reality."[112] As his description of the kind of reading demanded by *Les Fruits d'Or* also reveals, the literary strategies he finds at work in these texts invite "new habits of reading":

> The movement connecting the various sequences is not immediately discernible; the *tone*, the irony that baffles and refuses certainty, may not be instantly caught. The complex interweavings of sounds, meanings, and images, will certainly not instantly leap to the eye. If, however, the reader is patient enough to read with the attention he would give a poem, the results are richly rewarding [. . .]. Nathalie Sarraute's fictional world may at times seem bleak, [. . .] yet her texts embody a prodigious act of faith that in and through language the human spirit may continue to perform that act of creation which is its unique privilege.[113]

In spite of Minogue's call for new ways of reading, he can also be viewed as a traditionalist because he derives a theme from his reading of Sarraute's work, an affirmation of the value of human creativity. Like other thematic critics, Minogue admits that though Sarraute's intention is not to moralize, he finds in all her work a "clear moral concern and effect."[114] His analysis of the poetic qualities of Sarraute's language enriches any reader's habits of reading and any critical discussion of the practice of reading, at the same time that it serves in the end his own preoccupation with Sarraute's "pursuit of the universal."

At the end of his study Minogue addresses "problems in the pursuit of the universal," most specifically the criticism by Sartre and others that Sarraute "claims to pursue in her work that which is universal and impersonal, but the specific and particular elements attached to the writer's words [. . .] create a social specificity that may be seen as endangering that project." Minogue argues that the socially specific details of bourgeois life which are attached to the words Sarraute uses do not deny the universality of tropistic movement represented: "It is the human movements which organize them for human purposes which are universal."[115] Sarraute is not ignoring historical reality, Minogue explains, she simply gives it less importance than did "la littérature engagée," for example, because she is engaged in representing the universal creation and expression of the self by means of the banal details of that reality.

Minogue cites a similar misreading of Sarraute's portrayal of women as reflecting some form of feminism, stating that "her presentation of women is no more partisan than her presentation of men, children, the middle-class, etc." Her "characters" may have a specific referent in society at large, but that specificity is secondary to the universal inclination presented. In addition, "the effect of her writing is to break down simplistic categorizations and divisions into age, class, sex and so forth. [. . .] It is indeed by virtue of their universality that these novels are far from irrelevant to the realities of the world."[116]

The principal aim of Minogue's approach is to show the "various self-questioning modes [which] replace the authoritative narrator" in Sarraute's first five novels. He notes that the power of Sarraute's language is due to her imagery, "drawn from our first experience of the world, from physical pleasure or disgust, recollections of childish games, references to the warmth of childish security, or the childish terror of isolation." The magic and fairy-tale images found throughout Sarraute's work are "reminiscences of that great source of childish compensation for the inadequacies of reality and the self."[117]

Unlike Cranaki and Belaval, Minogue does not look to Sarraute's childhood as the source for this imagery. In an earlier article on childhood imagery in her first novel, he describes it as a means of universalizing the complex experience of tropisms which could otherwise alienate the reader because it "illuminates for the reader the uncertain situation of the narrator in relation to the world." By placing the narrator outside the security of the "lieu commun," Sarraute "strips him of all authority," which allows her to present a "particular, non-authoritative version of human life to the reader" and perhaps to "persuade [the reader] to acknowledge it as his own."[118]

For Minogue, a destabilization of narrative authority is largely effected by Sarraute's use of poetic language which allows the reader a more intimate experience of tropistic reality. Whereas Newman interprets the use of a poetic, performative language within the novel form as part of an evolving "poétique du roman," Minogue reads this language and technique as a refusal of superiority on the author's part which allows for a text in which "everyone and no one is the writer": "Maintaining resolutely an ambiguous and interrogative mood, Natha-

lie Sarraute shows the disruptive presence of tropistic activity in the
narrator and the creator, binding them in common humanity to their
creations and to the reader."[119] The material of these novels becomes
"the writer's own consciousness, and that consciousness must be capable of observing its own movements both beneath and towards verbal
formulation." Through an "emphatic recreation of the movements that
ultimately emerge as words or gestures" the reader is also divested of
the role of spectator, becoming instead "a creative participant." The
absence of individuated subjectivity that Ruth Levinsky noted earlier
in her comparative study of Dostoevsky and Sarraute is seen by Minogue as one of Sarraute's textual strategies for representing tropisms:
"The area of reality uncovered is thus inter-personal rather than individuated. It is an area where the writer is everyone and no one, articu-
lating by imagery and analogy a level of inarticulate experience in
which the reader in turn will recognize his own movements of consciousness [. . .]." The reader participates in the psychological process
of self-creation which is ultimately also the process of self-expres-
sion.[120] This self-reflective narrative world is both liberating and constraining for the reader: constraining in that the reader is made
continually aware of the arbitrary exclusions inherent in the narrator's
activity within the text, and liberating in that it marks the arbitrariness
in such a way as to guarantee its subjectivity. Put another way, although
the "matter" of the narration is constraining, the "manner" liberates.

In his 1980 study of *L'Oeuvre romanesque de Nathalie Sarraute*,
André Allemand also thematizes what he finds to be "une espèce de
retour au sens du langage" [a kind of return to the sense of language]
in *Tropismes*, which he traces chronologically in her novels. Where
other critics use dichotomous categories to describe the reality in these
novels, Allemand dismisses these categories as simply a means of "dis-
tribuer les éléments de notre monde en deux séries parallèles et de
signes opposés" [distributing the elements of our world in two parallel
series of opposing signs]. He finds that the power of Sarraute's work
lies in that which is not categorizable, what he calls "l'innommable"
[the unnameable]: "Chez Nathalie Sarraute le mot n'est pas seulement
en rapport avec le contre-mot, qui le nie ou l'infirme, mais avec ce que
nous pourrions appeler le non-mot, c'est à dire l'innommable, l'in-
nommé" [In Sarraute's work the word does not exist simply in a relationship with its opposite, which denies it and invalidates it, but in a
relationship with what we could call the non-word, that is, the unnameable, the unnamed].[121]

According to Allemand the valorization of "l'innommable" not only
breaks apart dichotomies but also allows the reader to appreciate that
what appears to be "déformé" [deformed] or "inachevé" [unfinished]

in these novels is actually an invitation to creation, that is, to take part in the last possible opportunity for human freedom in the modern world: "[L'oeuvre d'art] seule nous offre encore l'image d'un monde en expansion, expansion qui permet à l'homme de vivre avec l'espoir de pouvoir changer la vie" [(The work of art) alone still offers us the image of a world in expansion, an expansion that allows man to live with the hope of being able to change life].[122] Thus it is that although nothing seems to "happen" in her novels, Allemand finds that there is a lot to say about them because "les choses conservent leur secret, [. . .] elles sont irréductibles à la pensée [. . .], parce que les points de vue, d'où elles sont considérées, ne cessent de changer" [things conserve their secret, they are irreducible to thought (. . .), because the points of view from which things are considered are continually changing].[123] Allemand concludes that Sarraute's writing "parle pour que nous prenions parti, pour que nous nous prononcions sur elle" [speaks so that we might take part, so that we pronounce ourselves on it].[124]

As irreducible as Allemand finds these novels to be, he nevertheless ends by presenting them chronologically in a schema which represents the five different discours he finds there: "le discours assujetti" [a subject's discourse] of the first two novels, "le discours superficiel" [superficial discourse] in Le Planétarium, "le discours global" [global discourse] found in Les Fruits d'Or, a totalizing "discours poétique" [poetic discourse] in Vous les entendez?, and finally "le discours despotique ou arbitraire" [the despotic or arbitrary discourse] in "disent les imbéciles."[125] Allemand interprets the variety of the discours represented as evidence that Sarraute's initial project to present subsurface reality does not change as her novels evolve, it is only enriched and transformed by its expression through first one, then many narrating voices.[126]

Allemand concludes by describing Sarraute's oeuvre as "une hypothèse de travail" [a working hypothesis], an image which suggests to this critic that life itself and identity are similarly hypotheses, continually in movement because of our relation to discourse: "Ainsi, dans ce monde 'en instabilité,' où rien n'est jamais définitivement pareil à soi, il n'y a plus de 'il,' parce qu'il n'y a plus de 'je' ni de 'tu.' Plus exactement, il n'y a plus de 'il' parce que tout peut devenir 'il,' 'je' ou 'tu'" [Thus, in this world "in instability," where nothing is ever definitively the same unto itself, there is no longer a "he," because there is no longer either an "I" or a "you." More precisely, there is no longer a "he" because anything can become "he," "I" or "you"].[127]

Like Allemand, Sabine Raffy identifies the plurality of Sarraute's subjects, but she uses it as a model for a "lecture plurielle" [plural reading] which places her project against the linearity of other studies. Raffy explains that what she finds most remarkable in Sarraute's work is not its "possibilité théorique" [theoretical possibility], but the possibility of "une pluralité d'interprétations" [a plurality of interpretations] corresponding to "l'épaisseur subjective de cette écriture" [the subjective thickness of this writing] and "la complexité de ses références culturelles" [the complexity of its cultural references]. Raffy describes her approach as that of intellectual history, where "la sociologie, la philosophie, l'anthropologie, et la psychanalyse mêlent et en même temps protègent leurs langages" [sociology, philosophy, anthropology and psychoanalysis mingle, while at the same time protecting their languages].[128] Each disciplinary approach is presented independently in separate chapters which proceed from the most exterior (the sociological) to the most interior (the psychoanalytic). Raffy explains that the separation of the chapters is maintained in order to encourage a "simultaneous" application that corresponds to the way in which the subject in Sarraute's world is constituted by reference to several codes at the same time.

Raffy concludes that an investigation of the codes at work in Sarraute's work reveals a denunciation of all masks, "sociologiques, mythiques, idéologiques, et fantasmatiques" [sociological, mythic, ideological and fantasmagoric], which separate us from "notre propre vérité" [our own truth], "une pure essence humaine" [a pure human essence]: "Structuré d'abord selon des cristallisations de l'inconscient, le sujet se constitue un soubassement imaginaire fondant ses relations au monde, élabore une idéologie justifiant son existence et lui donnant un sens, et s'intègre dans un milieu social qui lui confère un personnage représentatif. C'est dans la nécessité de ce trajet constitutif de l'être que semblerait résider la preuve, s'il en est, d'une universalité de la psyché humaine, et la possibilité même de la communication" [Structured at first by the crystalizations of the unconscious, the subject constitutes for itself an imaginary base establishing its relations with the world, elaborates an ideology justifying its existence and giving it meaning, and integrates itself in a social milieu which confers it with a representative character. It is in the necessity of this constitutive journey of a being that proof would seem to be founded, if proof there is, of the universality of the human psyche, and even the possibility of communication].[129]

In the studies by Calin, Newman, Minogue, Allemand, and Raffy, criticism on Sarraute gradually moves away from the reconstruction of an author through her works, as it was problematized by Cranaki and Belaval, and toward an investigation of the way in which Sarraute's reader is constituted by the act of reading. These critics join Cranaki, Belaval, Micha and Rous-Besser to identify the reader as experiencing "le même fond commun" or "l'instinct humain" shared by all. This universal meeting place is characterized by uncertainty and often paralleled to the experience of a child in an adult world, or it is identified with a creative potential which we all share as we seek to give meaning to our lives.

With the exception of Newman, who avoids the temptation altogether, none of these critics can refrain from assigning that quality some attribute analogous to "universal." Raffy's formulation of "la *nécessité* de ce trajet constitutif de l'être" moves a step beyond these attributes to return our attention to the *process* of making meaning and of establishing identity. Her insistence on this necessity allows for the *different* experiences of what may be considered universal to present themselves. The chapters that follow represent an investigation of one of those experiences.

2

A Feminist Reading *Tropismes*

My "discovery" in 1979 of Nathalie Sarraute's *Tropismes* resonated within current discussions among feminists about a woman writer's relationship to literary tradition and the difference between writing by women and men.[1] Some feminist literary critics in this country were analyzing the stereotypical roles assigned to female characters in men's writing and others were engaged in (re)discovering writings by women. The "revolutionary" qualities of Sarraute's work seemed to embody the challenge to patriarchal "norms" that these critics found in writings by women.

In critical studies about her work Sarraute was called a "founder/ member" of the *nouveau roman*, but critics also noted that her mimetic intentions isolated her within that group.[2] All the other writers designated as *nouveaux romanciers* were men, and I attributed Sarraute's isolation to the fact that she was a woman. When I came upon the preface to *L'Ere du soupçon*, I read Sarraute's personal statements about writing through my own desire to identify her as a rebel against patriarchy:

> Les textes qui composaient ce premier ouvrage *[Tropismes]* étaient l'expression spontanée d'impressions très vives, et leur forme était aussi spontanée et naturelle que les impressions auxquelles elle donnait vie.
>
> Je me suis aperçue en travaillant que ces impressions étaient produites par certains mouvements, certaines actions intérieures sur lesquelles mon attention s'était fixée depuis longtemps. En fait, me semble-t-il, depuis mon enfance.[3]

> [The texts that composed this first work were the spontaneous expression of very vivid impressions, and their form was as spontaneous and natural as the impressions re-created.
>
> I perceived while working that these impressions were produced by cer-

---

A version of this chapter was given as a paper at a conference entitled "Feminism and/in French Literature" at the University of South Carolina. The proceedings for the conference were published in *French Literature Series*, 16, 1989.

tain interior actions which had attracted my attention for a long time. In fact, it seemed to me, since my childhood.]

The line between lived and literary reality appeared to collapse with the last sentence of this passage. I read Sarraute's insistence on the spontaneous and natural quality of her work as not simply an answer to critics who called the *nouveaux romanciers* "des froids experimen-teurs" [cold experimenters], but also as a reflection of her desire as a woman writer to present her specific view of reality.

In addition, here was a French woman whose writing broke apart patriarchal conventions: her works decentered the narrative voice, they disrupted narrative and syntactical order, their images were corporeal, and their language poetic. These were the qualities of writing which Hélène Cixous was making polemics in the 1970s, as noted by Toril Moi: "For Cixous, feminine texts are texts that 'work on the difference,' as she once put it, strive in the direction of difference, struggle to undermine phallogocentric logic, split open the closure of binary opposition and revel in the pleasures of open-ended textuality."[4] When Cixous further specified that the term *l'écriture féminine* was "a dangerous and stylish expression full of traps," because such naming simply reinforced the binary logic which imprisons us, I agreed intellectually, but my body did not listen.[5] Sarraute was a woman, I was a woman, so I set about to characterize her writing within my own definition of *l'écriture féminine*: writing by a woman which in its form disrupts patriarchal logic and language, and in its content addresses the "other side" of the established order. I realize now that I was reading Sarraute from a position that Julia Kristeva describes as "second generation feminism" emerging after 1968: "Essentially interested in the specificity of female psychology and its symbolic realizations, these women seek to give a language to the intrasubjective and corporeal experiences left mute by culture in the past."[6]

As yet unresponsive to Kristeva's theory, which also complicates the elision of "feminine" and "female," I was still responding *personally* to Nathalie Sarraute, the French woman writer. I was reading her work as what Patrocinio Schweickart would later call "a manifestation of the subjectivity of the absent author—the 'voice' of another woman."[7] Reading more about this woman writer, however, I soon discovered a troubling remark she made in an interview: "Any good writer is androgynous, he or she has to be, so as to be able to write equally about men and women."[8] Simone de Beauvoir had accused Sarraute of ignoring the social, historical context in her work, and I knew that I could read her refusal to be labeled a woman writer as an extension of that accusation: this woman writer was denying what I felt to be her feminine specificity. That reading would unfortunately lead me to the same end as de Beauvoir, that is, to dismiss Sarraute for polemical reasons. Sarraute's work was too significant and too poignant to be dismissed, but I needed a paradigm with which to explain my growing suspicion that the impersonal voice narrating *Tropismes* was Sarraute's means of hiding her specificity.

In the same year that I found Sarraute, Sandra Gilbert and Susan Gubar published *The Madwoman in the Attic: The Woman Writer and the Nineteenth-Century Literary Imagination*. Their study addressed precisely the specificity I wanted to investigate, and in a vocabulary both theoretically and personally accessible to me at the time: "Since his is the chief voice she hears, does the Queen try to sound like the King, imitating his tone, his inflections, his phrasing, his point of view? Or does she 'talk back' to him in her own vocabulary, her own timbre, insisting on her own viewpoint? We believe these are basic questions feminist literary criticism—both theoretical and practical—must answer [. . .]."[9] In an effort to establish a theory of women's literary creativity, Gilbert and Gubar alter Harold Bloom's formulation about male poets who are pushed to creativity by an "anxiety of influence." These critics proposed instead that the nineteenth-century woman writer suffered an "anxiety of authorship," "a radical fear that she cannot create, that because she can never become a 'precursor' the act of writing will isolate or destroy her."[10]

In her critical writings Sarraute refers frequently to her "precursors," especially Flaubert, Joyce, Proust, and Woolf, and to the notion of "le psychologique" that she feels links the works of Dostoyevsky to those of Kafka and her own. I thus understood Sarraute's re-reading (and re-writing) of the novel's tradition to be nothing less than a woman writer's effort to redefine masculine tradition in order to make a place for her (specifically feminine) view of reality. The extremely ironic style she adopts in these essays also appeared to exemplify the woman writer's subversion as Gilbert and Gubar describe it: "Thus these authors managed the difficult task of achieving true female literary authority by simultaneously conforming to and subverting patriarchal literary standards."[11] An application of this theory to my French woman writer, however, suppressed both Sarraute's desire not to be named a "woman writer" and Cixous's refusal to limit her concept of the "feminine" to writers who are women.

Adding an ironic twist to the dilemma, what do I do with this woman writer Nathalie Sarraute, were the opening words of the first book-length critical work on Sarraute's novels, "L'Homme et l'oeuvre?" [The man and the work?]. The practice of using the term *homme* to refer to the (male or female) individual was criticized by feminists in the

1970s,[12] but in 1965, Mimica Cranaki and Yvon Belaval were offering a variation on the current critical approach as a way of introducing their own dilemma: "L'homme vrai, ce n'est pas pour elle, l'enveloppe sociale, ce que nous voyons à distance [. . .]. Le 'personnage' ou 'caractère' individue cette substance (anonyme comparable au sang) à laquelle on attribue alors un nom: par exemple, Nathalie Sarraute" [The real man is not for her, the social envelope, what we see at a distance (. . .). The "personnage" or "character" individuates that substance, (anonymous as blood) to which we then attribute a name: Nathalie Sarraute, for example].[13] With the Death of the Novel well under way, the Death of the Author and the Death of the Subject were soon at hand; Cranaki and Belaval were writing at the height of a critical self-consciousness that was in part provoked by the innovations found in the works of Sarraute and the other *nouveaux romanciers*.

In time I would come to realize that my own dilemma was similarly part of a larger debate, the one between American and French feminist literary and cultural critics which could be schematized by a transformation of Cranaki and Belaval's question, "la femme ou l'oeuvre?" If both groups have at some point asked the same question—"What is *the difference* of women's writing?"[14] and "Existe-t-il une écriture féminine?"[15]—each has dealt with the question differently. Critics in the United States tended toward what has been called "a woman-centered approach," that is, concentrating on studies of "Images of Women in (Male) Fiction" or compiling anthologies of women writers in order to formulate a theory of their creativity; in France, critics were investigating "theories of the feminine" and "Woman" as a cultural construct, that is, the product ("l'oeuvre") of male desire.[16] This difference in approach sometimes created division between feminists in the United States and France, but in the last ten years the relationship has become more of a dialogue which has been articulated by, among others, Alice Jardine, Toril Moi, and Rita Felski.

The disruption of linguistic and narrative conventions that led me at first to identify Sarraute's writing as "l'écriture féminine" opens onto another aspect of her work that I had experienced personally but had not yet adequately analyzed critically, and that is the practice of reading. Cranaki and Belaval's question, "Que faire avec Nathalie Sarraute," resonated within my more North American oriented search for "la femme" and A. S. Newman's later question, "Comment lire Nathalie Sarraute," directed my attention back to "l'oeuvre."[17] More importantly, Newman's question took me away from defining Nathalie Sarraute as a particular kind of writer and toward an investigation of myself as a reader. My first reading of Sarraute had been made as a desire to be liberated *from* silence. I had thus inflected her texts with my own sex(uality) and mistaken her work as primarily an expression of female experience.[18]

In an effort to explore more theoretically the ways in which the apparently impersonal narration of *Tropismes* solicited such a personal involvement, I began a close textual analysis of Sarraute's first work. This investigation revealed that the use of language in these prose pieces invites the reader into both a complicitous relationship with an outside (objective) observing narrator and a more intimate (subjective) relationship to the psychological reality of those observed. These two positions can also represent two ways of knowing as they are discussed by Lynn Sukenick in her article "Women and Fiction." Analytical knowing is characterized as "moving around the object," while intuitive knowing is similar to Henri Bergson's "intellectual sympathy," "entering into the object," and to Helen Deutsch's explanation that in intuitive knowing "the other person's mental state [is . . .] emotionally and unconsciously 're-experienced.'"[19]

The dichotomy analytical-intuitive has traditionally been a gendered one and inspired feminist critiques on both sides of the Atlantic, from Susan Griffin to Hélène Cixous.[20] The anonymity of the narrator in *Tropismes*, however, leaves these two ways of knowing conspicuously ungendered, which serves to bracket the gender of this woman writer. The shifting position of the reader in relation to the narration of these prose pieces also enacts a breakdown of that dichotomy because the reader is moved between these two ways of knowing.

Although none of the pieces is presented in a first-person narration, a relationship between the first two persons (I, you) of the verb is established on an imaginary level by the use of the singular or plural third-person pronoun: *I-narrator* tell *you-reader* about *her, him* or *them*. The singular or plural third person is excluded from the narrator/reader relationship and occupies instead the position of the one talked about.[21] The majority of the pieces begin with *Ils, Elles, Il,* or *Elle,* and the distance by which the narrator describes "them" invites the reader into the narrator's position as observer, seen in the following examples: "Ils semblaient sourdre de partout, éclos dans la tiédeur un peu moite de l'air, ils s'écoulaient doucement comme s'ils suintaient des murs, des arbres grillagés, des bancs, des trottoirs sales, des squares" [They seemed to spring up from everywhere, hatched in the slightly damp warmth of the air, they were pouring out softly as if oozing from the walls, the fenced in trees, the benches, the dirty sidewalks, the town squares] ("Tropisme I"); "Elles baragouinaient des choses à demi exprimées, le regard perdu et comme suivant intérieurement un sentiment subtil et délicat qu'elles semblaient ne pouvoir traduire" [They were jabbering about half-expressed things, their look lost and as if following internally a subtle and delicate feeling that they seemed unable to translate] ("Tropisme IV"); "Le matin elle sautait de son lit très tôt, courait dans l'appartement, âcre, serrée, toute chargée de cris, de gestes, de halètements de colère, de 'scènes'" [In the morning she would jump out of bed very early, run through the apartment, acrid, tight, all full of cries, of gestures, of gasps of anger, of "scenes"] ("Tropisme VI").

The I-you dyad initially assures the reader a secure position and announces a communicative, descriptive function, but as the reader seeks to "comprehend" the text, the narration sets up a network of deferred referentiality and takes on a creative power of its own. By means of this and other textual stimuli, the communicative description merges with a performative one. As following chapters discuss, however, the deferral of meaning which has come to be one of the identifying features of a modernist text, in that it plays with the reader's desire for meaning, will be more liberating in Sarraute's novels than in the prose pieces of this first work. Here, the reader's invitation to experience the problematic nature of making meaning is in the service of a representation of tropisms, that is, of (the woman writer) Nathalie Sarraute's perception of reality. Rather than announcing the (feminine) specificity of that perception with the use of a narration in the first person, Sarraute inscribes her specific view of reality in the activity of the narration itself, in the manipulation of the reader in and out of an I-you dyad, between an implied narrator and the reader, and back and forth between being a semi-active participant in a (descriptive) dialogic situation to being a passive-active participant in a creative (performative) one. Tropistic movement is thus represented in *Tropismes* not as an (gender specific) activity to be observed (judged, analyzed, appropriated or dismissed as such), but as a (nongender specific) phenomenon to be experienced. Once Sarraute establishes tropisms as a reality by means of the manipulative narrative authority in this first work, she goes on to investigate that very authority in the novels that follow.

A textual reading of "Tropisme III" offers a more specific example of this movement and manipulation.

Ils étaient venus se loger dans des petites rues tranquilles, derrière le Panthéon, du côté de la rue Gay-Lussac ou de la rue Saint-Jacques, dans des appartements donnant sur des cours sombres, mais tout à fait décents et munis de confort.

On leur offrait cela ici, cela, et la liberté de faire ce qu'ils voulaient, de marcher comme ils voulaient, dans n'importe quel accoutrement, avec n'importe quel visage, dans les modestes petites rues.

Aucune tenue n'était exigée d'eux ici, aucune activité en commun avec d'autres, aucun sentiment, aucun souvenir. On leur offrait une existence à la fois dépouillée et protégée, une existence semblable à une salle d'attente dans une gare de banlieue déserte, une salle nue, grise et tiède, avec un poêle noir au milieu et des banquettes en bois le long des murs.

Et ils étaient contents, ils se plaisaient ici, ils se sentaient presque chez eux, ils étaient en bons termes avec Mme la concierge, avec la crémière, ils portaient leurs vêtements à nettoyer à la plus consciencieuse et la moins chère teinturière du quartier.

Ils ne cherchaient jamais à se souvenir de la campagne où ils avaient grandi, ils ne voyaient jamais surgir en eux, quand ils marchaient dans les rues de leur quartier, quand ils regardaient les devantures des magasins, quand ils passaient devant la loge de la concierge et la saluaient très poli-ment, ils ne voyaient jamais se lever dans leur souvenir un pan de mur inondé de vie, ou les pavés d'une cour, intenses et caressants, ou les marches douces d'un perron sur lequel ils s'étaient assis dans leur enfance.

Dans l'escalier de leur maison, ils rencontraient parfois 'le locataire du dessous,' professeur au lycée, qui revenait de classe avec ses deux enfants, à quatre heures. Ils avaient tous les trois de longues têtes aux yeux pales, luisantes et lisses comme de grands oeufs d'ivoire. La porte de leur apparte-ment s'entr'ouvrait un instant pour les laisser passer. On les voyait poser leurs pieds sur des petits carrés de feutre placés sur le parquet de l'entrée— et s'éloigner silencieusement, glissant vers le fond sombre du couloir.[22]

[They had come to live in the little, quiet streets, behind the Pantheon, next to rue Gay-Lussac or rue Saint-Jacques, in apartments opening onto dark courtyards, but completely decent and equipped with modern conveniences.

They were offered that here, that, and the freedom to do what they wanted, to walk as they wanted, in any get-up, with any expression, in the modest, little streets.

No behavior was demanded of them here, no group activities with the others, no feeling, no memory. They were offered an existence at once stripped and protected, an existence like that in a waiting room at a station in a deserted suburb, a bare room, gray and tepid, with a black stove in the middle and wooden benches along the wall.

And they were content, they enjoyed themselves here, they almost felt at home, they were on good terms with Madame the concierge, with the dairywoman, they took their clothes to be cleaned at the most conscientious and the least expensive cleaners in the neighborhood.

They never tried to remember the countryside where they grew up, they never saw suddenly surging up in their minds, when they walked in the streets of their neighborhood, when they looked at the shop windows, when they passed by the concierge's room and spoke very politely to her, they never saw rise up in their memory a part of a wall inundated with life, or the paving stones of a courtyard, intense and tender, or the soft steps of a stoop where they used to sit in their childhood.

In the stairway of their house, they would sometimes meet "the tenant from downstairs," a high school teacher, who was returning from class with his two children, at four o'clock. They all three had long heads with pale eyes, shiny and smooth like big, ivory eggs. The door of their apartment would open for an instant to let them pass. One saw them put their feet on the little felt squares found on the floor of the entranceway—and silently withdraw, slipping toward the dark end of the hallway.]

Like the little quiet streets located in the shadow of the Pantheon, the figure of *ils* is shadowed by progressively qualifying indicators of place which limit the volition suggested by the opening clause, "Ils étaient venus se loger. . . ." *Ils* come to live "dans des petites rue tranquilles"; these streets are then positioned "derrière le Panthéon," which are vaguely "du côté de la rue Gay-Lussac ou de la rue Saint-Jacques." By the middle of the sentence, *ils* have been deposited "dans des appartements," but the qualification continues. These are apartments "donnant sur des cours sombres, mais tout à fait décents et munis de confort." The qualifying spatial indicators central to this paragraph ("dans," "derrière," "du côté de," "donnant sur") operate as deictic indicators do, that is, like demonstrative adverbs or adjectives they organize the spatial and temporal relations in the passage and announce some subject as "point de repère" [orientation point].[23] The reader is at first invited to perceive this scene with an implied subject outside the textual space, but by the end of the sentence, the reader has been dislocated conceptually by these indicators within that space.

The first paragraph also dislocates the reader semantically, in the sense that an effort to locate the meaning of the words "tranquilles" and "sombres" by means of a referentiality to some "objective real" outside the text is problematized. *Ils* (and the reader) are at first moved from place to place by the spatial indicators, and now the reader experiences a further manipulation as the significance of these modifiers is dislocated, or relocated, to have a qualified meaning in this text. The adjective "tranquilles" modifying "rues," when it is read on a denotative level signifies "immobiles, silencieux." Its connotation implies "une idée de paix et de sécurité."[24] Given the mobility within the paragraph which the reader has experienced conceptually, however, the word's semantic meaning is destabilized. The concept of tranquility is again destabilized when the word "sombres" is not left to lie in its semantic state out of which the reader may derive meanings ranging from the quality of light to the disposition of the soul. The reader is immediately told that although the courtyards are "sombres," the apartments are "tout à fait décents et munis de confort," thus qualifying the qualifier.

The loss of volition on the part of *ils* enacted by the narration in the first paragraph is now represented syntactically in the opening clause of the second in which this subject is now an indirect object: "On leur offrait cela ici. . . ." Another dislocation of signification begins with the use of the word "cela" [that], indefinite in its antecedent, and continues through the use of repetition. Extending the tension created in the first paragraph between the semantic function of "tranquilles" and the conceptual mobility of the indicators surrounding it, the semantic presence of the word "ici" [here] in the phonetic repetition, "cela, ici, cela et la . . . ," is surrounded by the homonymic equivalence of its opposite, "là" [there]. This repetition creates a tension between these two spaces which will enter the text more explicitly in the penultimate paragraph. The repetition of words and syntax as the sentence continues joins two pairs—"de faire ce qu'ils voulaient, de marcher comme ils voulaient, dans n'importe quel accoutrement, avec n'importe quel visage"—while the images themselves compound the vagueness introduced at the beginning of the sentence by "cela." The paragraph offers a description of "la liberté [qu'on] leur offrait," and indeed the phrase, "la liberté de faire ce qu'ils voulaient," suggests a freedom which the reader might desire or recognize. The singsong repetition of the sound "la" that precedes this phrase does not feel like mockery until the appearance of the paired pairs in the following phrases. The repetition of sounds, words, and phrases combines with the indefinite "cela" to create the sense of an empty, circular freedom. The one-sentence paragraph ends with the phrase "dans les modestes et petites rues," but the literal meaning for this phrase that might find its referent in one that is similar in the first paragraph, "dans des petites rues tranquilles," is no longer functional.

Repetition again structures the opening sentence of the next paragraph, again in reference to "la liberté," and the word comes to signify a negative freedom: "Aucune tenue . . . aucune activité . . . aucun sentiment . . . aucun souvenir." The phonetic, semantic and syntactic repetitions of the preceding paragraph join with this repetition of negatives to circle in on the meaning of "liberté." Without the explicit mediation of a narrator who defines the constraint of this freedom, the narration itself becomes constraining for the reader, like "la liberté [qu'on] leur offrait."

This negative freedom might best be described by the word that ends the preceding paragraph, "modeste"—"ce qui est simple, sans faste ou sans éclat"—but the text offers its own description, "une existence à la fois dépouillée et protégée."[25] This description is then given an analogy which displaces the space so detailed in the first paragraph and replaces it within a metaphorical space: "une existence semblable à une salle d'attente dans une gare de banlieue déserte, une salle nue, grise et tiède, avec un poêle noir au milieu et des banquettes en bois le long des murs." The mobility of spatial indicators found in the first paragraph is similarly replaced by a proliferation of adjectives that undermine any signification the reader might have applied to the adjectives found in the beginning of the piece—"déserte," "nue, grise et tiède," "un poêle noir," "des banquettes en bois," bear no resemblance to "tranquilles" or "tout à fait décents et munis de confort." At this point in the text, the "poêle noir" and the "banquettes en bois" seem to have more substance than either *ils* or "la liberté."

The reader can only be skeptical of the *meaning* of the words beginning the fourth paragraph ("Et ils étaient contents, ils se plaisaient ici. . . .") because a tension has been created in the reading experience between making meaning by referentiality outside the text and making meaning by means of a referentiality within the text. The textual strategies thus far—that is, the accumulation of spatial indicators in the first paragraph; the phonetic tension between "ici" and "la/là," which conveys a metaphorical tension between places in the second; and finally, perhaps the center around which these tensions turn, "la liberté de faire ce qu'ils voulaient"—all combine to create an unnamed anxiety for the reader because of the possibility of a troubling interior reality beneath the surface of this "existence à la fois dépouillée et protégée." The following phrase, "ils se sentaient presque chez eux," extends that anxiety, which is only aggravated by the neat, modest daily life described in the rest of the sentence here. The tension between "ici" and "là" represents a surface-depth dichotomy in the second paragraph, and in the one that follows, it becomes a more dialectical movement between the present (surface "ici") and the past (depth "là").

The figure of *ils* begins this paragraph in the position of subject as it did in the preceding paragraph, but the reader's suspicion aroused about the meaning of "ils se sentaient presque chez eux," that is, about the unified nature of this subject, is here compounded by the use of negation and repetition: "Ils ne cherchaient jamais à se souvenir, [. . .] ils ne cherchaient jamais à retrouver, [. . .] ils ne voyaient jamais se lever [. . .]." The repeated negative terms diminish the presence of the objects of the negation ("se souvenir," and so on). The earlier tension created between "ici" and "là" now enters the text more fully: a temporal and spatial *ailleurs*, that is, an other place, *là*, is represented by the objects of negation, whereas a sense for *ici* is contained by the negation itself, and the figure of *ils* is split between them. As the sentence continues, "ici" is further composed of the images introduced by "quand" which interrupt the series of negations: "quand ils marchaient dans les rues de leur quartier, quand ils regardaient les devantures des magasins, quand ils passaient devant la loge de la concierge. . . ." Just as the repetitions and negations circled in on the signification of the word "liberté" in the preceding paragraphs, the present situation of *ils* "ici" circles and constrains a past "là" which nevertheless surges up to finish the sentence. This tension between "ici" and "là" can serve as a model not only for the reader's position, never allowed to remain one of unified subjectivity "là" outside the text, but also for that of the figures who people Sarraute's subsequent novels to be discussed later.

One way the reader has been replaced in the I-you dyad throughout the piece has been by the use of the possessive adjective "leur" [their]. As we have seen, however, the deferral of meaning and the textual strategies in this piece have served at the same time to create a textual tension for the reader and to disrupt that dyad. In the opening phrase of the final paragraph, "Dans l'escalier de leur maison, ils rencontraient. . . ," the metaphorical tension between "ici" and "là" identified with *ils* is given a concrete image (the figure of *ils* positioned on the stairway between two floors), and the reader's textual tension is brought to a halt by the (concrete) literalness of the language. The I-you dyad seems to be reestablished, but the dislocation which has characterized this text throughout operates in the last paragraph to dislocate that dyad one last time.

The dislocation begins with the object of the verb phrase "ils rencontraient parfois" set off by quotation marks, "'le locataire du dessous,'" which designates "le locataire" as the one talked about. "'Le locataire'" is joined by "ses deux enfants" as "ils" in the next sentence, "Ils avaient tous les trois . . . oeufs d'ivoire," and in the following sentence the referent to *leur* is established. The subject *on* which begins the following sentence is the only personal pronoun in French which theoretically can refer to any of the three persons, singular or plural, of the verb. The presence of this pronoun earlier in the text, "on leur offrait," established the authority of the observing narrative voice and invited the reader into that position. Given the positions established in the final paragraph, however, *on* could represent any of the following: *tu*, the reader addressed by the narrating voice; *nous*, the reader and the narrating voice; or, moving *ils* into a position with the reader and the narrating voice, *nous* could refer to all three observing this new group "ils"; or *vous*, which thereby effects a shift by the narrating voice to move the reader and *ils* into position together. It is even conceivable that *on* could represent the implied narrative *je*. This indefinite personal pronoun which effectively eludes any definite referentiality figures all dislocating gestures within this piece.

In contrast to the unspecific nature of *on* is the very specific composition of the group now represented by "ils": "professeur au lycée, qui revenait de classe avec ses deux enfants, à quatre heures." The presence of this group gives the pronoun *ils* another position: *ils*, the ones talked about now talk about "ils," and the reader is left looking for another point of orientation in the final image: "On les voyait poser leurs pieds sur des petits carrés de feutre placés sur le parquet de l'entrée—et s'éloigner silencieusement, glissant vers le fond sombre du couloir." A new spatial indicator is introduced in this image, "sur," and is then repeated in such a way that the reader is neither dislocated spatially in the paragraph nor allowed to remain as an observer outside the text, but is instead moved more and more directly into the space described.

That movement is represented by the phrase which precedes this indicator ("On les *voyait poser leurs pieds*") and contains three elements counteracting the mobility and tension introduced at the beginning of "Tropisme III" and sustained throughout. With the verb "voyait" the narrating voice directs the reader's point of view to a specific scene; the reader's view is "posée," like the feet of the professor and his children; and finally, the object of this gaze is "leurs pieds," feet placed solidly "sur des petits carrés de feutre." The hard sounds of the vowel and consonants of *sur* further substantiate this feeling of solidity or immobility. This image and the language by which it is represented free the reader from the tension between "ici" and "là" that has been felt textually. Similarly, the word "sombre" at the end of the sentence is not marked by any qualifications as it was in the first paragraph of the piece, leaving the reader free to return to a referentiality outside the text where "sombre" denotes "peu éclairé."

The reader has thus been aligned with the observing narrator in an I-you dyad established by the position of *ils* as the ones talked about, and because of certain textual strategies has shared with *ils* the anxiety of dislocation and tension between "ici" and "là." The I-you dyad splits at a certain point, is reestablished in the last paragraph, but is finally deposited in the indefinite (plural, singular?) *on*. Similarly, the reader now diverges from identification with the psychological reality of *ils*. While in the final image the figure of *ils* is left imprisoned in the text, on the stairway between floors, the other figure of "ils," described as having "de longues têtes aux yeux pâles, luissantes et lisses comme de grands oeufs d'ivoire," escapes ("s'éloigner silencieusement, glissant vers le fond sombre du couloir").

The reader is thus left with another surface-depth dichotomy from which there is no escape, its image corresponding to the one Sarraute gives to her concept of "tropismes": "des mouvements indéfinissables qui glissent très rapidement aux limites de notre conscience."[26] Unlike *ils*, "ils" is given both an antecedent, "[le] professeur et ses deux enfants," and a physical description, which allows this group to function very schematically as a character. In "Tropisme III," Sarraute has thus not only exercised her narrative authority in such a way as to give the reader an experience of her (specific) perception of reality, she also has introduced the question of surface-depth dichotomy into her own larger discussion of the nature of conventional character, which serves as the focal point of her first two novels.

Like *Tropismes*, however, Sarraute's fourth novel, *Les Fruits d'Or*, concentrates less on character and more on an investigation of tropistic reality. Narrative language is manipulated in *Tropismes* to give the reader an experience of tropistic depth beneath the surface of description. In *Les Fruits d'Or*, the reader is thrown immediately into a surface of discourse that originates not in characters as individuals but in voices as centers of different states of being also represented in *sous-conversation*. Whereas Sarraute's first two novels, *Portrait d'un inconnu* and *Martereau*, introduce masculine figures who by virtue of their first-person narration tempt the reader to succumb to the tendency to create characters, the fourth novel, *Les Fruits d'Or*, undercuts that temptation at every turn. Interlocutors speak, but phrases and words which might serve to character-ize a voice appear to be used by other voices from one chapter to another. This novel resists the creation of characters, just as Cranaki and Belaval strive to do in their study of Sarraute, and creates instead a mirror which reflects the reader's desire, much like my reading of "Tropismes III." Because the narrative figures in *Les Fruits d'Or* are divested of any characterization except gender, a discussion of the qualities that the different gendered figures come to represent in this novel will precede the investigation of the role gender plays in the identity quests found in Sarraute's first two novels.

3

Readers Talking: *Les Fruits d'Or*

Les Fruits d'Or follows a certain linearity as it traces the rise and fall in popularity of an imaginary novel called "Les Fruits d'Or" (which for the purposes of this discussion will be designated by quotation marks). At the same time, however, the conversation and *sous-conversation* which make up the narration of Sarraute's fourth novel are so marked by generalities from beginning to end that the reader can open to any chapter in Proustian fashion and become engaged in the circularity of discourse.

Les Fruits d'Or thematizes both Sarraute's sense of the evolutionary nature of literary works and the relativity of their reception. Sarraute said in 1968 that "un aspect des *Fruits d'Or*, c'est le besoin, l'impossibilité de saisir dans une oeuvre d'art une valeur absolue" [one aspect of *Les Fruits d'Or* is the need, the impossibility, of seizing an absolute value in a work of art]. "Elle se dérobe constamment," she continues, "un seul lecteur arrive, à la fin, à établir avec l'oeuvre un contact direct, à préserver la fraîcheur de sa sensation, comme s'efforce de le faire un écrivain" [It is always elusive. A single reader arrives at the end to establish direct contact and to preserve the intact freshness of his sensation, as the writer tries to do].[1] The qualities embodied in this "single reader" lead Jaccard to call him "an ideal reader," and Minogue to conclude that *Les Fruits d'Or* "reasserts [. . .] the vitality of literature": "Those who assimilate literature into their very fibres will preserve its creative power, while those who use it briefly to decorate socially presentable images of themselves, will in the end destroy it in their ceaseless and frenetic oscillations between one bright star and another."[2]

The few modifiers which appear in the last chapter of *Les Fruits d'Or* identify the final reader who emerges as masculine, which can be explained by Sarraute's words cited earlier: "I often prefer *he* to *she* because *he* is neutral but *she* is only female." In a discursive text that depends almost uniquely on personal pronouns to identify speakers, and one in which masculine pronouns are considered "neutral," feminine pronouns stand out as something "other." When a reader who is "only female" attempts, in spite of herself, to create characters with whom to identify, that desire necessarily shifts attention to the way in which feminine pronouns are used in this novel. A voice identified as feminine opens *Les Fruits d'Or*, and several feminine voices speak throughout. Some of the qualities that these feminine figures represent ultimately characterize the (masculine) ideal reader, but when embodied by feminine figures these qualities are rebuked by masculine figures. When the (masculine) ideal reader is accorded these (feminine) qualities, they are in effect "neutralized." This kind of neutralization remains an issue for a feminist analysis in the first two novels, but as discussion of the later novels will show, such gender differences eventually dissipate in Sarraute's work.

The neutral position of the ideal reader is not established until certain battles are engaged between gendered positions that are both traditionalist and modernist. The former is marked by an aggressive masculine figure in opposition to a timid, polite feminine one. This is the relationship that begins the novel. In order to highlight the gendered nature of certain positions, my English translation of the French pronoun *elle* will be *it/she* or an equivalent, depending on syntax. This translation will also be found in my discussion of the later novels to mark what I find to be a gendered dynamic between two figures in the narration.

In the first three chapters of *Les Fruits d'Or*, the reader is introduced to several levels of discourse which can be identified as the "optique" of one of three figures.[3] In Chapter 1 a feminine and a masculine speaker are entertained by another masculine figure, the "host." When he brings out a reproduction of a Courbet painting for the couple's admiration, each speaker has a different response to this representation of "le lieu commun." The feminine speaker opens the novel with the words, "'Tu étais terrible [. . .], je suis polie'" ["You were terrible (. . .), I am polite"]. *Elle* describes the host's gesture as "touchant" [touching] and considers it an effort to "partager" [share], "'il m'a fait tout à coup terriblement pitié'" ["he suddenly made me pity him"].[4] The feminine figure's interlocutor, on the other hand, scorns the host's gesture: "'Il était ulcéré parce que je ne me suis pas extasié comme ils font tous, parce que je ne me suis pas prosterné . . .'" ["He was appalled because I did not get ecstatic like the rest of them, because I did not prostrate myself like they all do . . ."] (5).

The feminine figure's position comes to characterize that of most other feminine figures in this novel: "'Moi, j'ai si peur [. . .], je ne sais pas où me mettre. Il me semble toujours . . .'" ["I am so afraid (. . .), I don't know where to put myself. It always seems to me that . . ."]—the

ellipsis marks an interruption in her discourse, for the masculine voice
is the more aggressive of the two (6–7). As Minogue notes, in the "play
of pronouns" between these two figures, "if 'she' does not accept the
proffered solidarity, she risks being joined with 'them' in a destructive
'you'" (115). "'Oui, ça m'a amusé de te voir,'" *il* tells *elle*. "'Tu te con-
duis comme avec les fous. Tout le monde, d'ailleurs, avec lui joue cette
comédie. Vous me faites tous penser à cette pièce de Pirandello [. . .]'"
["Yes, it was amusing to watch you" (. . .). You act like you are with
someone who's disturbed. Everyone plays that act with him. You all
make me think of that play by Pirandello (. . .)"] (7).

The masculine figure's scorn for *elle*, and "everyone else" who plays
this game with the host, is resumed in the passage in which "la tête de
chien" [the head of a dog] is the object of wild adoration. The term is
then represented by a feminine pronoun, which puts those who are
subject to such adoration in a feminine camp and those who are not
in the camp of the aggressive masculine figure: "[. . .] en elle réunis . . .
délices . . . communion, fusion des âmes . . . [. . .] Le voilà. Il tombe en
transes, le Dieu le possède, il se convulsionne, [. . .] l'écume aux lèvres"
[(. . .) in it/her united . . . delights . . . communion, fusion of souls . . .
(. . .) There he is. He falls into a trance, God possesses him, he goes
into convulsions, (. . .) foaming at the mouth] (9).

The feminine figure who opens the novel is thus identified as timid
and polite and is joined by her pity for the host to those who "fall into
trances" over a work of art. In an exchange after the aggressive masculine figure has scorned the host, *elle* speaks in marked discourse: "'Tu
ne peux pas comprendre . . . J'espérais qu'on discuterait . . . Je ne pouvais pas supporter que tous les ponts soient coupés . . .'" ["You can't
understand . . . I was hoping that we would discuss it . . . I can't stand
for all bridges to be burned . . ."] (13). In the passage that follows, this
desire for discussion and the fear of being ostracized are represented
by another feminine noun "la flamme" [the flame]. This designation
further inscribes the gendered tension already established, and as the
image is elaborated it could just as easily be a description of the feminine figure's earlier reaction to the scorned host: "[. . .] la flamme tout
à coup vacille, elle se penche, elle s'éteint, l'autre qui ne la quitte jamais
des yeux [. . .], sachant qu'on ne le laissera pas [. . .] s'égarer dans l'obscurité [. . .], l'autre vers elle vaillamment avance" [(. . .) the flame suddenly flickers, it/she is leaning, it/she is going out, the other one who
never takes his eyes off it/her (. . .), knowing that they would not leave
him (. . .) wanders around in the darkness (. . .), the other toward it/her
valiantly advances] (13). This passage ends with words spoken by the
feminine figure, or rather cried out to the host who was left in the

darkness, "'Les Fruits d'Or . . . vous m'entendez? Qu'en pensez vous?'"
["'Les Fruits d'Or'. . . do you hear me? What do you think about it?"]
(14).

After this opening scene, *elle* returns to see the host to confirm
whether or not he truly likes "Les Fruits d'Or." All the drama of the
above scene is dissipated by his reaction. The narration appears to be
from the consciousness of the figure of *elle* in the one-sided exchange
that follows in *sous-conversation:* "Ah, il n'y avait rien, c'est cela? Vous
ne pensiez rien. Les Fruits d'Or—c'est bien. Vous pensiez cela. C'est
tout. [. . .] C'est cela que vous me donnez, cette menue monnaie [. . .].
Ce sont des pièces que vous avez sans doute rapportées d'un pays
étranger où je ne suis jamais allée . . . Elles n'ont pas cours ici, où je
vis, vous le savez bien [. . .]" [Ah, it was nothing, is that it? You didn't
think anything. "Les Fruits d'Or"—it's good. That's what you think.
That's all. (. . .) That's what you give me, this little coin (. . .). One of
those coins you must have brought back from a foreign country where
I have never been . . . They are worth nothing here where I live, you
know that very well] (16–17). Like this feminine figure at the end of
Chapter 1, the ideal reader in the last chapter constitutes an identity
not in opposition to the figure of *ils,* as the aggressive masculine
speaker does earlier ("'je ne me suis pas extasié comme *ils* font tous'"),
but in relation to the imaginary novel, "Les Fruits d'Or."

At the end of Chapter 2 the narration returns to the nocturnal visit
elle makes to see the host, and it presents his *sous-conversation* as he
tries to explain what is "admirable" about "Les Fruits d'Or." What
began as a guest-host relationship in Chapter 1 of Sarraute's novel becomes one between student and master in Chapter 2, which characterizes the other feminine-masculine relationships in this novel.
"'Excusez-moi, je vous ai dérangé'" ["Excuse me, I bothered you"], *elle*
tells the host at the end of this chapter. "'Mais à certains moments,
vous savez, je deviens très égoiste, je ne peux pas m'en empêcher, il
faut absolument que je vous voie'" ["But at certain moments, you know,
I become very selfish, I cannot stop myself, I absolutely must see you"]
(28). Chapter 3 begins after *elle* has visited the host, and the character-
ization of her visit as an intrusion in his order introduces the modernist
component of the feminine-masculine relationships in the novel: "[. . .]
tout ce qui en lui, à l'arrivée de l'intrus, avait fui, [. . .] se regroupe,
s'organise, rentre dans l'ordre" [(. . .) everything in him that had fled
with the arrival of the intruder regrouped, organized, itself, returned
to order] (29). On a narrative level, feminine voices arise to interrupt
masculine discourse, like various masculine figures do later in the
novel. These interruptions insert some form of subjectivity into a discussion which represents an attempt to be objective, and they are analo-

gous to "poetic language" as Kristeva describes it. This is a language which breaks codes "to find a specific discourse closer to the body and emotions, to the unnameable repressed by the social contract."[5]

The feminine speaker disappears at the beginning of Chapter 3, and the host moves into a more powerful role of a critic in the process of writing an article about "Les Fruits d'Or." The description of the feminine figure's departure originates in the masculine figure's consciousness, as seen initially in the reference in *sous-conversation* to "la vieille machine," presumably the typewriter at which he was working. The language and images used to describe *elle* in this passage recall Sarraute's description of tropistic reality as well as poetic language which is "closer to the body and emotions, to the unnameable." These also are qualities that later mark the ideal reader's description of his response to "Les Fruits d'Or": "Même l'image qu'a laissée, l'espace de quelques secondes, la longue forme étroite et sombre qui descendait les marches de l'escalier, s'est évanouie. Il ne reste plus rien, pas même une sensation de soulagement. Il n'y a rien à redresser, à effacer, aucun dommage à réparer. Pas le moindre dégât, aucune éraflure, tache, poussière, fine buée sur les rouages lisses et brillants: le vieille machine admirablement construite, solide, inattaquable, très bien huilée et préservée, s'ébranle doucement, se remet à tourner" [Even the image it left, within the space of a few seconds, the long, narrow and somber form which was descending the stairway, has disappeared. Nothing is left any more, not even a feeling of relief. There is nothing to redress, to erase, no damage to repair. Not the least waste, no scratch, spot, dust, fine mist on the smooth and bright gears: the old, admirably constructed machine, solid, unassailable, very well oiled and preserved, takes off softly, begins to turn again] (30).

At the end of this passage "la vieille machine" is unscathed by the intrusion, and in its "solid, unassailable" state it serves as a figure for the kind of language the host turned critic admires: "[. . .] cette langue écrite qui [. . .] ordonne, structure, durcit ce qui doit durer" [(. . .) that written language which (. . .) orders, structures, hardens what must endure]: "Elle [. . .] ne laisse jamais passer ce qui est mou, flou, baveux, gluant" [It/She never lets pass what is soft, vague, slobbery, slimy]. The text assigns other attributes to "cette langue écrite" which are feminine nouns in French: "quelle exquise courtoisie," "quelle pudeur, quelle fière modestie" [what exquisite courtesy, (. . .) what decency, what proud modesty]. The feminine figure as a subject represents an "intrusion," but when this masculine critic looks for abstractions in which to contain a language that is desirable, these abstractions are feminine. "On est entre gens de bonne compagnie" [One is among good company], the text says, that is, back in the master's discourse where noth-

ing from the body or the emotions erupts in tropistic disorder, and
where the feminine falls easily into abstraction (31).

The fourth chapter of Les Fruits d'Or is the longest in the novel,
about forty-five pages. In each of the subsequent ten chapters, ranging
from roughly four to fourteen pages, the novel's theme is dramatized
as the "optiques," and thus the figures involved, are multiplied to create
the "vacarme" that the ideal reader seeks to escape in the end. Among
the variety of "optiques" in this weighty fourth chapter are four feminine speakers who represent the gamut of the abstraction Woman seen
in Sarraute's novel: a disciple figure like the one who "disappeared" at
the beginning of Chapter 3, a critic of the "realist" approach whose
remarks are ridiculed and then appropriated for masculine arguments,
a solitary voice who speaks for the "little people" but is ultimately
rejected as a madwoman, and finally, a possible partner for a solitary
il.

Chapter 4 opens in the middle of a discussion about "l'article de
Brulé sur les Fruits d'Or" [the article by Brulé about "Les Fruits d'Or"]
which is judged by the speakers present to be "de tout premier ordre"
[first-class], "parfait" [perfect]: "Les vraies valeurs triomphent. Les
honnêtes gens peuvent respirer" [True values triumph. Decent people
can breathe]. The "enemy" is here identified in terms recalling the
tension between a master discourse and a dissenting one:

> Les révoltés, les fortes têtes, vous tous, là-bas, qui vouliez faire table rase, qui
> dansiez sur les belles terres plantureuses que vous aviez dévastées vos danses
> sauvages, poussiez vos cris, vous le savez maintenant, la fête est finie. [. . .]
> Maintenant on apprendra à tous les paresseux, les ignorants, les enfants de
> la nature, les forts tempéraments, à marcher droit. A respecter les règles du
> savoir-vivre, de la bienséance. On leur apprendra—ah, c'est dur, n'est-ce
> pas?—que la littérature est un lieu sacré, fermé, où seul un humble appre-
> ntissage, l'étude patiente des maîtres peut donner le droit à quelques rares
> élus de pénétrer (33, 34).

> [The rebels, the hotheads, all of you over there, who wanted to make a clean
> slate, who were dancing on the beautiful, fertile lands that you devastated
> with your wild dances, spewing your cries, you know now that the party is
> over. (. . .) Now we will teach all the lazy, the ignorant, the nature children,
> the hard-headed ones to tow the line. To respect the rule of *savoir-vivre*, of
> *bienséance*. We will teach them—ah, it is difficult, isn't it?—that literature
> is a sacred place, closed up, where only humble apprenticeship, a patient
> study of the masters gives a few rare and chosen ones the right to penetrate.]

What makes this passage particularly powerful is that the exaggeration
of the language not only mocks itself, it connects at the same time to
the distortion that this point of view takes on for someone who has
been oppressed by even one of its elements. The pedantry represented

here has led to monumental efforts by feminists in this country to establish a tradition of women writers precisely because the domain of literature has traditionally been "sacred"—and "closed"—that is, male.[6]

As the discussion in the opening pages of Chapter 4 continues, the objectification of the literary work enacted by this point of view becomes clear. Another voice adds that "Les Fruits d'Or" is "admirable," and the feminine noun ("une petite chose") that *il* uses to describe his joy about the novel enhances the gender inflection in his remarks: "Admirable. Un vrai joyau . . . la main amoureusement caresse dans l'air une forme arrondie . . . Une petite chose parfaite. Refermée sur elle-même. Ronde. Pleine" [A real plaything . . . the hand lovingly caresses a rounded form in the air . . . . A perfect little thing. Closed in upon itself/herself. Round. Full] (35). The ideal reader's later intimacy with "Les Fruits d'Or" is based on a subjective interaction rather than on this kind of objectifying gesture, and such a gender-specific description never appears in the consciousness of a feminine speaker.

As the discussion continues among masculine figures in Chapter 4, a feminine figure enters the narration in *sous-conversation*. Her response is marked by the same outrage at indiscretion as that of the feminine speaker who opened the book: "Mais perdent-ils donc la tête? [. . .] . . . comment osent-ils? ont-ils donc oublié qu'il est là, qu'il écoute, replié sur lui-même. . ." [But have they lost their minds? (. . .) . . . how dare they? Have they forgotten that he is here, listening, turned in upon himself . . .] (35). And like the first figure, this feminine figure asks the question, "'Dites-nous . . . Qu'en pensez-vous?'" ["Tell us . . . What do you think of it?"]. The question is not asked in this passage as an attempt to save anyone; it is posed by a disciple at the feet of a "Maître," imploring him to share his revered opinion, even though the text notes the "dédain" with which he receives this adoration (37).[7] *Elle* had earlier confided to the Master that she found the style of "Les Fruits d'Or" to be "rigide" and "froid" [cold], but now he praises these same qualities as evidence of the work's modernity: "'Elle [cette oeuvre] reflète parfaitement l'esprit de notre temps'" ["It/She reflects perfectly the spirit of our times"] (38).

In such a traditional master-student relationship it is the student who must "se soumettre" [submit herself], "il faut s'arracher de tout ce qu'elle aime" [she must tear herself away from everything that she loves] in order to become "droite et pure" [straight and pure]:

Il faut s'arracher [. . .] à ces tièdeurs intimes où, repliée sur elle-même, elle se laissait couler toujours plus bas vers quelles moiteurs douceâtres, quelles fades, honteuses, délicieuses odeurs . . . Il faut oublier tout cela. [. . .] Devant elle s'étend quelque chose de gris, de froid. . . cryptes, voûtes, sépulcres, musées où un jour blafard tombe sur les dalles, les colonnes brisées, les sarcophages de marbre, les statues aux poses hiératiques, aux yeux opaques, aux visages figés. Elle a envie de s'écarter, de s'enfuir, de retourner là-bas, vers les molles tiédeurs, avec les autres, ses proches, ses semblables, ils la tirent [. . .]. Ecartez-vous. J'entre. [. . .Je] contemple (39–40).

[She must tear herself away from that intimate warmth where, turned inward, she would let herself flow always deeper toward some sweet dampness, some sickly, shameful and delicious odors . . . She has to forget all that. (. . .) Something gray, cold, stretches out before her . . . crypts, arches, sepulchers, museums where a pale light falls on the stone floor, the columns broken, marble sarcophagi, statues in hieratic poses, with opaque eyes, frozen faces. She wants to break away, to flee, to return to the languid warmth, with the others, her kin, they pull her (. . .). Leave me alone. I am going in. (. . . I) contemplate.]

The renunciation *elle* makes is described in terms of space ("devant elle s'étend," "elle a envie de s'écarter, de s'enfuir, de retourner là-bas," "J'entre"). These spatial images serve to connect this figure of *elle* to the feminine figure at the end of Chapter 1 who refuses the "menue monnaie" that the host offered her because "elles n'ont pas de cours ici, où je vis." The spatial imagery also recalls the description of literature at the beginning of Chapter 4 as the "lieu sacré, fermé." The juxtaposition of the masculine and feminine figures' use of spatial imagery effects a gendered opposition. The terms used to describe what *elle* renounces, "moiteurs douceâtres, quelles fades, honteuses, délicieuses odeurs," can be similarly juxtaposed with "la vieille machine admirablement construite," which represents the host turned critic in Chapter 3. The (masculine) ideal reader in the last chapter, however, does not use the imagery associated with the masculine figures in Chapters 3 and 4; he describes his appreciation for "Les Fruits d'Or" in terms closer to the sensual imagery describing what *elle* must here renounce.

The space *elle* enters is animated by "des formes pétrifiées qui se dressent dans le jour blafard" [petrified forms, which stand up in the pale light]. At the same time, "un souffle tiède" [a tepid breeze] brings "une familière intime, rassurante bouffée" [an intimate, familiar, reassuring breath]. What is "familiar" to *elle* in this space are the flat images of women in fashion magazines and portraits of noble women which she contemplates and which ennoble the feminine role as disciple to a masculine figure. This role is not described as such; it is suggested by sensual imagery: "Une onde tiède la parcourt, une douce vibration, l'exquise titillation de l'humilité, de la dévotion" [A tepid wave runs over her, a sweet vibration, the exquisite titillation of humility, of devotion] (40). The renouncement is complete with the female disciple's words marked by quotes: "'Ah que ça fait du bien de savoir que vous

aimez ce beau livre, mon cher Lucien'" ["Ah, it's good to know that
you like this beautiful book, my dear Lucien"] (41).

This is the kind of passage that Rous-Besser would interpret as a
"satire of women's position in society," but such an interpretation represses the power of the sensual imagery and dramatic language in the
passage which not only takes a reader into that world and sits her
down in front of those magazines, but also reveals the feminine figure's
ambivalent relationship to the tropistic world she leaves behind, to the
world (as "lieu sacré") that she enters, and to the role that is cast for
her there, as seen in the *sous-conversation* which precedes the above
renouncement: "Bien sûr, ceux qui [. . .] veulent se reconnaître, ceux
qui veulent toujours retrouver partout leurs propres sentiments, restent
sur leur faim" [Of course, those who (. . .) want to recognize themselves,
who always find their own sentiments everywhere, are stuck with their
hunger (. . .)] (41).

The exchange above between *elle* and her mentor is observed by
another "optique" at the beginning of the next passage: "Les arguments
d'autorités. [. . .] Une copie, il avait envie de lui crier cela . . . [. . .] Ce
n'est rien Les Fruits d'Or. Un pastiche" [Arguments about authorities.
(. . .) A copy, he felt like screaming that to her . . . (. . .) It's nothing "Les
Fruits d'Or." A pastiche] (41). While this figure of *il* mocks the female
disciple's desire for authority, he also asserts his own desire. The *sous-
conversation* of this figure represents a space which resembles "le lieu
sacré" of literature: "Nobles villes aux dômes étincelants, aux places
harmonieuses [. . .] . . . là il s'est toujours vécu. [. . .] Un nouveau monument s'élève [. . .] . . . une demeure à son goût, à sa mesure, à la mesure
de l'homme . . . il s'y sent chez lui . . ." [Noble cities with shining
domes, peaceful town squares (. . .) . . . that's where he has always lived.
(. . .) A new monument is going up (. . .) . . . a dwelling in accordance
with his taste, a worthy match, a match for any man . . . he feels at
home there . . .] (43).

This figure then addresses *elle* in *sous-conversation*, pointing out to
her what constitutes "une oeuvre d'art" [a work of art]: "D'abord parce
qu'elle est vraie. [. . .] Un style souple, puissant qui soutient [. . .] les
grands, les vrais sentiments . . . ceux de tous les hommes normaux,
sains, pas ceux de quelques névrosés [. . .], les miens, les vôtres, ma
chère amie" [First because it/she's true. (. . .) A supple style, powerful,
which supports (. . .) the great, true, feelings . . . those of all normal
men, healthy ones, not those of some neurotics (. . .), my sentiments,
yours, my dear friend] (43). The gendered nature of this discussion is
highlighted by the audience, no longer a single feminine figure but a
plural one, *elles*, which listens to the pronouncements made by this
masculine figure.

The narration of the reaction of this plural is characterized by the scorn of a critic disgusted by the likes of Madame Bovary, those who look for their own "truth" in a novel.[8] *Il* gives an example of a moment of "truth" in "Les Fruits d'Or," when "la naissance de l'amour" [the birth of love] is summed up by the male character's simple gesture of laying a shawl on the female character's shoulders, and it is at this point that a singular feminine figure enters the narration: "Elle rassemble toutes ses forces, elle crie . . . 'C'est faux. Moi je vous le dis. Archifaux. C'est ça la fausse vérité des romans'" [She gathers all her strength, she cries out . . . "That's false. I'm here to tell you. Utterly false. That's the false truth of novels"]:

> "Ce geste [. . .] peut signifier mille choses . . . ou rien. Une simple gentillesse, sans plus . . . Pierre, tenez, mon mari, mais c'est quelque chose qu'il fait tout naturellement, pour n'importe qui [. . .]. Mais les romanciers choisissent n'importe quoi . . . [. . .]. Un geste qu'ils ont remarqué [. . .], ils le prennent et ils se disent: [. . .] il va signifier la naissance du grand amour. On pense que lui, il sait. Et on dit: mais comme c'est vrai. Et on le retrouve dans la vie . . . Bien sûr qu'on l'y retrouve, puisqu'on l'y a mis . . . Puisqu'on on voit la vie à travers les romans . . . Il y a des gens marqués pour toujours par ces vérités-là. Moi, tenez, je connaissais une pauvre fille . . ." (46–47).

> ["This gesture (. . .) can mean a thousand things . . . or nothing. A simple politeness, nothing more . . . Pierre, listen, my husband, but this is something that he does completely naturally, for anyone (. . .). But novelists choose anything . . . (. . .) A gesture that they've noticed (. . .), they take it and they say to themselves: (. . .) this is going to mean the birth of great love. (. . .) We think that surely he knows. And we say: look how true it is. And we find it in life . . . Of course, we find it there, they've put it there . . . Because we see life through novels . . . There are people marked forever by these truths. Listen, I knew a poor girl . . ."]

Instead of looking to the novel to tell her the truth about life, *elle* looks to her life to judge the truth of the critic's judgment of this "moment of truth" found in "Les Fruits d'Or." The positions represented by the feminine speakers in this chapter thus far are antithetical. The disciple looks to popular art to find a "truth" for her life, and the figure in the passage above looks from her life to judge the "truth" of a literary work. The latter position, however, opens onto a certain compassion for the position of the first ("There are people marked forever by these truths. . . . I knew a poor girl"). This compassion is also a quality found in the ideal reader. Like the second figure of *elle*, the ideal reader does not hold a position in *opposition* to another; he has instead an affective relationship to his own and other positions.

The question about the relationship of art to life is raised by another feminine figure in Chapter 5, where its gender inflection is parodied in the narration. The exchange is recounted by an admirer of a writer named Orthil, and it takes place between the writer and a figure identified as "Madame," "la pauvre" [the poor thing]: "'Il fallait l'entendre, la brave dame, elle était toute rouge, toutes ses plumes hérissées: 'Mais Monsieur, moi je trouve Les Fruits d'Or factice . . . C'est trop littéraire . . . Ce n'est pas ça, la réalité . . .' [. . .] Il fallait la voir, c'était tordant: [. . .] 'Ce que nous appelons la réalité aujourd'hui—c'est bien autre chose'" ["You should have heard her, the good lady, she was all red, all her feathers ruffled: 'But Monsieur, I think that "Les Fruits d'Or" is artificial . . . It's too literary . . . That's not reality . . .' (. . .) You had to see her, it was a scream: (. . .). 'What we call reality today is something else entirely. . . .'"] (79). Madame's interlocutor responds: "'Ah, Madame, il hoche la tête d'un air faussement pensif et grave . . . qu'est-ce donc que la réalité?'" ["Ah Madame, he shakes his head in a falsely pensive and serious way . . . what then is reality?"] (80). In Minogue's interpretation, Madame's words "effectively parody much of the critical accompaniment to the new novel, and caricature even the author's own view."[9]

At the same time, however, the entire narration is framed at the end by the admirer's unbridled adoration of Orthil which appears in *sous-conversation*: "Il est l'intelligence même, la sensibilité. La sensibilité de l'intelligence . . . ce qu'il y a de plus rare . . ." [He is intelligence itself, sensibility. The sensibility of intelligence . . . which is what is so rare about him . . .] (81). If the feminine figures are ridiculed for looking for themselves in the novels they read, the masculine figures who scorn this tendency are equally mocked within the narration itself. The above scene marks a moment when figures of both genders are presented in a negative light. The irony in the treatment of the masculine figures, however, undermines their scorn for the position represented by the feminine ones. These positions thus remain in a state of irresolution: looking for art in life or life in art and the reading subject's relationship to literature. For the feminist critic the representation of these positions by feminine figures in Les Fruits d'Or resonates within literary studies which specifically address women's writing. Masculinist critics have traditionally scorned writing by women for its sentimentality, its preoccupation with "trivial" matters. Many feminist critics in this country have set for themselves the task of re-discovering writing by women precisely because it represents a reality repressed by patriarchal notions of what constitutes "literary" material.[10] In addition, feminist investigations of the questions raised by this writing about the relationship of art to life have greatly contributed to the evolution of literary criticism in the last two decades.[11] The critical "value" which the feminist reader might place on the irresolution of the above questions in *Les Fruits d'Or* is abruptly displaced by disturbing images as this scene continues.

The feminine figure's ambivalent relationship to the master's discourse is dramatized when the audience of *elles*, which witnesses the objection of the singular *elle*, is shocked and surprised by her outburst: "Comment ose-t-elle? Elle perd la tête . . . Elle si timide, toujours silencieuse, quelle mouche l'a piquée?" [How could she? She's lost her head . . . That timid one, always so silent, what bee got in her bonnet?] (47). The colloquial expression and indirect discourse suggest that this observation is made by *elles*, intimidated by the authorities present, and the discourse of the next voice enters the text directly, using a different language: "'Ma chère enfant, c'est très touchant [. . .], ces gens [. . .] qui voient leur propre vie à travers les romans. Mais c'est leur faute à eux. Pas celle du romancier. [. . .] Ceux qui lisent les romans comme cette pauvre fille dont vous parlez n'ont que ce qu'ils méritent. Ils n'ont pas la moindre notion de ce que c'est qu'une oeuvre d'art'" ["My dear child, that is very touching (. . .), those people (. . .) who see their own life through novels. But it's their own fault. Not that of the novelist. (. . .) The people who read novels like that poor girl you speak of only get what they deserve. They haven't the slightest idea of what a work of art is"] (47).

If a single *elle* can disrupt male discourse, a plural *elles* risks going out of control. This threat to order is represented earlier in the novel by another (the same?) plural feminine. When *elle* in Chapter 1 is on her way to see the host, her fear of being rejected is summed up in a nightmare image that deserves to be cited in full: "Dans la salle commune des femmes échevelées aux longues mèches rêches se frappent la poitrine, grimacent, rient, soulèvent leurs jupes, montrent leurs cuisses grises, agitent leur arrière-train, des femmes, le bras tendu, au milieu du tintamarre, restent immobiles, figées comme au jeu des statues, catatonie, épilepsie, hystérie, camisole de force, couches, coups, féroces gardiens . . . Mais cela ne fait rien, cela ne compte pas, je n'ai pas peur [. . .]" [In the commonroom the frenzied women with long, coarse locks beat their chests, they frown, laugh, raise their skirts, show off their gray thighs, wag their tails, women, arms outstretched, in the middle of the racket, remain immobile, frozen as in the game of statues, catatonia, epilepsy, hysteria, straightjacket, showers, blows, ferocious guards . . . But that's nothing, it doesn't count for anything, I'm not afraid (. . .)] (15).

The collective *elles* in Chapter 4 is equally disturbing after the dissenting *elle* has raised her objections. "Elles [. . .] s'engouffrent, se poussent, elles se bousculent, elles fouillent . . . Comme aux soldes des grandes maisons de couture [. . .], elles sortent et essaient . . . est-ce à leur taille?" [The women (. . .) rush in, push and elbow one another, they comb through . . . Like at big department store sales, they take out and try on . . . is it their size?] (48). If the doors are opened to these female readers who "voient leur propre vie à travers les romans" [see their own life through novels] where will it all end? The figure of *elles* searches through their "mental reference-book of 'admirabilia' (from classical sculpture to racehorses)," as Minogue describes it, to see if the image of the heroine of "Les Fruits d'Or" is "lifelike."[12] In the presence of such authorities as the male critics, however, this plural feminine figure is brought back to order. As they nod their heads in agreement, their collective voice pronounces: "'Marcel a raison . . . Ce qui est bon dans un roman . . .'" ["Marcel is right . . . What is good in a novel . . ."] (48).

Another masculine voice comes forth to admire the "tempérament puissant" [powerful temperament] of the dissenting feminine figure, and he appropriates her outburst for his own ends in *sous-conversation:* "Qu'elles s'écartent. Qu'on disperse ce troupeau hébété. Et qu'on m'amène le coupable" [Get them out of here. Disperse this useless herd. And bring the guilty one to me] (48–49). A regular inquisition of taste takes place as everyone is called on to give an opinion of the matters at hand. Voices come from every imaginable sector, praising the novel in varying degrees, but this barrage is once more interrupted by a feminine voice: "Mais elle n'est pas lâche comme eux. [. . .] Elle ne fera pas semblant de ne rien voir [. . .]: 'Eh bien . . . sa voix tremble un peu . . . eh bien, vois pouvez dire ce que vois voulez, mais moi, Les Fruits d'Or, je n'aime pas ça. [. . .] Moi j'aimerais bien que quelqu'un me le prouve, le livre en main'" [But she is not cowardly like they are. (. . .) She will not pretend not to see (. . .): "Well . . . her voice trembles a little . . . well, you can say what you like, but as for me, 'Les Fruits d'Or,' I don't like it. (. . .) I would like someone to prove it, book in hand"] (58, 59).

This feminine figure's outburst opens the narration up to the non-critics, "le menu peuple" [the humble folk], the ones who need explanations about such matters (60–61), and to the voice that scorns them for their literalness (61–62); then the narration closes up again to reject her: "mais c'est passé, effacé—un bref sursaut, aussitôt réprimé. Rien n'a affleuré au-dehors, qui eût pu permettre de déceler une complicité, même timide et sournoise, avec cette folle, cette tête brûlée" [But it's over now, erased—a brief fit, immediately repressed. Nothing showed, nothing that could have revealed a complicity, even a timorous, indirect one, with that crazy woman, that hothead] (63).

Later in *Les Fruits d'Or*, the narration describes a feminine voice who is disturbed to find a certain critic's name, Mettetal, signed to an article praising "Les Fruits d'Or" and claiming to have liked Bréhier's work from the beginning. *Elle* remembers that Mettetal had earlier had a different response, a violent rejection of "ce livre étrange" [that strange book]. *Elle* mentions this discrepency to Mettetal in an offhand way, so as not to create a great disturbance, and like one of the critics above, Mettetal is described as treating the observation made by *elle* "comme font les grandes personnes quand les enfants terribles, ah, ces petits diables incorrigibles, se livrent à une de leurs facéties" [like adults do when horrifying children, ah, those little, incorrigible devils, give in to one of their pranks] (85). Harmony is restored by Mettetal's response; that is all *elle* wanted, the text tells us, but it is too late, this *elle* is also rejected: "Qu'est-ce que c'est que cette folle, [. . .] qui parcourt la terre, pieds nus et en haillons, crie sur les places publiques [. . .]. On l'entoure. Leurs regards la lapident. Elle est repoussée, expulsée. Le cercle des fidèles se referme" [What is it with this crazy woman, (. . .) who runs around, barefoot and in rags, crying out in town squares (. . .). She is surrounded. Their looks stone her. She is repulsed, expulsed. The circle of the faithful closes] (85–86). Here, as in Chapter 4, the narration returns from a tropistic depth to the surface conversation of masculine speakers represented by marked discourse.

At the end of Chapter 4 a lone figure emerges amid the tumult of voices and announces in *sous-conversation*, "moi je tiens bon" [I hold on tightly] (72). Having pulled away from the other critics, *il* narrates the tale of his journey to enlightenment. The tale, characterized by a neat, marked linearity comes to certain judgmental conclusions: "Ils se sont enfermés à triple tour. Seuls avec une autre image qu'ils n'ont plus cessée de contempler, une image d'eux-mêmes aux proportions gigantesques [. . .]. Leur langage plus que jamais dirigé vers eux seuls [. . .]. Et puis j'ai vu les autres, maintenus au-dehors [. . .]. Ils se sentaient mis au ban [. . .]: ils étaient exclus. [. . .] C'est ainsi que tout a commencé. C'est ainsi que tout s'est déroulé, j'en suis certain" [They have closed themselves in with triple locks. Alone with another image that they continue to contemplate, an image of themselves in gigantic proportions (. . .). Their language more than ever directed toward themselves alone (. . .). And then I saw the others, kept outside (. . .). They felt banished (. . .): They were excluded. (. . .) That's how everything started. That's how it happened, I am certain of it] (67–71). With the words of this masculine figure, all the confusion provoked by earlier masculine authority and represented by the feminine figures up to this point comes to a halt. A critique of the master's discourse is thus articulated by a masculine figure, while feminine figures remain at the level of experiencing its totalitarian effect.

In spite of having become the dominant voice, the lone figure still wants a witness to his tale and finds one in a feminine figure: "[. . .]

là, presque en face de lui, il ne l'avait pas remarquée, elle se tient si effacée [. . .]" [(. . .) there almost in front of him, he hadn't noticed her, she is keeping herself so hidden] (73). *Il* is attracted to *elle* because he senses that she, like him, is not crazy about "Les Fruits d'Or," and *elle* affirms this in the *tête-à-tête* which takes place while the others go on with their pronouncements. *Elle* is not only like *il, elle* embodies the masculine figure's best image of himself: "[. . .] son âme pure, forte [. . .] s'étalant avec une parfaite innocence, une touchante confiance dans ses grands yeux transparents, dans ses larges joues, dans son sourire d'une enfantine candeur [. . .]. Il est prêt à tout abandonner, à renoncer à toutes les richesses qu'il a amassées [. . .], pour être semblable à elle, fait de la même substance, modeste, humble, et fort d'une inébranlable confiance dans la victoire finale du bien, dans le triomphe de la vérité. [. . .] Il est avec elle [. . .], elle, sa soeur" [(. . .) her pure, strong soul (. . .) laying itself out with a perfect innocence, a touching confidence in her great transparent eyes, in her large cheeks, in the childish candor of her smile (. . .). He is ready to abandon everything, to renounce all the riches he has amassed (. . .) to be like her, made of the same substance, modest, humble and strong in an unshakable confidence in the final victory of good, in the triumph of truth. He is with her (. . .), her, his sister] (75–76). *Elle*, however, does not accept his adulation—"'Oh moi, vous savez, je n'y connais rien . . . Qui suis-je, moi, pour juger?'" ["Oh me, you know, I don't know anything about all this . . . Who am I, to judge?"] (76). The narration that had joined the pair now separates them as *il* observes that *elle* has the "visage d'extatique, de fanatique" [face of an ecstatic, a fanatic], that her head is full of "quelles croyances . . . absurdes . . . Christian Science . . . sciences occultes . . . yoga" [such beliefs . . . absurd . . . Christian Science . . . occult . . . yoga] (76).

Just as *elle* had been the mirror of his aspiration, the feminine figure now reflects his ostracism. Resorting to mockery, the villains of *Les Fruits d'Or* lump *il* and *elle* together with the look they cast on the pair: "'Ha, ha, encore . . . Vous discutez toujours des Fruits d'Or?' Côte à côte, les deux grands, les deux pairs [. . .] les ont frôlés, les ont regardés d'un air malicieux. Ils ont vu les deux âmes pures, les deux innocents. Ils l'ont associé, lui, avec cette demeurée" ["Ha, ha, still . . . You're still discussing 'Les Fruits d'Or?'" Side by side, two adults, two comrades (. . .) passed, rubbed up against them, gave them a malicious look. They saw the two pure souls, the two innocents. They associated *him* with that half-wit] (75–76).

Toward the end of *Les Fruits d'Or* in Chapter 11, another male/female couple enters the fray but the tables are turned. In the *sous-conversation* of the feminine figure, the masculine figure named *Jacques* represents her aspiration to be joined with him as one of "les premiers résistants" [the first *résistants*] against the unanimous praise of "Les Fruits d'Or." The description of this figure's admiration of Jacques resembles the one the lone figure gives of *elle* in Chapter 4, that is, as having a certain moral character: "Elle ne se lassera jamais de l'admirer . . . Ce sont des gens comme lui, si purs, si intègres, si forts, grâce à qui ont toujours pu s'affirmer les vraies valeurs" [She will never tire of admiring him . . . It's because of people like him, so pure, so upright, so strong, that the true values could always be affirmed] (120–21). Unlike the scene between the dissident and *elle* in Chapter 4, where the reader is given no access to the tropistic depth of the initially admired feminine figure, in Chapter 11 Jacques's thoughts are revealed by his *sous-conversation* in which this feminine figure is presented as someone to be pitied: "Il la regarde, impuissant, paralysé, il ne peut rien pour elle (. . .), pauvre petit étourneau . . ." [He looks at her, powerless, paralyzed, he can't do anything for her (. . .), poor little birdbrain . . .] (124). All of the heterosexual pairs in *Les Fruits d'Or* end up in separation, preparing the way for a pair of gendered "equals" or "neutrals" to achieve the union that the various feminine figures and the lone masculine figure sought unsuccessfully in Chapter 4 through a heterosexual bond.

After the sundering of the union between *il* and *elle* at the end of Chapter 4, *elle* as Madame begins Chapter 5 and *il*, who admires Orthil, ends it. Admirer and master critic, *elle* and Mettetal, appear as a pair in Chapter 6, where the (feminine) admirer is ostracized for questioning the (masculine) critic's change in opinion. As if to fill up the emptiness left by the admirers' exile of *elle* from their group, personal dramas recede in Chapter 7 and slogans praising "Les Fruits d'Or" follow one another in isolated paragraphs.

Chapter 8 begins with the words of one who calls himself "un provincial" [a provincial], "un paysan" [a peasant] who asks his city friend about "Les Fruits d'Or," the "le dernier dada" [latest rage] in Paris (92). The "provincial" designates those who adore the novel "ces crétins" [those morons] because he finds "Les Fruits d'Or" to represent a "grande banalité de pensée, de sentiments" [great banality of thought, of sentiments]. This judgment sends the city friend into spasms of laughter: "'Mais voyons, comment ne voyez-vous pas que ce côté banal, ce côté plat dont vous parlez, cela, justement, Bréhier l'a voulu, il l'a fait exprès'" ["But look, how can you not see that this banal side, this flatness that you speak of is precisely what Bréhier wanted, he did it on purpose"] (93–95). The narration of the discussion that follows is straightforward, two distinct voices separated syntactically in the text, ideologically in their disagreement, slipping into *sous-conversation* and images of a jousting match with an audience of observers, then returning to the surface (95–102).

Once the two friends find a critic they mutually dislike, the narration becomes a more tropistic interaction which joins the two discussants as *ils* and *nous*—"Collés l'un à l'autre, ne faisant qu'un seul corps comme le cheval de course et son jockey, [. . .] encore cette dernière haie, nous allons la franchir, à nous deux, nous sommes sûrs de vaincre, rien ne peut briser notre élan [. . .]" [Stuck to one another, making only one body like the racehorse and his jockey, (. . .) and still that last hurdle, we are going to jump over it, the two of us, we are sure of winning, nothing can break our stride (. . .)] (103). Dialogue continues, marked by dashes in the text but not separated by paragraphs, their voices are indistinguishable. When their paths threaten to part again the narration does not separate the pair, the two are joined by an acknowledgment that serves the theme of Sarraute's novel: "'Ah, c'est bien étrange, ces engouements . . . ces partis pris, tout à coup, pour n'importe quoi . . . Cette passion, cet acharnement des gens . . . Et puis ça se défait, on ne sait trop comment'" ["Ah, it's really strange, these fads . . . these opinions, suddenly, for just anything . . . This passion, this fierce determination of people . . . And then it disintegrates on its own, it's hard to know how . . ."]. The other voice agrees: "'Oh ça se défait . . . Il faut parfois des années, il faut parfois une ou deux générations . . .'" ["Oh it disintegrates . . . it sometimes takes years, sometimes one or two generations . . ."] (104).

Their discussion digresses from the domain of critics and "Les Fruits d'Or" to move on to personal taste. A line of poetry is offered for scrutiny: "'[. . .] qu'en dites-vous, ça, tenez [. . .]'" ["(. . .) what do you say about this, here take this (. . .)"] (105). *Ils* may never agree in their taste, but they continue to meet one another halfway: "'Attendez, je vous suis . . . On ne peut pas se quitter ainsi, quand on a, dans une fusion si parfaite franchi tant d'obstacles [. . .]. On ne lâche pas si brutalement son fidèle compagnon . . . Je ne peux pas supporter de me retrouver seul comme avant [. . .]'" ["Wait, I'm with you . . . We cannot leave one another like this, when we have, in such a perfect fusion overcome so many obstacles (. . .). Such a faithful companion is not so brutally dropped . . . I can't stand the thought of being alone as I was before (. . .)"] (105). Even when *ils* almost separate again, the chapter ends with an image of (male) camaraderie, *ils* finally separating into *je* and *tu*, but in a narration which leaves them indistinguishable:

Rires obtus de brutes, bavardages d'ivrognes . . . Grosses tapes sur l'épaule, penchés l'un vers l'autre, titubant, enlacés . . . Ho, ho, . . . ils disent que c'est

fait exprès . . . Ho, ho, comme c'est tordant . . . Dis-moi le grand docteur,
qu'est-ce que tu en penses? C'est fait exprès? Eh bien, attends . . . le doigt
mou trace une courbe dans l'air, se pose sur le nez . . . Mais ça ne tient pas
. . . je vais t'expliquer . . . Voix grasse . . . hoquets . . . et lui-même, avec son
visage béat, sa bouche entrouverte, son oeil luisant et son rire satisfait d'idiot
(106–7).

[Dull-witted, brutish laughter, drunks' chatter . . . Heavy slaps on the shoulder, leaning into one another, staggering, entwined . . . Ho, ho . . . they say
that it's there on purpose . . . Ho, ho, that's a scream . . . Tell me, you the
great doctor, what do you think? Is it on purpose? All right, wait . . . the
limp finger traces a curve in the air, lands on his nose . . . You say that it's
on purpose, old pal? But that doesn't hold any water . . . let me explain . . .
Thick voice . . . hiccups . . . and him, with his blissful look, his mouth half-
open, his shining eyes and his satisfied idiot's laugh.]

As this masculine plural figure finds a common ground and stays there,
"Les Fruits d'Or" moves to the background, preparing the way for the
final chapters in which the imaginary novel returns to the foreground
only to be attacked. This discussion between two masculine voices in
Chapter 8 not only offers some relief from the din of praise, but more
importantly, the concluding moment of unity is both founded upon a
shared mockery of that discourse and represented as mocking itself.

The popularity of "Les Fruits d'Or" begins to disintegrate in Chapter
9. Awkwardly trying to prove the novel's greatness, a critic called Parrot
reads one passage after another. This situation is at first described as
if from a group perspective but then slips into a feminine figure's consciousness: "[. . .] le pauvre bougre attend qu'on lui donne quelque
chose . . . chacun hésite, un peu confus, chacun fouille, mais elle . . .
voilà, j'ai ce qu'il faut, tenez, mon brave, prenez: 'C'est très beau'" [(. . .)
the poor devil is waiting to be given something . . . everyone hesitates,
a little lost, everyone ponders, except her . . . here, I have what you
need, here, my good man, take this: "It's very beautiful"] (113). Like
the host at the beginning of the novel, though more pointedly, Parrot
rejects the lifeline: "'Non, je crois que vous exagérez. [. . .] Et après
tout, peut-être me suis-je trompé . . .'" ["No, I think you're exaggerating.
(. . .) And after all, perhaps I am wrong . . ."] (114).

At this point in the novel gender lines have been clearly drawn. In
Chapter 1, masculine figures are represented by an aggressive guest and
a timid host. This host becomes an authoritarian critic in Chapter 3
who subscribes to an objectifying master discourse which ridicules
tropistic reality. Chapter 5 presents the (ironized) admirer of Orthil,
and Chapter 6 the critic Mettetal whom the crowd adores. Feminine
figures are represented by the polite one in Chapter 1 who tries to save
a masculine figure from being thrown out of a group, the figure of a

mythologized mother in Chapter 2, who saves the host from the scorn of the aggressive guest. In Chapter 4, feminine figures interrupt masculine discourse and are represented by a disciple who changes herself to enter a masculine critic's territory, a reader of the realist approach whose argument is appropriated for a masculine figure's discourse, a critic who wants proof (book in hand) and is thrown out as a madwoman, and the mirror of a lone hero's aspiration and then of his paranoia. In Chapter 6, a feminine figure is a disciple who is ostracized for daring to challenge a masculine critic's authority.

The tension between an authoritarian discourse which admires itself and a dissenting though confused discourse is represented respectively by masculine and feminine figures. All these positions are presented in a tropistic narration characterized by *sous-conversation*. At the same time, all are drenched in varying degrees of irony, such that *Les Fruits d'Or* privileges none of them. The lone masculine figure who emerges in Chapter 4, with his conclusions about discourse which admires itself, begins the construction of the ideal reader who ends the novel. Like several of the feminine figures, this reader is one who dissents, but beginning in Chapter 10 that dissention is represented only by masculine figures. That is, in order for the reader to scrutinize this dissent, Sarraute's narrative strategy neutralizes it. Nathalie Sarraute, woman writer, is everywhere and nowhere in this novel.

A dissenting masculine *je* opens Chapter 10 with a demand for clarification:

"Je voudrais qu'on m'explique [. . .]. Je sais que je suis ridicule. C'est ridicule de jouer les Alceste, mais ça m'est bien égal, tant pis [. . .], eh bien, comment se fait-il qu'à tout moment on assiste à ces extraordinaires revirements sans que personne paraisse s'en étonner [. . .] . . . c'est comme des hallucinations collectives, ces énormes engouements sans qu'on sache très bien pourquoi . . . et du haut en bas de l'échelle littéraire [. . .]. Tenez, en ce moment . . . pour Les Fruits d'Or . . . [. . . il] y a comme un revirement [. . .] . . . Pourquoi tout à coup? Que s'est-il passé?" (115–16).

["I would like someone to explain to me (. . .). I know that I'm ridiculous. It's ridiculous to play Alceste, but it doesn't matter, too bad (. . .), well, how is it that at any moment we witness these extraordinary reversals and no one seems to be surprised (. . .) . . . it's like collective hallucinations, these terrific fads for no good reason . . . and from both ends of the literary ladder (. . .). Now, for example . . . for 'Les Fruits d'Or' . . . (. . . there) is a kind of reversal (. . .) . . . Why so suddenly? What happened?"]

Like the feminine figures who have objected at various moments in *Les Fruits d'Or*, *il* is treated like a child when he makes these observations. In this passage, however, the source of that treatment is itself introduced with a certain irony: "Et voilà que la masse inerte en face de lui se met à remuer, se soulève: [. . .] 'Vous ne vieillissez pas. Vous avez les exigences, les indignations des adolescents'" [And there is the inert mass in front of him which begins to twitch, to raise up: (. . .) "You never grow up. You have the demands and indignation of an adolescent"] (116).

This marked discourse originating from the "masse" explains, as Sarraute did in an interview cited earlier, that "'l'Art, comme vous dites, une oeuvre d'art n'est jamais une valeur sûre'" ["Art, as you call it, never has a fixed value"] (118). Unlike Sarraute, however, this voice uses the phrase to dismiss the dissident's question and to establish another "lieu commun": "'C'est bien connu, c'est évident. [. . .] Les goûts changent. Il y a à certain moments, certains besoins. Et après on veut autre chose. [. . .] Durera-t-il? Comment savoir? . . . Et, entre nous, quelle importance?'" ["Everyone knows that, it's obvious. (. . .) Tastes change. There are certain needs at certain moments. And then we want something else. (. . .) Will it last? How can we know? . . . And, just between us, is that so important?"] (118–19). This response throws the "childish" hero into a world he fears, onto what he calls "ces terres spongieuses" [those spongey lands] that resemble a land an earlier *elle* was reluctant to leave. Unable to tolerate "ces terres spongieuses," the dissenting masculine figure quickly rises to the surface and engages in the discourse begun by "la masse": "'Les Fruits d'Or, [. . .] vous avez l'air de ne pas l'aimer . . . Moi je l'ai toujours soutenu. J'ai peut-être eu tort'" ["'Les Fruits d'Or,' (. . .) you seem not to like it . . . for myself, I've always supported it. Perhaps I was wrong"] (118).

Chapter 11 digresses to the scene between Jacques and *elle*, one of the shaky heterosexual unions discussed above. Chapter 12 begins with a declaration denouncing the value of "Les Fruits d'Or," and in the *sous-conversation* that follows as unmarked discourse the text says that "ceux qui, encore aujourd'hui, admirent Les Fruits d'Or sont des sots" [those who, even today, admire "Les Fruits d'Or" are stupid] (132). A masculine subject (the same as above or another?) arises to protest in *sous-conversation*: "Mais moi, ça me brûle [. . .] . . . Cette fraternelle and innocente confiance, [. . .] elle va me faire mal au coeur, la tête me tourne, elle va me donner une insolation [. . .]" [But for me, that kills me (. . .) . . . That fraternal and innocent confidence, (. . .) it/she's going to make me sick, my head is swimming, it/she's going to give me sunstroke] (132). The dissident in Chapter 4 looked for someone to share his opinion and found a feminine figure, but that figure's perception of *elle* as a subject problematized their brief union. The masculine dissident in the scene above, like the host who turns critic in Chapter 3, interacts with an abstraction of the feminine. This dissident denounces first one *elle* ("cette fraternité") then attaches himself to another, "ma sottise" [my stupidity] (134).

This *moi* passes through various stages before the chapter ends. First he marvels at "ma sottise," how it spreads all over him and everything he touches. Then he redescribes it as something that is not "fatal" or "congenital," that is, not "quelque chose d'irréparable comme la couleur de la peau" [something irreparable like the color of one's skin] (134–35). The next stage introduces the sense of intimacy that characterizes the ideal reader's relationship to "Les Fruits d'Or," but here that intimacy is described with the use of a feminine abstraction and unites this dissident to the other masculine figures. This dissident's relationship to "Les Fruits d'Or" is described as an exchange, "cette ondulation, cette modulation" [that undulation, that modulation], that passes "des Fruits d'Or à moi," "d'eux à moi et de moi à eux" [from them to me and from me to them], "entre nous cette osmose" [between us that osmosis]: "Aucune parole venue du dehors ne peut détruire une si naturelle et parfaite fusion. Comme l'amour, elle nous donne la force de tout braver. Comme un amoureux, j'ai envie de la cacher" [Not a word from outside can destroy such a natural and perfect fusion. Like love, it/she gives us the strength to confront everything. Like a lover, I feel like hiding it/her] (136). From within this "fusion," the narrator as *je* goes deeper into his own mythology. Something lifts him up, described as "quelque chose d'aussi impérieux que les voix qui commandent à ceux qui le Ciel a élus de tout abandonner" [something as imperious as the voices that command those whom Heaven has elected to abandon everything]. *Je* joins "missionnaires" and "révolutionnaires" sent to evangelize among "les peuplades sauvages" [wild people], "les masses illettrées" [illiterate masses] (137).

What topples this subject from his lofty position are the words, "'Ah on voit bien que vous ne connaissez pas Bréhier'" ["Ah, it's very obvious that you don't know Bréhier . . ."] (138). With this direct address, *nous* who have denounced "Les Fruits d'Or" invite the rebellious *moi* into "solidarité": "Venez donc près de nous, un peu plus près, serré les uns contre les autres, [. . .] vous allez voir, vous serez étonné . . ." [Come on over here next to us, a little closer, squeeze in together, (. . .) you'll see, you'll be astonished] (138). The dissident does not give in to the evidence offered by *nous* that proves the author of "Les Fruits d'Or" is a fake. The image representing the rejection of the dissident creates the feeling of a person being stoned by villagers: "Je protège mon visage, je courbe le dos" [I protect my face, I bend my back] (143). The feminine disciple who criticized Mettetal in Chapter 6 was also expelled from a group with the same imagery. The difference between these two expul-

sions is in their representation in the text. In Chapter 6 *elle* is the
object—"On l'entoure. Leurs regards la lapident" (86)—whereas here,
je is the subject. For the feminist reader, this difference moves the text
in three directions simultaneously. This masculine figure is not any
different from other masculine figures in the novel because of his use
of a feminine abstraction, and the action of expulsion has been "neutralized" in Sarraute's terms in that it is operated on a masculine figure.
At the same time, through the use of a first-person narration this figure
is personalized and unmarked by gender.

In Chapter 13, an omniscient voice which is never identified describes the dissident from a position of superiority. The terms of the
dissident's intimacy with the novel resemble those later used by the
ideal reader: "le contact direct, spontané" [direct, spontaneous con-
tact], "cette sensation [. . .] fraîche, intacte, neuve" [that sensation (. . .)
fresh, intact, new], and "nourrie de ce qui se cache au plus secret de
lui-même" [nourished by what hides in the most secret part of him]
(145). The difference between this dissident and the ideal reader is the
sense of ownership by which the former seeks to distinguish himself
from others. That sense of possession is made clear in the passage
which begins the penultimate chapter of the novel: "Ah, le pauvret,
comme il se débattait . . . [. . .] Tous les experts du monde pouvaient
lui donner tort . . . il ne cesserait jamais d'affirmer qu'ils se sont tous
trompés [. . .]. Ce qui les distingue de tout ce qui a jamais été écrit,
c'est à lui, lui seul [. . .], depuis son enfance le contact s'est établi,
direct, spontané . . . c'est sa sensation à lui [. . .]" [Ah the poor thing,
how he carries on . . . (. . .) All the experts in the world can prove him
wrong . . . he will never stop affirming that they are all wrong (. . .).
What distinguishes (Les Fruits d'Or) from all the others that have ever
been written, is his, his alone (. . .), since his childhood the contact has
been there, direct, spontaneous . . . it's his sensation (. . .)] (144). The
efforts made by *il* to do battle with *their* weapons and to individuate
himself by his literary preferences can only fail in the context of *Les
Fruits d'Or*. The text, represented above by an anonymous voice, mocks
the dissidents who seek singularity. The ideal reader separates himself
from the critics and turns his attention to his own subjective reaction
to "Les Fruits d'Or." The novel he reads becomes an extension of himself and the ultimate union achieved seems to be that of self to self,
beyond the categories of "le lieu commun" or of gender.

The figure of the ideal reader who emerges from the fray at the end
does not express himself in the critical vocabulary that marks the novel
throughout. Speaking in the first person, this figure admits in *sous-
conversation* that he can only use "pauvres mots" [paltry words], "complètement usés à force d'avoir servi à tous et à tout" [completely used

up from having been used by all for everything]. The figure of *je* adds with a certain irony that "il me faudrait posséder le vocabulaire perfectionné de ces savants docteurs" [I would need to have the perfected vocabulary of those learned doctors] (152). There is a candor in this voice, and an absence of the dramatic images which tend to embalm the novel's other speakers in their own phantasmagoric scramble for identity. The ideal reader admits that he once envied those "savants docteurs," but that "la curiosité" [the curiosity] and "cette sincérité qui est, soit dit sans me vanter, ma principale qualité" [that sincerity which is, all vanity aside, my main characteristic] pushed him to decide for himself about the value of a literary work. "Je ne sais pas bien ce que c'est" [I don't know very well what it is], the narrating subject explains, and describes it with metaphors derived from the senses:

> . . . je ne sais pas bien ce que c'est . . . c'est quelque chose comme ce qu'on sent devant la première herbe qui pousse sa tige timidement . . . un crocus encore fermé . . . c'est ce parfum qu'ils dégagent, mais ce n'est pas un parfum, pas même encore une odeur, cela ne porte aucun nom, c'est une odeur d'avant les odeurs . . . Il me semble que c'est cela . . . C'est quelque chose qui me prend doucement et me tient sans me lâcher . . . quelque chose d'intact, d'innocent . . . comme les doigts fluets d'un enfant [. . .]. Une candeur confiante se répand partout en moi . . . chaque parcelle de moi en est impregnée . . . (152–53).

> [. . . it is something like what one feels before the first blade of grass sprouts timidly . . . a crocus before it blossoms . . . there is a perfume that they release, but it isn't a scent, not yet an odor, it does not have a name, it is an odor from before odors . . . It seems to me to be that . . . It is something that takes me gently and holds me without letting go . . . something intact, innocent . . . like the slender fingers of a child (. . .). A confident candor spreads throughout me . . . every part of my self is impregnated with it . . .]

The difference between the "quelque chose" that this reader cherishes and the "vocabulaire perfectionné des docteur savants" who make pronouncements on the novel is a difference in scale: small is beautiful, big threatens to efface detail—"Qu'importent les bâtiments et les constructions aux dimensions du monde si elles ne contiennent pas le crocus encore fermé, la main d'enfant . . . Est-ce là ou non? C'est toute la question" [What good are the buildings and constructions built to the world's dimensions if they do not contain the still closed crocus, the child's hand . . . Is it there or not? That's the only question] (153). Small is also personal, emotional, sensation, back to childhood where the scale of the world invests the simplest thing with grandeur, and small is closer to tropisms. This ideal reader not only escapes the irony which mocks other dissidents, he also values what Sarraute values.

This reader's more intimate relation to "Les Fruits d'Or" remains unproblematized by the irony that characterizes the presentation of more intellectual discourse throughout the novel. When this subject asks the question—"'Et Les Fruits d'Or?'"—it is in an effort to find "une autre voix" [another voice], a companion in his solitary praise of the novel. Other figures pose this question throughout *Les Fruits d'Or*, and the question usually brings on a barrage of discourses. In the last chapter, however, those discourses are themselves described in terms that could represent a theme of this novel: "Mais le plus souvent ils n'entendent même pas . . . C'est qu'ils sont si affairés, il y a toujours chez eux un tel vacarme. Ce sont toujours les mêmes cris, les mêmes pâmoisons . . . Et toujours cette certitude chez eux, qui chaque fois me surprend. Des noms défilent sans cesse, je ne cherche même pas à les retenir" [But most of the time they don't even hear . . . It's because they are so busy, there is always such a ruckus with them. Always the same cries, the same swoonings . . . And always that certitude with them, which astonishes me each time. Names file by endlessly, I don't even try to retain them] (151). The same question—"'Et les Fruits d'Or?'"— appears in the final paragraph, but the ideal reader recognizes it as the "mécanisme" in place to dispute the value of the novel. The narrator notes that this is the same question *ils* used to ask "autrefois, au temps où de prononcer votre nom faisait retenir aussitôt des cris d'admiration" [before, when as soon as your name was pronounced, cries of admiration sounded] (158).

Narrated by the ideal reader, the final chapter of *Les Fruits d'Or* takes on a very personal tone. Unlike any of the previous chapters it begins immediately with *nous* and *je*, pronouns which throughout the text have been used after third-person pronouns, that is, already identified by another speaker in some way, usually as part of an attack or defense. In the opening lines of the final chapter, identification reaches outward, and the first-person plural seems to refer to all of us, those who are figured in this novel about a novel and those who are at the end of reading it: "Oui, c'est bien le cas de le dire, nous sommes mal partis. Nous voilà réduits à un piteux état. Et seuls, si seuls, c'est à ne pas croire" [Yes, this is really a case in which we got off to a bad start. Here we are reduced to a pitiful state. And alone, so alone, unbelievable] (151). If Sarraute's reader identifies as part of this plural, however, a passage several pages later destabilizes that identification. The figure of *je* is addressing "Les Fruits d'Or": "Nous sommes si proches maintenant, vous êtes tellement une partie de moi, qu'il me semble que si vous cessiez d'exister, ce serait comme une part de moi-même qui deviendrait du tissu mort" [We are so close now, you are such a part of me, that it seems if you ceased to exist, it would be like a part of myself had become dead tissue] (157).

The ideal reader's discourse as *je* joins him to "Les Fruits d'Or" in a plural "nous," but the division between "us" and "them" loses the violent ostracism that it carried in previous chapters: "Nous sommes si fragiles et eux si forts. Ou peut-être, je sens cela aussi par moments, peut-être ai-je, sans bien m'en rendre compte, la certitude que c'est nous, vous et moi, les plus forts, même maintenant. Ils me font peut-être un peu pitié . . . Je ne sais pas . . ." [We are so fragile and they are so strong. Or perhaps, I think that also at times, perhaps, without realizing it, I am certain that we, you and I, are the strongest, even now. Perhaps I pity them . . . I don't know . . .] (154). In addition, Minogue notes that the style of this discourse is not authoritarian. It is characterized by a "modesty" which "is maintained by keeping the always dangerous 'moi' down to the level of 'des gens comme moi' [people like me], so that the adjectives are plurally distributed rather than reserved for the individual."[13]

This *je/il* may effect a neutral position and may ultimately achieve a universal status by the use of the first person as this novel ends. In the earlier chapters, however, the figures of discourse marked by the masculine pronoun represent either a divided subject situated between the *ça* and the *on*, that is, between a personal, intimate response to "Les Fruits d'Or" and an authoritarian, critical response, or a subject who sets himself up as an authority outside of this tense division. Feminine pronouns in the singular represent figures who are self-consciously aligned with emotions or sensations, confused by the discourse of masculine figures representing the *on*, or drawn to the security of their authority. The feminine pronoun appears only twice in the plural. In the beginning, this pronoun represents the *on*, identified in a nightmarish image of tropistic fear, and toward the end of *Les Fruits d'Or* the plural *elles* represents the *on*, an audience which ultimately subscribes to masculine authority.

The final (masculine) narrator emerges on the side of the *ça*, that is, his non-authoritative judgment is derived from direct contact with "Les Fruits d'Or," as represented by his address discussed above. In addition, this reader joins with the novel he is reading in a union much like the one between two masculine figures earlier in the novel, the city dweller and the provincial. Whereas the union of feminine and masculine figures throughout Sarraute's novel is undermined by the *sous-conversation* of one or the other, usually characterized by fear in the former and scorn in the latter, the union between the two masculine figures is shaped by personal intimacy and poetry, values of the ideal reader.

Les Fruits d'Or maps out traditional and modernist gendered terrains: feminine figures remain in private realms and masculine figures in public ones; feminine figures enact interruption of masculine "surface" discourse and represent the "unnameable," the interior world of tropisms. The roles played by the feminine elements that emerge from *Les Fruits d'Or* raise certain questions for the feminist reader. Does *elle* represent the intuitive (tropistic) against the intellectual, that is, in Cranaki and Belaval's vocabulary, the *ça*? Is this tropistic element transferred to an *il* so that it ends up being more "neutral" and "universal"? Does this neutralization of what appears to be a feminine element in her novels represent Sarraute's desire to hide her feminine specificity? What does this mean for a feminist critic? Judith Gardiner offers one interpretation: "When a feminist critic looks into a woman writer's mind, she often sees anger and self-doubt. Some critics extend this approach to the generalization that what unifies women's writing is the psychology of oppression, the psychology of women living under patriarchy."[14] There are studies which look for and find the "psychology of oppression" in women's writing, but these studies are usually interpretations of the use of characters or the presence of a "sub-plot." *Les Fruits d'Or* offers neither. By virtue of the first-person narration of the final chapter and the paucity of gender-designating modifiers in that narration, the ideal reader becomes less an identifiable figure, that is, a "character," and more a signifying space. Because Nathalie Sarraute will not call herself a "feminist," the "neutralization" of what appears to be "feminine" elements invites an interpretation such as the one Gardiner identifies. To draw such a conclusion, however, returns to the act of categorizing, which is continually problematized by Sarraute's style.

What Sarraute offers in her novels is access to the space in which we all signify (and classify) ourselves. An illumination of this space is particularly significant for the feminist reader. In *Les Fruits d'Or* the issue is seen most poignantly at a moment when the plural feminine figure of *elles* discusses the female *personnage* drawn by a male author:

> —Moi aussi ça m'a surprise . . . la jeune femme, l'héroïne, Estelle, elle a de grosses jambes. —Mais où? Je ne me souviens pas . . . —Si, si c'est vrai, rappelez-vous [. . .], c'est dit en toutes lettres: 'Il regardait ses jambes lourdes, aux chevilles épaisses . . .'" Leurs regards songeurs parcourent des salles de musée, des temples antiques, grimpent sur l'Acropole, palpent les contours des Vénus, des Dianes chasseresses, des cariatides, fuient vers les pistes où s'avancent avec une "grâce royale," sur leurs fines chevilles frémissantes les chevaux de course . . . (48).

> [—That also surprised me . . . the young woman, the heroine, Estelle, she has big legs. —Where?? I don't remember that . . . —Yes, yes it's true, remember (. . .), it's all over the place: "He looked at her heavy legs, with thick ankles . . ." Their dreamy looks race through museums, classical temples, climb the Acropolis, run their fingers along the contours of all the Venuses,

the hunters Diane, the caryatids, flee toward the race course where they move forward with "royal grace," on their fine, quivering ankles, race horses. . . .]

A critique of the idealization of feminine beauty takes place in this passage at the intersection of the images, such that even though every reader may not immediately see it, a critique is ultimately possible. The objectification implied by a notion of ideal beauty which directly affects women in particular, however, is given overall scrutiny in *Les Fruits d'Or*; that is, it is experienced by both masculine and feminine figures. Feminine objectification by a masculine subject is often considered to be only a "woman's problem," particular and specific, but in this novel it is brought into another arena which is represented by a "neutral" (masculine) subject. Each of these terms will be investigated in the chapters that follow.

In Sarraute's first two novels, *Portrait d'un inconnu* and *Martereau*, the neutrality of the masculine narrator is continually undermined, and the third, *Le Planétarium*, invites an investigation of subjectivity as it is constructed by both masculine and feminine figures. Sarraute's fifth novel, *Entre la vie et la mort*, identifies the principal figure as masculine and recreates the union seen at the end of *Les Fruits d'Or*. The play of pronouns enacted in the third and fifth novels continues in the sixth and seventh, *Vous les entendez?* and *"disent les imbéciles,"* opening the way for an experience of subjectivity beyond the boundaries of gender.

4

Identity Quests: Male

Portrait d'un inconnu

(The prose pieces in *Tropismes* are especially powerful because of the absence of an identified narrator. The evocative language and images associated with poetry combine with the narrative authority of prose to move the reader in and out of tropistic moments without the mediation of any narrative figures. As seen in the discussion of *Les Fruits d'Or*, Sarraute's representation of tropistic reality in the longer form of the novel necessarily led to an exploration of narrative perspective. This later work utilizes the shifting points of view already found in *Tropismes* to create the effect that Sarraute feels is basic to the novel, the successive accumulation of experience inherent in the reading of a longer prose work. It is "chacun de ces étapes," she writes, "celle de chaque paragraphe, de chaque phrase—qui d'abord retient, stimule l'attention, provoque la satisfaction du lecteur, bien avant les rapports des différentes parties entre elles et que la construction globale, dont je ne nie pas l'importance, prenne sa forme définitive" [each of these stages, of each paragraph, of each sentence—which at first retains, stimulates the attention, and provokes the satisfaction of the reader, well before the relationship of the parts to one another, the global construction, the importance of which I do not deny, takes its definitive form].[1] Instead of accumulating physical descriptions with which to compose characters in *Les Fruits d'Or*, Sarraute's reader accumulates an effect created by discourse.

A traditional realist text constructs a reality by means of characters and setting. In this sense, even the modernist works of Proust, Joyce, and Woolf create inner worlds and worlds sometimes identifiable in lived reality, re-constructed, as it were, in their texts. These works involve characters who represent the fluid and complex modernist subject. The reader is brought into the flux of a character's perceptions through the use of stream of consciousness, interior monologue and free indirect discourse. Although the representation of character in these works constitutes a challenge to the notion of the fixity or unifor-

100

mity of the human subject, characters are finally there as modernist subjects with whom the reader may identify in one way or another. Sarraute's novels also contribute to the modernist investigation of the uniformity of the subject. Unlike the characters found in the works of Proust, Joyce, and Woolf, narrator and character in her novels are formal figures which act as a vague center from which tropistic movement radiates or is perceived.

In *Portrait,* character equals mask, the mask that each figure wears for the other and the mask that the narrator risks placing on two other narrative figures. The reality that the narrator seeks beneath the mask of character, and of language itself, is associated with authenticity: "Il est inutile de tricher. [. . .] Ils ne sont pas pour moi, les ornements somptueux, les chaudes couleurs, les certitudes apaisantes, la fraîche douceur de la 'vie'" [It is useless to fake it. (. . .) They are not for me, the sumptuous ornaments, the warm colors, the soothing certitudes, the fresh softness of "life"].[2] By the middle of the novel the narrator has given up his quest for the true nature of the other narrative figures, "les masques m'ont perdu" [the masks defeated me]: "Je suis rentré dans le rang. Il le fallait. On ne peut impunément vivre parmi les larves. Le jeu devenait malsain" [I've returned to the ranks. I had to. One cannot live with impunity among the larvae. The game was becoming unhealthy] (68).

The reader who joins the narrator on his quest also flounders in the space between and around the desire to character-ize and the tropistic movement which is necessarily frozen by that gesture. At the same time, the self-reflection which the interrogative nature of this novel offers invites the feminist reader to investigate the role played by what comes to be identified as "feminine" in this narrator's quest. In his quest for the true, tropistic identity of the two other narrative figures, tropistic perception does not remain an undifferentiated entity.

The narrating figure is, in Sarraute's terms, gender neutral, a young male who interacts with a male-female pair, an old father and his daughter. The narrator wishes to distance himself from the "unhealthy" side of tropisms, identified with the daughter and often represented by a plural feminine, *elles.* A more romantic, dualistic side is identified with *le vieux,* with whom the narrator seeks to make a bond. This aspect of tropisms also inspires the narrator's creative mode. At the end of *Portrait* tropistic perception in all its configurations is nullified by the entrance of a character, Monsieur Dumontet, the daughter's fiancé, "right out of the traditional novel." Sarraute tells Germaine Brée in an interview, "he was to destroy all the movements, and everything would fall back again into the norm, into the classical novel."[3] The narrator is then left with *le vieux* and accepted by *elles* in "le lieu commun," which pretends to a gender neutrality because the gender constructs there are traditional. *Elle* takes on her female role as fiancée, and Monsieur Dumontet represents the male role of protector-provider. The narrator's struggle with tropisms subsides, and with it the dilemma experienced by this male narrator who has assigned the positions *self* and *other* to the old man and the daughter respectively.

The narrator's ambivalent relationship to character-izing, language, and the tropistic reality that they hide is represented throughout the novel by his use of certain "realist touchstones." These touchstones serve to orient the reader and to identify the narration as a construct by which the narrative *je* takes control of his narration after moments of doubt about his perception. Such a moment opens the novel: "Une fois de plus je n'ai pas pu me retenir, ç'a été plus fort que moi, je me suis avancé un peu trop" [Once again I could not control myself, it was stronger than I was, I went too far] (17). Alone at the beginning of Chapter 2, the figure of *je* describes losing this anxiety as language comes to his rescue: "Cette fois, comme cela m'arrive presque toujours quand c'est allé un peu trop loin, j'ai eu l'impression d'avoir 'touché le fond'—c'est une expression dont je me sers assez souvent [. . .], cela m'apaise toujours" [This time, as almost always happens when I have gone a little too far, I had the impression of having "touched bottom"— that's an expression I often use (. . .), that always calms me] (26).

In spite of such touchstones, the narrator's authority is also circum-scribed by the tentative nature of his effort to recount his own "paysage intérieur" [interior landscape] and that of the objects of his quest. This undermining gives the reader a critical handle with which to read the novel as a story told by an unreliable narrator. As Valerie Minogue has pointed out, "Through N [the narrator] Nathalie Sarraute submits her tropistic view of life to maximal questioning, stripping it deliberately of authority and even appeal."[4]

The narrator's sense that there is something beneath the surface of *elle* and *le vieux* leads him in the opening pages of the novel to seek affirmation about his point of view from an amorphous group identified as *ils*, those who represent the conventional way of interacting with others through maxims and clichés. Both *elle* and *le vieux* can also operate in that world, but through the narrator's projection onto his "characters," *je* also attributes them from the beginning with knowl-edge of tropistic "jeux" [games]. These "jeux," however, have two sides.

After seeing a "spécialiste" to cure him of the unhealthy side of tropistic perception, the narrator takes a trip and ends up in a museum where he sees "Le Portrait d'un inconnu" (also identified as "Le Portrait de l'homme du pourpoint" [Man in the doublet]). The narrator experi-ences an "appel" [call] from the portrait that inspires him to set out once again on his quest. Before his visit to the museum where he sees the portrait, both *elle* and *le vieux* are endowed with the same "pressentiments" [premonitions] that *je* has, but *le vieux* is better at manipulating them to ensure his power because he is more conscious of them than *elle* is: "je me souviens de lui, une fois . . . Il est beaucoup plus fort qu'elle dans ces jeux . . . Parfois même très subtil" [I remember him, once . . . He is much stronger than she is in these games . . . Sometimes even very subtle] (36). In the post-portrait section of the novel, *je* is less questioning, and in a more creative mode is able to represent his empathy with *le vieux* by entering completely into his consciousness.

The tropistic perception attributed to *le vieux* is characterized by a romantic duality, the "exaltation" of an affinity with the world around him and the "tourment" that gives him depth. *Elle*, on the other hand, comes to represent only one side of tropistic games, the "malsain" [unhealthy] aspect that drives *je* to a "spécialiste" for a cure. When *elle* assumes the mask of "le lieu commun," *je* covers her with his own mask of generalization as one of *elles*, an ambiguous entity representing at once the "unhealthy" side of tropisms and the rigidification of "le lieu commun." What *je* admires and seeks to emulate in *le vieux* is his ability to move willfully between depth and surface reality. When *je* fails to form a union with *le vieux* or to "tame" *elle*, he returns to the conventional realist touchstones discussed above or questions his own authority. This questioning of his own point of view continues throughout the novel, but after his encounter with the portrait, his quest for the tropistic reality of *elle* and *le vieux* becomes a more specific quest for the self. *Je* no longer seeks approval from the amorphous *ils* of the first chapter, though he will refer to *ils* as "les gens de là-bas" [the people down there], and his projections on *le vieux* and *elle* become more identifiable as projections of Self and Other.

In her critical articles Sarraute describes the undermining of narrative authority represented in her novels as a necessary function of her particular desire to represent tropistic reality. As seen in Chapter 1, this undermining is also read in the context of innovation practiced by the other *nouveaux romanciers*. Robbe-Grillet and Roland Barthes, among others, unveil the class identity of the so-called omniscient narrator of the nineteenth-century novel, and feminist critics have extended this unveiling to reveal the gender bias of these novels.[5] *Portrait* offers the feminist reader not only a useful example of the instability of the norm represented by a male narrator, it also presents a male narrator who, in his interpretation of the female figure in this novel, enacts what Luce Irigaray calls "specularization."

Toril Moi clarifies Irigaray's term as she uses it in her critique of

Freud: "'Specularization' suggests not only the mirror-image that comes from the visual penetration of the speculum inside the vagina; it also hints at a basic assumption underlying all Western philosophical discourse: the necessity of postulating a subject that is capable of *reflecting* on his own being. [. . .] It is this kind of specul(ariz)ation Irigaray has in mind when she argues that Western philosophical discourse is incapable of representing femininity/woman other than as the negative of its *own* reflection."[6] In *Portrait d'un inconnu*, Sarraute's questioning of the conventions of narrative point of view and character by means of a tentative narrator introduces the more complex nature of tropisms than her collection of prose pieces did. The added element of the narrator introduces the relationship between self and other, and the role that the narrator's perception of tropistic movement plays in that relationship.

In the beginning of the novel, *elle* is described as similar to the narrator: "Pour elle aussi, sans doute, c'est contraire aux règles du jeu, invraisemblable que je la suive, que j'ose l'aborder en ce moment. Elle a aussi, sûrement, en ce qui me concerne, ses pressentiments infaillibles, ses signes" [For her also, no doubt, it is contrary to the rules of the game, unbelievable that I would follow her, that I would dare to approach her. She also has, surely, as concerns me, her infallible premonitions, her signs] (32). At a later point in the novel *elle* is described as "l'Hypersensible" [the Hypersensitive one], and *je* says that he hates her for implicating him in her games: "Je ne peux jamais éviter de percevoir, venant d'elle, les décharges les plus légères, et de vibrer à l'unisson. C'est pour cela aussi qu'il m'est arrivé souvent de la haïr, pour cette complicité, cette promiscuité humiliante qui s'établit entre nous malgré moi, cette fascination qu'elle exerce toujours sur moi et qui me force à la suivre à la trace, tête basse, flairant à sa suite d'immondes odeurs" [I can never avoid perceiving, coming from her, the slightest discharges, and from vibrating in unison. It's also for that that I often find myself hating her, for that complicity, that humiliating promiscuity which establishes itself between us in spite of my efforts, that fascination that she always exercises on me and which forces me to follow in her footsteps, head bowed, behind her sniffing the foul odors] (129–30).

The narrator sees *elle* and *le vieux* in the café at the end of the novel and says he hardly recognizes them, but it is *elle* who *je* singles out as more unlike her former self: "Elle surtout presque méconnaissable. [. . . Son] visage avait cet aspect lisse et net, cet éclat un peu figé que donnent les fards" [She especially, almost unrecognizable. (. . . Her) face had that smooth, clean look, that brilliance, slightly frozen, that cosmetics give] (198). *Elle*, now engaged to Monsieur Dumontet, resembles "non-man," *elles,* and she is devoid of the subsurface rumblings that had earlier been the source of the narrator's uneasy connection with her: "Sur son visage maintenant rien d'autre que cette expression d'absence confiante qu'elles ont—il n'y a qu'à regarder ces visages de femmes assises autour de nous aux autres tables—cet air de paisible et vague rumination qu'elles ont toujours pendant que les hommes, près d'elles, parlent d'affaires, discutent de chiffres" [On her face now nothing but that expression of confident absence that they have—you only have to look at the faces of the women seated near us at other tables— that look of peaceful and vague rumination that they always have while the men, nearby, talk about business, discuss figures] (204–5).

Elle is also the object of Monsieur Dumontet's tender mockery in this scene, which wraps the narrator in male complicity: "'Ah! les femmes, hein c'est bien ça . . .' Tous les trémoussements, tous les tapotements ont disparu comme par enchantement: en moi les petites bêtes effarouchées, les petites couleuvres rapides s'enfuient; je hoche la tête, amusé et je ris" ["Ah! women, eh? that's really it . . ." All the wiggling, all the tapping has disappeared as if by magic: the little wild beasts, the swift little grass snakes in me have fled; I nod my head, amused and I laugh] (206). *Elle* is finally categorized as Other, and with that categorization "les petites bêtes" of tropisms also vanish, that is, the side of tropisms that has been problematic for *je* throughout the novel.

The reader's identity with *elle* or *le vieux* is thus always manipulated by the narrator, this is, after all, his quest. There are moments in this text, however, when the point of view represented by *je* is suspended, held out of reach, as the reader becomes lost in dreamlike fashion in another more general reality marked by plural pronouns and closer to the prose poems in *Tropismes.* These moments have a function in the narrative. In the case of *elle,* they serve to distance her from the reader and to transform *elle* into an abstraction, both of which unite the narrator with the old man in the romantic duality of tropisms. When *je* pluralizes the experience of *le vieux,* it is more often than not marked by the first-person plural, *nous,* which invites the reader to empathize with the old man as *je* does. The first moment of a pluralization of *elle* occurs early in the novel after *je* has accosted the daughter in the park, taken her by surprise, and she just as quickly returned to "sa coquille" [her shell], "sa carapace où elle se tient à l'abri" [her carapace where she keeps herself protected] (38).

This section is at first grounded in the narrator's consciousness: "Elle est bien protégée, inattaquable, fermée, gardée de toutes parts . . . Personne ne peut l'entamer. Personne ne la reconnaît, quand elle passe [. . .]" [She is well protected, unassailable, closed, guarded from every direction . . . No one can break it down. No one recognizes her, when she passes (. . .)] (38–39). After a break in the page the figure of *je* disappears, and the text elaborates a more general image: "Personne ne les reconnaît, quand elles sortent et vont, comme elle, longeant les murs, avides et obstinées. Elles se tiennent derrière les portes. Elles sonnent. Le nerveux-de-la-famille, replié au pied de son lit, tapi au fond de sa chambre [. . .], entend leur coup de sonnette. [. . .] Personne ne les reconnaît, sauf lui, quand elles se tiennent sur les seuils [No one recognizes them, when they (feminine) come and go, like her, sliding along the wall, avid and obstinate. They stand on the other side of doors. They ring the bell. The nervous-one-in-the-family, curled up at the foot of his bed, hidden at the bottom of his room (. . .), hears their ring. (. . .) No one recognizes them, except him, when they wait at the doorway (. . .).] (39). The male figure at the end of this passage could be the narrator or *le vieux*. The interchangeability is significant because it prefigures the identification the narrator makes with the old man after *je* has experienced the "appel" [call] of the portrait in the middle of the novel.

The passage above departs form the narrator's quest in such a way that when the first person reappears at the end of the passage, the observation that follows resembles a passage from *Tropismes* more than it does the other passages the reader has so far encountered in *Portrait*:

Il m'est arrivé parfois, étant assis près d'elles dans une salle de spectacle, de sentir [. . .], tandis qu'elles écoutaient près de moi, immobiles et comme pétrifiées, la trajectoire que traçaient à travers toute la salle ces images, jaillies de la scène, de l'écran, pour venir se fixer sur elles comme des parcelles d'acier sur une plaque aimantée. J'aurais voulu me dresser, m'interposer, arrêter ces images au passage, les dévier, mais elles coulaient avec une force irrésistible droit de l'écran sur elles, elles adhéraient à elles, et je sentais comme tout près de moi, dans l'obscurité de la salle, immobiles, silencieuses et voraces, elles les agglutinaient (42).

[Sometimes it has happened to me, sitting near them (feminine) at the theater, to feel (. . .), while they were listening near me, motionless and petrified, the trajectory that these images, spewing from the stage, the screen, were tracing throughout the room, attaching themselves to them like iron dust on a magnet. I would have liked to get up, to interject myself, to stop these images in flight, to divert them, but they were flowing with an irresistible force straight from the screen to them, they adhered to them, and I felt it like it was right next to me, in the darkness of the room, motionless, silent and voracious, they stuck to them.]

This image of *elles* functions to solicit the reader's intellect and imagination to experience a reality larger than the narrator's quest. In the global construction of *Portrait*, however, its presence in the narration of *je* at this point serves to categorize *elle* and wrap her up with *elles* as part of an easily influenced group of women looking for the masks to wear in the world. For the feminist reader this paragraph resonates within the works of feminist film critics who have discussed the female spectator's dual role in a male narrative film. In the role of spectator she identifies with the male protagonist at the same time that she identifies with the images of the passive female on the screen.[7]

Shall we say that this is a female reality described in a female writer's text? Such identification is always problematic in Sarraute's works. In turnings that are as subtle as tropistic movement itself, Sarraute's particular view of reality as it was represented in *Tropismes* is tucked into a text narrated by the most "normal" of all narrators, the self-conscious male artist speaking in the first person. By taking us out of his narrative moment, his quest, Sarraute's particular point of view is tied neither to the "normal" (male) narrator nor to what could be considered her "particular" (female) one.

Sarraute has described the function of all personal pronouns in her works as linguistic rather than nominal demarcations, emphasizing that these plurals could just as easily be turned around.[8] The word "images" in the passage above, for example, is a feminine noun in French, such that the phrase with a male subject, "ils adhéraient à elles," is not as poetic as "elles adhéraient à elles," the image of figures adhering to one another is reinforced by a repetition of the pronoun "elles." This passage places the female reader in between the principle of interchangeability which Sarraute says she applies to pronouns, chosen only for the sake of variety or poetry, and the very *real* nontextual reality that the reader who identifies herself as *elle* cannot help but look to it to represent. In the latter case, we (*elles*) are locked hopelessly in the male-female dichotomy, *elles* (not *ils*) adhéraient à *elles* (les images); in the possibility of the former, we (*elles*) can imagine this image applying to them (*ils*) as well.

Pre-portrait, *je* is still a more tentative narrator, represented by his hesitant style. The image he wishes to adhere to becomes clearer in a scene which introduces a figure whom *je* calls his "alter" [alter-ego]. After the narrator's encounter with *elle* he rushes to a café for a rendez-vous with this friend. On the way he sees himself through the eyes of passers-by in the street, which serves as a kind of realist touchstone for the reader: "Je devais avoir un air un peu bizarre; je m'en apercevais aux regards légèrement étonnés, amusés des passants" [I must have looked a little strange; I noticed it in the slightly surprised and amused looks of passers-by] (42–43). *Je* can afford this kind of reflection; he is sure his "alter" will understand him: "Je marchais très vite, je courais presque, comme cela m'arrive dans mes moments d'excitation, quand je m'abandonne à des divagations de ce genre, à mes 'visions,' comme j'aime les appeler pompeusement. Je devais sourire tout seul" [I was walking very quickly, almost running, that happens to me in my moments of excitement, when I abandon myself to ramblings of this sort, to my "visions," as I like to call them pompously. I must have been smiling to myself (. . .)] (43).

Je represents the earlier scene in the park to his "alter" in a linear narrative in the present tense. "Je lui raconte tout" [I tell him everything], the narrator says, and in this recounting je is not an actor but an interpreter: "'Je t'assure, il me semble que maintenant je les vois: tous ces remous en eux, ces flageolements, ces tremblements, [. . .] ce que nous appelions autrefois leurs 'petits démons,' un seul mot, une seule bonne grosse image bien assenée, dès qu'elle pénètre là-dedans, c'est comme une particule de cristal qui tombe dans un liquide sursaturé: tout se pétrifie [. . .]. Ils se recouvrent d'une carapace'" ["I assure you, it seems to me now that I see them: all that bustling in them, that quaking, those tremblings, (. . .) what we used to call their 'little demons,' a single word, one single good, big image, well placed, as soon as it penetrates, it's like a piece of crystal that falls in a super-saturated liquid: everything is petrified (. . .). They cover themselves with a carapace"] (46).

Je uses his encounter with elle to hypothesize about le vieux as well, but "l'alter" points out the difference between the two, reminding the narrator that he resembles the daughter: "'Tu te rappelles son mot, quand elle flairait [. . .] quelque chose d'un peu douteux, son mot: c'est du réchauffée . . . ça fait cliché [. . .]. Curieux, au fond, que ce soit aussi un mot que tu affectionnes . . . ton mot à toi . . .'" ["You remember her word, when she would sniff out (. . .) something a little dubious, her word: that's old hat . . . that's cliché-ridden (. . .). Odd, really, that this would also be a word that you are attached to . . . your very own word . . ."] (47). Reinforcing the earlier observation made by je that the old man is better at tropistic games, the friend warns the narrator that le vieux is more dangerous than his daughter: "'Je t'assure qu'il n'est pas dupe, il n'y croit pas [les catégories]. A ta place, je me méfierais'" ["I assure you that he's no dupe, he doesn't believe (in the categories). If I were in your shoes, I'd be careful"] (47).

This scene provides a reflective pause and introduces an important figure for the questioning that had been restricted to the narrator. The figure identified by je as "l'alter" assumes much more narrative authority than Monsieur Dumontet does at the end. Dumontet is merely a cardboard figure, the kind the text teaches its readers to mistrust as much as the narrator does even when je must renounce his quest. This "alter", on the other hand, has authority because he embodies the suspicions the reader might have about the narrator's point of view without dismissing them.

Whereas *je* seeks approval from *ils*, his relationship with "l' alter" is described in more intimate terms, similar to those used to describe the provincial and the city friend in *Les Fruits d'Or:* "[. . .] il ne faut à aucun prix laisser se refroidir cette eau torpide et douce où nous nous sommes plongés—notre intimité—ce bain tiède [. . .]" [I mustn't at any price let that torpid and sweet water that we jumped into grow cold— our intimacy—that warm bath (. . .)] (48). Even though *je* must abandon the opinions of "l'alter" in order to pursue his own quest, this figure serves as a model for the relationship *je* seeks with *le vieux*. "Nous nous neutralisions en tout cas, lui et moi," the narrator tells the reader, "au contraire de moi qui exerce toujours sur eux une influence mystéri- euse [. . .], lui, [. . .] il les tient [. . .]" [We neutralize one another in any case, him and me, unlike me who always exercizes on them a mysteri- ous influence (. . .), he holds them tightly (. . .)] (50). For the narrator, "l'alter" represents a balance between "les larves" and "les clichés." He also perceives "les larves," but at the same time he recognizes his friend's projections onto *elle* and *le vieux*.

Je is self-questioning when "l'alter" is present; he describes his point of view as "négligeable," "un peu infantile et fruste, inculte" [a little childish and rough, unrefined] (50). Left alone with *elle*, however, *je* resumes his battle for control. The power struggle between the narrator and the daughter represented in the narrative also operates between reader and narrator, because his perception of her tropistic movement is used as a weapon rather than as a call for empathy. Consequently, the reader has difficulty identifying with *elle*. She is carefully kept from us as "our character"; we cannot, we do not identify with her. When *je* says the words that bring tears to her eyes (54), there are no tears in ours, we are lost instead in *looking* at her tears and in recogniz- ing the force *je* used to cause them.

Throughout this text, and most especially during the argument be- tween *elle* and *le vieux* in Chapter 10, the reader's identification with one or the other of these figures depends on the narrator. When readers join *je* in the position of voyeur, they find themselves WATCHING the violence and unable to be FOR or AGAINST either the old man or his daughter. There is a discomfort in reading in Chapter 10, for example, that "la douleur, la volupté ont atteint leur point culminant" [the pain, the voluptuousness have reached their climax] (179), because the por- nographic side of our reading raises a problematic head. Much has been made of the discomfort of reading Sarraute's novels from a conventional reader's point of view; this is the characteristic that places her work in

the critical category of the *nouveau roman*. What separates Sarraute
from the other writers in this category, however, is her adherence to the
psychological, and in the dramatization of that content is a style which
puts her readers in this uncomfortable position of watching the intimacy and the violence of tropistic warfare with the same "volupté
particulière" [particular voluptuousness] that *je* describes in the first
pages of this novel, "toujours ce mélange d'attrait et de peur" [always
that mixture of attraction and fear] (32).

At this point in the novel, however, the violence has not yet reached
its climax, and the reader's penchant for voyeurism is more comfortably
contained by the narrator's fairy-tale imagery: "Je regarde. Comme dans
les contes de fées, dès que l'incantation magique a été prononcée, le
charme opère, la métamorphose se fait: [. . .] son visage devient tout
plat, sa tête s'affaisse dans ses épaules et pend un peu en avant vers
moi d'un air quêteur, ses yeux se remplissent de larmes [. . .]" [I watch.
As in a fairy tale, as soon as the magic words are spoken, the charm
does its work, the metamorphosis takes place: (. . .) her face becomes
completely flat, her head sinks into her shoulders and hangs forward
a little toward me with a needy look, her eyes fill with tears] (54). The
anger *je* feels toward *elle* for playing the role of "martyred victim" is
rendered in the same fairy-tale imagery; he says he wants to take her
by the neck and throw her over the rooftops: "[. . .] je voudrais la voir,
comme les sorcières des contes de fées, voler par-dessus les cheminées,
poussant des cris aigus, tricotant l'air de ses jambes crochues" [I would
like to see her, like witches in fairy tales, fly above chimneys, letting
out shrieks, pedalling the air with her legs]. "Mais nous ne sommes
pas malheureusement, dans un conte de fées," *je* tells the reader, "je
dois maîtriser en moi le dégoût, la haine qui monte" [But unfortunately,
we are not in a fairy tale, I must overcome the hatred and disgust that
rises up in me] (54). The narrator's desire for violence is contained by
the imagery, and with it, our voyeurism.

What is not contained, however, is the resemblance of *je* to *elle*, a
resemblance which he does not recognize, but which seeps through his
narration when he describes that *elle* tries to avoid "ce qui pourrait
étonner ou paraître anormal, déplacé" [what could surprise or appear
abnormal, out of place] (55–56). *Elle* seeks the advice of others, "elle a
si peur de se tromper, elle n'ose se fier à elle-même" [she is so afraid
of being wrong she doesn't dare have confidence in herself], which is
exactly the position *je* is in when the novel opens. In the scene with
"l'alter," *je* describes himself as "si influençable, [. . .] si suggestible"
[so easily influenced, (. . .) so suggestible]: "L'impression que les gens
ont de moi détient sur moi tout de suite, je deviens tout de suite et

malgré moi exactement comme ils me voient" [The impression that people have of me spreads out over me all at once, I become immediately and in spite of myself exactly as they see me to be] (50–51).

After the narrator has recounted to his friend the scene in the park with elle, she walks over to their table in the café, and je is left watching the two converse "normally." Je tries to join the conversation but his voice comes out "timide et mal posée, cette voix que j'ai toujours dès que je ne me sens pas sûr de moi" [timid and out of place, that voice that I always have as soon as I feel unsure of myself]. This uneasiness creates in him what he calls "ce besoin de l'amadouer, de la séduire" [that need to tame her, to seduce her] (51). Je detests in the Other what he detests in himself.

Later in this chapter the narration betrays the discomfort felt by je as he describes how others respond to the need for approval he sees expressed in elle. The passage begins with a "general" masculine pronoun: "Avec eux rien de mordant, d'agressif [. . .]. Aussi ils s'y trompent toujours, ils ne se méfient jamais" [With them, nothing biting, nothing aggressive (. . .). They are also always wrong, they never distrust (her)]. In the next sentence this neutral becomes a more specific female group: "Les femmes qui se croisent sur le seuil de leur porte ou bien dans l'escalier, leur filet à la main, la regardent avec sympathie. Rien de louche en elle, rien d'indécent, de vaguement inquiétant, ne les incite à se méfier" [The women who pass one another at their doorways or else in the stairway, their shopping bags in hand, look at her with sympathy. Nothing fishy about her, nothing indecent, nothing vaguely disquieting, incites them to distrust (her)] (57).

On one hand, any sarrautien narrator would detest the group designated as elles, because their phrases bring tropistic movement to a halt: "'Si ce n'est pas malheureux de voir ça . . . Un homme de son âge et si peu raisonnable . . . Et quand je pense qu'il n'a que vous au monde'" ["If it weren't so unfortunate to see . . . A man of his age and so unreasonable . . . And when I think that you're the only one he has in the world (. . .)"] (57). On the other hand, the narrator's loss of control at this moment in his narration, represented by his image being given over to a feeling of scorn for the gossiping group of women, marks his own anxiety about their distrust of him. The anxiety is only suggested in this passage but becomes clearer later in the novel when je describes "les fées protectrices" [the protective fairies] who stand behind elle during her argument with le vieux in Chapter 10: "Les bonnes femmes aux visages placides—celles-là mêmes que j'avais, moi aussi dans mes moments de détresse, tenté de solliciter, mais en vain, de moi elles se méfient, je ne sais pas leur inspirer confiance" [The kindly women with the placid faces—the very ones whom I myself, in moments of distress, had attempted to solicit, but in vain, they don't trust me, I don't know how to inspire their confidence] (155).

Je leaves *elle* joined with this group at the end of Chapter 2: "Elle absorbe avec avidité leurs mots lourds comme du plomb qui coulent au fond d'elle et la lestent. Elle s'abandonne, toute lourde, inerte entre leurs mains—une chose inanimée qu'elles vont pousser, qu'elles vont lancer sur lui, qui avancera sur lui avec le mouvement précis, aveugle, inexorable, de la torpille qui suit sa trajectoire. Rien ne l'arrêtera, ne la fera dévier" [She absorbs avidly their words, heavy like the lead that flows to her bottom and balances her. She abandons herself, all heavy, inert between their hands—an inanimate thing that they are going to push, that they are going to throw at him, that will come toward him with precision, with the blind, inexorable movement of a torpedo following its trajectory. Nothing will stop it, nothing will divert it] (58). The figure of *elles* represents a formidable, plural Other. The obvious referent to "lui" in the passage above is *le vieux*, but left as it is, unidentified, it resonates between the two male figures. The mysterious danger that ends Chapter 2 dissipates, or is suspended by the chapter that follows.

As seen earlier, when *je* contains the threat that *elle* represents by generalizing her behavior in the passage "Elles adhéraient à elles," the threat of "le lieu commun" represented by *elles* at the end of Chapter 2 is contained in a description of how such generalities resemble the mask that individuals put on for one another. The example offered in Chapter 3 is that of *le vieux*. Given the relationship the narrator has created between the old man and his daughter (represented by the threatening *elles*), the mask is seen as this character's crafty means of protection: "Le masque—c'est le mot que j'emploie toujours, bien qu'il ne convienne pas très exactement, pour désigner ce visage qu'il prend dès qu'elle entre, ou même avant qu'elle n'entre" [The mask— that's the word that I always use, even if it is not all that apt—to describe the face that he takes on as soon as she enters, or even before she enters (. . .)] (59).

Similar to the way in which the narrator's perspective in the passage "elles adhéraient à elles" slips into a narration more reminiscent of a prose piece from *Tropismes*, this discussion of "le masque" leaves *je* behind halfway through the chapter and veers toward a more literary discussion of character that could be found in *L'Ere du soupçon*. More dramatically separated from the text, the reflections on the literary character which fill Chapter 3 not only continue the analogy of the narrator's quest to that of a writer, but the nature of the discussion allows the reader to put Sarraute in this narrative position with *je*. Just as Sarraute explains to Brée how "very enjoyable and amusing" it was to draw the character of Dumontet at the end of *Portrait*,[9] the narrator describes that "je voudrais leur voir aussi ces formes lisses et arrondies, ces contours purs et fermes, à ces lambeaux informes, ces ombres tremblantes, ces spectres, ces goules, ces larves qui me narguent et après lesquels je cours . . ." [I would also like to see in them those smooth, round forms, those pure and firm contours, instead of those unformed scraps, those trembling shadows, those ghosts, those ghouls, those larvae that drown me and which I pursue] (66). In the passage about *elles*, Sarraute's particular tropistic view is generalized by a narration that resembles that of *Tropismes*. In the passage that ends Chapter 3, her view of character and of her own enterprise is described by a *je* who is just enough removed from the male narrator of *Portrait* that it seems to enter the text ungendered: "Là je m'accroche, j'appuie. Et je sens alors soudre d'eux [ces gens 'vivants,' ces personnages] et s'écouler en un jet sans fin une matière étrange, anonyme comme la lymphe, comme le sang, une matière fade et fluide qui coule entre mes mains, qui se répand . . . Et il ne reste plus, de leur chair si ferme, colorée, veloutée, de gens vivants, qu'une enveloppe exsangue, informe et grise" [There I hang on, I push. And then I feel spring forth from (these 'lifelike' characters) in an endless spray a strange matter, anonymous as lymph, like blood, a sickly, fluid matter that runs between my hands, that spreads . . . And nothing remains, of their skin so firm, flushed, velvety, these lifelike people, except a bloodless envelope, gray and shapeless] (66–67). This represents to the narrator the "dangerous" side of tropisms. Chapter 4 begins with the words, "J'ai renoncé" [I've renounced] (68); *je* is not a sarrautien writer, he is a romantic.

"Vivre parmi les larves," the malady for which *je* sought a remedy from the specialist, is described from the beginning as "une volupté particulièrement, extrêmement douce et en même temps atroce et louche" [a particularly and extremely sweet voluptuousness and at the same time atrocious and suspect] (32). Although *je* is ready to renounce the side of tropisms that is "atroce et louche," he is reluctant to abandon the "sweet" side. This side is characterized by a traditionally romantic harmony with the world around him, and by the image with which he describes his emotions when he considers his renunciation: "Comme l'amoureux qui, autrefois, sentait son coeur bondir, ses mains trembler rien qu'à entrevoir sur un visage inconnu la ligne d'un sourcil ou l'arrondi d'une joue lui rappelant vaguement le visage de sa bien-aimée, s'aperçoit avec étonnement, quand son amour pour elle a disparu, qu'aucun de ses traits [. . .] ne signifie plus rien pour lui" [Like the lover who, before, felt his heart leap, his hands tremble just at the sight of the trace of an eyebrow on an unknown face or the roundness of a cheek, reminding him vaguely of the face of his beloved, recognized with surprise, when his love for her has vanished, that none of her traits (. . .) mean anything to him any more] (76).

For the feminist reader, the recognition of her role in this image can flow below the surface of her reading as forcefully as tropistic movement does for Sarraute. Patriarchal society has set the male subject up as norm and woman as the object of his desire. Like this narrator, the feminist reader is constantly aware of the struggle for power just below the surface of what is considered a benign, normal world. On one hand, the dichotomous division of the world and the individual into tropistic depth covered by superficial masks fits neatly into a gender analysis: gender is one of many social constructs, a mask covering the human world of tropisms we all share. This is Sarraute's universalist view. On the other hand, given the roles (masks) assigned, the particularity assigned to women in society leaves us doubly masked, as seen in the passage above.

When the specialist in *Portrait* gives the narrator advice about slipping back into his "illness," that is, the sweet side of his desire for the hypersensitively perceptive world of tropisms, the feminist reader can once again superimpose her experience onto his. There are moments in the feminist critique of patriarchy when a woman is reluctant to take either mask. She could thus read the narrator's "illness" as her own desire to escape the hypersensitivity that is attributed to the Woman-mask by slipping into the more comfortable Man-mask, especially when the doctor says: "'Le malheur des gens comme vous [. . .], c'est qu'ils se mentent à eux-mêmes. Leur désir de guérir se double le plus souvent d'une répugnance non moins grande à renoncer aux avantages, aux satisfactions (hé oui, il faut bien le dire, malgré les souffrances, très réelles, je ne le nie pas) que leur procure leur maladie'" ["The unhappiness of people like you (. . .), is that they lie to themselves. Their desire to be cured is doubled, more often than not, by a repugnance, which is no less powerful, to renounce the advantages (. . .) (ah yes, it must be said, in spite of the very real suffering, I don't deny it) that their illness affords them"] (75).

The trip to the specialist ends with his final advice, given in Gide's terms, "'soyez Nathanâel, goûtez aux "nourritures terrestres"'" ["be Nathanial, partake of 'earthly pleasures'"]. *Je* describes this advice as given with "son sourire gêné et un peu moqueur" [his embarrassed and somewhat mocking smile] (77). The mockery of this tone extends to the narration of the trip *je* takes as well, now subject to the author's irony. Whereas Sarraute's male narrator seeks to divest himself of tropistic perception, his own flight will be rendered in a tropistic text. That is, the "dangerous" side of tropisms is identified with a feminine narrative figure, *elle*, and the literary side exploited by Nathalie Sarraute, woman writer.

The narration takes on the style of a Baudelairean poet as *je* describes that the city he visits "avait toujours été pour moi, la ville de *L'Invitation au Voyage*" [had always been for me, the city of "Invitation au Voyage"]: "Ses navires imperceptiblement balancés (Baudelaire avait songé aussi à dire: dandinés, il avait hésité, mais il avait trouvé à le dire mieux encore), [. . .] tout saignait dans une sorte de douceur exaltée" [Its ships imperceptibly balanced (Baudelaire had also thought of saying: waddling, he hesitated, but he found an even better way to say it), (. . .) all bathed in a kind of exalted sweetness] (77–78). The sweet side of tropistic sensitivity is characterized by this "heureuse exaltation" of the romantic poet projecting his emotions onto the world around him.

While in this Baudelairean town *je* returns to the museum to look at a favorite picture, "Le Portrait d'un inconnu." There he finds the inspiration he needs when something in the portrait resonates within his self: "Et il me semblait, tandis que je restais là devant lui, perdu, fondu en lui, que cette note hésitante et grêle, cette réponse timide qu'il avait fait sourdre de moi, pénétrait en lui, résonnait en lui, il la recueillait, il la renvoyait, fortifiée, grossie par lui comme par un amplificateur, elle montait de moi, de lui, [. . .] m'emportait. [. . .] 'L'Homme au pourpoint,' comme je l'appelais, m'avait délivré" [It seemed to me, while I stood in front of him, lost, fused with him, that this hesitating and frail note, this timid response that he had made spring up in me, was penetrating in him, resonating in him, he gathered it up, he sent it back, fortified, enlarged by him as if by an amplifier, it rose from me, from him, (. . .), carried me. (. . .) "The Man in the Doublet," as I called him, had delivered me] (81). Renewed by the "sweet" side of tropistic perception and inspired by his romantic interpretation of the "heureuse exaltation" he finds in the Baudelairean town, the narrator lingers momentarily on his earlier romantic style before returning to the quest: "L'eau s'ouvrait avec un bruit de soie froissée sous l'étrave du bateau. De minces crêtes d'écume blanches couraient, frémissantes d'allégresse . . ." [The water opened up with the sound of crumpled silk beneath the front of the boat. Thin crests of white foam were running, quivering with jubilation] (85). This style represents the narrator's retrieval of his voice after the visit to the "spécialiste." Armed with his romantic interpretation of "le doute" and "le tourment" that he has seen embodied in the portrait, *je* now returns to create *le vieux* in his own image.

"'Assez! Taisez-vous! Assez!'" ["Enough! Shut up! Enough!"] (85). These are the words that greet him, words of *le vieux* reported to *je* by a mutual friend, words that set off the narrator's empathy and projection, similar to the "appel" he felt coming from portrait:

> Il devait le sentir confusément, que ces mots allaient m'atteindre, que c'était vers moi, que c'était à moi surtout que ces mots étaient lancés comme un appel ou comme un défi. Je sais qu'il devait le sentir. [. . .] Il s'est senti, lui aussi, tout à coup agrippé, saisi par quelqu'un qui le narguait de loin [. . .], et il avait senti tout de suite, [. . .] le contraste exaspérant entre ce cadre fabriqué, verni comme un joli jouet, et cela se mettait à se dérouler en lui—ses tourments, sa fille, sa vie (87, 90).

> [He must have felt it awkwardly, that these words were going to reach me, that it would come toward me, that it was especially to me that these words were thrown, like a call or a challenge. I know that he must have felt it. (. . .) He too felt suddenly gripped, seized by someone who was drowning him from afar (. . .), and he had felt all at once, (. . .) the exasperating contrast between this fabricated frame, polished like a pretty toy, and that started it rolling in him—his torments, his daughter, his life.]

In the scene je recreates around these words, le vieux is still not an alter ego; rather he serves as the model for a kind of strength that is later identified as male. At the end of this scene je is more aligned with elle, "l'Hypersensible," the figure who like je is "si influençable," "si suggestible," and whose mere presence is "un défi" [a challenge] to le vieux: "Il mêlait tout ensemble dans le même sac, [. . .] sa fille enfin et moi qui le défiions maintenant de loin, en train [. . .] de faire les parasites, pâmés devant 'les chefs-d'oeuvre'" [He was putting everyone in the same sack (. . .), his daughter finally, and me who were defying him now from a distance, (. . .) being parasites, swooned before "masterpieces" (. . .)] (92–93).

This defeat does not discourage the narrator because he has his male mentor in the portrait, "l'Inconnu me servait d'écran, me protégeait" [the Unknown Man served as a screen for me, protected me] (94). And since seeing the portrait, je also has a "jouissance nouvelle" [new pleasure], a romantic pleasure derived from "mes fétiches, les objects de mon culte" [my fetishes, the objects of my cult] which seek to "établir un contact" [establish contact] with him. The places he visits recall "certains décors de mon enfance" [certain scenes from my childhood], and the narrator feels "une drôle de satisfaction" [a funny kind of satisfaction], "une sensation très intime et douce de repliement sur soi" [a very intimate and sweet sensation of going into oneself], "une exaltation confuse" [a confused exaltation] (96). Gone is the "volupté," "ce mélange d'attrait et de peur" that he felt earlier when he sensed the presence of elle; it is replaced by the "jouissance," and becomes "une attente inquiète" [a disquieting wait], "ce mélange d'appréhension et d'espoir" [that mixture of apprehension and of hope], more characteristic of the writer seated before the blank page.

The reader now encounters *le vieux* for the first time in the novel. While *je* is at the railroad station, he says that he senses "leur présence" [their presence], "comme toujours, avant même de les apercevoir" [as always, even before seeing them] (97). "Leur présence," however, does not refer to *le vieux* and the daughter as the reader might expect. *Elle* disappears from the narration for several scenes, roughly thirty pages, while *je* focuses his interest on the old man.

Le vieux is at the station with the wife of a friend, and this feminine figure appears harmless at first. Still influenced by the "exaltation heureuse" inspired by the portrait, *je* projects it hesitantly onto *le vieux*: "[. . .] sûrement comme je suis venu portant avec moi mes trésors, il est venu" [(. . .) surely as I have come bringing with me my treasures, he has come]. In his description of *le vieux* the narrator uses the same comparison that he had earlier used for himself, "il y a dans tout cela quelque chose, sûrement, qui l'excite, lui procure une sensation semblable à celle du bourgeois cossu qui se promène à la Foire aux Puces" [there is in all this something, surely, that excites him, affords him a sensation similar to that of the well-to-do bourgeois who walks around at the Flea Market] (99).

This "sensation" is the romantic tendency to anthropomorphize the objects around him: "[. . .] une intuition déjà, un pressentiment, avait attiré mon attention sur ce baluchon, sur cet air, surtout de sollicitude, avec lequel il lui avait pris le baluchon des mains. Il y avait là autre chose encore que la sollicitude [. . .], il aurait pu enlever son chapeau et s'agenouiller" [(. . .) already an intuition, a premonition, had attracted my attention to this bundle, to that look, especially the solicitude, with which he had taken the bundle from her hands. There was still something more there than solicitude (. . .), he could have taken off his hat and gotten down on his knees] (101). As his narration continues, *je* inserts the daughter parenthetically, awkwardly, but quickly interjects the friend's wife instead: "Il aime cela, venir ainsi de temps en temps baiser un pan du vêtement de leur déesse à tous les deux (lui et sa fille): ils se ressemblent. Seulement il joue un jeu dangereux. Elle est toute-puissante, la vieille qui est avec lui—une vestale du culte" [He likes that, to come like this from time to time to kiss the hem of the robe of their goddess, the one they share (him and his daughter): they are alike. Only he is playing a dangerous game. She is all-powerful, the old woman who is with him—a vestal of the cult] (101).

In the narrator's first reference to an *elles* figure, the passage ending with "elles adhéraient à elles" served to contain the daughter's "unhealthy" tropistic games. At the end of Chapter 2, the narrator joins *elle* to *elles*, a group which constitutes a threat to *le vieux* because their words freeze his "true" tropistic reality. The "vieille amie" in the scene at the railroad station in Chapter 7 introduces a contrasting image and is described in ambivalent terms. This feminine figure's words are described as "toutes-puissantes" [all-powerful], even though she "semble être, comme les élus que la Divinité choisit pour accomplir de saintes missions, la pureté, l'innocence même" [seems to be, like the elected that the Divine chooses to carry out holy missions, purity, innocence itself] (101–2).

The "paroles" pronounced by *elle* can break through the surface that *le vieux* constructs, allowing *elle* to push on "le point sensible" [his sensitive spot] (102). This figure of *elle* is dangerous to the old man, for like the "fées protectrices" [protective fairies] who stand behind the daughter during the argument in Chapter 10, *elles* can provoke *le vieux*, make him vulnerable to the emotions that make up his tropistic reality. When *elles* push on his "point sensible," the narrator says that it is like "un drain par où une partie de lui-même, sa substance allait s'écouler" [a drain through which a part of himself, his substance was going to flow out] (157).

Whereas *le vieux* was described earlier in the novel as "fort" in "ces jeux" [strong in these games], in the narrator's "characterization" of *le vieux* at this point the two share a weakness: "[. . .] cette extrême sensibilité à l'impression que les autres ont de lui, [. . .] qui lui donne toujours la sensation pénible [. . .] de jouer avec tous la comédie, de n'être jamais 'lui-même'" [(. . .) that extreme sensitivity to the impression that others have of him, (. . .) that always gives him the painful feeling (. . .) of playing the comedy with everyone, of never being "himself"] (104). *Je* earlier attributes this same trait to *elle*, but without the qualifiers which here join it to the younger male narrator and which extend it to become a more general (human) characteristic, "'un trait, dirait mon spécialiste, fréquent chez les nerveux'" ["a trait, so my specialist says, common among nervous types"] (104).

The narrator notices that *le vieux* is not yet aware of the feelings the two of them share. *Je* thinks that if he stood before *le vieux* and told him that *elle* ("la vieille amie") had touched his "point sensible," he would dismiss the narrator's observation as childish babbling, a "langage dément" [demented language] (104). *Je* notices that *le vieux* is no different from *elle* or everyone else in this denial, "c'est leur moyen de défense à tous" [it's their defense]. This recognition, however, does not stop *je* in his quest to make *le vieux* a different kind of adult. Like a child, *je* imagines following the old man into his house to observe him: "Il me semble que je suis maintenant près de lui, tandis qu'il est assis là sans bouger, pareil au Petit Poucet, quand il épiait, effrayé, le sommeil de l'Ogre" [It seems to me that I am close to him now, while he sits there without moving, like Tom Thumb, terrified, as he spied on the sleeping Giant] (106). The fairy tale imagery gives over to the insect image of tropisms and marks the narrator's control of the text: "Je sais maintenant ce qui me faisait toujours penser [. . .] qu'il était comme une grosse araignée immobile dans sa toile. Ce n'est pas seulement cet air qu'il a toujours, [. . .] c'est aussi sa position: au centre—il est au centre, il trône, il domine—l'univers entier est comme une toile qu'il a tissée et qu'il dispose à son gré autour de lui" [I now know what always made me think (. . .) that he was like a large, motionless spider in his web. It's not simply that way he always has, (. . .) it is also his position: in the center—he is in the center, he lords over, he dominates—the entire universe is like a web that he has spun around him and that he manages at will] (107–8).

Although the narrator is in control of the text, his boychild self still wishes to emulate the control the old man seems to have. After this observation the voice of the narrator as child is represented when *je* recognizes that he is of little interest to *le vieux*, "il a d'autres passe-temps" [he has other pastimes], "d'autres jeux plus attachants" [other, more attractive games]: "[. . .] les recherches, les découvertes les plus récentes, les théories, les constructions [. . .]: de grands bonshommes, [. . .] de très forts bonshommes" [(. . .) research, the most recent discoveries, theories, constructions (. . .): of great fellows, (. . .) of very strong fellows] (109–10). The modification of "de grands bonhommes" as "de très forts bonhommes" suggests an irony which could go in both directions: the childlike narrator mocking the adult who ignores him, or the adult narrator mocking the trivial pastimes of the old man. In either case, the irony represents some kind of personal investment in the old man on the part of the narrator.

As if responding to this character-izing gesture, *je* says he must not be tempted by this image, "Mais attention, je sens que je serais assez tenté de m'attarder dangereusement sur cette image" [Attention, I feel that I would be tempted to linger dangerously on this image]: "Il y a toujours ainsi, comme dans les romans d'aventure, quelque chose au dernier moment qui me sauve. C'est un souvenir, cette fois, qui est venu me tirer de cet état de détente satisfaite auquel j'étais en train de m'abandonner paresseusement" [There is always something that saves me at the last minute, like in adventure novels. It's a memory, this time, which came to pull me out of that state of satisfied relaxation where I was abandoning myself lazily] (110, 111–12).

If "contes de fées" [fairy tales] speak childhood, "romans d'aventures" [adventure novels] speak men in combat with forces larger than themselves, often male rivalry as bonding in mythic proportions. Although fairy-tale imagery is usually as gender biased as that found in adventure novels, this reference to "romans d'aventure" inflects the "neutral" narrator with the male gender. The memory the narrator recounts not only establishes evidence of the tropistic side of le vieux, but more importantly, it is also a scene in which je perceives the two of them in a mythical, oedipal duel, with himself as the victor, that is, his child (boy) self assumes adulthood (manhood).

One element of the memory that is recalled is that the narrator is paired with the adolescent who accompanies the old man and another old friend on a walk. Le vieux talks about death, "et je sentais comme il se pelotonnait délicieusement en lançant sur l'adolescent et moi un regard de côté pour juger de l'effet produit" [and I felt as if he snuggled up in himself with delight while glancing at the adolescent and me to measure the effect it produced] (112). When the old man makes his pronouncement on life and death, citing the words of another friend's parrot—"Tout cela 'n'a vraiment aucune importance'" [All of that "has truly no importance"]—the narrator laughs out loud: "J'avais réussi à saisir, dépassant de l'armure solide, qu'il s'était fabriquée et où il se croyait bien en sûreté, quelque chose de vivant—sa main qui se tendait vers moi furtivement. J'avais saisi sa main au vol. Je le tenais" [I had succeeded in seizing, through his solid armor that he had manufactured and where he believed himself to be very safe, something alive—his hand that he was stretching out to me furtively. I had seized his hand in flight. I had him] (113–14).

Now that le vieux is in the narrator's grasp they are equals, and the narrator must bring the reader to share his empathy and identification with the older man. In the scene at the railroad station, je described le vieux in terms which brought the two figures together in their appreciation of "l'exaltation heureuse." The passage that follows is one that takes on larger proportions, as seen in the passage about elles, but in the opposite direction: "Des coups frappés quelque part au fond de nous, des coups étouffés, menaçants, semblables aux battements sourds du sang dans les veines dilatées, nous réveillent en sursaut. 'Mes réveils de condamné à mort,' c'est ainsi qu'il les appelait" [Blows struck somewhere in the depth of ourselves, muffled blows, threatening, similar to the deaf beating of blood in dilated veins, awakens us with a start. "My awakenings of a condemned man," that's what he used to call them (. . .)] (114). A plural in the third person would have separated the narrative situation from the reader. Here, "our" experience of "les tourments" of insomnia or "le vide" [the emptiness] of Sunday afternoons extends at the end of the sentence to include le vieux.

The agony of insomnia is then expanded by means of imagery that is less sweeping than the narrator's earlier nostalgic reveries inspired by deserted streets, more mysterious and haunting:

> Elle est là, plantée au coeur de l'angoisse, un corpuscule solide, piquant et dur, autour duquel la douleur irradie, elle est là (parfois il faut tâtonner assez longtemps avant de la trouver, parfois on la découvre très rapidement), l'image, l'idée . . . Très simple d'ordinaire et même un peu puérile à première vue, d'une un peu trop naïve crudité—une image de notre mort, de notre vie. [. . .] Notre vie, non pas telle que nous la sentons au cours des journées, comme un jet d'eau intarissable, sans cesse renouvelé, qui s'éparpille à chaque instant en impalpables gouttelettes aux teintes irisées, mais durcie, pétrifiée: un paysage lunaire avec ses pics dénudés qui se dressent tragiquement dans un ciel désert, ses profonds cratères pleins d'ombre (115–16).

> [It/She's there, planted at the heart of the anguish, a solid corpuscle, prickly and hard, from which the pain irradiates, it/she's there (sometimes you have to grope around for a fairly long time before finding it/her, sometimes you discover it/her very quickly), the image, the idea . . . Ordinarily very simple and even a little puerile at first, with a little too naive crudeness—an image of our death, of our life. (. . .) Our life, not the one that we feel as the days go by, like a inexhaustible fountain, always renewed, which scatters at every instant into impalpable droplets in iridescent shades, but hardened, petrified: a lunar landscape with its denuded peaks that rise up tragically in a deserted sky, its deep craters full of shadows.]

In a text where antecedents are often fleeting, the feminine pronoun *elle* which begins this passage remains poetically ambiguous and elicits several possible references before it is joined to "l'image, l'idée." In a similar reference earlier in the novel, the figure of the daughter is suggested by the context in which a phrase appears, "au moment où elle disparaissait à un tournant de l'escalier." As the sentence continues, however, the pronoun turns out to refer to another noun, "la ligne furtive de leur dos [. . .]" [in the moment when she/it disappeared at the turn of the stair, the furtive line of their back (. . .)] (31). The opening pronoun in the above passage carries with it traces of the daughter because she has been associated with "l'angoisse" of *le vieux*, but it also resonates with earlier references to the *elles*, those who judge him with their moral maxims (56–57), the *elles* of "elles adhéraient à elles" (42), the *elle* who pushed the old man's "point sensible" at the station (102–4) and whose voice nags him again in these moments of insomnia. All the threats that these figures represent to the narrator and to his projection on *le vieux* come to bear on this pronoun as we wait—menaced ourselves—for its antecedent.

Je says that this "tourment" is "quelque chose de miniscule—de si ridiculement petit, de si particulier à lui, que cela ne vaudrait même pas la peine d'en parler" [something so miniscule—so ridiculously small, so particular to him that it would hardly be worth talking about it], because "personne ne pourrait sympathiser, admirer, personne ne comprendrait" [no one could sympathize, no one would understand] (116). The narration describing this "parcelle," however, is far from "miniscule." Two long paragraphs with breathless sentences and graphic metaphors create an agony that once again inspires a more general sympathy, compassion, and understanding. "Il m'attendrit" [He moves me], the narrator has said earlier, and here it seems he does. Because of his identification with *le vieux*, *je* is able to recognize his "tourments" much more than those of *elle*, and at the end of this long passage, a feminine pronoun once again represents "le tourment": "Mais peu à peu, à mesure que le jour se lève, la petite boule dans son esprit ralentit son mouvement. Elle n'avance plus maintenant que par bonds espacés" [But little by little, as the day breaks, the little ball in his spirit slowed down its movement. It/She doesn't advance any longer now except in well-spaced leaps] (123). This is the dangerous side of tropisms, but in the absence of the daughter to embody it, *je* can contain it instead in an abstracted feminine entity and raise it to the status of a sentiment that he shares (and which he invites the reader to share) with *le vieux*.

The identification *je* establishes with *le vieux* disappears when the "obsessions" and "tourments" that joined them disperse with "le réveil paisible" [the peaceful awakening]: "Il n'y a plus de lien entre nous. Plus de signes de lui à moi. Aucun regard de connivence" [There is no longer any connection between us. No more signs from him to me. No look of connivance] (123). In spite of this separation, or because of it, *je* still retains a certain admiration for *le vieux*: "Il est même extraordinaire de voir combien dans les moments les plus dangereux des journées, il peut rester inconscient et calme" [It is, all the same, extraordinary to see how he can remain unconscious and calm in the most dangerous moments of the day] (124). Now that the tropistic line is broken, the narrator separates the reader from the *nous/on* experience of insomnia which had brought us all together; *je* singles out *le vieux* as the object of observation. "On peut l'observer," the narrator tells us, on Sunday afternoons, "[. . .] quand tant de gens sentent comme une crampe légère au coeur tandis qu'ils se laissent glisser sans pouvoir se retenir dans le vide, il marche d'un pas assuré tout au bord de la peur" [He can be seen (. . .) on Sunday afternoons, when so many people feel something like a slight cramp in the heart while they let themselves slide, unable to stop themselves, into the emptiness, he walks with a sure step at the very edge of the fear] (124–25).

In the scene the narrator describes, the old man is at a café with his friends, strutting about between stereotypical gender groupings: the waitresses and his cronies—"[. . .] elles sourient gentiment, attentives à lui plaire [. . .], elles frétillent légèrement, des êtres exquis, tout d'instinct . . . des abeilles, des papillons . . . c'est ainsi qu'il les appelle souvent . . ." [(. . .) they smile nicely, attentive to please him (. . .), they wriggle slightly, exquisite beings, all the instinct . . . of bees, of butterflies . . . that's what he often calls them . . .] (126); "les hommes, tous réunis d'un côté du salon, discutent comme il se doit de finances ou de politique" [the men, all gathered in one corner of the room, discuss, as they should, finances and politics (. . .)] (125); and le vieux, "il est apaisé, satisfait, son regard glisse sur elles distraitement, tandis qu'il se lève pour se rapprocher du groupe des hommes" [he is calm, satisfied, his distracted look slides onto the women, while he gets up to move closer to the group of men] (127); "le cercle des hommes, solides, rassurant, se resserre autour de lui [. . .], il a l'air détendu, sûr de lui, tout à fait dans son élément" [the circle of men, solid, reassuring, closes around him (. . .), he looks relaxed, sure of himself, completely in his element] (127).

When le vieux is in his element in this way, the narrator feels no connection with him because he has abandoned "la forme grotesque" [the grotesque form] of insomnia. Although the narrator tells us that he can "l'évoquer de nouveau, cette image tourmentée" [call it up again, that tormented image], their separation is marked by an abstraction represented by the pronoun elle ("cette image") which pulls away from le vieux and returns to its place in the narrator: "[. . .] il me semble que, pareille à mon ombre quand le soleil monte dans le ciel, elle diminue rapidement, se ramasse à mes pieds en une petite tache informe, se résorbe en moi-même" [(. . .) it seems to me that, like my shadow when the sun rises in the sky, it/she diminishes rapidly, gathers at my feet in a little shapeless spot, is reabsorbed into me] (127). Je admires le vieux because he is able to move between the surface (here represented as a gender construct, male) and the subsurface (represented by "l'ombre" and more on the side of the feminine). Je is not in the "cercle des hommes," and he is left alone with this feminine element.

The desire of je to be like le vieux is acted out in the next chapter at a luncheon "chez eux" [at their house]. Unlike the other scenes, which have slipped into a more timeless present of creation, this scene is recounted in the narrative past, which serves as a realist touchstone marking the narrator's more lucid, less tropistic moments. This lucidity is highlighted because it is preceded by several paragraphs in which elle is presented in the timeless present. She is identified with the "ombres" that je no longer sees around le vieux, but which the narrator

hates in *elle:* "Je sais qu'il lui faut si peu de chose, un rien la fait
trembler, l'Hypersensible, tapissée de petits tentacules soyeux qui frémissent, se penchent au moindre souffle et font qu'elle est sans cesse
parcourue d'ombres rapides" [I know that she needs very little, a nothing makes her tremble, the Hypersensitive One, covered with little silky
tentacles that quiver, bend at the least breath such that rapid shadows
run over her endlessly] (128, 129). During this luncheon *je* describes
himself as resolved to "me tenir à l'écart" [remain at a distance] (130),
which is similar to the way in which he described *le vieux* at the café
with his friends, "écoutant d'une oreille distraite" [listening with a
distracted ear] (125). When conversation begins between the guests, *je*
looks to *le vieux* for strength and for confirmation that a power struggle
is not about to take place: "[. . .] il se taisait, renfrogné, en tapotant
nerveusement la table" [(. . .) he remained quiet, scowling, nervously
tapping the table] (131).

Je is unable to remain calm and cannot help but resume "mon rôle,
ma qualité de corps conducteur à travers lequel passaient tous les
courants dont l'atmosphère était chargée" [my role, my skill as a con-
ductor through which passed all the currents of this charged atmo-
sphere]. In this role *je* joins the larger group of *nous*, the voyeurs
anticipating the battle, the guests, the narrator, and the readers all
rolled into one by the use of the plural *nous* (131). A young male
guest tries to engage *le vieux* in conversation: "[. . .] le jeune acrobate
avançait d'un pas léger sur la corde tendue et nous le regardions [. . .],
nous le regardions [. . .], le jeune fou, l'inconscient, l'innocent allait
venir s'écraser à nos pieds [. . .], mais non, rien n'arrivait . . . nous en-
tendions le vieux répondre d'une voix où nous seuls pouvions percevoir cette nuance un peu forcée, cette note un peu enrouée qui révélait
la réalité du danger, de la menace qui avait pesé" [(. . .) the young
acrobat came forward with a light step onto the tightrope and we were
looking at him (. . .), we were looking at him (. . .), the crazy young
man, the unconscious one, the innocent one was going to come crashing
down at our feet (. . .), but no, nothing happened . . . we heard the old
man respond with a voice which only we could recognize as having
that slightly forced nuance, that slightly rusty note that revealed the
reality of the danger, of the threat hanging over him] (133). The circus
imagery lends the battle a lightness and humor not seen in this novel
to such a degree in connection with a tropistic perspective, and when
the young man tries again he is identified as Saint George trying to slay
the dragon (*le vieux*) in order to save the princess (*elle*) (134). This
tone strips tropistic perspective of either the more romantic "exaltation
heureuse" experienced and projected in the scene at the station, or of

"le tourment" created by insomnia, and it marks the distance between *je* and *le vieux*.

When *le vieux* unexpectedly accepts the young guest's offer to teach his daughter to play golf, it is *elle* who upsets the balance with her refusal. The old man's scornful look joins the narrator with the daughter and the other guests and separates him from the old man: "Le vieux la regardait, elle sentait, nous sentions tous comme il la haïssait en ce moment, comme il nous méprisait, honteux pour nous, dégoûté [. . . . Il] se détournait d'elle tout à coup, de nous, il nous abandonnait à notre abjection. L'innocence, la pureté, l'insouciance l'emportaient . . . Il allait à elles, conquis, il se rangeait de leur côté [The old man looked at her, she felt, we all felt as if he hated us at this moment, as if he scorned us, was ashamed for us, disgusted (. . . . He) turned away from her all at once, from all of us, he abandoned us to our abjection. Innocence, purity, a carefree air took him away . . . He went to them (feminine), converted, he stood by their side] (134–35). The plural *nous* projected onto *je* throws him into resemblance to *elle* and to the voyeuristic public. *Nous*, we who were watching, have been caught in our voyeurism, and *le vieux* retreats with *elles*, that (mysterious) group of qualities that ends up with a plural feminine pronoun.

Throughout this novel the figure of *elles* represents contrary qualities, much like the virgin goddess and the whore do in patriarchal imagery. This figure both dangerously provokes the tropistic "substance" or dangerously contains it in maxims. Although *le vieux* is similarly ambivalent, slipping between "le tourment" of insomnia and the "Monsieur bien découpé" [the well-drawn Monsieur] which includes him in "le cercle des hommes," *je* attributes to him a sense of his own depths. *Le vieux* can exercise his will and control, usually "en se tenant à l'écart" [by keeping himself to one side], and he is not lost because of that depth as *elle* sometimes is. The description of escape to *elles* made by *le vieux* attributes to him a similar sense of control. *Je*, however, recuperates this retreat into a feminine plural by characterizing the old man's "conquis" in male images: "Avec cet air d'indulgence admirative et attendrie avec lequel les vieux serviteurs dévoués, les vieux 'butlers' des comédies anglaises sourient des facéties des fils de famille qu'ils ont connus tout petits [. . .], il souriait au jeune ami. [. . .] Il riait de son rire bonhomme. Rassurés, détendus, nous riions avec lui" [With that air of admiring and tender indulgence with which old devoted servants, the old "butlers" of English comedies smile at the pranks of the son of the family whom they have known since childhood, (. . .) he smiled at the young friend. (. . .) He laughed his goodhearted laugh. Reassured, relaxed, we laughed with him] (135).

The figure of nous looks foolish at the end Chapter 8 when "l'explosion," perhaps awaited with "une volupté particulière, un mélange d'attrait et de peur," does not take place; le vieux has controlled it:
"L'explosion, l'éruption que nous avions attendue, ramassés sur nous-
mêmes, l'effrayant déferlement de scories, de cendres brûlantes, de lave
bouillante, ne s'était pas produit" [The explosion, the eruption that we
had awaited, curled up together, the terrifying flood of scoria, of burning ashes, of bubbling lava, didn't happen] (135). The narrator is returned to his position of defeat: "Je m'étais démené inutilement, une
fois de plus" [I had uselessly exerted myself, once again] (135). This
experience of defeat leads the narrator back into a more analytical
mode.

In the series of short paragraphs that begin Chapter 9, je continually
refers to ils, the old man and the daughter, as a single unit. He describes
their "prudence" and explains that if he tries to force their tropistic
reality to the surface, "ils se solidifieraient d'un coup" [they would
solidify in one turn]. The narrator's quest, however, remains focused
on le vieux and the control he exerts: "Lui, comme il est prudent.
Comme il se tient en sûreté. On a du mal à le surprendre" [Him, how
prudent he is. How he keeps himself safe. It's hard to surprise him]
(137). As if reflecting on his own position, je imagines that this is the
quality which attracts others to le vieux, "comme des mouches" [like
flies].

Je turns his attention at this point away from the old man and his
daughter and examines another feminine figure, "la bonne" [the maid].
She is endowed with the same "volupté" that attracts the narrator to le
vieux, but she is deprived of its depth: "La vieille bonne, [. . .] se sent
aux heures trop calmes des débuts d'après-midi, [. . .] une crampe [. . .].
Ou peut-être sent-elle vaguement, au coeur de cette torpeur, comme
l'appel étouffé d'une sorte de lourde et louche volupté. Mais elle ne se
l'avoue pas, bien sûr" [The old maid, (. . .) feels during the too calm
hours of the afternoon (. . .) a cramp (. . .). Or perhaps she feels vaguely,
at the heart of that torpor, something like a muffled appeal to a kind
of heavy and suspect voluptuousness. But, of course, she doesn't admit
it] (138).

Even though je joins the daughter to her father in this power to attract
others, her power is not realized until after their argument in Chapter
10. The ignorance on the part of the maid of the significance of the old
man's power looks at first like another effort by the narrator to distinguish le vieux from others. The narration takes an unexpected return
to the surface, however, and transforms the scene into a tropistic farce.
After recounting the scene in a linear fashion with instances of indirect
discourse taking readers into the maid's consciousness, the text pulls

back to a more general experience, now familiar to readers in the narrator's treatment of le vieux. This digression presents the most prolonged
general view in Portrait which takes the readers out of the narrator's
quest, and it ends in his complete inability to remain with his character
in a tropistic depth.

The passage first describes "les moments dangereux" in the beginning of the afternoon as "une menace indéfinissable" [an undefinable
threat], elaborated with diverse images, "la fente miniscule" [the miniscule crack], "l'écaillure" [the flaking patch], "l'éraflure" [the scratch],
"ce gouffre" [that pit]. The group affected by this threat includes both
masculine and feminine figures, but the figure of elles takes over the
passage and then the old man's experience is linked to theirs:

> Des hommes solitaires, des femmes que "la vie", comme elles disent, a déjà
> malmenées, restées veuves, leurs enfants morts, l'un de scarlatine—"un
> amour, si vous saviez . . . pourquoi, disait-il, il faisait de ces réflexions, il
> était si mignon, pourquoi doit-on aimer les gens, puisqu'il faudra s'en séparer
> un jour . . . il avait des boucles blondes, [. . .] je le disais toujours, de si beaux
> cheveux pour un garçon"—des femmes aux yeux délavés, aux corps usés, se
> lèvent dès le petit jour . . . il faut courir, regarder . . . le trou est là . . . la
> tache [. . .] . . . elle se voit à deux mètres, elle est là, menaçante, hostile, à les
> narguer en plein milieu du salon, entourée de son cerne rougeâtre . . . il est
> toujours là [. . .]. C'est là, dans le mur . . . une vrai inondation . . . le mur est
> traversé . . . Il rajuste son lorgnon [. . .], il se penche, il s'agenouille, il se
> couche, la joue contre le carreau, pour mieux voir . . . (145–46).

> [Lonely men, women whom "life," as they say, has already brutalized, still
> widows, their children dead, one from scarlet fever—"a love, if you only
> knew . . . why, he would say, he thought about things, he was so cute, why
> should we love people, if we have to part with them some day . . . he had
> blond curls, (. . .) I always said, such beautiful hair for a boy"—women with
> faded eyes, with worn out bodies, up at the crack of dawn . . . must run,
> must look . . . the hole is there . . . the spot (. . .) . . . it/she's visible from two
> meters, it/she's there, hostile, threatening to drown them in the middle of the
> living room, encircled by its/her reddish shadow, it/he's always there (. . .).
> It's there, on the wall . . . a real flood . . . through the wall . . . He readjusts
> his pince-nez (. . .), he leans over, he kneels, he lies down, his cheek against
> the tile, to see better. . . .]

The weighty subject of life and death that introduces this passage is
ridiculed by the discourse surrounding it and then simplified by the
child's question, "pourquoi doit-on aimer les gens puisqu'il faut s'en
séparer un jour?" This is the narrator's theme, a romantic lament that
represents his desire for union with le vieux in "une menace indéfinissable," a moral anguish. The narration rips the lament apart by returning the image of this "menace" to that of "une tache" on the
bathroom wall, which then joins le vieux with "les femmes aux yeux

délavés." The narrator has difficulty maintaining a distance between the "unhealthy" side of tropisms and the "sweet" side, seen in this passage in which "la menace" is represented by a masculine and a feminine noun and pronoun ("le trou," "la tache").

Je does not give up in his effort to give this "tache" larger dimensions in the old man's consciousness. The narrator's paragraphs begin confidently: "Il sent" [He feels]; "Il lui semble que" [It seems to him that]; "C'est dans ces moments-là, je l'ai remarqué" [It's during moments like this, I've noticed]; "Le soulagement qu'il éprouve" [The relief he feels] (147–48). As the passage continues, however, the narrator's tropistic identification with *le vieux* is mocked by the realistic touchstone represented by *elle*, "la bonne": "Elle l'a saisi au collet et tiré hors de cette torpeur débilitante dans laquelle il était en train de macérer—au-dehors, au grand jour" [She grabbed him by the collar and pulled him out of that debilitating torpor he was wallowing in—outside, into the broad daylight (. . .)] (148). When the scene ends, "il est à quatre pattes, son derrière qui pointe en l'air tend son pantalon à le faire craquer—la bonne aurait envie de sourire, mais elle sait que le moment n'est pas aux plaisanteries" [he is down on all fours, his rear-end sticking up in the air stretches his pants to their limit—the maid must have wanted to smile, but she knows that this is not the time for jokes] (149).

There is a growing sense that the narrator separates the old man's world into gendered spheres: "Il a été arraché à son monde malléable, [. . .] il a été projeté brutalement dans son monde à elle, dur, agressif, implacable, sur lequel il n'a pas pris [. . .], dans cet univers hostile où il se sent étranger, menacé de toutes parts" [He was torn from his malleable world, (. . .) thrown brutally into her world, hard, aggressive, implacable, where he has no bearings (. . .), that hostile universe where he feels like a foreigner, threatened from all sides] (149–50). In the time that it takes to inhale the breath to say that *le vieux* in this scene represents the fluid world of tropisms and *elle* hard reality, the text brings these speculations to an ironic halt by returning entirely to the surface: *Le vieux* asks, "'Et les teintures? [. . .] Si l'on reteignait le rideau entièrement?' Elle hésite . . . 'Peut-être . . . il faudrait le montrer au teinturier . . . Mais alors . . .' elle sourit d'un drôle de sourire un peu moqueur où pointe en même temps comme une sorte d'appréhension dégoûtée [. . .]: 'Mais alors . . . le prix . . . ça . . .'" ["And the dye? (. . .) If we redye the whole curtain?" She hesitates . . . "Perhaps . . . we should take it to the cleaners . . . But . . ." she smiles a funny, slightly mocking smile which revealed at the same time a kind of disgusted apprehension [. . .]: "But . . . the price . . . now that . . ."] (149–50). Unlike the earlier passage about insomnia, which solicits the reader's empathy for *le vieux*, this passage begins similarly, but *je* loses control of tropistic empathy as the surface triumphs.

Breaking through that surface now, the old man's emotions rage out of control, a quality that the narrator fears. *Le vieux* begins screaming at the maid, telling her of waking in the night to turn off the faucet, and implying the daughter's guilt: "[. . .] le trou ne s'est pas fait tout seul" [(. . .) the hole didn't appear all by itself] (150). Faced with his character's loss of control, *je* reestablishes it in his narration by appropriating with his own vocabulary what he sees to be the old man's "douleur" [pain]: "[. . .] bien qu'assez forte encore, ce mélange d'une sorte du volupté" [(. . .) even though it is still fairly strong, it is mixed with a sort of voluptuousness] (150). The drama will quickly be over, the narrator explains, "tout rentrera dans l'ordre" [everything will fall back into place].

This order is marked by a return to the spider imagery which explicitly refers to *le vieux* but implicitly describes the narrator's own narration: "Soulagé, apaisé, il peut maintenant revenir à petits pas pressés, un peu gênés, dans son cabinet reprendre sa place au centre de cet univers qu'il s'est tissé, [. . .] le voir s'animer et se colorer de nouveau sous son regard" [Relieved, calmed, he can now return with little hurried steps, slightly annoyed, to his study to resume his place in the center of that universe that he has woven (. . .), watch it take on life and color once again beneath his gaze (. . .)] (152). The point of the reader's identification, tropistic emptiness felt during the silence of some afternoons and its metaphor "la tache," transforms into an image of *le vieux* literally down on his hands and knees looking at a hole in the wall; this image marks the failure of *je* to remain with the *le vieux* on a level deeper than this spider image.

That failure is realized in Chapter 10, a scene of confrontation between father and daughter. In his narration of their argument, *je* begins in resemblance to the daughter who also responds to "l'appel" that comes from *le vieux* (154), but she is just as quickly distinguished from both male figures in that she is supported by "les bonnes femmes" (157–58). It is from *elles* that the daughter has learned "petit à petit à mieux connaître en lui les endroits douillets, les points sensibles" [little by little to recognize in (the old man) the downy spots, the sensitive points] (158). As the passage proceeds, *je* attributes the now familiar tropistic "jouissance" to the old man in an image of father and daughter walking in the park in younger days: "[. . .] et il sentait, tandis qu'il l'entraînait plus loin, pressant très fort dans ses doigts la petite main, arrachant de lui, écrasant les doux tentacules mous qui s'accrochaient à lui timidement, une sorte de jouissance douloureuse, une drôle de

satisfaction au goût âcre et légèrement écoeurant" [(. . .) and he felt, as
he was leading her farther away, pressing very strongly between his
fingers the little hand, tearing away from him, crushing the soft, limp
tentacles which were hanging onto him timidly, a sort of sad pleasure,
a funny kind of satisfaction with a bitter taste and slightly nauseating]
(159). Joined to le vieux by this "jouissance douloureuse," the narrator
can separate himself from elle, represented by "la petite main." This
image is then replaced by "les tentacules," a synecdoche used earlier
that marked the disgust je identified when he felt elle soliciting his
complicity in "unhealthy" tropistic games.

When the battle begins le vieux and elle remain separate. Le vieux
is on his guard and elle "l'observe" [observes him], just as she had done
with je before their first power struggle (159, 160). The battle lines are
clearly drawn between genders, elle and her "fées" on one side, who
represent both the danger of "la substance" and the moralizing power
of maxims which negate "la substance"; and on the other, le vieux with
his "cohorte protectrice" [protective cohorts] (160–61). This feminine
noun is never represented as a pronoun in this passage but is instead
elaborated with other designations representing both feminine and
masculine nouns: "sa vieille garde" [his old guard], "ses vieux amis"
[his old friends]. The figure of elles is considered dangerous, because
their words generalize the narrator's attempts to establish both himself
and le vieux as individuals. This feminine figure represents an amorphous domesticity throughout the novel. Je as narrator invents both
groups, but where the image of elles is provoked by fear, the image of
ils is provoked by desire, as seen by the way in which this group is
introduced into the battle scene.

Whereas the figure of elles is described in ambiguous terms, the
reader learns about "ses vieux amis" through a brief narrative which
establishes them easily in the reader's mind: "[. . .] il les sent derrière
lui—un appui solide . . . Le samedi, quand il va le rejoindre au restaurant, ce vieux Jérôme,—un bon restaurant cossu, car il a fait du chemin,
lui aussi, le bougre, depuis les trajets sur l'impériale, c'est devenu un
Monsieur, comme on dit—quand il va déjeuner avec lui et quelques
vieux amis d'autrefois" [(. . .) he feels them behind him—a solid support . . . Saturdays, when he goes to meet him at the restaurant, old
Jerome,—a good, ritzy restaurant, because he has done his work, he has,
this fellow, since the days of riding those double-decker buses, he's
become a Monsieur, as they say—when he goes to lunch with him and
a few other friends from the old days] (161). The narrator observes that
what is reassuring about the group with le vieux is that it does not
tolerate "la substance": "[. . .] sous leur regard placide, ce regard si
assuré, toujours un peu indifférent, il lui semble qu'il se remplit tout

entier d'une matière consistante qui le rend compact et lourd, bien stable, 'un Monsieur' [. . .]" [(. . .) beneath their placid look, so self-assured, always a little indifferent, it seems to him that he is completely filled up with a consistent matter which makes him compact and heavy, very stable, "a Monsieur" (. . .)] (162). At the same time, however, je notes that le vieux is different from the others in that he elicits tenderness: "Le maître d'hôtel sourit et le regarde dans les yeux [. . .] que le maître d'hôtel aime bien, pour avoir surpris en eux [. . .] un reflet ému, caressant et attendri" [The maître d'hôtel smiles and looks him in the eye (. . .), which the maître d'hôtel likes very much because of the moving reflection, caressing and tender, that he happens to see there] (163).

On his quest for their "mouvements secrets," je pursues both elle and le vieux, but in the triangle that takes shape in the narration of that quest, je and le vieux operate on the same plane. The two male figures are at the base of a triangle that is inverted to place elle alone beneath them occupying the "malsain" world of tropisms with its "immondes odeurs." Je as narrator creates the "character" le vieux with both a "male" surface and a "feminine" depth. The narrator puts the mask of masculinity on le vieux ("le cercle des hommes" which exists in opposition to elles), at the same time he attributes to le vieux the knowledge of tropistic games ("Il est beaucoup plus fort qu'elle dans ces jeux"), as well as the experience of "jouissance douleureuse" and "l'exaltation heureuse," another side of tropisms.

By giving le vieux access to these two poles, je can attribute to him the characteristic that je finds in the portrait, that of a male figure with depth in whom he can find resonance as described earlier: "Les lignes de son visage, [. . .] de son pourpoint, de ses mains, semblaient être les contours fragmentaires [. . .]. On dirait qu'ici l'effort, le doute, le tourment avaient été surpris par une catastrophe soudaine" [The lines of his face, (. . .) of his doublet, of his hands, seem to be fragmented contours (. . .). One could say that here the effort, the doubt, the torment had been surprised by a sudden catastrophe] (80). The figure of elles, never representing the harmony of these two poles, is either on one side or the other, immersed in "des immondes odeurs" or "attachées aux images."

During the battle in Chapter 10, father and daughter lose their distinctions when they leave the defending groups at the surface and fall "comme Alice au Pays des Merveilles" [like Alice in Wonderland] to a place "sans protection" [without protection] (167). For a moment it looks as if elle is going to commit the crime that will separate her from her father, "la Désinvolture" [Casualness], "ce crime qu'il agit sans cesse devant elle sans le nommer" [that crime that he waves in front of her endlessly without naming it]. But this too is an illusion. *Le vieux* and *elle* arise instead in a union which excludes the narrator; they are not separate, and *elle* is an image of *le vieux:* "Sa propre image grotesque. Sa caricature [. . .]—sa propre image ridiculement outrée, distendue, comme renvoyée par un miroir déformant . . . Non, il n'y a pas de danger. Pas avec elle" [His own grotesque image. His caricature (. . .)—his own image ridiculously exaggerated, distended, as if in a carnival mirror . . . No, there's no danger. Not from her] (173). *Le vieux,* created by *je,* has created *elle* in his own image: "Son produit immonde. Répugnant" [His vile product. Repugnant] (174). Both figures are surrounded by and identified with another group of *elles,* dangerous clichés: "[. . .] des formes hideuses, menaçantes," "la Maladie, La Misère, la Ruine [. . .]. Elles fermaient toutes les issues" [(. . .) hideous forms, threatening, (. . .) Sickness, Poverty, Ruin (. . .). They were closing all exits] (173–74). What *je* has failed to do is maintain the dichotomy self-other, male-female.

From the beginning of this argument *elle* has been compared to "un chien" [a dog], a comparison *je* had used earlier to describe her as "l'Hypersensible." The earlier image expressed his hatred of her "contorsions" when the complicity that they elicited in him prevented his desired union with *le vieux.* The comparison reappears in this scene with almost the same vocabulary that *je* had used earlier, but now it describes how *le vieux* trained *elle* as a child to be like him, so *je* attributes it with "une sorte de sens spécial, pareil au sien" [a sort of special sense, like his]. This "special sense," however, is nothing as complex as tropistic perception; it refers to the daughter's stinginess. Still intent on making *le vieux* in his own image, the narrator gives him the power to see beneath the surface: "Bien sûr, à qui le dis-tu, il la connaît, se privant, rognant sur tout, le nez dans la crasse, fouillant, flairant partout, toujours à l'affût de quelques sous à gratter . . ." [Of course, what's new, he knows her, depriving herself, cutting down on everything, nose in the grime, digging around, sniffing everything, always ready to scratch up a few pennies] (175).

As seen earlier in the treatment of "la tache," where the word as metaphor for "le tourment" suddenly returned to the surface of the bathroom, the narrator's metaphor for the daughter's tropistic ferreting now refers to something less profound. Here, however, *je* transforms the diminishment into proof that *le vieux* still has the upper hand. When *le vieux* engages in a verbal battle with *elle,* *je* notes that words can still protect the old man from "la substance": "[. . .] ses paroles [. . .] semblent avoir aussi peu de rapport avec les sentiments confus qui bouillonnent au fond de lui" [(. . .) his words (. . .) also seem to have little relationship to the confusion of feelings that are boiling at his depths] (175). *Le vieux* then attacks with the words "'Trouve-toi un mari'" ["Find yourself a husband"], and the narrator's more confident style returns to recuperate his union with the old man: "[. . .] il éprouve cette jouissance de maniaque, douloureuse et écoeurante, qui coupe la respiration, [. . .] une volupté étrange, une drôle de volupté qui ressemble à la souffrance" [(. . .) he feels that manical pleasure, sad and nauseating, that knocks the breath out of you, (. . .) a strange voluptuousness, a funny voluptuousness that resembles suffering] (178).

In a world where nothing remains stable, the narrator's efforts can only fail; he cannot deny the tie that binds this pair as one. Their "games" unite them, so *elle* is described as adept at these games. "L'Hypersensible," *je* asks, "Qui la reconnaîtrait?" [Who would have recognized her?] (180). *Elle* is also attributed with "voluptuousness" that the narrator earlier shared only with *le vieux*. The sensual image of their union is a maternal one, a harmonious paradise found which excludes any masculine construct: "La douce saveur du lait nourricier. La tendre tiédeur du sein. [. . .] Elle la sent, j'en suis sûr, elle la hume avec volupté, calfeutrée ici avec lui [. . .]. C'est juste pour l'exciter un peu plus qu'elle se débat ainsi" [The sweet taste of mother's milk. The tender warmth of the breast. (. . .) She feels it/her, I'm sure, she breathes it/her in with voluptuousness, snuggled here with him (. . .). It's just to excite him a little that she is fighting like this] (181). The complete union that *je* has desired with *le vieux* is now conferred on *elle*, and the narrator can only experience it vicariously as (potential) voyeur: "[. . .] elle se blottira contre lui, les douces palpitations de son coeur battant à l'unisson du sien" [(. . .) she will curl up next to him, the soft palpitations of her heart beating in unison with his].

This union does not last because *le vieux* is about to give himself over to "la substance," to the "unhealthy" side of tropisms which separates people from one another. The angry discourse of *le vieux* fills the page, and the narrator can hardly believe that the old man is making himself so vulnerable: "Mais non . . . il me semble tout à coup, tandis que je le vois qui se jette sur elle, [. . .] qu'il n'y a rien d'autre en lui qu'une impulsion aveugle, une sorte de fureur opaque" [But no . . . it seems to me all at once, when I see him throw himself at her, (. . .) that there is nothing in him but a blind impulsion, a sort of opaque fury] (182).

The response *elle* makes is simply to "lever le nez très haut" [raise her nose very high], and *je* is not at all sure of anything: "Mais il ne doit pas croire à son jeu [. . .]. Ou bien peut-être, au contraire, a-t-il impression tout à coup que c'est vrai" [But he must not believe her game (. . .). Or perhaps, on the contrary, he suddenly has the impression that it's true] (183). *Elle* has the upper hand, and although *je* notices that "elle a un peu peur" [she is a little afraid], the laughter of *le vieux*

is "comme un rire de dément" [like that of a crazy person] (184). Word
games are over, and le vieux can only resort to a physical response: "Il
la pousse contre la porte. [. . .] Il lui donne un coup dans la poitrine
qui lui fait lâcher le chambranle [. . .]. Il l'a poussée si fort qu'elle vient
heurter avec son dos la porte de l'entrée juste en face de la porte du
bureau. [. . .] Il a fermé sa porte à clé" [He pushes her against the door.
(. . .) He hits her in the chest, which throws her against the doorframe
(. . .). He pushed her so hard that her back hits the front door just in
front of the study. (. . .) He locks himself in] (185–86).

The reproach of silence follows. The silent polishing by the concierge
in the stairwell, the maid stacking plates in the kitchen, "des bruits
dans ce silence, angoissants, menaçants, comme le son distant d'un
tam-tam" [sounds in the silence, agonizing, threatening, like the distant
sound of a tom-tom]. It is as if the figure of elles has materialized and
come to the daughter's rescue, as seen in the daughter's words when
she whispers to her father through the door: "Ouvre vite, c'est ridicule,
on nous entend" [Open quickly, this is ridiculous, they can hear us]
(186). Le vieux opens the door enough to toss out the money she had
requested; elle takes it and runs down the stairs: "La concierge, le dos
tourné, occupée à frotter les barreaux de la rampe, s'écarte légèrement
pour la laisser passer" [The concierge, her back turned, busy polishing
the bannister, steps lightly aside to let her pass] (187). The surface
the concierge is polishing is the one where the narrator finds himself,
defeated.

Elle hurries to a date at the museum and je almost grabs hold of her
coat to be pulled along by her solidity. Her victory over le vieux has
thrown her out of the categories je had been using to describe her, or
is it that as his character she has gotten away from him, she has had
an experience with le vieux that he has not? Following elle through
the streets, je looks at her image as it is reflected in storefront windows:
"[. . .] un oeil impartial et frais pourrait trouver dans la ligne sèche de
son profil une certaine pureté, peut-être même de la noblesse, presque
une certaine beauté" [(. . .) an impartial and new eye could see in the
dry line of her profile a certain purity, perhaps even nobility, almost a
certain beauty] (188). It is only now that je gives his readers a look at
himself: "J'évite de regarder [. . .], ce bonhomme 'sur le retour,' à la
mine négligée [. . .], un peu chauve, légèrement bedonnant. [. . .] Jamais
mes paupières fatiguées, mes yeux ternes, mes joues affaissées, ne m'étaient apparus aussi impitoyablement que maintenant, près de son image à elle, dans cette lumière crue" [I try not to look (. . .), this fellow
"in decline," somewhat disheveled (. . .), a little bald, slightly paunchy.
(. . .) Never had my tired eyelids, my pale eyes, my flaccid cheeks, ap-

peared to me as pitiful as now, next to her image, in that harsh light]
(189).

The touchstone of this physical image reflected in the store window
serves to stabilize all the questioning narration up to this point in the
novel. The narrator's moment of self-reflection is given a further element of "outside reality" by his description of the daughter's image as
it would be seen by "un oeil impartial et frais," a perspective the reader
could share. The creative confidence that the portrait had inspired in
je, to allow him to create his bond with le vieux, is gone. Elle is given
the power of "un oeil objectif," judging him unfavorably, reducing him
to "une image," a feminine noun: "Elle la voit, elle aussi, dans la glace,
cette image aux lignes molles, un peu avachies—le fruit malsain d'obscures occupations, de louches ruminations, que fait-il au juste toute la
journée? à quoi peut-il passer son temps?" [She sees it/her also, in the
window, that indistinct image, a little sloppy—the unhealthy fruit of
dark preoccupations, of suspect ruminations, what does he actually do
all day long? how could he spend his time?] (189). Now it is elle/l'image
which adheres to "ce bonhomme," the narrator, an inversion of the
earlier "elles adhèraient à elles."

This perspective is other than the obsessive one that has forced the
reader to rely completely on the narrator's observations throughout the
major part of the novel, and it prepares the way for the following scene,
a scene of confession. The narrator reveals to the daughter, not to le
vieux but to the Other, his view of art, no longer the romantic view
seen earlier but a modernist view closer to that of Sarraute: "Je préfère,
je crois, aux oeuvres les plus achevées, celles où n'a pu être maîtrisé
. . . où l'on sent affleurer encore le tâtonnement anxieux . . . le doute
. . . le tourment . . . [. . .] insaisissable qui échappe quand on croit la
tenir . . . le but jamais atteint . . . la faiblesse des moyens" [I prefer, I
think, instead of the most finished works, works where (it) could not
be mastered . . . in which one feels rising to the surface still the anxious
groping . . . doubt . . . torment . . . (. . .) unattainable which escapes
when one thinks it's caught . . . the goal never reached . . . the failure
of means . . .] (192).

The narrator lingers on the possibility of union with elle, and like
the one that he had imagined between himself and the portrait and, by
extension, le vieux, it depends on a certain interiority: "Je la regarde:
il me semble qu'elle m'observe d'un regard grave et pénétrant que je ne
lui ai encore jamais vu; elle détourne les yeux, [. . .] mais je sens que
c'est en elle-même qu'elle regarde, et elle sourit doucement [. . .]. Je me
sens soulevé tout à coup dans un élan de reconnaissance, d'espoir" [I
look at her: it seems to me that she looks at me with a serious and

penetrating eye that I have never seen in her; she turns her eyes away,
(. . .) but I feel that she is looking into herself, and she smiles sweetly
(. . .). I suddenly feel raised up in a thrust of recognition, of hope . . .]
(193). For the first time in the novel the narrator projects a self-reflecting
subjectivity onto the figure of *elle*, thus realizing the authority he had
attributed to her image above in the store window.

For the moment *je* does not need to bring in the generalizing container of the plural feminine. He recalls instead a tropistic image which
he feels he shares with *elle*, the moment when her father would not
open the door. His union with *elle* depends on a rejection of the maxims pronounced by *elles* and on *le vieux* being strong enough to resist
them. "S'il n'ouvre pas," the narrator says, "quelque chose va sa produ-
ire, quelque chose de définitif, [. . .] tout va se pétrifier [. . .], elles vont
surgir triomphantes [. . .]: 'Voyez, je vous l'avais dit, un égoïste, un
avare'" [If he doesn't open up, something is going to happen, something
definitive, (. . .) everything is going to be petrified (. . .), they are going
to rise up triumphantly (. . .)]: "See, I told you, an egotist, a miser" . . .]
(193). The narrator's union with *elle* depends on *le vieux* not allowing
such a thing, a desire which the narrator projects onto the daughter as
one they both share: "[. . .] mais il ne le permettra pas, ce n'est pas vrai,
elle le sait bien, ils le savent bien tous deux, il va ouvrir . . . elle le
verra de nouveau, tel qu'elle le connaît, tel qu'elle l'a toujours connu,
non pas cette poupée grossièrement fabriquée, cette camelote de bazar
à l'usage du vulgaire, mais tel qu'il est en vérité, indéfinissable, sans
contours, chaud et mou, malléable" [(. . .) it's not true, she knows it,
they both know it, he is going to open up . . . she will see him again,
as she knows him, as she has always known him (. . .), not the roughly
made doll, that cheap stuff everyone gets at the market, but as he truly
is, undefinable, without contours, warm and flabby, malleable] (193).

In this replay of the argument, the union between *je* and *elle* can
come about if *le vieux* does not allow himself to be resumed by surface,
feminine images ("cette poupée," "cette camelote"), but instead appears
"tel qu'il est en vérité," a male figure with a (feminine) tropistic interior,
"indéfinissable, sans contours, chaud et mou, malléable." Throughout
this passage the barriers between good and bad tropistic perceptions
are let down. *Elle* no longer threatens, the narrator joins her to himself
and to his projections onto *le vieux*, and the image of a pre-Oedipal
exaltation of unity is repeated: "[. . .] elle pourra de nouveau, serrée,
blottie contre lui, sentir, battant à l'unisson, leur pulsation secrète, faible et douce comme la palpitation de viscères encore tièdes" [(. . .) she
will once again, pressed, curled up next to him, be able to feel, beating
in unison, their secret pulsation, weak and soft like the palpitation of
still warm entrails] (193).

Below the surface of their discourse, however, this union is dissolved by a look, "un regard fermé et dur qui me repousse, me maintient à distance" [a closed and hard look that pushes me away, keeps me at a distance]: "'Ah! oui, c'est bien ça . . . C'est ce que tu pensais . . . Cette façon de juger la peinture [. . .]. Méfiez-vous, c'est très malsain, [. . .] ce contact trop personnel . . . la recherche de ces sortes d'émotions'" ["Ah yes, that's it . . . That's what you were thinking . . . That way of judging painting (. . .). Be careful, it's too unhealthy, (. . .) that too personal contact . . . the search for those kinds of emotions . . ."] (194). *Elle* no longer embodies "unhealthy" tropistic perception, and she warns the narrator about the "danger" of such a point of view. The split between self and other which had been momentarily suspended now returns, but the terms are reversed.

This reversal prepares for the last chapter of the novel. As noted earlier, when *je* runs into *elle* and *le vieux* at a café, *elle* is "peu reconnaissable." The "dangerous" Other now embodies the "lieu commun." This final separation from *elle* returns the reader to the larger drama that has been at work throughout the novel, the one composed of the young narrator's relationship to the old man, child to adult, but more importantly younger male to older male, and of the association of a certain side of tropisms with a feminine figure (singular and plural). Once *elle* assumes the traditional role as fiancée and leaves the two men alone, the narrator's desired tropistic union with *le vieux* is realized as a physical and emotional one: "[. . .] nous ne bougeons pas, assis l'un en face de l'autre, le vieux et moi" [(. . .) we do not move, seated opposite one another, the old man and me]: "Je devais lui ressembler, j'avais aussi cet air abandonné, quand j'étais affalé ainsi dans la salle de l'exposition [. . .]. Ils ont été trop forts pour lui aussi" [I must have resembled him, I also had that abandoned look when I was similarly slumped on the bench at the museum (. . .). They were too much for him too] (208).

The masculine figures are united, but far away from the "tourments" that the narrator imagined united them earlier: "Il n'y a plus rien en moi maintenant qui l'excite, qui l'incite à me provoquer. J'ai beau tendre l'oreille, je ne perçois plus dans les paroles que nous échangeons ces résonnances qu'elles avaient autrefois, ces prolongements qui s'enfonçaient en nous si loin. Des paroles anodines, anonymes, enregistrées depuis longtemps. Elles font penser à de vieux disques. Nous devons ressembler, assis côte à côte sur la banquette, à deux grosses poupées qu'on vient de remonter" [There is nothing more in me now that excites him, that incites him to provoke me. In vain, I strain my ear to hear, I no longer hear in the words we exchange the resonances that they had before, those effects which used to plunge so far into us. Harmless, anonymous words, recorded long ago. They (feminine) make you think of old records. Seated side by side on the bench, we must look like two big dolls that they have just put back on display] (209). As the passage continues, "les paroles" (elles) of the above passage, those which inspired the narrator's desire for tropistic union with *le vieux*, are now replaced by the masculine noun, "les mots": "Ces mots qu'il a l'air de dévider mécaniquement doivent avoir à la longue ce pouvoir apaisant, exorcisant qu'ont sur les croyants les paroles simples, monotones, des prières. [. . .] Ils n'attendaient que cela, je le sais bien, ils ne demandent qu'à m'accueillir. [. . .] Ils m'attendent. Je n'ai qu'à venir" [Those words that he seems to empty out mechanically must finally have the calming, exorcising power of the simple, monotonous words of believers' prayers. (. . .) They (masculine) wait for only that, I know it well, they only want to welcome me (. . .) They are waiting for me. I only have to come] (211). The old man's words (ils) soothe and welcome the (younger, male) narrator, metaphorically, linguistically, and in the final paragraphs he is also accepted by "les femmes aux visages un peu effacés" [the women with the slightly faded faces]. "Je suis des leurs," the narrator says, "Je mêlerai pieusement ma voix aux leurs" [I'm one of them, I will mix my voice piously with theirs] (211–12).

The ambivalent nature of *elles* has disappeared, and the two male figures are contained by a feminine image, "deux grosses poupées," imposed by the surface world which the figure of *elles* now represents. At the end of the novel this narrator, often called "childlike," returns home, not to his biological parents who sent him to be cured by the specialist, but to a world where both the old man and the amorphous *elles* live by "les mots," not by the problematic "paroles." The gender distinction in French between these two nouns and the feminine quality attributed to tropistic sensitivity, much more evident in *Martereau*, invite a reading in terms of gender that will continue in our discussion.

Martereau

The young male figure's desire for union with an older male in *Portrait* is amplified in Sarraute's second novel, *Martereau*. Here the male narrator interacts not only with his uncle, aunt, and occasionally their daughter, but also with Martereau and occasionally his wife. Sarraute describes this novel as a continuation of the first, and in a sense it begins where *Portrait* left off. Early in *Martereau* the narrator describes that, as a child, he thought tropisms came from the things around him but soon realized that they are provoked by people, "un sourire, un regard" [a smile, a look], and "cela surgissait tout d'un coup de n'importe où [. . .]—l'atteinte secrète, la menace" [it would rise up all of the sudden from nowhere (. . .)—the secret attack, the threat] (22–23). The progression found in *Portrait* from perception of tropisms to a defeat represented by order moves in the opposite direction in *Martereau*. At the end of the novel the narrator's union in "le lieu commun" with either the uncle or Martereau is more problematic than it is in the first novel because the narrator cannot escape tropistic perception. As in *Portrait*, however, this perception also inspires creativity for the narrator of *Martereau*.

Martereau adds to the literary context found in the first novel the machinations of the family. The narrator is a sickly young man staying with his aunt, uncle, and cousin. Even though this narrator recognizes from the beginning the destructive power that resides in the tropistic world and the illusion of union that it offers, his psychological journey from boyhood to manhood is not any easier. In his discussion on this novel, Valerie Minogue remarks the uncertainty and "inwardness of the narrative," where "prosaic understanding" is given over to a "poetic deepening of the moment": "a deepening effected by ironic inflections and by rapid changes in pitch and tone, as the voice shifts between observation and rumination, transporting the immediate to the emblematic." Minogue notes that this novel is best understood as a "demand for collaboration in uncertainty."[10]

This uncertainty is due in part to the increased number of narrative figures. Although the nephew is probably about the same age as the narrator in *Portrait*, in this familial arrangement he remains the young one, "mon petit," his uncle calls him. In addition, the narrator's fairy-tale imagery further places him at the bottom end of this familial hierarchy where the aunt and uncle fight one another for power. The world in this novel is reduced to a familial setting where a magnified gender battle characterizes his quest for identity. The text veers away only once from the narrator's particular preoccupations to present a more general view of tropisms; but more often, uncertainty arises as the narrator enters into the consciousness of these figures. He too is on a quest, but not for "true characters"; this is a childlike quest for identity. His "observations and ruminations" move between those of a young nephew, a reader of the adult world, and those of a narrator who takes on characteristics of a writer giving tropistic and gendered qualities to the adults. As discussed earlier, tropism is described in opposition to "le lieu commun," but here that common place divides between male and female constructs. The nephew perceives tropistic struggles in both the aunt and the uncle, but as in *Portrait*, he is more drawn to the male figure. His aunt's maneuvers frighten him and he ultimately rejects the complicity she solicits. His response to his uncle is more complicated.

The nephew wants to join the uncle in the male "lieu commun" which the older man creates in opposition to *elle/elles*. When his uncle rejects him, the nephew despises his "feminine" tropistic perceptions and internalizes his uncle's scorn of it by self-denigration.

The familial relationship in this novel suggests the image of an isosceles triangle tilted at its base so that it stands on one point. The longest side leans off to the left, the aunt is at the end of it, separated from both males and higher up because the narrator fears her power more than he fears that of his uncle. The uncle occupies the point on the right, above the nephew, but below the aunt. The distance between the uncle and the nephew is shorter because he moves back and forth along that line, seeking resemblance with his uncle where he only rarely seeks it with his aunt. The daughter exists as the narrator's accomplice in one scene, an extension of the aunt in others, and enlarges the group of *vous* when the uncle attacks the three of them. At times the narrator places Martereau with the uncle in his position of power, but Martereau's power comes from outside the triangle. It comes from the narrator's imagination as he tries to dismantle the triangle and make it into a straight line, a mythical world on another plane. The figure of Martereau offers the nephew a way out of the familial dilemma. He is the white page on which the narrator writes his own myth of manhood and draws an image of a nurturing male, that is, where he composes his own arrangement of clichés from "le lieu commun." In a novel based on the uncertainty and flux of the identity process, however, Martereau's own "épaisseur subjective" cannot be repressed.

As the novel opens, the nephew is listening to his aunt tell him about her life: "J'observe scrupuleusement les règles du jeu. Je me tiens dans la position voulue" [I observe scrupulously the rules of the game. I remain in the desired position].[11] The aunt gives her confidential view of herself in the audience of this passive narrator: "Elle se sent en confiance maintenant, très à l'aise, elle pose la main sur mon bras" [She feels she can speak in confidence now, very relaxed, she puts her hand on my arm] (11). He is not her husband, he is her nephew, not a son, but the age of a son. If she had been confiding in another woman, her confidences would have been "entre femmes." Instead, by addressing a "neutral" narrator, a traditional "norm," the aunt's view is unmediated by the danger or mockery implied by women speaking among women in *Portrait*. Her discourse is characterized by her own fairy-tale imagery, and in this respect, *Martereau* begins an investigation of the myths that construct *both* female and male identity through the consciousness of a male narrator.

The aunt presents herself in the opening scene as "la princesse lointaine, la dame à la licorne" [the faraway princess, the lady of the unicorn]. The nephew joins her in her imagery; they are like two children whose gender identity has not yet been constructed. This kind of intimacy between these two figures never occurs again in the novel. Once tropistic rumblings interrupt the aunt's unself-conscious discourse, her dangerous side shows itself: "Mais il se passe quelque chose. [. . .] Elle a senti quelque chose, [. . .] ce qu'elle sait, ce qu'elle a surpris en moi: [. . .] rien ne lui échappe, elle voit tout—[. . .] ou encore—c'est ce qui me fait le plus peur—quelqu'un a déposé cela en elle, glissé cela en elle insidieusement [. . .] je n'en sais rien [. . .]" [But something is happening. (. . .) She feels something, (. . .) what she knows [about me], what she has surprised in me: (. . .) nothing escapes her, she sees everything—(. . .) or what's more—and this makes me the most afraid—someone has placed that in her, slipped that in her insidiously (. . .), I know nothing about it (. . .)] (13–15). When the aunt's discourse abandons the fairy-tale imagery and takes on more conventional phrases from "le lieu commun," her interaction with the narrator becomes gendered and their experiences different: "'Vous ne savez pas ce que c'est, ce sentiment pour une jeune fille'" ["You don't know what this is, this feeling for a girl . . ."] (16–17). The nephew now assigns a more ironic image to their relationship. The aunt is compared to one of "ces grandes dames ouvrant leur coeur généreusement à quelque petit-bourgeois éperdu" [those great ladies opening their heart generously to some lost petty-bourgeois] (17).

Whereas the narrator in *Portrait* is often described as a writer apprehending his characters, the nephew in *Martereau* begins as a reader. In the presence of his aunt he admits to being easily manipulated by the seductive stories of "les grandes dames": "J'acquiesce avec sympathie, je suis touché malgré tout, vaguement flatté [. . .]: elles le savent et jouent à coup sûr" [I give in with sympathy, I'm touched in spite of everything, vaguely flattered (. . .): they know it and play with a sure hand] (20). The nephew's vulnerability to these stories feminizes him in turn. He identifies himself in this interaction with a feminine image, "la petite bête" [the little beast]: "La petite bête qu'elle n'a cessé de taquiner, qu'elle a réussi enfin à enfumer, rampe honteusement hors de son trou" [The little beast that she doesn't stop teasing, that she has finally succeeded in smoking out, frolics shamelessly outside its/her hole] (21).

In a later scene in Chapter 1, where he is walking in the meadows with his uncle, the narrator describes how he offers himself as a subject of conversation. In the image drawn he again transforms himself into a feminine figure, "la victime": "Il n'écoute pas les explications embrouillées que je lui présente en bafouillant. [. . .] L'occasion est vraiment trop belle. La victime assoiffée de sacrifice, toute titubante déjà de la volupté du martyre, est venue d'elle-même, pantelante et nue, se livrer à sa merci" [He doesn't listen to the confused explanations that I give him, stammering. (. . .) It's too good to be true. The thirsty, sacrificial victim, already all staggering with the voluptuousness of martyrdom, comes on its/her own, nude and panting, to deliver it/herself to his mercy] (39). The "volupté" that the narrator identifies in this passage is a trait not found in the masculine world of the uncle, and it character-izes the narrator's "feminine" side.

This sickly young man corresponds easily to the male romantic artist in nineteenth-century French literature, a male feminized by his sensi-tivity to feelings.[12] The term *feelings* in Sarraute's early novels also means perception of tropistic movement. The narrator of *Portrait* at-tempted to use that perception as an access to a dualized romantic bond with *le vieux*. As seen at the end of the argument between the old man and his daughter, tropisms as a psychological force cannot be idealized, neither can it be controlled. In that crucial familial scene, *le vieux* no longer has the power to move between surface and depth; the depths leave him unarmed and his daughter wins. Where the figure of *elles* is ambivalent throughout *Portrait,* in the end all three characters join the side of *elles* represented simply as "le lieu commun."

At the beginning of *Martereau,* the aunt is similarly joined to a plural feminine figure and is often coupled with her daughter in opposition to the male couple of the uncle and his nephew. Both the aunt and the uncle represent dangerous tropistic power. In both scenes discussed above, the nephew disclaims the significance of his "feelings." He gen-eralizes his interaction with the aunt, a representative of these "grandes dames"—"Non, il n'y a pas moyen de se défendre contre eux, de leur résister, ils sont trop fort" [No, there is no way to defend oneself against them, to resist them, they are too strong]. In the scene above where he offers himself to his uncle, the nephew also recuperates the tropistic power of their relationship: "C'est un jeu entre nous, rien de plus. Un simulacre" [It's a game between us, nothing else. A fake] (42). The nephew seeks the solace of "le lieu commun," and in the uncle's house it is a male construct constituted in opposition to a female one. The uncle continually places a female construct on the nephew, which serves to keep the two males apart.

The desire for myth on the part of the nephew, represented by his vulnerability to the aunt's tale, transfers to the uncle and to Martereau. This mythic world of union is suggested in the novel's only passage which digresses from the familial setting: "Ils traversent les prairies. Ils enjambent d'un même pas les ruisseaux. [. . .] C'est une véritable volupté que j'éprouve à les contempler. En eux je nous retrouve, je nous reconnais. C'est notre image, notre portrait telle qu'un peintre bien doué aurait pu le dessiner. Ils possèdent ce qui nous manque, à nous autres, modèles informes, chaos où s'entrechoquent mille possibilités—le style, l'outrance révélatrice, la simplicité et la netteté audacieuse du trait" [They walk through the meadows. They cross streams in the same step. (. . .) It is a veritable voluptuousness that I feel in contemplating them. In them I find us. I recognize us. It is our image, our portrait as a gifted painter would have drawn it. They possess what we lack, us the other ones, shapeless models, the chaos where a thousand possibilities bang into one another—the style, the revealing extravagance, the simplicity and the audacious cleanness of line] (34). The "véritable volupté" referred to in this passage has exactly the opposite signification for this narrator than it did for the narrator in *Portrait*. In order to calm the "volupté confus" experienced by that narrator when he recognized tropisms, the term "volupté" was interpreted as a call to a romantic tropistic world which he transferred from the portrait to *le vieux*. In the passage from *Martereau* above, the narrator experiences the "volupté" of leaving the "chaos" behind, of rising above tropisms to take on a shape. That shape will be a myth.

The general mythic image above narrows after a break in the page to join the uncle and his nephew as *nous*: "Nous traversons les prairies. Nous enjambons d'un même pas les ruisseaux" [We cross the meadows. We cross the streams in the same step] (34). As the sentence continues the pronoun *il* is slipped in and its referent soon identified as the uncle, "il parle, avec lui on n'a jamais fini de parler" [he talks, with him, the talking never ends]. His monologue resembles the aunt's seen earlier in that the narrator does not at first insert himself. The narrator recognized the aunt's fairy tale and participated momentarily in that myth in *sous-conversation*. The discourse of the masculine world of the uncle represents one which excludes the narrator, as seen by its telegraphic treatment in the narration: "[. . .] j'ingurgite, il parle, [. . .] sociétés anonymes, conseils d'administration, bénéfices et pertes [. . .]" [I ingest, he speaks, (. . .) anonymous companies, boards of directors, profits and losses] (34–35). This is the same talk from "le cercle des hommes" that the narrator "overheard" in *Portrait* but did not try to join in, preferring to meet *le vieux* among "les ombres" or "l'exhaltation heureuse."

Instead of attempting to participate in this "male talk" from "le lieu commun," the narrator of *Martereau* inserts his own romantic view of nature. This view does not represent tropistic depth; it is a different "lieu commun": "Parfois, dans un moment d'intrépidité subite," the nephew says, "je m'arrête tout à coup, et là, [. . .] au bord du ruisseau, j'ose, dilatant mes narines, humer l'odeur de l'herbe fauchée, regarder au loin les collines [. . .], et dire . . . 'Ecoutez ça . . . ces clochettes . . . cette source . . . Regardez là-bas la ligne des bois . . . le chalet'"

[Sometimes, in a moment of sudden intrepidness, I stop all of the sudden, and there (. . .) at the edge of a stream, I dare, flaring my nostrils,
to suck in the odor of mown grass, to look at the distant hills (. . .) and
to say . . . "Listen to that . . . those church bells . . . this stream . . . Look
over there at the line of the woods . . . the chalet . . ."] (35).

The nephew's romantic tendency is less tropistic than it was for the
narrator of *Portrait*. It is not a desire for tropistic fusion with the world
around him, it is a poet's love of nature which he tries to share with
his uncle. In the silence that follows the nephew narrates what he
imagines to be the uncle's inner thoughts which would mock such
"unmanly" preoccupations: "Le sentiment de la nature, hein? La petite
fleur bleue? La pureté? . . . Les rêveurs, les ratés qui marchent dans
les prairies humant l'odeur des fleurs, [. . .] les imbéciles, [. . .] qui se
permettent de dédaigner [. . .] l'univers solide et dur où de vrais hommes se battent pour eux, pour les incapables, les paresseux, les petits
énervés, les dégoûtés, les 'esthètes' . . . il les connaît, [. . .] c'est eux qui
lui apprendront à vivre, qui lui donneront l'exemple de la pureté, du
détachement, non vraiment c'est à mourir de rire" [The feeling for
nature, is that it? The little blue flower? Purity? . . . Dreamers, losers
who walk in the meadows sucking in the odor of flowers, (. . .) fools,
(. . .) who allow themselves to scorn (. . .) the solid, hard universe where
true men fight for them, for the ones who are useless, lazy, the little
nervous types, the fussy ones, the "aesthetes" . . . he knows them, (. . .)
they're the ones who will teach him how to live, give him examples of
purity, of detachment, no really, it's enough to make you die laughing]
(36). The nephew describes the remorse he feels for having uttered the
words that could have done such damage (37). Where the narrator in
Portrait is both disgusted by and drawn to *le vieux*, this nephew is
afraid of and empathetic toward his uncle. If *elle* in *Martereau* represents the danger of one who brings the nephew into her camp by spinning seductive tales, *il* elicits a more complex reaction. The narrator
says that only rarely does he try to intervene in the uncle's discourse,
"c'est plutôt un rêve, un jeu de l'esprit" [it's more like a dream, a trick
of the mind]; most of the time "je lui facilite plutôt les choses de mon
mieux" [I help him instead, the best I can] (38).

The childish, sado-masochistic quality of the narrator's relationship
to his uncle does not escape scrutiny in the narration: "Je me suis
souvent demandé quel démon [. . .] me pousse . . . Le goût de la souffrance, me dira-t-on . . . une soif morbide d'humiliation" [I have often
asked myself what demon (. . .) pushes me . . . A taste for suffering,
some would tell me . . . a morbid thirst for humiliation] (38). More than
the narrator of *Portrait*, the nephew is aware that he might be seeking
some kind of union with the older man: "[. . .] ou peut-être [c'est] l'es-

poir enfantin de parvenir à lui ressembler pour me sentir à l'aise auprès de lui, pour être encouragé, admis, pour me trouver moi aussi en lieu sûr, blotti douillettement contre lui dans son refuge [. . .], ou encore l'espoir insensé de lui en imposer, de le battre par ses armes, sur son propre terrain? . . . tout cela à la fois, sûrement" [(. . .) or maybe (it is) the childish hope of succeeding in resembling him so that I'll feel comfortable around him, to be encouraged, admitted, so I too could be in a safe place, curled up snugly against him in his refuge (. . .), or maybe it's the mad hope of imposing it on him, to fight him with his own weapons, on his own turf? . . . all of that at the same time, surely] (38).

Later in the novel when he proposes to the uncle that Martereau act as a consultant in their search for a country house, the narrator is similarly aware of his motive in relation to the uncle: "[. . .] je veux le séduire, lui prouver que je suis avec lui, comme lui, comme il prétend être, du bon côté, dans le monde des vrais hommes" [(. . .) I want to seduce him, to prove to him that I am with him, like him, like he pretends to be, on the good side, in the world of true men] (105–6). This union continues to be frustrated in the novel because the uncle perceives the nephew through terms from "le lieu commun" which identify him as a feminized male. In the passage above, the nephew also uses vocabulary from "le lieu commun," a mythical vocabulary of father-son battle for power like the one engaged in by the narrator in a memory scene in *Portrait*.

The uncle in *Martereau* can be as aggressive in his defense as *le vieux* in *Portrait*. The nephew frequently feels reduced by what he perceives to be his uncle's judgment of his "unmanly" behavior, as seen above, or his complicity with his aunt and female cousin. At dinner in a restaurant, the uncle shouts at the three of them, lumping them together as "'Vous' . . . 'Vous' . . . 'Vous' . . . et nous nous ratatinons, nous nous blottissons l'un contre l'autre, nous nous tenons serrés, pressés les uns contre les autres comme des moineaux effrayés" ["You . . ." "You. . . ." "You" . . . and we draw in, we curl up next to one another, we squeeze together, pressed against one another like frightened sparrows] (25).

The narrator knows the power of the uncle's "vous" because he is often dumped there with *elles*. The images the nephew uses to describe its effect not only reveal the fear this gesture inspires, but also his own voyeuristic pleasure when it doesn't apply to him. In another scene when the uncle addresses the aunt and cousin, the observant narrator describes them as "enchaînées l'une à l'autre, bétail conduit pêle-mêle au marché; aussi différentes de lui dans leur ressemblance entre elles, leur impuissance, leur stupidité, que le sont de l'homme et les animaux" [chained to one another, beasts lead pell-mell to market; as different from him in their resemblance to one another, their powerlessness, their stupidity, as animals from man] (129). Even when the nephew is scooped up with his aunt and cousin in this way, he continues to be "amazed" by the older male figure, "tous ses coups m'émerveillent par leur sûreté" [all his blows amaze me for their precision] (25), "mais surtout, je l'admire, [. . .] comme auprès de lui je me sens faible et maladroit" [above all, I admire him, (. . .) how weak and awkward I feel when I am near him] (144).

Male-female battle lines are always drawn in the presence of the uncle, and the nephew takes pleasure in being on the male side. In one of the restaurant scenes he imagines how the uncle must perceive these dinners together as "ces corvées qu'elles lui imposent . . . ces sorties en famille [. . .], il n'y a rien qu'il déteste autant" [these chores that they impose on him . . . these family outings (. . .), there is nothing he hates as much] (25). In the same scene the two males are described as seated together opposite *elles:* "[. . .] assises côte à côte en face de nous deux poupées: la fille déjà une reproduction de la mère [. . .], peintes toutes les deux, apprêtées, [. . .] revêtues toutes deux comme il se doit des insignes de sa force à lui, portant tous les coûteux colifichets, [. . .] elles se penchent l'une vers l'autre avec des sourires complices" [(. . .) seated side by side opposite us two dolls: the daughter already a reproduction of the mother (. . .), both of them painted, affected, (. . .) both of them dressed up properly as emblems of his strength, wearing all the costly baubles, (. . .) they lean close to one another with complicitous smiles] (26–27). The aunt-daughter couple represents a female construct which repulses and terrifies its male counterpart, as seen in the rambling enumerative style of the passage as it continues. Sentences are separated only by ellipses, breathlessly "overdescribing" the conventional "poupée" [doll], the princess, spoiled by the "papa gâteau" [sugar daddy]. The passage fills in the image that the aunt had used to describe the life she wanted to leave behind when she spoke to the narrator earlier, "un oiseau dans une cage dorée" [a bird in a golden cage], "un objet de luxe" [a luxury item] (15). The above scene in the restaurant is told from the uncle's perspective, however, such that the "sincerity" of the aunt's desire becomes suspect.

As the scene continues, the narrator imagines the uncle trying to "educate" his daughter to be more like him. The language used in the passage further scorns feminine "frivolity": "[. . .] il avait gambadé à quatre pattes dans la nursery pour l'inciter à jouer à la chasse dans la forêt vierge, [. . .] il lui avait donné des soldats de plomb . . . Mais pensez-vous . . . De la marchandise à l'étalage—rien d'autre . . . elles ne pensent qu'à se marier, tout le reste, tous ces cours, ces diplômes, ces leçons à prix d'or, de la frime tout ça, une façon de passer le temps . . . qui croient-elles tromper?" [(. . .) he had frolicked around on all fours in the nursery, trying to incite her to play the hunter in a virgin forest, (. . .) he had given her tin soldiers . . . But imagine . . . Showing her stuff—nothing else . . . they think of nothing except getting married, all the rest, courses, diplomas, lessons that cost a fortune, all an act all that, a way of passing time . . . who are they kidding?] (27–28). The narrator expresses fear that the uncle's disgust with *elles* might get out of control in this scene, but when *elles* look to the nephew to join in their games, he risks being thrown out of the masculine camp: "J'hesite, [. . .] le moindre mouvement maintenant de ma part, [. . .] mon dédain—c'est ce qu'il attend de moi, ce coup de tampon apposant [. . .] le masque de fer que nous venons de leur forger—et il maintiendra le masque plaqué brutalement sur leur visage, il leur écrasera la bouche, il leur aplatira le nez, elles étoufferont" [I hesitate, (. . .) the slightest movement now on my part (. . .), my scorn—that's what he's waiting for, the stamp of approval confirming (. . .) the iron mask that we have just forged for them—and he will keep the mask stuck brutally on their face, he will crush their mouth, he will flatten their nose, they will suffocate] (28–29).

The nephew feels "gêné, honteux" [awkward, ashamed] by the situation, declaring that "il faut à tout prix essayer de l'arrêter" [he must be stopped at any price]; but in the next moment he is transformed from the gallant defender of *elles* to a suspicious male, like his uncle: "Je me tourne, quelque chose me pousse . . . mais ce n'est pas le besoin de les protéger contre lui, ce n'est pas ça . . . je sais ce que c'est . . . c'est d'elles que j'ai peur, plus peur que de lui" [I turn around, something pushes me . . . but it isn't the need to protect them against him, it's not that . . . I know what it is . . . it's them I'm afraid of, more afraid of them than of him . . .] (29). In spite of the nephew's desire to separate himself from this female group, the uncle continues to see the aunt and the nephew as a unit organized against him and his male world; and the nephew continues to internalize the older male figure's view of him. In the *sous-conversation* that follows, the male voices overlap completely, the image the young man has of himself converges with the older man's condescending view of him as a "greluchon stupide" [stupid gigolo] (30).

This self-image characterizes the narrator as nephew, male-child seeking male-adult affirmation, at the same time that the narrator also operates as a more distant observer of tropistic movement. In the scene above the narrative voice pulls away from the familial drama to explain that these feelings are "exprimé non avec des mots, bien sûr, mais évoqué plutôt par des sortes de signes très rapides contenant tout cela, le résumant, [. . .] je ne peux que [. . .] traduire gauchement par des mots ce que ces signes représentent" [expressed not with words of course, but evoked instead by something like very rapid signs containing all this, resuming it, (. . . .) I can only (. . . .) translate awkwardly with words what these signs represent] (30–31). The strength elicited by the clarity of such an observation, that is, the equilibrium established in the text as the narrator interrupts the uncle's discourse, is undermined by a return to a narration more characteristic of the nephew as boy-child when the uncle's violent discourse interrupts the narrator's text (31). When he sees the aunt's defense against her husband, the cold stare and the silence, the narrator as nephew returns to express his loyalty to the uncle: "[. . .] je voudrais implorer, le protéger, qu'elle pardonne, qu'elle ne fasse pas attention, il est si bon, juste maladroit, nerveux" [(. . .) I would like to implore, to protect him, she should pardon him, she shouldn't pay attention, he is good, just awkward, nervous] (32).

Even though at the end of this scene the nephew contains the group in fairy-tale imagery, "petits cochons innocents qui dansent sous l'oeil du méchant loup" [little innocent pigs who dance under the gaze of the mean wolf] (33), he still prefers the uncle's violence to what he perceives to be the manipulation of the aunt. In another restaurant scene in Chapter 1, the narrator's use of vous includes the reader with the uncle and himself in an image of defenselessness before the aunt's powerful regard: "[. . .] un oeil en elles, auquel rien n'échappe, impitoyable, glacé, à tout moment vous jauge, vous juge . . . un demi-sourire sur leur visage, [. . .] et vous savez que vous êtes condamné sans appel . . ." [(. . .) an eye in them, from which nothing escapes, pitiless, icy, at any moment sizes you up, judges you . . . a half-smile on their face, (. . .) and you know that you are condemned without appeal . . .] (46). When the aunt gets the upper hand, the narrator wishes for a return of the uncle's domineering pose: "Quel soulagement ce serait [. . .], s'il se métamorphosait soudain et redevenait tel qu'il était, assis ici à cette même place, elles en face de nous, des poupées [. . .], quand il laissait jaillir et nous écorcher son 'vous' sifflant, brûlant . . . Je préférais cela" [What a relief it would be, (. . .) if he were to transform suddenly and become what he was before, seated here at the same place, them facing us, dolls, (. . .), when he was letting it spew out and scorch us with his whistling, burning "you" . . . I would prefer that] (46–47).

In Portrait the narrator's relationship to the world was judged as a sickness, and in the end it is described as the "Malin" [Evil] which the old man's words exorcise. In Martereau, the narrator perceives his illness from the opposite direction as "cette impossibilité de prendre parti en face d'eux, [. . .] de les aimer pour de bon ou de les haïr" [that impossibility to have an opinion of them, (. . .) to love them well or hate them] (43). Others seem to have "lignes de conduite si bien tracées, d'un dessin si net, si pur" [well outlined designs of conduct, so neat, so pure]; it is an "instinct de conservation" [survival instinct]. The narrator says that "c'est grâce à cela [. . .] que je leur envie tant" [it's because of that (. . .) that I envy them so much] (44).

Throughout the first part of Chapter 1 the uncle represents this ability to control, but as in the case of the argument scene in *Portrait*, when the older male figure slips out of control the narrator can no longer identify with him. At one point the narrator perceives that the regard of *elle* makes the uncle vulnerable, and the narration turns uncharacteristically to the aunt's perspective. The nephew remembers an earlier moment when the uncle showed his optimistic side, that is, his blind adoration for his wife: "[. . .] il l'aime, au fond, c'est cela, il l'a toujours aimée, rien d'autre n'a vraiment compté" [(. . .) he loves her, that's basically it, he has always loved her, nothing else has really mattered] (48). During "ses moments d'attendrissement" [his moments of tenderness], the uncle's voice takes on "ce ton enfantin, désarmé, naïf" [that child-like tone, disarmed, naive], and the nephew identifies with the aunt: "[. . .] il lui semble—je le sais, je l'éprouve comme elle chaque fois— qu'en elle aussitôt tout se hérisse comme les poils sur le dos du chat" [(. . .) it seems to her—I know it, I feel it like she does every time—that as soon as that happens everything in her bristles like the fur on a cat's back] (48). The nephew not only says that he feels the same "gêne" [uneasiness] and "répulsion" that the aunt does, but solicits the reader's complicity in those feelings with the use of *vous*: ". . . cette intonation cajolante, humide et molle s'insinue en vous, cherche à vous atteindre aux endroits les plus secrets, les mieux gardés, c'est un manque de décence, un manque criminel de respect, une tentative de viol" [. . . that cajoling intonation, moist and muffled, insinuates itself into you, tries to reach you in the most secret, well-guarded places, it's a lack of decency, a criminal lack of respect, a rape/robbery attempt . . .] (48). When the nephew is alone again with the aunt, this alignment dissolves.

In a later passage after this scene, the narrator is preparing to leave the house. He describes opening and closing his door "le plus silencieusement possible" [as silently as possible], and as the passage continues the threatening presence of *elle* is sensed by the reader: "[. . .] son ouïe aussi exercée que celle des prisonniers dans leurs cellules capte aussitôt et reconnaît autour d'elle dans la maison le plus faible bruit" [(. . .) her sense of hearing, as keen as that of prisoners in their cells, as quickly seizes and recognizes the slightest noise around her in the house] (49). The use of the present serves to enact the narrator's effort to escape from *elle*, but finally he says, "je cède" [I give in] (50).

The aunt wants to talk to the narrator about her daughter's relationship with one of her friends. The two girls are in the daughter's room laughing. The aunt's monologue goes on for almost ten pages and is distinctly different from the one that opens this novel, because her discourse is here framed by more of the narrator's commentary on what she is saying. The *rapprochement* established with the uncle between the first talk with the aunt and this one prevents the narrator from joining her. Whereas her earlier stories were surrounded in the text by the images they provoked in the narrator's mind, this monologue is received from more of a distance. In one of the narrator's digressions he identifies the aunt's preoccupation with the giggling she hears coming from her daughter's room: "[. . .] il faut tâter cela, le palper, bien l'examiner de toutes parts, presser comme on tâte sans cesse et presse un endroit douloureux pour se rassurer, pour s'irriter, et plus en appuie, plus ça gonfle" [(. . .) she has to feel that, finger it, examine it closely from all sides, press like one feels endlessly and presses a painful spot to reassure oneself, to irritate it, and the more one pushes, the more it swells . . .] (52). Although he qualifies the aunt's obsessions as "c'est ce qu'ils font toujours" [it's what they always do], referring to both the aunt and the uncle, when *elle* solicits the narrator's affirmation of her tropistic perception he refuses: "Mais un dégoût me prend, un désir de l'arracher de moi, je refuse l'alliance, je ne veux pas entrer dans son jeu . . ." [But a disgust seizes me, a desire to pull her off me, I refuse the alliance, I do not want to enter into her game . . .] (54).

From this distance the narrator becomes more analytical of the role the aunt is playing, and he generalizes it as the attentiveness of all mothers to their children, contained as "leur regard avide adhérant à chaque mouvement de l'enfant" [their avid look adhering to each of the child's movements], which turns them into "une bête avide de carnage" [a starved beast avid for carnage] (56–57). The narrator earlier described the uncle as a demanding parent. But the uncle's effort to "educate" his daughter was presented from his/the narrator's point of view and that description denigrated the daughter. These images of the mother as "avide" also originate from the nephew, but they embody the fear that *elle* provokes because he imagines that her tropistic perception is similar to his.

The distance that the narrator has maintained by means of the textual digressions above appears justified when he later sees the aunt returning from a shopping trip with her daughter. All tropistic uneasiness between the two female figures has disappeared, and the nephew becomes the object of their judgment. As in the uncle's discourse, their words about the narrator question his manliness: "[. . .] elles se penchent l'une vers l'autre: 'Tu sais, par moments, il m'inquiète [. . .]. Quand on pense à l'âge qu'il a . . . Songe donc . . . Non, mais imagine un homme comme ton père, à son âge . . .'" [(. . .) the women lean into one another: "you know, sometimes he worries me (. . .). When you think about how old he is . . . Really, imagine . . . No, but imagine a man like your father, at his age . . ."] (64).

In the final scene of Chapter 1 the narrator again separates from the nephew's story and reflects momentarily on the "complexe d'infériorité" [inferiority complex] which "tout le monde partage avec nous" [everybody shares with us]. He explains that it expresses itself in a need for "le dénigrement" [the denigration] of others (64). The narrator's confidence, represented by this moment of reflection, cannot be maintained in the presence of his uncle. When the two of them are together again the nephew accepts the denigration he feels coming from his uncle: "C'est lui le maître. Il commande. Je feins de croire que je cède comme on cède aux caprices d'un enfant malade ou au regard suppliant d'un chien. Mais le chien ici, c'est moi" [He's the master. He rules. I pretend to believe that I give in like one gives in to the caprices of a sick child or the supplicant look of a dog. But the dog, here, is me] (65). The nephew has refused his aunt's tropistic games, but in his desire to identify with his uncle, he lets the uncle "achever la fête" [play the game out], "tout prêt à croire à son innocence, à ma culpabilité [completely prepared to believe in his innocence, in my guilt] (71).

In the last scene with the uncle in Chapter 1 the narrator is passive; there are no digressions like the ones that marked the aunt's monologue. His uncle can be excused for being overly sentimental and childish, and the nephew wants to believe his tropistic attacks are merely games. The aunt frightens the nephew because she "presses on the painful spots," just as he fears he does. In the last two pages of Chapter 1, the narrator separates from the nephew to reflect on his tropistic tendencies: "J'ai honte (c'est pour cela que je les cache si bien) de mes tressaillements [. . .]. Il me semble quand je tressaille que c'est moi le coupable; [. . .] moi qui pêche en eau trouble [. . .], qui vois dans l'air le trajectoire invisible de Dieu sait quels cailloux que personne ne m'a lancés, et qui rapporte ce que personne n'attend; moi qui sans cesse éveille ce qui veut dormir, excite, suscite, guette, quête, appelle; moi l'impur" [I am ashamed of my quiverings (that's why I hide them so well) (. . .). It seems to me that when I quiver, I am the guilty one; (. . .) I who fish in troubled waters, (. . .) who see in the air an invisible trajectory of God knows what stones that no one has thrown to me, and who report what no one awaits; I who endlessly awaken what wants to sleep, excite, incite, await, lie in wait for, call up; me, the impure one] (72–73).

Chapter 1 begins and ends with the child-reader of adult texts. Adults' words wash over the nephew-narrator, elicit images, amuse or terrify him. Whereas we as readers were more or less excluded from the narrator's more literary quest in *Portrait*, though never from tropistic movement, we are invited in *Martereau* to experience this world as readers who were once children. When the narrator interjects himself into the monologues of his uncle or aunt, interrupting their discourse with his own narration, or when he manipulates his discourse to align himself with either of the older figures, it is the child mingled with the young man who is in search of his adult identity. The last words of the chapter cited above mark the subtle movement that has been made by the nephew from a passive to a critical reader who cannot give up his tropistic perspective.

In his quest for identity in the first chapter the narrator looked for a hero, and in boy-child fashion he tried to align himself with his uncle. In a style that recalls the short mythical passage in Chapter 1, the opening lines of the second chapter reveal once again that the narrator is not naive about the nature of his quest: "Ce n'est pas par hasard que j'ai rencontré Martereau. [. . .] J'ai toujours le sentiment que c'est nous qui les faisons surgir: ils apparaissent à point nommé, comme faits sur mesure, sur commande, pour répondre exactement (nous ne nous en apercevons souvent que bien plus tard) à des besoins en nous, à des désirs parfois inavoués ou inconscients" [It is not by chance that I met Martereau. (. . .) I always have the feeling that we conjure them up: they appear at a certain time, as if made to order, to respond exactly (we often do not perceive this until much later) to our needs, to our sometimes unconfessed or unconscious desires] (74). The narrator also describes Martereau in terms that recall a child's idealized relationship to the mother: "J'ai toujours cherché Martereau. Je l'ai toujours appelé. C'est son image—je le sais maintenant—qui m'a toujours hanté sous des formes diverses. Je la contemplais avec nostalgie. [. . .] Il était la patrie lointaine dont pour des raisons mystérieuses j'avais été banni; le port d'attache, le havre paisible dont j'avais perdu le chemin; la terre où je ne pourrais jamais aborder, ballotté que j'étais sur une mer agitée, déporté sans cesse par tous les courants" [I have always been looking for Martereau. I have always called him. It's his image—I know that now—which always haunted me in various forms. I looked upon it with nostalgia. (. . .) He was the faraway homeland from which for mysterious reasons I had been banished; the port of call, the peaceful harbor, to which I had lost the way; the land where I would never be able to set foot, tossed about as I was on an agitated sea] (74–75). The nephew not only puts Martereau as the nurturing male hero in the position traditionally reserved for the mother, but he also transfers from the uncle to Martereau his desire for identification with an older male figure. Martereau's presence protects the narrator, much like the narrator in *Portrait* was protected by the portrait.

With the arrival of Martereau, the narrator is no longer the passive reader of his aunt's seductive stories and he begins to write his own. He is unable to leave his childlike tendencies behind, so his creation is drawn from a child's "lieu commun." First, a domestic scene in Holland is the site of his tale: "Je l'observais, caché sous le porche. Tout pareil à l'enfant loqueteux qui contemple dans la vitrine illuminée l'énorme bûche de Noël" [I was watching him, hidden under the porch. Just like the child in rags who stares into the lighted shop window at the enormous *bûche de Noël*] (76–77). Then he imagines Martereau in England, "une belle poupée articulée, au visage souriant et agréablement teinté" [a beautiful, jointed doll, with a smiling and agreeably colored face]. The narrator frames these "stories" with a reflection on the subjective nature of his mythologizing. He says he calls forth "toute une imagerie faite à mon goût [qui] soutenait mes rêveries, apaisait ma faim" [a whole imagery made to my taste, (which) supported my reveries, soothed my hunger] (77). As the image-making continues, the ages of man march across the page in socially constructed manly images: "[. . .] mannequin héroïque franchissant sous nos yeux d'un pas admirablement réglé, égal et ferme, toutes les étapes: poupon aux longues robes de dentelles sur les genoux de sa mère-grand; enfant espiégle et prince charmant; combattant sur le front; jeune officier tenant la main de sa fiancée; heureux père faisant sauter sur ses genoux son premier-né; fils conduisant tête nue et à pas lents le deuil de son père; lui-même enfin sur son lit de mort" [(. . .) heroic mannequin leaping with an admirably firm, ordered, paced step, before our eyes all the stages: little baby with long lace robes on the knees of his grandmother; mischievous child and prince charming; fighting at the front; young officer holding the hand of his fiancée; happy father bouncing his first born on his knees; son following slowly his father's casket, head bare; finally him, on his deathbed] (77–78). The hero comes to life, "Martereau était là, [. . .] en chair et en os, meilleur cent fois que les plus beaux jouets [. . .]. Martereau que je connaissais depuis longtemps" [Martereau was there, (. . .) in flesh and blood, a hundred times better than the most beautiful toys (. . .). Martereau whom I had known a long time] (78). Like the words of *le vieux* at the end of *Portrait*, Martereau's words and gestures are soothing, "sa poignée de main forte et cordiale, sa tape sur l'épaule: 'Et comment va, jeune homme?'" [his strong, cordial handshake, his slap on the shoulder: "How's it going, young man?"].

The narrator calls these details "le signe de croix qui fait fuir le malin" [the sign of the cross that chases evil away] and describes "le malin" in feminine terms similar to those used by the uncle: "[. . .] la demi-inaction à laquelle je suis condamné, 'la mère de tous les vices,' qui entretient en moi ces ruminations oiseuses, qui me donne cette sensibilité—la faiblesse physique aidant—de femme hystérique, ces sentiments morbides de culpabilité" [(. . .) the demi-inaction to which I am condemned, "the mother of all vices," that fosters in me those trifling ruminations, that gives me that sensitivity—my physical weakness contributing—of a hysterical woman, those morbid feelings of guilt] (79–80, 81). Unlike the uncle, however, Martereau chases this "malin" away because he has "les vrais sentiments" [true feelings], "les grands sentiments tout simples qui donnent leur valeur et leur signification à la seule chose qui compte: nos actes" [great feelings, quite simple ones which give value and meaning to the only thing that counts: our actions] (82). The uncle's emotion has been shown to be violent, but that of Martereau is described as "légère, tendresse virilement contenue qui convient" [light, tenderness contained in a virile, fitting way]. He thus encourages the narrator to be "raisonnable" [reasonable] (86).

In one scene in this chapter the narrator presents a marvelously idealized evening homecoming of the man of the house. The narrator is there, "pareil à l'enfant qui grandit dans un taudis au milieu des cris et des coups quand il s'assoit sur les bancs de l'école du dimanche, écoute la leçon du maître, [. . .] feuillette les livres saints [. . .]" [like the child who grows up in a slum amidst screams and blows when he sits down at Sunday school, listens to the master's lesson, (. . .) looks through the holy books (. . .)] (84). This is a cozy patriarchy, "la certitude, la sécurité se trouvent là" [certitude, security are there] (83). The narrator recognizes both "ce besoin qu'il éveille en moi de perfection, d'absolu" [that need that he awakens in me for perfection, the absolute] and that Martereau surely has "d'autres aspects [. . .], comme tous les hommes" [other sides, (. . .) like all men] (88).

These "other aspects" are presented in the last paragraph of Chapter 2, one long, breathless sentence with no quotation marks to indicate the source of reflections. The narrative disorder is brought back into line at the end of the passage by the image of Martereau as what might be called a "red-blooded" male: "[. . .] qui sait, et qui cela étonnerait-il qu'un bel homme comme lui ait eu quelques passades [. . .], il l'aime, elle le sait bien, alors pourquoi faire des histoires, avec les femmes on ne sait jamais comment ça peut tourner, bien que sa femme à lui aurait probablement compris et pardonné" [(. . .) who knows, and who would be surprised if a handsome man like him had had a few affairs (. . .), he loves (his wife), she knows it, why make a fuss, with women you never know how it will end, even though his wife would probably understand and pardon him] (89). This slight suspicion, contained by "tous les hommes sont ainsi," returns in a later chapter when the narrator begins to doubt Martereau and imagines that he is having an affair with the aunt.

In Chapter 4 Martereau joins the uncle and the nephew on a visit to a country house which the uncle wants to buy. The nephew had proposed this excursion and, like a matchmaker or an artist, he takes pride in having brought these older men together: "[. . .] je les regarde, [. . .] ils sont mon oeuvre, c'est mon oeuvre, la réunion de ces braves gens qui s'entendent si bien, qui parlent la même langue . . . l'enfant de parents divorcés qui les voit enfin réunis doit éprouver ce même ravissement" [(. . .) I look at them, (. . .) they are my work, it's my work, the reunion of these good people who understand one another so well, who speak the same language . . . the child of divorced parents who finally sees them reunited must feel this same ecstasy . . .] (107). The young man calls himself their "trait d'union" [hyphen] and describes the pleasure their union inspires in childlike terms which recall the mother projection he made earlier in his description of Martereau: "J'ai envie de m'étirer de bien-être. Je vais m'assoupir là près d'eux, m'endormir d'un sommeil heureux d'enfant" [I feel like stretching out in comfort. I am going to go relax there next to them, fall into the sleep of a happy child] (107). Artist, matchmaker, child, the narrator is all of these in the "lieu commun" he creates, but the presence of his tropistic rumblings forces him to add to this list the label "le trouble-fête" [killjoy]: "[. . .] je sais bien que si je n'étais pas là, tout serait différent, ce serait entre eux ce calme plat dont je rêve, cette entente parfaite" [(. . .) I know very well that if I were not here, everything would be different, there would be between them that flat calmness that I dream of, that perfect understanding] (107).

The source of this fear that he is a "killjoy" becomes clearer in the scene that follows. The uncle scorns the aunt for suggesting that Martereau had been upset by something said to him in an earlier visit. In his tirade, the uncle claims that Martereau is like him, "ce n'est pas une femme, un petit énervé" [he's not a woman, a little nervous type]. This accusation leads the nephew to reflect that "c'est ce que nous sommes, elle et moi" [that's what we are, her and me] (113). He also imagines that if Martereau had been there, "il serait écoeuré" [he would be nauseated], "il serait contre nous avec lui" [he would be against us with him]: "Ils seraient ensemble, du bon côté, celui des hommes sains et forts, nous ne sommes pas des femmelettes, n'est-ce pas?" [They would be together, on the good side, the side of healthy, hearty men, we're

not little biddies, are we?] (113–14). The struggle within the narrator
between the young man self, self-reflecting and autonomous, and the
boy-child self who seeks (male) adult affirmation is clear in this passage. Taking a more analytical mode, he notes that Martereau's words
are like coins that you put in a vending machine, you pull the lever
and a candy bar drops out, "fade nourriture, bon-bons insipides" [taste-
less food, insipid bonbons] (114–15). But when the narrator as child
recalls words spoken by Martereau to reassure him that something his
uncle had said was not insulting, the narrator says, "je me sens [. . .]
purifié," "rentré dans le droit chemin" [I feel (. . .) purified, (. . .) returned to the right road] (118–19). Like the narrator in *Portrait*, the
nephew in *Martereau* is "impressionable," and he doubts his character-
ization of himself and of others.

Up to this point in the novel, this doubt is represented by the move in
the narration between reflective moments of observation and dramatic
moments in the presence of the adult figures. Chapter 4 ends with the
event that brings this doubt to the surface. The uncle has concocted a
plan to buy a country house without paying taxes. To win his wife's
approval of the idea, the uncle suggests that their daughter learn a little
about business by realizing his plan. She is to go to Martereau with
money to buy the house in the uncle's stead, and the aunt suggests that
the nephew accompany his cousin on this mission (129–37). In spite of
the "responsibility" accorded to the "children," the narrator describes
himself and his cousin in fairy-tale imagery in which both the narrator
and his cousin are given a feminine role: "tandis que nous marchons
côte à côte, portant le précieux paquet, sages petits Chaperons Rouges
allant chez leur mère-grand, je me sens délicieusement en règle, en
ordre [. . .]" [While we walk along side by side, carrying the precious
package, good little Red Riding Hoods going to their grandmother's
house, I feel delightfully proper, neat (. . .)] (139). The innocence of this
image prepares the way for the disillusionment the narrator experiences in Chapter 5. The narrator had compared himself to a child from
the slums and a child in rags who is blessed by the presence of Martereau. For this male narrator, however, to be a child is to be feminized,
and when his uncle is not denigrating him for this role, as seen above,
it suits the narrator very well.

He has described his desire to prove to his uncle that he is like him
in "le monde des vrais hommes" (106), but the quality that keeps the
narrator out of this world is his (over)sensitivity to a situation, a quality
characterized by the uncle as that of "une femme, un petit énervé"
(113). At the same time that the uncle sets himself apart from this
world by explicitly placing himself in a "man's world," the narrator
also feels the uncle implicitly participating in it. When he is "sensitive"

to a situation, the narrator describes him as "maladroit" because the narrator senses his tropistic side. The ambiguity of the uncle's relation to the sensitive world of tropisms leads the narrator to "invent" Martereau, who with his smooth surface and coin-like language disperses such ambiguity. With his "émotion légère" and his "tendresse virilement contenue," Martereau represents a "purer" masculine model than the uncle does. In Martereau's presence the narrator says, "je sais où je suis, qui je suis" [I know where I am, who I am] (80).

Chapter 5 is the site of revelation, realization and recognition as sensations that the narrator felt earlier begin to connect and give meaning to what he is reading. The chapter begins six weeks after the money has been given to Martereau. The uncle returns home from a business trip and asks the "children" if they had gotten a receipt for the money. When they answer in the negative, the uncle blames Martereau and maligns his honesty. As soon as this doubt has been sown, the narration digresses from this moment of difficulty to a moment in his childhood when the narrator discovered that things are not always what they seem. It is as if the trace of disillusionment has been in the narrator intact and unresolved until this moment. The memory digression to childhood serves to clarify the mother projection that the narrator has been using in his "invention" of the nurturing male figure of Martereau. The power of this passage comes from the way in which the present disillusionment in regard to Martereau is laid on top of a past disillusionment in regard to the narrator's mother. In the memory digression, the "pure" masculine model of Martereau is superimposed on a "pure" feminine one, that of the nurturing mother who comforts her son. This superimposition is represented in the narration by a weaving of gestures and words that are emblematic of the past (mother) moment and the present (Martereau) moment. The reader is left with the trace of a sensation, disillusionment, and with the superimposition of the image of the narrator's mother onto that of Martereau.

"Vous lui avez remis l'argent?" [Did you give him the money], the uncle asks, then turning to his nephew says, "Tu lui as demandé un reçu?" [You asked him for a receipt?] (144). These words shake from his memory the words of the kitchen help in his childhood home: "'Tiens, regarde un peu ce qu'elle nous a laissé [. . .]: rien que des tendons et des os'" ["Here, take a look at what she left us (. . .): nothing but gristle and bones"] (148). The narrator describes their words as "un vent glacé . . . tout vacillait . . . se défaisait . . . ce regard de ma mère à table quand elle examine les morceaux dans le plat, insiste: 'En veux-tu encore, prends-en, il y en a, il en reste bien assez pour la cuisine'" [a cold wind . . . everything vacillated . . . came undone . . . my mother's look at dinner when she examines the pieces left on the serving dish, insists: "Do you want some more, take some, it's there, there's plenty for the kitchen . . ."] (148). The timeless infinitive which introduces the next sentence and the sense of "froideur" [cold] link the two moments seamlessly: "Eprouver jusqu'au fond cette détresse . . . Tout en moi vacille et s'ouvre . . . j'ai froid . . . Ce geste de Martereau quand il a tourné la clef dans la serrure . . . Ses gros doigts replets qui retiraient la clef . . . Son air quand il s'est tourné vers nous" [To feel that distress deep inside . . . Everything in me vacillates and is opened . . . I'm cold . . . Martereau's gesture when he turned the key in the lock . . . His big, chubby fingers that took out the key . . . His look when he turned around toward us . . .] (148).

Faced with this sense of suspicion in the presence of his uncle, the nephew can only establish equilibrium in the narration. He fills the page with words and descriptions of gestures that reassure, and the original smooth surface of Martereau is joined to that of the mother in the passage that follows: "Revoir Martereau tout de suite: son bon sourire, le regard placide [. . .], sa solide poignée de main, sa bonne grosse voix." [See Martereau right away: his good smile, the placid look (. . .), his solid handshake, his big, good voice . . .]. Now the other image, the other voice:

Tout va sa remettre en place aussitôt, reprendre forme, ce n'était rien, qu'est-ce que c'était? un vilain rêve, de folles idées, mais qu'est-ce qu'il a encore, mon poussinet, mon grand nigaud . . . assise sur le bord de mon lit et moi blotti contre elle . . . la douceur soyeuse de sa peau si fine, plus soyeuse que la soie, ses doigts dans mon cou, sur mon front . . . Mais comme tu as chaud . . . Je me serre contre elle, je ferme les yeux, je m'assoupis, je hume la délicieuse odeur qui n'est qu'à elle, qu'à moi, mon secret, je l'ai découverte, inventée, c'est l'odeur de la certitude, de la sécurité . . . (149).

[Everything is going to fall into order soon, take form, it was nothing, what was it? a bad dream, crazy ideas, but what's the matter, my little pet, my big silly . . . seated on the edge of my bed and me curled up next to her . . . the silky sweetness of her skin so fine, silkier than silk, her fingers on my neck, on my forehead . . . You're so hot . . . I press against her, I close my eyes, I doze off, I breathe in the delicious smell that is hers alone, mine, my secret, I found it, invented it, it's the smell of certainty, of safety. . . .]

When his image of Martereau is threatened, the memory rephrases this present disillusionment and resolves it as it was resolved in the past. Just as he said he had invented Martereau, here the narrator admits inventing his mother's "odeur délicieuse." The invention of Martereau as the narrator's source of male security is joined with the female security he derives from the mother memory. Together, they separate him from the dangerous (because ambiguous) tropistic world of his uncle where male and female perceptions are antagonistic and separate.

When the digression is over, the narrator rushes to Martereau's house, as if to confirm that all is in order. No one is home, and as he sits on the steps awaiting Martereau's return, the young man begins to doubt again.

That doubt is described in an image which recalls that of Freud's castrating mother. When the male child learns that the mother has no penis, she represents lack and embodies his fear of castration. Sitting on the steps of Martereau's house, the narrator says "il faut se préparer à supporter ce que je redoute tant, cette sensation pénible" [I must be prepared to tolerate what I fear so much, that painful sensation]: "[. . .] à la place vide qu'a laissée l'enflure énorme du désir, de l'espoir—comme à la place où se trouvait un membre amputé—d'élancements sourds, de tiraillements" [(. . .) in the place left empty by the enormous swelling of desire, of hope—like where an amputated member was—dull, shooting pains, gnawing] (150). The narrator has to give up the desire for the "purely" virile world because his model Martereau is stained by the "woman game" of concealment, just as the uncle is. The metaphor of "un membre amputé" is easily read as representing a sense and fear of loss, but I do not want to restrict it to a Freudian reading. What is richest in Sarraute's work is that any number of passages can awaken any number of traces in the reader's imagination, critical or personal. The possibility of reading Martereau and the mother together, and of assigning the male figure the castrating mother role breaks apart the feminine specificity of that role, undoing it at its very origin. But as both her narrators in these first two novels have told us, anything we find is something we have already been looking for.

Martereau does not come home, but on leaving his house, the narrator sees him in the street. When Martereau fails to greet him, the narrator's tropistic perceptions take hold and he reads this oversight as a rejection. He then analyzes Martereau's gesture and recognizes it from an earlier moment when he was leaving the uncle's house. As in the memory digression, the earlier gesture has left a trace. Only now is it analyzed as "ce mouvement qu'il avait esquissé pour s'écarter" [that movement that he had made in order to distance himself]. The earlier gesture is superimposed on the gesture he has just seen Martereau make in the street: "[. . .] il a senti [. . .] qu'il lui faudrait, dès que je l'apercevrais, revêtir pour me faire plaisir le déguisement enfantin, [. . .] me servir ce que j'attendais, quêtais: le sourire bonhomme, le regard clair, le geste aisé [. . .]: il m'observe, il me manoeuvre . . ." [(. . .) he felt (. . .) that he would have to, as soon as I saw him, dress himself up to please me in a childish costume (. . .) and serve me what I was waiting for: the good-natured smile, the clear look (. . .): he is observing me, he maneuvers me] (154). This reflection leads the narrator to reread the

visit he made with his cousin to transact the business deal with Martereau and to see that they were nothing but "les appétissants petits cochons de lait venus dans l'antre du grand méchant loup" [appetizing
little pigs come to the den of the big bad wolf] (155). When he finally
does see Martereau, everything has changed, the mythic age has passed:
"Le temps n'est plus le temps de Martereau [. . .]. Non, le temps est
comme chez nous, une matière informe et molle" [The time is no longer
the time of Martereau (. . .). No, the time is like it is at our house, a
shapeless and limp matter] (162).

The stable ground beneath this male myth shifts, so the narrator
looks to his uncle for reassurance. As if trying to efface the earlier
memory which joined Martereau to his mother, the narrator's need for
security is now marked by another childhood memory and tied to his
uncle: "[. . .] j'ai envie de courir, comme je faisais autrefois quand je
courais à toutes jambes le long du couloir obscur vers le refuge de la
salle éclairée où se tenaient mes parents . . . Mon oncle [. . .] me regarde
par-dessus ses lunettes de ce bon regard d'homme vieillissant qu'il a
parfois et qui m'attendrit toujours" [(. . .) I feel like running, like I used
to do when I would run with all my might down the long dark corridor
toward the refuge of the lighted living room where my parents were
. . . My uncle (. . .) looks at me over his glasses with that good look of
an aging man that he gets sometimes and which always touches me]
(163).

Added to the flux of his identity between being a passive observer
and a reader of complex realities is another movement between constructs of security represented by childlike imagery. Even though he
has forged union with the uncle against Martereau, like a child returning to the safety of the familial nest, when he goes back to see
Martereau, he is once again tempted to make their home his own: "[. . .]
je retrouve l'émotion que je connais si bien, que j'ai si souvent éprouvée
en entrant chez eux—cet attendrissement du voyageur qui revient dans
sa maison natale" [(. . .) I find again the emotion that I know so well,
that I have so often felt upon entering their house—that tenderness a
traveler feels who returns to his native home] (166).

This flux is brought to a halt when he rushes back to report to his
uncle what has taken place. The terms of the uncle's reply efface the
security the narrator had created when he superimposed his memory
of running home to his parents with that of his uncle seated in the
living room. Now the uncle returns to his former self, and to the model
of masculinity which excludes the narrator: "'Martereau t'a fait pitié?
C'est effrayant, toutes ces natures sensibles . . . Heureusement que j'ai
le coeur dur, moi, [. . .] ce n'est pas permis, à ton âge, tu n'es pas une
femmelette [. . .]. Moi, vois-tu, mon petit, je ne suis pas de la race des

rêveurs. Tu le sais, ce qui compte pour moi, ce sont les faits. [. . .] J'aime les réalités solides'" ["You felt sorry for Martereau? It's frightening, all these sensitive types . . . Fortunately I have a hard heart (. . .), it's not permitted, at your age, you are not a little girl (. . .). You see, little one, I am not from a race of dreamers. You know, what counts for me are the facts. (. . .) I like solid realities"] (174–76). Given a choice between the "man's world" of facts and the "woman's world" of "ces natures sensibles," the narrator tries to prefer the former, "je dois l'avouer, sous son influence, je me suis presque mis à les aimer" [I must admit, that under his influence, I have almost begun to like (facts)] (176).

But something has changed. Instead of denigrating himself, he distinguishes himself from his uncle's "manly" brutishness that denies "ces nuances infimes où parfois gît la vérité" [those minute nuances where truth sometimes lies] (176). "J'accuse la ferocité de mon oncle" [I accuse the ferocity of my uncle], the narrator says, "son esprit fruste qui simplifie par goût secret d'une certaine brutalité" [his crude mind which simplifies by a secret taste for a certain brutality]; "il manque d'indulgence, de sympathie" [he lacks indulgence, sympathy] (176). In order to bring together the desires of his reflecting self and his nephew self, the narrator steps into the more independent role of creator of narratives—"j'ai besoin de réfléchir, [. . .] de ruminer encore un peu" [I need to reflect, (. . .) to ruminate a little more]. He adds that he is trying to "affaiblir" [weaken] his uncle, to "démolir" [demolish] him by "lui faire prendre conscience de sa brutalité, de sa simplicité enfantine, à l'attirer dans les terrains bourbeux qu'il a en horreur" [making him conscious of his brutality, of his childish simplicity, to attack him on the muddy ground that he abhors] (177). The twists and turns of the narratives that follow, all focused on Martereau, serve that purpose and achieve that end.

The first four "stories" play and replay a scene between Madame and Monsieur Martereau after the uncle has paid them a visit in their home. Once these "characters" are initially identified, they are referred to simply as *il* and *elle*, that is, taken out of the nephew's universe and into the world of a writer. Each tale goes deeper into a battle between husband and wife. The narrator enters the consciousness of both his characters but clearly identifies with the male role. In the first version he attributes tropistic perception to the husband who is relieved that "ce que Martereau avait pressenti vagument" [what Martereau had vaguely sensed] had not happened after the uncle left, "cette sensation [. . .] d'arrachement, de chute dans le vide" [that sensation (. . .) of wrenching, of falling into emptiness]. *Il* is left instead with a "confiance joyeuse" [joyous confidence], "de bonne humeur à dépenser" [in a good mood to share] (178). The narrator also attributes the wife with a sense of the depths, but the emotion expressed there is negative. She is described as "jalouse" [jealous], "elle hait l'intrus qui le tire loin d'elle dans un monde inconnu où elle n'a pas accès" [she hates the intrusion that pulls him away from her, into an unknown world which she finds inaccessible]; and the husband is the one who "ne veut pas jouer à ces jeux-là" [does not want to play these games] (182–83). The tale ends as they all do, with the husband going out for a walk, but each time the manner in which he leaves is different. In this first version, he leaves in order to preserve his "joie" [joy], to avoid her "détresse" [distress], and he is slightly perturbed: "'Tiens, j'en ai assez, je sors'" ["Listen, I've had enough, I'm going out"] (184).

The narrator is not convinced by his story, however, believing that his male character "se domine encore trop bien, il est trop heureux encore, il se sent trop fort" [still controls himself too well, he's still too happy, he feels too strong] (183). In the next version the narrator goes deeper into the husband's consciousness and lets him ruminate about his wife, though the use of free indirect discourse mingles their perspectives: "Il marche de long en large, les mains dans ses poches: elle trotte, apporte un plateau [. . .]. Elle ne le regarde pas [. . .]. Elle connaît sa vanité, sa coquetterie de jolie femme, ce besoin de se faire apprécier [. . .], mais il est comme tous les hommes, un grand enfant . . ." [He walks back and forth, his hands in his pockets (. . .) she trots around, carries a platter (. . .). She doesn't look at him. (. . .) She knows his vanity, his pretty woman's coquetry, that need to be appreciated (. . .), but he's like all men, a big baby . . .] (185). The wife is attributed with the no-nonsense stance more associated with the uncle. It is also identified with elles in this version, the women who work behind the scenes, for whom the immediate need to wash the body takes precedence over the death itself (186). Where the first version contained the husband's irritation in his discourse to the wife, this version contains it in the narrator's interpretation of his leaving for a walk: "S'échapper tout de suite, la fuir . . . Il ouvre la porte" [To escape right away, to flee from her . . . He opens the door] (189).

The flux seen earlier between impressionable nephew and observant narrator becomes more marked in the third version. Here the name "Martereau" designates the husband, and the narrator's text takes its readers beneath the name by attributing this character with tropistic reflection on the true meaning of the uncle's parting words. The character "Martereau" "se met à marcher de long en large . . ." [begins walking back and forth], ruminating on the mask he feels the uncle placed on him, "un homme de paille . . . c'est cela" [a front man . . . that's it]: "Il reste cloué sur place, pétrifié, calciné: un homme de paille [. . .]: il n'y a pas moyen de se tromper, il n'y a plus rien à découvrir [. . .]. Et je suis cela, moi, moi! Son homme de paille" [He remains rooted to the spot, petrified, reduced to ashes: a front man (. . .): there's no mistake about it, there's nothing left to know (. . .). And that's what I am, me! His front man] (191–92).

With her tropistic perception, the wife also sees beneath her husband's name: "Martereau marche de long en large [. . .], elle le voit sans le regarder" [Martereau walks back and forth (. . .), she sees him without looking at him]. It is no doubt because "Madame Martereau" can see without looking that her husband seeks her confirmation about the uncle: "Il est bougrement intelligent, tu ne trouves pas?" [He's awfully intelligent, don't you think?] (193). Adopting a more distanced narrative mode, the narrator now says that "Certains, que je connais bien, à la place de Madame Martereau, ici n'auraient pas résisté: [. . .] ils auraient collé leur bouche là où le sang tiède afflue, [. . .] ils auraient sucé, mordu . . ." [Certain people, whom I know well, in Madame Martereau's place would not have resisted: (. . .) they would have stuck their mouth there where the warm blood flows, (. . .) they would have sucked, bitten . . .] (196). This narrator, however, is determined to keep his character in character: "Mais Madame Martereau n'a rien du vampire" [But Madame Martereau is nothing like a vampire] (196). She is a good wife, she has "ce qui s'appelle un bon mari" [what is called a good husband], the narrator explains. At the same time, however, the narrator cannot resist having her tell her husband that "il t'a possédé" [he took you], and that the uncle knew it, "le vieux renard, il a bien su se servir de toi . . ." [the old fox, he knew how to use you . . .] (197).

The surface of the name "Martereau" opens up again after these remarks when the narrator describes their effects on *il*: "Il ne reste plus qu'à se retirer en bon ordre, à limiter les dégâts, à sauver devant elle au moins, s'il en est temps encore, la face . . ." [There's nothing left to do but return things to order, to limit the damage, at least in front of her, if there's till time, to save face] (197). Given this depth, the male character can no longer be referred to simply as "Martereau," and his parting words are similarly only a surface for the reader as this version ends: "'Ah! tiens, j'ai envie de sortir. [. . .] Tu dois être fatiguée. [. . .] Ne m'attends pas'" ["Listen, I feel like going out. (. . .) You must be tired. (. . .) Don't wait up for me"] (197–98).

The final version of the scene returns to the simple use of *il* and *elle* and to classic gender differences. The narrator isolates the subject this couple fights about, money. The tension centers on the stereotypical images that husband and wife have of one another and begins with a traditional exchange: "'Ecoute, ma chérie, dis-moi, [. . .] tout à l'heure, au moment où j'ai accepté de lui prêter de l'argent, il m'a semblé que tu m'as regardé . . .'" ["Listen, honey, tell me, (. . .) a little while ago, when I accepted to lend him some money, it seemed to me that you looked at me . . .".] Their *sous-conversation* also retains certain stereotypes. *Elle* notices that *il* has a "manie" [mania] about trying to change her, and *il* considers *elle* to be like "toute la fémininité avec sa longue patience, sa souffrance" [all of femininity with her long patience and suffering], playing the role of "la pauvre femme sans défense entre les mains d'une brute" [the poor, defenseless woman in the hands of a brute] (199–201). The narrator plays out the drama between "la brute" and "la femme" to perfection, the script for a western: "Une brute: elle a raison: un bourreau. [. . .] Qu'elle lui tire ses bottes quand il rentre en titubant du bistrot. Une brute avinée qui hoquette, se plante devant elle, lui barre le passage et éclate de rire en regardant ses yeux bleus que l'horreur dilate" [A brute: she's right: an executioner. (. . .) Let her take off his boots when he comes staggering home from the bar. A drunken brute who hiccups, plants himself in front of her, blocks her way and bursts into laughter as he watches her blue eyes dilate in horror] (201).

In the same brutish manner, the husband puts the question about the uncle to the wife one last time. The look on her face, however, described as "une expression sournoise de crainte et de défi" [a sly expression of fear and challenge], releases a tropistic matter, "ça a jailli, il le reçoit en plein dans les yeux" [it spurts out, he gets it right in the eye]; and the husband assumes the role of a male character who has tropistic perception but controls it: "Maintenant que la poche en elle est percée, elle va vouloir la vider jusqu'au fond. Mais ça non" [Now that the pocket in her is open, she is going to want to empty it entirely. But no she won't]. The husband's parting words reduce the "venin" [venom] he knows *elle* is capable of releasing by addressing her as a child: "'Ah! non, mon petit, je t'en prie, ne commençons pas. J'ai d'autres idées que toi là-dessus. Tiens, tu feras mieux d'aller dormir. Va donc te coucher, je sors. Ne m'attends pas'" ["Ah! no, my dear, I beg you, let's not get started. I have my own ideas about this. Listen, you'd best go to sleep. Go on to bed, I'm going out. Don't wait up for me"] (202).

Now that the narrator is fully receptive to the world of tropisms and immersed in creation, another repressed text rises to the surface of his narration. He recalls his own words when he visited the country house with his uncle and Martereau, "on dirait la scène finale du Procès de Kafka" [one would say the final scene in Kafka's *Trial*] (202). The narrator casts himself as a Kafkaesque hero, not a "petit Chaperon Rouge" [Little Red Riding Hood] as seen in an earlier moment, and the two older men as "Les Messieurs," "mon oncle et Martereau m'encadrant de chaque côté" [my uncle and Martereau flanking me on both sides] (202).

This is the first time the narrator uses an image from literature other than fairy tales. Although this characterization is no less one-dimensional, it represents the narrator's movement from the child's moral plane to an adult one. The reference to Kafka brings to the text the weight of Kafka's bleak fiction, as well as that of Sarraute's article "De Dostoïevski à Kafka," where she writes: "Ces 'messieurs' dont il est impossible de connaître même l'apparence, [. . .] avec qui vous ne pouvez espérer créer une sorte de rapport qu'en 'figurant sur un procès-verbal' qu'ils ne liront probablement jamais, mais qui, du moins, 'sera classé dans leurs archives,' n'ont [. . .] de vous qu'une connaissance distante, à la fois générale et précise, comme celle qui peut figurer sur les fichiers d'une administration pénitiaire" [Those "messieurs" with whom you cannot hope to create a relationship except by "taking part in a court report" that they probably will never read, but which, at least, "will be filed in their archives," only have of you (. . .) a distant knowledge, at once general and precise, as it might be found on prison forms in the warden's office] (60–61). At the end of this article Sarraute identifies these "Messieurs" as Nazis in Hitler's Germany and notes that "Kafka qui était juif [. . .] a préfiguré le sort prochain de son peuple" [Kafka who was Jewish (. . .) foretold the fate of his people] (64).

The nephew's two models of male behavior bear the weight of this image; that is, they are placed undifferentiated on the fictional plane of Kafkan thugs carrying out their evil deed and on a realist plane representing a lived reality. In this text the reference thus represents a general stereotype, as Minogue describes, "carrying a suitably high charge of emotional vehemence."[13] The reference is on one hand, light as a feather, given the nephew's penchant for dramatization, at the same time that it is a stereotype come to life, much like Martereau himself. The knowledge of both prevents the reader from diminishing either extreme, and the same can be said for the gender stereotypes introduced in this novel. So when the narrator admits that he was "fabricating" this image of the men, just as the husband and wife had fabricated images of each other, self-consciousness marks the gesture and the emotional reality of the desire remains; that is, the desire to create characters in order to embody lived reality. The narrator remains on an emotional plane, but he still makes certain reflections. He admits that he was fabricating this image of the older men as "les Messieurs," at the same time that he imagines that "Martereau savait où il me menait" [Martereau knew where he was leading me] (202–3). Martereau is still larger than life, but the narrator is no longer a disillusioned child. He becomes writer-detective and goes to see his cousin to get confirmation about what happened that afternoon when they went to give Martereau the money.

For the first time in the novel the narrator takes control in a conversation with another figure by dominating the discourse. Emulating the style he has attributed to Martereau, he is now the one who maneuvers: "'[. . .] ce jour-là, quand nous sommes allés chez lui . . . dis-moi . . . tu as parfois de ces divinations . . . est-ce que tu n'as pas senti . . . tu sens parfois si bien ces choses-là [. . .] que cet argent, tu ne le reverrais jamais?'" ["(. . .) that day, when we went to his house . . . tell me . . . you sometimes have these divinations . . . didn't you feel . . . sometimes you feel these things so well (. . .) that you would never see that money again?"] (205). The result excites him, "je la sens qui se serre contre moi, qui vibre à l'unisson . . ." [I feel her press up against me, vibrate in unison] (205).

When the daughter's discourse breaks out of character and veers into an analysis of her actions that are anything but childlike, the narrator leads her back. In his *sous-conversation*, he describes their collusion in fairy-tale imagery: "Nous avançons doucement, la main dans la main, le Petit Poucet et sa petite soeur qui cherchent leur chemin dans la forêt, nous retrouvons un à un les cailloux . . ." [We advance softly, hand in hand, Tom Thumb and his little sister making their way through the forest, one by one we find the stones . . .] (205). This imagery serves to reestablish the childlike role he has written for his cousin; and the male role of Tom Thumb that he gives himself marks the commanding role he has assumed. In the end he also imagines that she shares in his pleasure: "[. . .] nous sentons l'un et l'autre cette délicieuse titillation, cette volupté qu'on éprouve tandis qu'on descend" [(. . .) we each feel that delicious titilation, that voluptuousness that one feels on descending] (205).

The narrator reflects on this "délicieuse titillation" and decides that it is wasted on his cousin, so he goes to offer it to his uncle. As he anticipates their encounter, he designs the role he will play, that of "un enfant appliqué qui a bien su tirer parti des leçons de son maître" [an industrious child who learned well how to take advantage of his master's lessons] (208). In order to win his case against Martereau the narrator chooses "la méthode qui convient" [the suitable method], that is, he puts himself squarely in the uncle's camp, the world of facts. The "enfant appliqué" lists them dispassionately, noting that he is now his own source of "la sécurité exquise que Martereau m'a toujours donnée" [the exquisite security that Martereau has always given me] (207). The narrator ends his speech with the vocabulary of a good prosecutor: "'Les faits: il n'y a que ça qui compte. Et les faits parlent'" ["Facts: that's all that counts. And the facts speak for themselves"] (207). In the security of his new role he is no longer worried that his gift will be refused. "Je me suis laissé mener par le bout du nez" [I let myself be led by the end of my nose], he says, as he sits back and lets the uncle savor the power he has loaned him. The uncle's response is described in sensual terms, recalling the male narrator's childlike desire for a male caress: "[Il était] ravi, touché, son regard caresse mon visage, [. . .] il me pince affectueusement comme il fait à de très rare moments d'attendrissement" [(He was) thrilled, touched, his look caresses my face, (. . .) he pinches me affectionately as he does in very rare moments of tenderness . . .] (208).

Just as Madame and Monsieur Martereau change places in relation to tropistic perception in the earlier stories, now the uncle and the nephew do the same, marked by the uncle's repetition of the words that had earlier been reserved for the oversensitive nephew—"'Mais non, écoute, tout de même les choses ne sont pas si simples . . .'" ["But no, listen, all the same, things are not as simple as that . . ."] (208). The narrator is at the height of his authority, noting that "les rôles sont invertis" [the roles are inverted]. Now he can make his uncle like him: "[. . .] maintenant que nous sommes si près l'un de l'autre, [. . .] il peut se détendre, un peu, [. . .] me montrer qu'il est capable aussi, comme moi, de voir les demi-teintes, les nuances . . ." [(. . .) now that we are so close to one another, (. . .) he can relax, a little, (. . .) show me that he is also capable, like me, of seeing the half-shades, the nuances . . .] (209). The narration of the uncle in sous-conversation continues in this style, breathlessly presenting first one opinion about Martereau, refuting it, then presenting another.

At one point the uncle's ravings are separated in the narration by quotation marks, and the observant narrator again interjects his feelings: "J'éprouve, en l'écoutant, une sorte d'émerveillement mêlé d'effroi" [I feel, while listening to him, a kind of amazement mixed with fear . . .] (210). After this observation in which the speakers are separate, the narration falls unexpectedly into complete disorder, their two voices overlapping. The passage presents a phrase in quotation marks that the uncle has spoken to Martereau earlier in the novel, but it is unclear if the narrator is now remembering it or if the uncle is now saying it. This uncertainty continues in the sentence that follows when the antecedent for the possessive pronouns could apply to the uncle talking about Martereau, or to the narrator talking about the uncle: "Son indignation, sa fureur dans ces cas-là, quand nous voulons le démasquer" [His indignation, his fury in such cases, when we want to unmask him]. What the reader has been following as text, trying to distinguish between the uncle's discourse and the nephew's narration, has been the uncle's discourse interjected with phrases from one of his earlier monologues. The narrator's slow revelation, "en écoutant" [while listening], is the uncle's repressed text, for, like "nous" (the narrator and the aunt), he is now vampire-ishly attentive to tropisms. At the end of the passage the speakers divide—"je me sens propre tout à coup, nettoyé" [I suddenly feel proper, clean], the narrator says. When the narrator adds that "mon oncle est aux anges" [my uncle is on cloud nine], it seems they both are (210).

Their harmony is at a crescendo when the paragraph ends, but in the closing passage, "nous nous taisons brusquement . . ." [we abruptly fall silent . . .]. The aunt arrives, and the uncle has been caught playing childish games with his nephew. The male figures resemble the husband in one of the Martereau tales, described as a man on the moon who is scolded by his wife as she stands on solid ground: "'Encore? Ce n'est pas fini? Vous en êtes toujours à ça? Toujours Martereau? Mais mon pauvre ami [. . .] . . . méfiez-vous, à votre âge ça devient dangereux'" ["Still? It's not over? You are still talking about that? Still Martereau? But my poor dear (. . .) . . . be careful, at your age it gets dangerous"] (211). Even though the narrator notices that the uncle blushes like an adolescent, the aunt's remarks reduce him to an old man. In the final image, "les gamins lui jettent des pierres" [kids throw stones at him]. The uncle is transformed into a "pitre" [dunce] and the aunt is an arrogant queen: "La garce . . . elle relève sa jupe très haut et l'oblige à s'agenouiller devant elle pour lui enfiler ses bas" [The fool . . . she raises her skirt very high and obliges him to kneel before her to put on her stockings] (212). Still a child in relation to the aunt, the narrator is untouched by the ridicule, and with this youthful strength he leads his uncle away. "Mon coeur saigne" [my heart bleeds], the narrator says, the creator of all narratives in this novel (212).

The narrator's creative thrust is suspended momentarily as Chapter 6 opens with him in a hospital bed. The opening scene functions as a realist touchstone which returns the reader to a surface reality and further personalizes the narration in the preceding chapter. In this last section of the book, however, Martereau is returned to mythic proportions, because the narrator has not abandoned his creative mode. He invents roles for his aunt, uncle, and himself in the "Martereau myth." First, Martereau is cast as the aunt's lover, "quelque chose que chacun aussitôt reconnaît et nomme: un adultère" [something that everyone recognizes right away and names: an adulterer] (215–16). The aunt, uncle, and nephew are merely actors in a play put on for the amusement of Martereau, "le mari (mon oncle), la femme (ma tante), le neveu (c'est moi)" [the husband (my uncle), the wife (my aunt), the nephew (that's me)] (218–19). When the "nephew" leaves the set to go to his room, the curtain falls, and he resumes his writerly role alone, "derrière les coulisses, seul dans ma chambre" [in the wings, alone in my room] (219).

In another of his creations, the aunt is "la dame à la licorne" referred to in the first chapter, and Martereau plays "ce rôle qu'elle lui fait jouer: le chevalier, le protecteur des faibles" [the role she has given him to play: the knight, the protector of the weak]. He is described as "compréhensif, délicat et fort, [. . .] genéreux envers le rival vaincu qu'elle traîne devant lui pieds nus, enchaîné" [understanding, delicate and strong, (. . .) generous toward the vanquished rival she leads before him in chains] (220). Then Martereau is the "public," watching the scene now played between the "dame à la licorne" and her husband. The narrator seems to join Martereau in this position when the comment is made that "elle est touchante en ce moment, c'est émouvant de la voir ici, dans l'antre du dragon . . . douce proie . . . oiselet effrayé" [she is touching at this moment, it's moving to see her here, in the dragon's lair . . . sweet prey . . . frightened fledgling] (222). This moment of male union in opposition to *elle* prefigures the narrator's final gesture in the novel.

In another scene from the narrator's imagination, the aunt is assigned the role of "Madame Récamier" who crushes her lover with her class, "le petit ramoneur" [the little chimney sweep] (223). The uncle also enters this mythic tale: "[. . .] il est le chevalier revêtu de sa plus belle armure" [(. . .) he is the knight dressed in his most beautiful armor], armed with the knowledge that Martereau would never have the class to be his wife's lover, "sa dame dont il porte les couleurs" [his wife whose colors he wears] (225). The narrator seems to like this version, he says, "je ne peux m'empêcher de l'admirer" [I cannot stop myself from admiring him], and joins the royal couple to watch Martereau: "[. . .] nous avons honte de voir Martereau terrassé brutalement, humilié, nous demandons grâce" [(. . .) we are ashamed to see Martereau brutally defeated, humiliated, asking our forgiveness] (225).

The variety of portraits in the narrator's imagination is almost endless. Each is drawn in great detail, and as seen in the three "stories" about Madame and Monsieur Martereau, one image is superimposed on another such that a trace from any of the portraits for one character may remain as another is being drawn. The narrator reveals his awareness of this gesture of superimposition by having it recognized by Martereau, which may indicate that this is the quality he has most admired in his hero all along. When Martereau looks at the uncle dressed up as a ridiculous character in one of these "scenes," the narrator explains that, "comme en surimpression" [as in a super-impression], he sees "le clown grotesque" [the grotesque clown], "l'ennemi captif, traîné dans l'arène devant lui" [the captured enemy, dragged around the arena before him], and "un adversaire puissant, armé jusqu'aux dents" [a powerful adversary, armed to the teeth] (225). "C'est une chose qui arrive assez souvent," the narrator explains, "qu'on perçoive d'un même objet, à la fois plusieurs images très différentes" [This is something that often happens, that the same object is perceived in several very different images all at the same time] (225).

Having given Martereau access to such a perception, the narrator dramatizes his own shame at having been so naive, "vraiment ma naïveté m'attendrit, ma stupidité" [really my naiveté moves me, my stupidity] (226). As if reverting back to his childlike self, he now imagines that "s'il [Martereau] lui fallait choisir entre nous, c'est peut-être encore mon oncle qu'il choisirait" [if (Martereau) had to choose between us, it's perhaps my uncle that he would choose] (227). Replacing the dichotomies his uncle had once imposed, the narrator puts his aunt and himself on one side, "les révoltés impuissants" [the powerless rebels], and his uncle with Martereau on the other, "mon oncle lui répugne moins que nous" [my uncle repulses him less than we do] (227). In order to disrupt this union, however, he casts the uncle as a buffoon laughing with Martereau as he pushes "la princesse" along, but the narrator assures his reader that "Martereau lui réservait un sort assez semblable au nôtre" [Martereau reserved for him a fate similar to ours] (229).

Martereau still represents the "pure" masculine model in this tropistic, mythic world. By superimposing the visit the three male figures made to the country house, the narrator also endows Martereau with a masculine power in the surface world. This is the business world, and Martereau's power is manifested in a discourse earlier reserved for the uncle, one which passes judgment in the designation of others as "vous." While the nephew and his uncle examine faucets, Martereau discusses the financial details with the real estate agent and the narrator assigns the gendered values: "Il s'agit maintenant entre hommes—vous êtes exclu—de débattre du bénéfice, de la commission, du prix qu'on vous fera payer" [This is between men—you're excluded—discussing profits, commissions, the price you will have to pay] (231).

This sequence is broken by a realist touchstone—"On m'appelle. Ma tante m'appelle. La porte s'ouvre" [They are calling me. My aunt is calling me. The door opens]. Once again, all the narrative that has gone before dissipates as the narrator says that "tout est comme dans les rêves" [everything is like in a dream]: "Il n'y avait rien: rien que bulles d'air, billevesées, mirages, fumée, reflets, ombres, ma propre ombre après laquelle je courais, tournant en rond" [There was nothing: nothing except air bubbles, nonsense, mirages, smoke, reflections, shadows, my own shadow which I have been chasing, turning in circles] (236–37). As in the child's toy the narrator described at the beginning of the novel, he pulls up the plastic page and all he has drawn there with the stylus disappears, "il n'y a rien: une feuille de papier blanc" [there's nothing: a blank piece of paper] (237).

In the final chapter the narrator recognizes that "j'ai fait des montagnes de rien, mon oncle a raison: il n'y avait pas de quoi fouetter un chat" [I made mountains out of nothing, my uncle is right: there was nothing to make a fuss about] (238). When he returns to the surface reality of the country house, however, he can hardly leave Martereau's blank page alone. Martereau is outside, untying knots in his fishing line. As this literal "dénouement" [untying] takes place on the surface of their encounter, the narrator goes through his own dénouement. The superimposition of selves described in the previous chapter is enacted in this last scene as the movement which has characterized this novel throughout between the positions of observing narrator and male-child creator of (manhood) myths. As narrator he comes to conclusions which could offer a traditional dénouement: "Je reproduis comme toujours en moi tous ses mouvements," the narrator says, "ou bien est-ce que ce sont mes propres mouvements qui se répercutent en lui?—je ne sais pas, je ne l'ai jamais su: jeu de miroirs où je me perds—mon image que je projette en lui ou celle qu'il plaque aussitôt, férocement, sur moi, comme fait l'autre, mon oncle" [I always reproduce his movements as if they were my own, or perhaps my own movements resound in him—I don't know, I have never learned: a game of mirrors where I lose myself—my image that I project on him or the one that he right away sticks on me, ferociously, like the other one does, my uncle] (240–41).

As narrator, he can bring tropistic movement to a halt and reflect on his relationship to the character-izations he has been making. As boy-child, however, he imagines that Martereau now places on him the mask that his uncle had given him earlier, that of "greluchon délicat" [sensitive gigolo], and the mask puts tropistic perception into motion. The narrator becomes fascinated with his own enumeration of epithets for himself, "l'image que je vois en lui me fascine, je me penche . . ." [the image I see in him fascinates me, I lean forward . . .] (241). This fascination is described as a "jouissance" [sensual/sexual pleasure], "je veux voir les tourbillons, les remous" [I want to see the whirls, the swirls], and as "celle même, sûrement, que doit éprouver si souvent en pareil cas mon oncle" [the same one, surely, that my uncle must feel so often in such cases] (242). This is the "jouissance" of the "enfant appliqué" seen earlier, one who turns adult lessons to his own advantage.

In the breathless *sous-conversation* which overruns the few sentences uttered by Martereau in this scene, the narrator uses his creative energy to pit his two male models against one another. As in the earlier mythic tales, the grounds for this battle is class difference. He mentions that his uncle plans to go to Saint-Moritz in the winter. Then imagining the judgment that Martereau must be feeling on hearing this news, the narrator draws an image of Monsieur and Madame Martereau in their modest life. Martereau's discourse interrupts this narration—"'Ah! votre oncle va à Saint-Moritz . . . qu'est-ce qu'il y fait, votre oncle? il fait des sports d'hiver? du ski?'" ["Ah! your uncle goes to Saint-Moritz . . . what does he do there, your uncle? he takes in the winter sports? skiing?"] (245). When the uncle becomes the object of ridicule, the two male figures are like two boys making fun of a third, "un petit patin [. . .] vacillant sur ses jambes grêles, agitant les bras" [a little skier (. . .) waivering on frail legs, waving his arms] (245).

The narrator describes the fraternity that this shared mockery creates between him and Martereau, and the sensual terms of this description superimpose the earlier memory digression scene between the child and his mother onto a more sexual scene between lovers: "[. . .] quelque chose en Martereau me tire, m'aspire . . . plus près, se coller à lui plus près, chatouilles, agaceries, pinçons légers . . ." [(. . .) something in Martereau pulls me, breathes me in . . . closer, stick to him closer, gentle tickles, provocative gestures, light pinch-marks . . .] (245). This homoerotic union is followed by the words, "'Ma tante' . . . je la pousse tout contre lui . . ." ["My aunt" . . . I push her right next to him . . .]. The narrator says that Martereau's "regard" [look], "fixé sur l'hameçon qu'il tient en l'air s'adoucit, fragile petit oiseau des îles, douce escalve captive" [fixed on the fish hook he is holding in the air softens, fragile little bird of the islands, sweet captive slave] (245–46). The union is complete with the narrator's interpretation of Martereau's look, no longer blank, as he turns toward the narrator, and the aunt is passed from one man to the other: "[. . .] il rit . . . délicate, rougissante . . . la princesse captive, [. . .] aux mains de grosssiers geôliers . . . elle lève le nez fièrement, mais finies les délicatesses [. . .], il la tient serrée" [(. . .) he laughs . . . delicate, blushing . . . the captive princess (. . .) in the hands of vulgar jailers . . . (. . .) she raises her nose proudly, but no more pretenses (. . .), he holds her tightly] (246).

Their union depends on the capture and resistance of the aunt, the "princesse," though for a moment the narrator joins himself with her and other female figures in order to be grasped in Martereau's big, strong hands, "moi aussi, avec elles, serré, étreinte humide" [me too, with the women, tight, wet embrace]. Tropistic bursting can often be read in sexual terms, but in all of Sarraute's work it depends on the context. When the narrator described it in *Portrait*, the imagery was more of a wound breaking its scab. In this context of male union, already described in intimate terms characteristic of mother and child or of two lovers, the scene resembles the aftermath of a sexual encounter between "la brute" and "la femme": "[. . .] un seul mouvement pour me dégager, pour le repousser, [. . .] et quelque chose d'atroce, d'insoutenable se produirait, une explosion, une affreuse déflagration, nos vêtements arrachés, miasmes, mortelles émanations, toute sa détresse sur moi, son impuissance, son abandon . . . nos deux corps nus roulant ensemble enlacés . . . il me pose la main sur le bras, il émet une sorte de craquement satisfait 'aah'" [(. . .) a single movement to disengage myself, to push him away (. . .), and something atrocious (. . .) will happen, an explosion, a horrifying deflagration, our clothes torn, putrid fumes, mortal emanations, all his distress on me, his powerlessness, his abandon . . . our two nude bodies rolling together, entwined . . . he puts his hand on my arm, he lets out a kind of satisfied crackling "ah . . ."] (246–47).

Without a pause, the text recuperates the image and returns to the surface, "le cercle des hommes": ". . . il me montre l'hameçon qu'il tient en l'air [. . .], 'aah, voilà qui est fait. Tenez, jeune homme regardez . . .' une claque pour me rappeler à l'ordre?" [. . . he shows me the fish hook he is holding in the air (. . .), "aah, it's done. Here, young man, look . . ." a clap to return me to order?] (246–47). Martereau's discourse closes the text, "'Aidez-moi donc, tenez, à remporter tout ça'" ["Well help me out, here, carry all that in"] (247).

As seen in other moments when a realist touchstone framed the narrator's tropistic musing, Martereau's words bring the reader uneasily back to the surface. Unlike the surface of the "lieu commun" where the narrator of Portrait found himself at the end of the novel, this surface produces no solid character. The young male narrator's identity quest is not over, it has only been compounded and confounded by the myths and masks he has created for himself and others. The feminine construct of the aunt stays intact, as does the erotic embrace the narrator imagines with Martereau. The return to the surface at the end, however, contextualizes both images, as well as the "neutrality" of the male narrator. Le Planétarium continues this contextualization of gender constructs as both male and female figures seek to establish identity.

5

Identity at Play: Male-Female

Le Planétarium

However undermined by his own narration, the "neutral" narrator in Sarraute's first two novels remains the organizing point of view. The daughter or the aunt speaking as *je* in discursive situations remains Other. While the hysterical quality of tropistic depth is identified as a feminine Other by these male narrators, they also represent their models of masculinity as having that quality. Tropistic perception was interpreted as "sensibilité," "exaltation," "volupté," and "jouissance," a romantic or mythical ground where female figures were excluded as the young male narrator sought to create a bond with an older male figure. In the presence of these male narrators the feminine figures, singular and anonymous plural, end up as an undifferentiated part of "le lieu commun" and/or in opposition to the tropistic narrator. Each of these positions invites a gender analysis which parallels, respectively, Kristeva's first two generations, women are like men and women are defined in opposition to men.

In the first chapter of *Le Planétarium*, tropistic perception is represented through the consciousness of a feminine character, later identified as Aunt Berthe. *Elle* is fixated on decorating her apartment, but a hole in the door she has just purchased jeopardizes that project. The text takes the reader through her anticipation as she comes up the stairs after the workmen have been there, her horror at seeing the door, her scolding the workmen when they return from lunch, and her own tropistic reflection about how to present herself to them: "[. . .] une maniaque, une vieille enfant gâtée, [. . .] elle sent qu'il est préférable [. . .] de forcer encore grotesquement les traits de cette caricature d'elle-même qu'elle voit en eux" [(. . .) a maniac, an old, spoiled child. (. . .) she feels that it is preferable to force grotesquely the characteristics of that caricature of herself that she sees in them].[1] An anonymous *il* in Chapter 2, later identified as Berthe's nephew, Alain, an aspiring writer, tells a gathering of acquaintances this story about his aunt.

The hole in the door, like the spot on the bathroom wall in *Portrait*, is a domestic triviality which takes on ontological proportions in Le Planétarium. Minogue suggests that "everyone in this novel has Berthe's 'mania'; they are all creators, all trying to construct a world in their own image, and they find holes in the door."[2] This paradigm operates on a literary plane in Portrait and on a mythical one in Martereau. In Sarraute's third novel the initial attempt at appropriation, the novel's theme, takes place in the specifically domestic world of a female character, the world that le vieux in Portrait saw as alien, other, feminine. A feminine milieu is thus the pretext for the thematic and technical structure of Le Planétarium. The female-male dichotomy in this novel appears in the beginning to enact a traditional opposition between a female figure who experiences tropistic depth and a male figure who is capable of transforming it into discourse. In spite of the fact that Berthe is attributed with a sense of tropistic self-reflection in Chapter 1, it is the male figure of Alain who operates as a reflective being who, unlike his aunt, is capable of telling her story.

In Chapter 2 Alain tells the group assembled that he responded to his aunt's call to come and help with the door, and he explains why she was so obsessed with it, "'toute l'angoisse ramassée en elle se fixe là'" ["all the anguish gathered in her is fixated there"]. He describes how he soon attacked the project with the same vigor: "'Moi-même, j'avoue, au bout d'un moment je frottais, repeignais, [. . .] je luttais contre quelque chose de menaçant [. . .] . . . C'était tout un univers en petit, là, devant nous . . . Et nous, essayant de maîtriser quelque chose de très fort, d'indestructible, d'intolérable . . .'" ["I myself admit, in a moment I was polishing, repainting, (. . .) I was fighting against something threatening (. . .) . . . It was a universe in miniscule, there, before us . . . And there we were, trying to master something very strong, indestructible, intolerable"] (28). The male-female opposition that his telling her story suggests is undermined when it is questioned and mocked by other feminine figures in the group.

Alain's metaphorization is first checked by an elle who responds: "'Moi si j'avais des loisirs et de l'argent, je passerais bien mon temps à astiquer des portes [. . .]. Pourquoi pas?'" ["If I had the time and the money, I would certainly spend my time polishing doors (. . .). Why not?"] (31). Another elle also rises out of the audience to contest the male narrator's identification with his aunt's door—"'Ha, ha, ha, quel rigolo vous êtes [. . .] . . . Oh non, moi, je vous garantis que je ne suis pas comme vous, je ne mets pas tout le monde dans le même panier . . .'" ["Ha, ha, ha, what a joker you are (. . .) . . . Oh no, I guarantee you that I am not like you, I do not put everyone in the same basket"] (29–30). Their discourse reflects on his, which scurries to escape in sous-conversation beneath all discourse.

In the passage that follows, Alain's effort to universalize his particular identification is itself metaphorized into a spot on the door: "Mais au nom du ciel, ne vous laissez pas impressionner, ne l'écoutez pas. Le but est proche, [. . .] allons [. . .], 'Je vous assure, non mais vous riez, mais c'est vrai, [. . .] je cirais . . .' Allons, frottez avec nous, les trous disparaissent . . ." [But in the name of heaven, don't let yourself be impressed, don't listen. It's almost there (. . .), let's go (. . .), "I assure you, no, you're laughing, but it's true (. . .), I was waxing . . ." Come, rub with us, the holes are disappearing] (30). At first, the public, male, storytelling sphere and the private, domestic, female sphere appear to be separate, then to be reversed and rephrased: female voices represent "le lieu commun," and the male voice is the site of tropisms. Discourse originates in all narrative figures in the course of the novel, such that separation along gender lines breaks down as each character faces the socio-symbolic contract as a subject.

The narrative figures in Le Planétarium move between two positions—we are alike, we are not alike—thus allowing the reader to investigate the nature of the universality that Sarraute proposes.[3] The tropistic gesture that includes and excludes by means of myths is practiced by all figures, that is, it is shown to be universal, at the same time that each individual constructs a personal and sexual identity by choosing particular myths. The self-questioning seen above is present in both of the earlier novels, but Le Planétarium introduces more figures, male and female, who, like Berthe and Alain, set up and take apart personal and sexual identity constructs, of themselves and of others. These constructs are derived from patriarchy, the only system available, and they all, male and female, suffer from its limitations.

Le Planétarium is a novel of images, identity at work though still in process, and everyone speaks here, men, women, old and young, constructing and deconstructing identities by telling stories. Gender battles emerge in conventional terms, as they did in the first two novels, then disappear as each figure uses whatever means is available for personal affirmation. Without a central narrating figure, Le Planétarium joins Sarraute's later novels, which, as Newman describes, "abandonnent presque entièrement la syntaxe de subordination" [abandon almost entirely the syntax of subordination]. He characterizes the relationship between figures in these novels as one of "coordination, plus encore de juxtaposition" [coordination, even more, of juxtaposition]. By extension, the reader's relationship to narrating figures shifts as well. "L'interlocuteur n'est pas toujours désigné sans ambiguïté" [the interlocutor is not always designated without ambiguity], Newman observes; that is, reference to "locuteurs" is often established through synecdoche, reflecting an affect, an impression of perception, and a transference of traits from one character to another, as well as through repetition of the same moment of tension from different "optiques." All contribute to create a more instinctive, less reflected perception. The use of pronouns in the first novels is "fonctionnelle," the critic continues, because the pronoun establishes the particular traits of a figure. The proper name as well as name substitutes like "le vieux," "ma tante," "mon oncle" operate similarly as what Newman calls a "pronom motivé" [motivated pronoun]. The pronoun, synecdoche and "description affective," giving one's vision of oneself, for example, or "une manière d'être" [a way of being], are the techniques that dominate the later works and contribute to their effect.[4]

Although both of the first two novels remain within a structure of gender difference, *Martereau* moves beyond a literary arena and into a more personal one. In *Le Planétarium* the complexities of the relationship of self to other are amplified, as are the myths that structure gender. Thus it is that with *Le Planétarium*, Sarraute's novels begin to move into Kristeva's third generation, where the "very dichotomy manwoman as an opposition between rival entities" takes place on an ontological level. "What can 'identity,' even 'sexual identity,' mean," Kristeva asks, "in a new theoretical space where the very notion of identity is challenged?" Because of the ambiguity created by Sarraute's narrative techniques as Newman describes them, the reader often experiences the effects of personal and sexual constructs before they are attached to a speaker. It is in this way that "the implacable difference," as Kristeva calls it, between male and female, "the violence be conceived in the very place where it operates with the maximum intransigence, in other words, in personal and sexual identity itself, so as to make it disappear in its very nucleus."[5]

Martereau reveals and undermines a male myth in the making, and *Le Planétarium* does the same with the myth of heterosexual union. Alain and Gisèle, his Young Wife, both attempt to compose the respective myths that patriarchy offers them for the Young Married Couple. This myth implicates the myth of the Mother-in-Law as well. She functions as one who upholds "le lieu commun" and can hardly separate her identity from its constructs. In Chapter 3, the voice of a feminine figure reflects on the storytelling scene from the preceding chapter and on first reading the passage, the origin of the narration could be Gisèle or her mother: "Elle qui s'était imaginé qu'elle le poussait [à raconter les petites manies de sa tante] à petites tapes encourageantes, protectrices" [She who had imagined that she was pushing him (to tell about his aunt's manias) with little encouraging and protective taps] (39). The interchangeability of these two figures is important to the female myth-making in this novel. Mother attempts to make Daughter into an image of herself, and *elle* in the next chapter struggles between her identity as Daughter and as Wife; that is, Wife as Mother constructs it and Wife as Daughter does.

It is not until another voice speaks of "vos enfants" [your children] that the above speaker is clearly identified as the Mother-in-Law in Chapter 3. What is at play in this chapter is the conflict between the image the figure of *elle* has of herself as "une mère pleine de sollici-tude" [a mother full of concern] and the one she imagines originates from the union of her Daughter with her Son-in-Law: "Il maintient d'une main ferme ce masque qu'il lui a plaqué sur son visage dès le premier moment, ce masque grotesque et démodé de belle-mère de vaudeville, de vieille femme qui fourre son nez partout, tyran qui fait marcher sa fille et son gendre au doigt et à l'oeil" [He holds with a firm hand that mask that he stuck on her face from the beginning, that grotesque and outdated mask of a comic mother-in-law, an old woman who pokes her nose everywhere, a tyrant who makes her daughter and son-in-law toe the line] (42, 44).

As Mother-in-Law, *elle* attempts to put on another face with these insolent children, one she recalls her husband using, "elle peut être comme lui quand elle le veut" [she can be like him when she wants to]: "Voilà comme je suis. Je n'ai pas besoin que vous m'aimiez" [Here's how I am, I don't need you to love me] (45). This is the mask she prefers to wear, but it is in direct conflict with her role as Mother. The superimposition of the two roles is reflected in the narration when her recollections of Mother-Daughter discussions about "le grand jour [de mariage]" [the great day (of the wedding)] meld temporally with reflec-tions on the chairs that she wants to buy for the couple once they are married (51). In neither role does *elle* escape placing masks on the Daughter and the Son-in-Law—her daughter is a "tendre, douce enfant" [tender, sweet child], and on her wedding day her groom is "le vrai prince charmant" [the true prince charming].

As Mother-in-Law and Mother, the two roles can hardly be separated in this chapter, this *elle* continually mouths instructions about gender constructs from "le lieu commun." "Ton rôle de femme" [your woman's role], Mother tells Daughter, is to change her husband for the best, "'[. . .] Alain est très jeune . . . il t'écoute'" ["(. . .) Alain is very young . . . he listens to you"] (51). A man should be "'calme, fort, pur, détaché, préoccupé de choses graves et compliquées qui leur échappent à elles faibles femmes'" ["calm, strong, pure, detached, preoccupied with seri-ous and complicated things that are too much for weak women"] (52). And this Man certainly should not be worried about what kind of chairs to put in the living room, "'un homme a d'autres chats à fouetter,

il se moque de ces choses-là'" ["a man has other fish to fry, he laughs
at such things"] (52).

When the Daughter becomes Wife, that is, susceptible to her Husband's point of view, the Mother-in-Law as Mother brings up the memory of herself as "protectrice" [protective], represented in *sous-
conversation*, in order to combat the designation "autoritaire" [au-
thoritarian]. She recalls times when her Daughter was afraid at night
and would come to her mother's room: "[. . .] toute tremblante contre
elle [. . .] quand elle avait peur des voleurs [. . .] et venait se blottir dans
le lit de sa maman" [(. . .) all trembling against her (. . .) when she was
afraid of thieves in the night (. . .) and came to snuggle up in her
mother's bed] (52). That sensation carries over into the next chapter
where the Daughter similarly feels the ground falling out from beneath
her and recalls a walk she took as a Child with her Mother in the park.
In the Daughter's memory, Mother screams and covers the Child's face
as "un véhicule étrange, une haute et mince charrette de cauchemar,
remplie d'une poudre livide, répandant une atroce odeur, cahote lentement vers elles dans l'allée" [a strange vehicle, a tall, thin, nightmarish
cart, filled with a pale powder, giving off a foul odor, trundles slowly
toward them down the path] (56). Both of these memories preserve the
relationship between Mother and Daughter as a protective one between
Mother and Child. This relationship thus becomes a myth which continues to influence the perceptions these female figures have of one
another.

All of the young male figures in Sarraute's first three novels are identified as childlike, usually by fairy-tale imagery. The older figures
around them include a male and a female figure (in the case of *Portrait,
elles*), which suggests a parental relationship of some sort. Where *le
vieux* is represented by the narrator in *Portrait* as a cult-like male figure,
the uncle in *Martereau* is more ambiguous. The nephew assigns him
an authoritarian role, identifies him alternately as brutish and innocent,
divests him of this ambiguity in a kind of oedipal battle, then leads the
old man away. The aunt is given a castrating role in that scene, only to
be controlled by the nephew's last image of her as a "la princesse
captive" who, like him, is held in Martereau's hand.

The use of these terms would make Sarraute shudder, but they are
useful as a way of delineating the psychological myths that her work
brings to the surface as objects to be investigated. The success of that
intention becomes clearer in the third novel and is most apparent in
Gisèle's relationship to her parents. Her *sous-conversation* during a
later discussion with her Father, and the style of the narration which
presents her responses to her Mother in Chapter 3, achieve an affective

rendering of this female subject's experience when facing these figures as psychological myths. At the end of Chapter 3 the dialogue between Mother and Daughter is narrated from the Mother's consciousness, and their discourse is delineated by quotation marks interspersed with the Mother's *sous-conversation*. The Daughter's reaction at one point is described from the Mother's point of view, "la pauvre petite enfant pâlit, on dirait que le sol se dérobe sous elle, elle a peur, elle fait pitié" [the poor little child pales, you could say that the earth gives way beneath her, she's afraid, she's pitiful] (52). At another moment, an ironic tone from outside the Mother-Daughter pair gives the reader distance on their drama. "'Il faut regarder les choses en face'" ["Things must be looked at head on"], Mother says, and the next sentence reads, "Elles regardent" [They look] (53).

Chapter 4 begins with an *elle* spinning in vertigo: "Quelque chose en elle s'arrache et tombe . . . dans le vide en elle quelque chose palpite . . . Vertige . . . La tête lui tourne un peu, ses jambes faiblissent . . . Mais il faut se raidir, [. . .] juste encore un instant, offrir un visage placide aux baisers légers sur ses joues, [. . .] sourire, parler . . . 'Oui, à bientôt, au revoir maman . . .'" [Something in her pulls away and falls . . . in the emptiness within her something palpitates . . . Vertigo . . . Her head spins a little, her legs weaken . . . But she must brace herself, (. . .) just an instant more, offer a placid face to the light kisses on her cheeks, (. . .) smile, speak . . . "Yes, see you later, bye-bye Mama . . ."] (55). The address identifies the discourse as originating from the Daughter and presents only her side of the exchange. The reader's knowledge of Mother from the preceding chapter fills in the rest: "'Mais non, je ne suis pas triste, non je ne suis pas vexée, quelle idée . . . mais bien sûr, maman, je comprends, je sais . . .'" ["Why no, I am not sad, no, I'm not angry, what a silly idea . . . Why of course, Mama, I understand, I know . . ."] (55).

Gisèle's discomfort with the Parent-Child myth takes place in her interaction with her Mother and her Father; her self-doubt in relation to her Husband is at the level of personal and sexual identity. In Chapter 4 she questions her idealized image of her Husband and their marriage. "La belle construction" [the beautiful construction] begins to shake on its foundations when she sees "des deux vieilles maléfiques" [two evil old women] gossiping in a corner on her wedding day (58). The Young Wife then recomposes the image of their marriage to replace it with memories of Husband and Wife joined in laughter and criticism of everyone else in the world. At times her Husband's analysis of her Mother threatens her role as Daughter: "'Ta mère est surtout une autoritaire. [. . .] Elle a été frustrée probablement. Elle n'a pas réalisé sa vie comme elle aurait voulu'" ["Your mother is above all authoritarian.

(. . .) She's probably been frustrated. She hasn't lived her life as she would have wanted"]. To dispel this discomfort, the Young Wife brings up words from the wedding ceremony, "tu quitteras tes père et mère" [you will leave your father and your mother] (59–60).

It is in *sous-conversation* that this female figure reveals the corporeal nature of her doubt, something the Young Husband would probably not notice. "Le corps ne se trompe jamais," the Young Wife's narration reads, "il enregistre, il amplifie, il rassemble et révèle au-dehors avec une implacable brutalité des multitudes d'impressions infimes, insaisissables, éparses" [The body is never wrong: it registers, amplifies, assembles and reveals on the exterior with an implacable brutality a multitude of miniscule, fleeting, scattered impressions] (62). *Elle* also recognizes that the idea of "fusion complète" [complete fusion] with another is a myth, one of those "histoires qu'on raconte dans les romans" [stories they tell in novels], a myth that her later return to loving, supportive Wife represses. In the dramatic scene that interrupts these reflections in Chapter 4, the Young Husband returns home. In his presence, the Young Wife cannot maintain her reflective distance.

When the narration moves into their dialogue, the Young Husband's *sous-conversation* reveals his suspicions that his Wife is trying to bring him into her Mother's camp. Chapter 4 ends with these accusations brought into discourse, as he condemns the Women in his life and bristles at the gender roles the reader recognizes from the Mother-in-Law's narrative in the previous chapter: "'C'est bon pour ma belle-mère, pour ma femme, de penser à ces choses-là, c'est à elles de me construire un petit nid confortable où je pourrai m'épanouir'" ["It's good of my mother-in-law, of my wife, to think about these things, it's their job to build a little, comfortable nest where I can blossom"] (70). The Young Husband is always better in external discourse than the Young Wife in this novel.

As seen above after the Mother-Daughter encounter, Gisèle's construction of a personal identity wavers between the myths her Mother gives her and the ones she constructs with her Husband. In Chapter 7 the young couple has a meal in the Young Wife's parents' home where the Daughter tries to establish her own personal and sexual identity in relation to her Father. In the end, however, she cannot abandon her role as Dutiful Daughter. The subject of discussion is a writer named Germaine Lemaire whom the Father has described as "une jolie femme" [a pretty woman]:

. . . "une jolie femme" . . . brève formule, [. . .] elle développe la formule instantanément: une jolie femme, ha, ha . . . voilà votre triste situation, à vous autres, votre tragique condition, mais il faut s'y plier. C'est pénible . . .

[. . .] n'est-ce pas, hé, hé, mes tendres, faibles oiselets? . . . Mais Dieu vous a ainsi faites, que voulez-vous. [. . . Est-ce que] vous pouvez vous plaindre de quelque chose, ta mère et toi? [. . .] C'est beau leur égalité [. . .], déguisées en homme [. . .], vieilles femmes à quarante ans . . . éteintes, ridées, monstres, bas-bleus, objets de risée, de répulsion (101).

[. . . "a pretty woman" . . . a curt expression, (. . .) she develops the formula instantaneously: a pretty woman, ha, ha . . . that's your sad situation, your pitiful condition, but you must submit to it. It's painful . . . (. . .) isn't it my tender, weak little fledglings? . . . But God made you this way, what do you want. (. . . Do) you and your mother have any complaints? (. . .) It's beautiful their equality (. . .), disguised as men (. . .), old women at forty . . . faded, wrinkled monsters, blue-stockings, objects of ridicule, of repulsion.]

The anger expressed in the Daughter's *sous-conversation* seems to give her the courage necessary to come to Lemaire's defense: "'Elle est mieux que jolie. Elle est belle. Tout le monde le dit . . . il y a des hommes qui se sont tués . . .'" ["She's better than pretty. She is beautiful. Everyone says so . . . there are men who have killed themselves . . ." (102).

The Daughter's mounting anger at her Father continues to remain available only to the reader, for it is unrealized in the conversation around the table: "Elle le hait [. . .], elle sent que si elle se laissait aller, eh bien, elle aussi, peut-être, dans cette camelote qu'il faut détester, dans ces poupées de coiffeur . . . elle trouverait . . . il n'y a pas si long-temps, elle-même . . . mais elle ne veut pas, il peut tirer aussi fort qu'il voudra, rien à faire . . ." [She hates him (. . .), she feels that if she lets herself go, well, she also, perhaps, in that schlock that she's supposed to detest, those coiffured dolls . . . she would find . . . not so long ago . . . herself . . . but she doesn't want that, he can pull as hard as he wants, nothing doing . . .] (102).

Armed with the resolution seen in the above *sous-conversation*, the Daughter responds openly to her Father's remarks: "'Il y a une autre idéal de beauté, figure-toi. [. . .] Et elle répond à cet idéal-là, Germaine Lemaire, que tu le veuilles ou non. Et je ne suis pas seule à le trouver. Sa tête par Barut—mais tu ne l'as pas vue, ça ne t'intéresse pas [. . .]'" ["There is another ideal of beauty, imagine. (. . .) And she corresponds to that ideal, Germaine Lemaire, whether you like it or not. And I'm not the only one who thinks so. Her head by Barut—but you haven't seen it, that doesn't interest you (. . .)"]. The Father's words now appear in the text inflected with the Daughter's anger: "—Si . . . i . . . son si est long sifflement, si . . . [. . .] il siffle comme un serpent . . . [. . .] il ri-cane . . ." [—Yes . . . s . . . his ss is hissingly long, yes . . . [. . .] he hisses like a snake . . . [. . .] he sniggers . . .] (102). The Father continues to attack the Daughter's model for ideal beauty. He calls Lemaire "une tête brûlée" [a hothead] and mocks her for "carrying on" as she does at her age.

Finally the anger expressed in *sous-conversation* erupts: "'Elle a ton âge et elle est plus jeune que toi'" ["She's your age and she's younger than you are"]. The Daughter's pain at her outburst falls beneath discourse: "Elle a envie de pleurer . . . mais qu'on l'aide enfin, que quelqu'un vienne donc à son secours . . ." [She feels like crying . . . someone help her already, someone come help her] (103). In direct conflict with this discomfort at speaking to her Father in this way is another attack which also remains below the surface: "C'est un pauvre gâteau. Il fait plutôt pitié. Un vieux jaloux . . ." [He's an old sugar daddy. He's pitiful. A jealous old man] (103).

The Daughter cannot be left with such a pitiful image of her father, however, so she constructs another: "Le roi Lear. Le père Goriot. Sa tendresse timide. Sa pudeur. Seul, vieux, abandonné, inconnu, exclu, rejeté par elle, sa fille chérie, son unique enfant . . . Mais elle l'aime, il le sait bien . . ." [King Lear. Père Goriot. His timid tenderness. His decency. Alone, old, abandoned, unknown, excluded, rejected by her, his dear daughter, his only child . . . But she loves him, he knows it]. The text continues to recount all her favorite things about him, synechdochical details of her affection, his "peau chaude sur le dos de sa main" [warm skin on the back of his hand], "son odeur à lui" [his odor], "ses bouclettes blanches" [his little white curls] (104). How could the Daughter let a Stranger separate her from her Father? In order for him to be "son père omniscient, bienveillant" [her omniscient, benevolent father], she must be the Good Daughter: "Il lui donnerait son approbation. Elle recevrait, [. . .] inclinée devant lui comme il se doit, sa bénédiction . . . 'Maman a raison. [. . .] Je suis folle. Pardonne-moi, Papa'" [He would give her his approval. She would receive it, (. . .) bowed down before him as it should be, his benediction . . . "Mama's right. (. . .) I'm crazy. Excuse me, Papa"] (104). In this familiar role, Gisèle appeases her father by telling him about the apartment they hope Aunt Berthe will offer them, and by asking for his advice (105). Gisèle as Daughter leaves the novel in Chapter 7, and although all the emotion of the earlier *sous-conversation* is wrapped up narratively by the straightforward exchange between Father and Daughter in the end, the effect of the exchange lingers.

In a scene in Chapter 8, the Young Wife talks her Husband into going to look at the apartment they hope Aunt Berthe will give them. Here the Young Wife plays out the appeal she knows she has for her Husband. After introducing the chapter with their well-delineated dialogue, the text slips into the Husband's consciousness: "Elle fait penser à un renardeau, elle ressemble à un jeune loup [. . .], la convoitise fait luire son oeil . . . c'est cela qu'il aime en elle, cette intensité, [. . .] toutes ses forces ramassées dans son regard" [She makes him think of a little fox, she resembles a fox cub (. . .), covetousness makes her eye shine . . . that's what he loves about her, that intensity, (. . .) all her strength gathered in her look] (107–8). The Young Wife's thoughts appear in the next paragraph in almost the same terms: "[. . .] elle sait ce qu'il voit: elle le fait penser à un petit renardeau, à un petit animal de bois, sauvage, capricieux" [(. . .) she knows what he sees: she makes him think of a little fox cub, a little animal, wild, capricious]. This perception of herself differs slightly from his. Whereas the Husband thinks that his wife's covetousness makes her eyes shine, her *sous-conversation* says that "ses yeux deviennent plus sombres quand elle fixe quelque chose ainsi avec cette intensité" [her eyes become darker when she fixes on something like this with that intensity] (108).[6] Gisèle's knowledge of the look in her eyes, however, is not her own; it comes from elsewhere, a formula she carries around with her, "le grand garçon blond qui avait l'air d'un Suédois lui avait dit cela" [the big blond who looked Swedish had told her that] (108). These words pronounced by an absent Other Man are the source of her power in this scene. In the end Gisèle plays the Childish Wife, "elle retrousse sa lèvre" [she curls her lip], and points out the window where she wants sunlight. Her Husband leans toward her, hugs her to him and explains where the sun rises. "Il sait tout" [he knows everything], she concludes, and her *sous-conversation* identifies the mask she is wearing, "les hommes savent toutes ces choses-là" [men know all those things] (108).

Chapter 9 begins with Gisèle's affective response to another man, "son sourire de Bouddha" [his Buddha smile], "son silence . . . elle ne sait pas ce que c'est . . . c'est son charme . . . il est charmant" [his silence . . . she does not know what it is . . . it's his charm . . . he's charming]. This male figure is identified in the next sentence with someone else's voice: "Ton beau-père a du charme, tu ne trouves pas?" [Your father-in-law has charm, don't you think so?] (112). This statement comes from *elles*, and their words upset the Young Wife because she keeps waiting for them to compare her Husband to his Father and *elles* never do.

Gisèle's argument with her Father raised questions about what it means to be a "woman," and in the preceding scene, Gisèle played her own version of the Childish Wife. When she visits her Father-in-Law, however, to ask his help in getting Aunt Berthe to give the Young Couple her apartment, she is up against a different sort of man. The Father-in-Law is described as a man who enjoys making women angry and enjoys watching them. The narration appears to originate from the Young Wife, though it also carries language more characteristic of *elles*: "Lui seul,

à travers toutes les apparences, tous les obstacles, lui—fort, viril, indé-
pendant" [Him alone, through all appearances, all the obstacles, him—
strong, virile, independent] (114). A man with the power to make
women "women": "[. . .] il se penche avec tendresse, c'est à lui, au fond
de leurs yeux son regard le caresse et elles se sentent vivre plus fort
. . . c'est sa chose, sa création . . . cela tremble, palpite doucement—la
vie même, [. . .] elles deviennent cela" [(. . .) he leans over with tenderness, it's his, in the depth of their eyes his look caresses it and they
feel themselves living more strongly . . . it's his thing, his creation . . .
it trembles, palpitates softly—life itself, (. . .) they become that] (114).
Words from the Father-in-Law's point of view slip into this sexually
charged text, which in turn inflects the exchange that follows with
sexuality: "Elle est gentille, ma bru" [She's nice, my daughter-in-law]
(114).

In her surface and interior discourse Gisèle winds in and out of the
roles of Daughter-in-Law and Woman: "'Voilà, je voulais vous parler
. . . Alain ne saurait jamais . . . Moi j'ai dit: "Je n'ai pas peur . . ."' Elle
rit et il l'encourage, elle sent sur sa joue la pulpe chaude et sèche de ses
doigts. 'De quoi n'avez-vous pas peur, mon petit enfant?' [. . .]" ["There, I
wanted to talk to you . . . Alain would never know . . . I said to myself:
'I'm not afraid . . .'" She laughs and he encourages her, she feels on her
cheek the warm and dry pulp of his fingers. "What are you not afraid
of, my little one?"] (114). It is the role of Daugher-in-Law that receives
the coldest review, and it appears to come from the consciousness of the
figure of il: "[. . .] elles sont toutes pareilles, chères petites Madames, il
les connaît, c'est pour ça qu'elles se marient" [(. . .) they're all alike,
dear little Madames, he knows them, that's why they get married] (115).

As the tropistic exchange continues, origins of discourse become
indistinguishable. The Young Wife and the Father-in-Law are "entre
nous, entre vieilles gens qui en savent long, qui connaissent la vie, pas
de ménagements, n'est-ce pas?" [between friends, between old folks
who have known each other a long time, who know about life, no cares,
right?] (117). This intimacy does not keep the Daughter-in-Law from
carrying out her business, that is, to secure Aunt Berthe's apartment.
The Young Husband is the sacrifice in the exchange: "[. . .] un poupon,
c'est vrai, un nourrisson couvé, sans force . . . un gosse capricieux"
[(. . .) a little baby, it's true, an over-protected, unweaned child, no
strength . . . a capricious kid]. The text that follows suggests that these
words came from elle: "[. . .] elle sent qu'en lui tout bouge et se déplace,
elle a frappé juste, [. . .] il fait penser à un taureau ensanglanté qui
baisse la tête et fait face au matador" [(. . .) she feels everything move
and shift in him, she hit the target, (. . .) he looks like a bloody bull
who bows his head and faces the matador] (117). "'C'est vrai, vous avez

raison,'" Alain's Father says, "'Il était déjà comme ça quand il était
haut comme une pomme [. . .]. J'ai tout essayé, croyez-moi. Mais rien
ne peut lui donner confiance en lui. C'est un grand timide, Alain, un
anxieux [. . .], il est comme ça, que voulez-vous?'" ["It's true, you're
right. (. . .) He was like that when he was knee-high to a grasshopper
(. . .). I tried everything, believe me. But nothing could give him confidence in himself. He's awfully shy, Alain, a worrier (. . .), he's just like
that, what do you want?"] (117).

Among the spoils of the Daughter-in-Law's victory is a noble role for
herself as Woman: "Il y a eu comme de la tendresse dans sa voix [. . .].
C'est leur sort à toutes . . . éternelles sacrifiées, tristes victimes . . .
Marie Stuart, Marie-Antoinette . . . belles princesses qui font rêver les
poètes, les guerriers . . . livrées à des gamins . . ." [There was something
like tenderness in his voice (. . .). It's the fate of all those women . . .
eternally sacrificed, sad victims . . . Marie Stuart, Marie-Antoinette . . .
beautiful princesses who make poets and warriors dream . . . handed
over to children.]. In the end the Father-in-Law places his hands on the
Young Wife's shoulders, and his words, "'Alors, ma petite Gisèle [. . .]'"
["Well, my little Gisèle (. . .)"], are described as "courageux" [coura-
geous]. *Il* is designated "le compagnon digne d'elle que le sort aurait
dû lui donner" [the companion she deserves, that fate should have
given her] (118).

When she sees her Husband after this exchange, the Daughter-in-Law
chooses the role of Mature Wife who deceives her Husband for his own
good. The difficulty of that deception becomes clear when she returns
to their "nid" [nest] to report the good news that his Father will intervene with the Aunt: "—Ton père est un amour. Je l'adore, tu sais, Alain
[. . .], ton père t'adore, je t'assure'" [—Your father is a love. I adore him,
you know, Alain (. . .), your father adores you, I assure you"] (118–19).
In his interpretation of the visit, the Young Husband tries to bring his
Young Wife back into the childlike role that he does not realize she
has left: "— [. . .] Pas un mot, pas un mordillement. Le loup a léché
tendrement le doux petit agneau venu lui-même gentiment'" [— (. . .)
Not a word, not a nibble. The wolf licked the sweet, little lamb tenderly,
who came so nicely to see him"] (119). When the Young Wife protests
her Husband's use of these terms, the picture he draws of himself in
response is undermined by her earlier *sous-conversation* with the Father-in-Law in which *he* is designated "le compagnon digne d'elle":
"— [. . .] Oh! qu'on a honte de mentir. Oh! que c'est méchant de raconter
des blagues à son amour, à son meilleur copain . . . Mais pourquoi le
cacher, puisque je sais toujours tout. Une voyante extra-lucide, voilà ce
qu'il est, ton petit Alain'" [— (. . .) Oh, we should be ashamed to lie.

Oh! it's naughty to tell stories to your love, your best friend . . . But why hide it, since I always know everything. A clairvoyant, that's what he is, your little Alain"] (119–20). The disparity between the Young Husband's words and the Young Wife's "small deception" can only be expressed by the body and repressed by words: "—Mais qu'est-ce que tu as, Gisèle? Tu pleures?' —Non, Alain, je t'aime. Tu es mon amour'" [—What is it, Gisèle, are you crying?" —No, Alain, I love you. You are my love"] (120). These are the last words spoken by the Young Wife in the novel. The denial resonates in the reader's experience of Gisèle's visit to see Alain's father, connecting the reader to the Young Wife as to no other figure in the novel, especially the Young Husband. For him, she remains "Gisèle . . . mon amour" [my love], "ma femme" [my wife] —he repeats her name when he needs "l'apaisement, c'est la sécurité" [a calming down, it's security] (91).

Alain's self-questioning takes place in terms of his aspiration to be a Writer. This is the object of his quest for approval from the writer Germaine Lemaire. After the earlier fight with his Wife about how she colludes with "ma belle-mère" [my mother-in-law] to exclude him from decorating the apartment, the Young Husband leaves in a huff and runs to Germaine Lemaire, "vers la délivrance" [toward deliverance] from such bourgeois pettiness. Lemaire plays the role of "belle femme" for Gisèle, when as Daughter, she praises the older woman as one who inspires men to action—"'Il y a des hommes qui se sont tués. . . .'" This is similar to the one that Gisèle constructs for herself as she leaves the "charming" Father-in-Law.

The vacillation the Young Wife feels toward "la belle construction" she has made of her Husband, "le vrai prince charmant," is the same doubt the Young Writer feels about Lemaire, here described as "belle," "et cette courbe un peu molle, un peu ingrate . . . pauvre . . . vulgaire . . . des ailes du nez, du menton, ce n'est rien, il faut faire juste un petit effort, et la grâce, la force captées sur les têtes des statues aztèques?" [and that slightly flabby curve, somewhat unattractive . . . weak . . . common . . . the wings of the nose, the chin, it's nothing, you only have to make a little effort, and the grace, the strength, captured on the heads of aztec statues?] (78). This is the *Martereau* scenario with an older female figure displacing the male one, and professional replacing personal identity. The different sites of the Young Couple's respective identity quests remain in a traditional arena marked by gender, female (private)/male (public), but the distinction is undermined by the way in which the text treats the figure of Alain and Gisèle. Inverting the characteristics of their quests, Gisèle's myth of her father is drawn from more serious literary images than Alain's myth of Germaine Lemaire—

the Young Wife who vacillates between Girl-Child and Adult Woman refers to Shakespeare and Balzac, and the Young Writer aspiring to write Serious Literature uses the epic imagery of a Boy-Child.

The Aspiring Young Writer opens the door to Lemaire's courtyard and imagines "les grands laquais en livrée, figés sur les marches de l'escalier d'honneur" [the tall retainers in livery, frozen on the steps of the main staircase] (77). Alain as Storyteller continues to describe this encounter in epic imagery which marks his affective response to the scene. The visitor whom "la reine" [the queen] is entertaining when the Young Writer arrives is first described as "ce grand garçon dégingandé" [that big, lanky boy], then as "le grand type" [the big guy] (79). When this visitor says something that displeases Her Highness, he becomes "le fou de la reine" [the queen's jester], but as he leaves there is no "trace" of the "buffon" that remains in the "jeune homme." He is now described once again as "dégingandé," but "au visage fin, au regard grave et droit" [with a fine face with a serious, correct look], because at the end of the scene the Young Writer realizes that he could learn a lesson from this visitor, "il faut être lui, il faut avoir son savoir-faire exceptionnel, son habileté, pour s'offrir ces sortes de plaisirs" [I must be him, I must have his exceptional know-how, his skill at offering himself these kinds of pleasures] (90).

Like Gisèle with her Father-in-Law, Alain finds in Germaine Lemaire "un public digne de lui" [an audience worthy of him], but as in the storytelling about his aunt, he goes too far (86). Alain tells "la reine" about his decision to abandon all efforts to obtain his aunt's apartment, to abandon such bourgeois concerns: "—Je vais briser avec tout ça pour toujours. M'échapper. Et c'est vous qui m'aurez aidé'" [—I am going to break with all that forever. Escape. And you are the one who will help me"]. When the telephone rings, the realist touchstone breaks his enthusiasm: "[. . .] elle revient vers lui [. . .], il sait que le spectacle est fini" [(. . .) she comes back toward him (. . .), he knows that the show is over] (88). This is the moment of "débâcle, d'écroulement" [debacle, of collapse], and "il sent qu'il serait dangereux de s'attarder, [. . .] il y a quelque chose de menaçant dans son amabilité un peu mondaine, distante . . . [he feels that it would be dangerous to linger, (. . .) there is something threatening in her politeness, slightly urbane, distant]. The Young Writer describes feeling "rejeté" [rejected] and "dégradé" [degraded], and at the end of the scene runs home, resolved to be "un homme" [a man], angry at himself for being affected by "la célébrité, la gloire" [fame, glory]. Chapter 6 opens with the Young Husband returned, his Young Wife's name on his lips: "Gisèle . . . mon amour, ma femme . . . Gisèle . . . Ce nom exorcise" [Gisèle . . . my love, my wife . . . Gisèle . . . That name exorcises] (90–91).

The myth of total union is a constant preoccupation for the figures in Sarraute's novels. It is perhaps because the myth in which two people become one is so prevalent in images of heterosexual marriage that her couples are particularly susceptible to it, and that the irony with which it is treated is so recognizable. The exchange between the Young Husband and Wife in this chapter represents a desperate attempt to recuperate his estrangement from his Literary Idol by reconstructing the "love nest"; much as Gisèle tries and fails to do when she experiences a similar separation from her Mother. Here Wife and Husband reverse roles and play out a scene she had hoped for during her earlier retreat to her imagination (69). "'Je me sens comme le renard poursuivi par les chasseurs,'" the Husband says, "'on disait toujours que c'était toi mon renardeau, mais cette fois c'est moi qui suis traqué, je viens me réfugier, prends-moi dans tes bras . . .'" ["I feel like the fox chased by the hounds (. . .) . . . they always say that you are my little fox cub, but this time, it's me who is being hunted, I come to take refuge, take me in your arms"] (91).

From the safety of his Wife's arms, the Young Husband describes his afternoon with Germaine Lemaire. The Young Wife's responses break into his discourse and represent her role as "protectrice" [protective] of her Husband's fragile ego, alluded to in her conversation with his Father. The role of Young Wife becomes that of Mother, and she resembles her own as she rephrases his emotions within that "lieu commun": " —Tu vois, Alain, mon chéri, tu vois ce que je te disais, tu vois comme tu étais fou . . . Alors comment c'était?'" [—You see, Alain, my dear, you see what I told you, you see how crazy you were . . . Well how was it?"] When he admits that Lemaire has "une sorte de majesté" [a kind of majesty], Gisèle appropriates the characterization for her own narrative of adoration: "'—Quand je pense qu'Irène me disait l'autre jour qu'il n'y a personne au monde qu'elle admire autant . . . elle donnerait n'importe quoi pour la voir trois minutes, pour l'entendre parler . . .'" " ["—When I think that Irene was telling me the other day that there isn't anyone in the world she admires as much . . . that she would give anything to see her for three minutes, to hear her speak"]. The Young Husband tries to explain how "'tout un coup on se sent surveillé'" ["all of the sudden you feel like you're being watched"], and his Young Wife reassures him: "'Alain, [. . .] je sais pourquoi je t'aime, entre autres choses, mon chéri . . . c'est pour ce genre de choses-là, [. . .] j'aime en toi, cette pureté, cette intégrité . . .'" ["Alain, (. . .) I know why I love you, among other things, my dear . . . it's for this kind of thing, (. . .) I love in you that purity, that integrity"] (92–93).

This exchange inspires the Young Husband to reassert the myth of total union, the one that the Young Wife renounced earlier: " — [. . .]

le bonheur, c'est ça le seul vrai bonheur, cette confiance absolue, cette fusion . . . un seul être . . . je ne sais plus où je finis, où tu commences . . . ils ont raison avec tous leurs vieux mythes'" [— (. . .) happiness, that's the only true happiness, this absolute confidence, this fusion . . . one single being . . . I no longer know where I end and where you begin . . . they are right with their old myths"]. This myth, however, is immediately undermined when the Young Husband confides to his Wife that he told Lemaire "cette histoire de fauteuils" [that thing about the chairs]: " — [. . .] j'ai voulu indirectement lui raconter, à Germaine Lemaire, voir ce qu'elle en penserait . . .'" [— (. . .) I wanted to tell it to her, indirectly, to Germaine Lemaire, to see what she thought about it"]. The Young Wife then becomes defensive of her Private Life, much like her Mother: "—Tu lui as parlé des fauteuils?'" [—You talked to her about the chairs?"] (95). The myth of total union is displaced by an ironic return to the surface.

   The Young Husband's desire for total union with his Wife completely dissipates as the novel continues and is itself displaced by the same desire in relation to Germaine Lemaire. That displacement is felt most acutely in the transition between Chapters 8 and 9. Chapter 8 ends with the Young Wife's words, "'Non, Alain, je t'aime.'" The conflict represented by these words and the tears accompanying them appear to be resolved momentarily as Chapter 9 begins: "Un air de surprise heureuse. Au air d'abandon, de grâce tendre. Les mots se forment n'importe comment, ils jaillissent, transparents et légers, bulles scintillantes qui montent dans un ciel pur et s'évanouissent sans laisser de traces . . ." [A look of happy surprise. A look of abandonment, of tender grace. The words are formed in any fashion, they spurt out, transparent and light, sparkling bubbles that rise in the clear sky and evaporate without leaving a trace . . .] (121). As the sentence continues, however, marked discourse indicates that this passage refers to words that follow, not to the ones preceding it: "'Ah tiens, mais comme je suis content, quelle chance de vous rencontrer [. . .]'" ["Oh, look, how happy this makes me, what luck to run into you (. . .)"] (121). This disorientation marks the chapter throughout and prefigures later moments of tension told from different points of view.[7]

   Alain and his Father run into Germaine Lemaire at a bookshop in Chapter 9, and the point of view is at first from the Son's consciousness: Father is described as looking "si fin, si intelligent" [so fine, so intelligent], the Son observes, "Ils ont l'air de tant s'aimer . . ." [They look like they like each other so much]. An observation about Germaine Lemaire corroborates that all is going well, and though the discourse is unmarked, it appears to be from the Father's point of view: "Mais elle est encore très belle, Germaine Lemaire, tu ne m'avais jamais dit ça [. . .] Une femme courageuse [. . .] qui a dû travailler dur toute sa vie, et si directe, si bon garçon" [But she is still very beautiful, Germaine Lemaire, you never told me that (. . .). A courageous woman (. . .) who must have worked hard all her life, and so direct, such a good chap] (122). Finally marked discourse breaks the overlay of this dual point of view, as the Writer appears to speak for herself: "'Je suis content de vous connaître, Monsieur, j'aime tant votre fils'" ["I am happy to meet you, Monsieur, I like your son so much"] (121–22). The last image which sums up the opening scene undermines the calmness which her phrase provokes in the Young Writer; the image is more characteristic of Alain the Storyteller than Alain the "modest" Young Writer: "Sourire heureux . . . [. . .] scène exquise, . . . délicieuse comédie que jouent à ravir des partenaires si bien assortis" [Happy smile . . . (. . .) exquisite scene, delicious comedy which well-matched partners play beautifully] (123).

The scene is repeated with the point of view in Alain's conscious-ness, that is, Alain the Storyteller who shifts the "comédie" tropis-tically as Alain the Son imagines the Father's possible reaction to the Great Writer:

> Et il s'en est fallu d'un rien [. . .], rien n'aurait pu empêcher qu'au lieu de l'heureuse surprise, [. . .] cette expression de crainte, de désarroi quand elle est apparue [. . .]—derrière la porte vitrée de la librairie. Son père l'observe un peu surpris et, se tournant pour suivre la direction de son regard devenant déjà quelque chose—[. . .] son père voit s'avancer vers eux [. . .] une grosse femme curieusement attifée, les traits taillés à la serpe, l'air d'une marchande à la toilette ou d'une actrice démodée vêtue de bizarres oripeaux (123–24).

> [And a nothing is all it would have taken (. . .), nothing would have been able to prevent, instead of happy surprise, (. . .) that expression of fear, of confusion when she appeared (. . .)—through the windows of the door to the bookstore. His father watches him, a little surprised and, turning to follow the direction of his look, already guessing something—(. . .) his father sees coming toward them (. . .), a big woman, curiously decked out, with craggy features like a shopkeeper who hasn't finished dressing or an actress past her prime wearing peculiar rags.]

The opening negative ("il s'en est fallu d'un rien") and gradual develop-ment of the scene create the threat of tropistic eruption which leads in the end to a dethroning of "la reine." This change divests the Young Writer of the earlier role he imagined for himself as one who is "prêt à exterminer les ignorants, les infidèles" [ready to exterminate the igno-rant ones, the infidels] who threaten the palace of the Queen (78–79). Now he is "un cadavre étalé sur la table de dissection et son père, rajustant ses lunettes, se penche . . ." [a cadaver laid out on the dissec-tion table and his father, readjusting his glasses, leans over . . .] (123–

24). The dissection of the Young Writer's adoration of Germaine Lemaire is carried out by Father and Son. At first the narration barely distinguishes them as the Son investigates images of himself from both points of view.

The operation leads to a renunciation of the Young Writer's adoration of Germaine Lemaire: "Cette fois, tout est fini. Finis les doutes, les craintes, les efforts [. . .]" [This time, it's over. Finished, the doubts, the fears, the effort (. . .)] (127). In spite of that renunciation, the Young Writer cannot help creating epic roles for himself. He moves from identifying himself as a "courtisan abject" [despicable courtier] "à la table d'un tyran cruel" [at a cruel tyrant's table] to being the one who tames "le monstre" [the monster] (128–29). Quotation marks suggest a dialogue between this Hero and his Lady, but the discourse is so overshadowed by the tropistic *sous-conversation*, at times set off only by ellipses within the quotation marks, that any simple identification of interlocutors is difficult and the two figures merge. When the passage ends, the epic remains. The other members of the Lady's party arrive to take her away from her adoring servant: "Ils ont été surpris, [. . .] les barbares les entourent, ils vont les séparer, elle serre sa main dans la sienne, elle retient encore un bref instant sa main tandis qu'ils l'entraînent . . ." [They have been surprised, (. . .) the barbarians surround them, they are going to separate them, she squeezes his hand in her own, she holds his hand a brief instant more as they take her away] (133).

At the end of this chapter the narration returns to the beginning scene at the bookstore where Son and Father run into Germaine Lemaire. The text takes the reader down slowly after the epic crescendo. Parts of the story are replayed, some are downplayed, until the Young Writer commits himself to Lemaire's oblivion: "Peut-être tout de même qu'un jour, même dans plusieurs années, son nom prononcé devant elle [. . .]: 'Alain Guimier [. . .] Qu'est-il devenu, au fait? Il ne manquait pas de talent, [. . .] il préparait un travail, une thèse, sur quoi déjà? . . . Oui, il était très timide, [. . .] bizarre, un curieux garçon . . .'" [Perhaps, all the same, one day, even a few years from now, his name pronounced in her presence (. . .): "Alain Guimier (. . .). What actually happened to him? He didn't lack talent, (. . .) he was working on something, a thesis, now what was it? . . . Yes, he was very timid, (. . .) bizarre, a curious boy"] (136). Even though Lemaire's words appear to be autonomous when read on their own in marked discourse, they are part of the Young Writer's narrative. Most of Alain's *sous-conversation* reflects on his adoration of Germaine Lemaire, and because that depth is represented by imagery from an epic "lieu commun," his reflections remain more limited than those seen in figures which appear to be independent of Alain's consciousness.

In Chapter 10, Alain's father goes to see his sister Berthe to talk about this business of giving the Young Couple her apartment. All the narration stays in his consciousness as he plays out the role he feels she has given him of "père dénaturé, bourré de préjugés ridicules, d'idées préconçues, saugrenues, de 'principes,' je vous demande un peu . . ." [unnatural father, stuffed with ridiculous prejudices, preconceived, preposterous ideas, "principles," I ask you . . .] (137). Alain's Father as Brother also passes through sentiments that are expressed by the details he notices, "ce regard sous les paupières usées, fardées, un bon regard d'où ruisselle une tendre émotion" [that look beneath her worn-out eyelids, dolled up, a good look where a tender emotion flows] (140). His emotions move from one extreme to another, as seen in the progression of the following passage: "Tandis qu'elle le précède à travers l'entrée, le salon, il regarde sans pouvoir en détacher les yeux sa vieille nuque fragile, le petit creux livide [. . .], un endroit très vulnérable, s'offrant innocemment, où plongerait sans rencontrer de résistance le poignard de l'assassin . . ." [While she leads him through the hallway, the living room, he looks without being able to take his eyes away at the old, fragile nape of her neck, the little pale hole (. .), a very vulnerable spot, offering itself innocently, where would plunge, without meeting any resistance, the assassin's knife] (140–41). This encounter between Brother and Sister is treated with a different kind of sensuality than that seen when Brother was Father-in-Law with his "bru." The violence and emotion expressed in *sous-conversation* in this scene also escape the ironic mockery sensed in encounters between the Young Husband and Wife. In this discussion of the Children's lust for Berthe's apartment, Brother and Sister are also joined against "'ces petits monstres [. . .] tu sais bien comment ils sont . . .'" ["those little monsters (. . .) you know very well how they are . . ."] (142).

This chapter began in the Brother's consciousness in *sous-conversation*, but in the end the Brother is immobilized and "petite Berthe" has the last word: "Il fait un geste de la main comme pour l'écarter, la chasser, il pousse une sorte de mugissement, mm . . . mm . . . Elle rit et pose la main sur son bras: '[. . .] Allons, tiens, je vais te faire goûter à mon eau-de-vie de prune, tu m'en diras des nouvelles. Ou tu préfères peut-être que je te prépare une bonne tasse de thé, juste comme tu l'aimes, bouillant, bien infusé . . .'" [He makes a gesture with his hand as if to keep her away from him, to chase her away, he lets out a sort of mooing, mm . . . mm . . . She laughs and puts her hand on his arm: "(. . .) C'mon, here, I am going to give you a taste of my prune brandy, you'll love it. Or would you prefer perhaps a nice cup of tea, just like you like it, boiling, well steeped . . ."] (145–46).

In Chapter 14 the scene between Brother and Sister is repeated from

Berthe's point of view, and it carries the similarly conflicting sentiments. "Le pli de sa bouche" [the fold of his mouth] seems at first
to be hiding "quelque chose d'un peu sournois" [something a little
underhanded], but when "elle regardait la peau trop fine de ses mains
un peu boursouflées" [the overly fine skin of his slightly puffy hands],
"le traître" [the traitor] disappears: "Elle voyait assis devant elle un
vieil homme seul comme elle, abandonné, son frère, son vieux Pierrot
. . ." [she saw seated before her an old man, alone like she was, abandoned, her brother, her old Pierrot] (177–78). In this second version of
their encounter Pierre finally tells Berthe that the Children will have
their way, and that "'tout ce que je veux c'est qu'on me fiche la paix
. . .'" ["all I want is that they leave me the hell alone . . ."]: "'Vous y
viendrez un jour de vous-même, allez, vous verrez ça . . .'" ["One day
you'll come around all by yourself, come on, you'll see . . ."] (183). This
chapter also ends with Berthe's response, but it is not as discourse. She
is described by an image which takes shape after discourse: "Elle se
raidit, se redresse. . . . Eh bien, ils verront. [. . .] Immobile, tassée sur
elle-même, lourde, calme, elle les attend comme le vieux sanglier quand
il se retourne et s'assied face à la meute" [She stiffens, straightens up
. . . All right, they'll see. (. . .) Motionless, settled into herself, heavy,
calm, she waits for them like the old boar when he turns around and
sits down to face the pack] (183).

Le Planétarium begins in Berthe's consciousness as she composed
the "caricature" she would offer to the workmen. The treatment given
both Berthe and Pierre in the above two passages is one in which the
perceptions each has of the other are superimposed in sous-conversation which reflects on those perceptions and thus problematizes any
neat character-ization of either figure by the other or by the reader.

Alain's characterization of himself is also undermined by his Aunt
Berthe. In Chapter 15 she presents another side of her Nephew, and
although it is marked by her dramatic imagery, there is little the reader
has learned about Alain to conflict with this perception: "Attention,
grand fou, qu'est-ce qui lui prend, attention, il va tout renverser, il va
me faire mal, il va me décoiffer, elle s'écarte, elle le repousse légèrement, comme autrefois, quand il était petit" [Look out, big fool, what's
gotten into him, look out, he's going to mess up my hair, he's going to
hurt me, he's going to scalp me, she steps back, she pushes him away
lightly, like in the old days, when he was a child] (184–88). At the end
of their encounter, the Nephew threatens to "bring in the law" if Berthe
does not give the apartment to the Young Couple. The Old Aunt's sous-
conversation explodes with images of "prisonniers évadés, des résistants, des juifs cachés" [escaped prisoners, resistance fighters, hidden
Jews], those who are denounced by people who object to breaking the

law, and her final discourse resonates within that image: "'Mais fais-le donc. Fais-le, tu en es capable. Ça ne m'étonne-ra-pas-de-toi'" ["Well do it. Do it, you're capable of doing it. It would-not-sur-prise-me-one-bit"] (188).

Just as Alain felt his adoration for Lemaire being dissected by his Father in Chapter 9, Germaine Lemaire's group takes the construct "les Guimier" apart in Chapter 16 (189–98). In Chapter 12, however, Lemaire dissects herself after she has read that someone compared her to "Madame Tussaud" (156). Lemaire has been called the master of "realism": "On croit entendre parler vos personnages . . . On les voit si bien, ils sont si vivants . . ." [One almost hears your characters speak . . . you can see them, they are so life-like] (155). The Great Writer's loneliness raises its head with the same ferocity as the Young Writer's timidity, the Young Wife's uncertainty, or the Aunt's defensiveness: "Elle est seule. Aucun recours. Aucun recours de personne" [She is alone. No recourse. No help from anyone] (157). The passage which describes Lemaire looking through her work for a spark of life is written in a prosaic style with short, clipped sentences, and the repetition of the words "figé" [frozen] and "vide" [emptiness] recreate her desperation (155–57).

On one level, Lemaire's reluctance to accept the Crown of Madame Tussaud and her search for "life" in her "realist" writing dramatize Sarraute's critique of what are considered "lifelike" characters in realist novels. At another level, however, this writer's designation as Madame Tussaud puts her uncomfortably in the company of realist (Male) writers, at the same time that the perception other figures in the novel have of her single her out as a Woman. Gisèle's father attacks her as a Woman trying to be a Man, and Gisèle idolizes her as a Beautiful Woman, telling everyone at dinner that "'Je serais rudement contente de lui resembler'" ["I would be quite happy to be like her"] (101–2). When Lemaire recalls the "encounter" with Alain's father, it is Germaine Lemaire as Woman who narrates this version: "Elle s'était sentie soudain exposée, rosissant, frissonnant sous ce regard d'où coulait sur elle [. . .] un mépris d'homme choyé, comblé depuis longtemps de grâce, de jeunesse, de beauté, un dégoût d'amateur délicat pour une femme . . . mais elle n'avait pas l'air d'une femme, elle était [. . .] un monstre" [She had suddenly felt exposed, blushing, shivering beneath that look which poured onto her (. . .) the scorn of a pampered man, filled for a long time with grace, youth, beauty, a delicate, amateur disgust for a woman . . . But she didn't look like a woman, she was (. . .) a monster] (164).

The Young Writer's adoration of the Great Writer is similar to the nephew's adoration of Martereau. Whereas the nephew reconstructs Martereau through his desired image of masculinity which combines

certain qualities designated as "feminine," especially sensitivity and
nurturing, with a "masculine" control of emotions, Alain's image of
Lemaire moves between set images of Woman. When he describes Lemaire as "la reine," Alain can thus cast himself as her Servant, but that
mythic image is superimposed onto the dichotomous image in Chapter
9 where he sees her through his Father's eyes as "une actrice démodée."
When Lemaire and her entourage leave Alain's apartment after a surprise visit, he remarks that "elle lui offre une dernière fois son visage
amical, presque tendre" [she offers him one last time her friendly face,
almost tender]. This "friendly" tenderness diffuses the earlier images
of Lemaire as authoritative and powerful, and that myth is further undermined when Lemaire offers to help Alain furnish his new apartment
should his aunt offer it to him. "'Je vous aiderai à le meubler, j'adore
ça'" ["I'll help you furnish it, I love that"], are Lemaire's parting words,
"'Nous irons à la Foire aux Puces'" ["We'll go to the Flea Market"].
"'Oui, moi aussi, c'est ma passion'" ["Yes, mine too, it's my passion"],
Alain responds, "'on se comprend . . .'" ["we understand one another . . ."] (175).

For each of the figures who describes her, Alain, Gisèle and her father, Lemaire is perceived first as a Woman. Whereas Sarraute's male
writer figures are constantly plagued by self-doubt about the "trueness"
of their art, this single female writer figure gives imagery to the docu-
mented anxiety that many women writers have expressed about their
position as artist in a male-dominated domain. This is an anxiety
which Sarraute has reportedly not experienced, and she should be
taken at her word. The presence of the figure of Lemaire in Sarraute's
novel, however, opens up the space of that reality.

Germaine Lemaire visits the Young Couple in the final chapter. Gisèle
is there as well, silently preparing the tea. From within the Young
Husband's sous-conversation, the Young Wife is blamed for the re-
straint he feels in Lemaire's presence: "Ce n'est pas sa faute à lui [. . .].
Voilà, il le sait, ce qui empêche ses sentiments de couler forts, libres,
chaleureux, dans ses mouvements, c'est cette masse inerte, là, près de
lui, ce bloc lourd . . ." [It's not his fault (. . .). There, he knows what it
is that keeps his feelings from running strong, free, warm, in his movements, it's that inert mass, there, near him, that heavy block . . .] (239).
Given the reader's experience of both Alain and Gisèle, however, the
neatness of this image is undermined. Gisèle has already assumed a
certain "épaisseur" because of her earlier sous-conversation. Like Aunt
Berthe, Gisèle is silent now. The reader's effort to character-ize this
figure is displaced by the variety of perceptions through which she has
been represented. It is Alain's sous-conversation which dominates the
last chapter and which reveals that his adolescent side is still the origin
of his perceptions.

Any reader's desire for an ending to this novel is fulfilled when the tour of the Young Couple's recently acquired apartment ends up at the famous door. Lemaire recognizes it: "'C'est celle qui a tant fait souffrir votre tante?'" ["Is this the one that upset your aunt so?"] (242). That story is far away now, empty compared to all the chapters of tropistic movement and introspection that followed from it. Now the door is the object of Alain's tropistic response to Lemaire: "En un instant la plus étonnante, la plus merveilleuse métamorphose se produit. Comme touchée par la baguette d'une fée, la porte [. . .] était apparue, enchâssée dans les murs d'un vieux cloître, d'un couvent [. . .], il fait une pirouette joyeuse [. . .]" [In the most surprising instant, the most marvelous metamorphosis takes place. As if touched by a fairy's wand, the door (. . .) appeared, set in the walls of an old cloister, of a convent (. . .), he does a joyous pirouette] (243).

Alain is given more space in this novel than any of the other figures, but the reader's sense of his "épaisseur subjective" has suffered for it as each of his constructions falls tumbling down. The complexity of Alain's identity is only maintained in the various versions of the encounter between Father, Son, and Lemaire in Chapter 9. As Young Husband his desire for total union with his Wife is undermined by her visit to see his Father. As Young Rebellious Artist, his attempt to escape bourgeois life is revealed to be a farce when he threatens to "call in the law" if his Aunt does not give him her apartment. The role the Young Writer has cast for Lemaire appears to be constructed in order that he might have a role as Adoring Servant.

That role is threatened toward the end of the last chapter when Alain mentions to Lemaire that he has seen a critic whom they both know, Lebat. Just as Berthe tried to get rid of the spot on the door, Alain tries at first to efface the animation he notices on Lemaire's face when Lebat's name is mentioned. When Lemaire defends Lebat, the exchange is presented without Alain's *sous-conversation*; but when he changes his approach and admits that he would like Lebat to be his friend, that depth reality is reopened: "Mais qu'elle le rabroue, qu'elle se dégage, qu'elle refuse de se courber, de s'agenouiller avec lui devant l'autre, l'étranger, qu'elle se redresse donc, qu'elle le force lui aussi à se redresser . . ." [But let her rebuff him, let her break free, let her refuse to bow down, to kneel with him before the other, the stranger, let her straighten up then, so that she can force him to straighten up as well . . .] (251). Alain is left looking to others for his perception of himself, at the same time that he criticizes Lebat for appearing to care about others' perceptions of him.

Lemaire's response to Alain's criticism of Lebat ends the novel. She has the last word, and all the other perceptions of her recede as her discourse assumes its presence. The banality of her statement, like her

offer to look for furniture at the Flea Market, also deflates all the constructions Alain has been projecting on Lemaire and others throughout
the novel: "'Oh ça, vraiment . . . Tout en lui, tout autour de lui se défait
. . . Vous êtes sévère. Je crois que nous sommes bien tous un peu comme
ça'" ["Oh, now really . . . Everything in him, everything around him
comes apart . . . You are severe. I think that we are all a little bit like
that"] (251).

Entre la vie et la mort

Le Planétarium takes the reader into the universality of "le lieu commun," a place of mythical constructs by which all narrative figures
constitute gender identity, familial and marital relationships. The tropistic representation of these myths reveals that they are used in several
different situations. Gisèle as Daughter effaces her separation from her
Father by making him into King Lear. The creation of myths expresses
as well the longing for an unattainable ideal when the Young Wife
vacillates between perceptions of Young Husband as "le beau prince
charmant" [the handsome prince charming] and "un nourrisson
couvé" [an over-protected, unweaned child], and when the Young Artist
moves between his vision of the Great Writer as "la reine" [the queen]
and "une actrice démodée" [an actress past her prime]. The tropistic
representation of the encounter between Berthe and Pierre exposed
conflicting myths of love and anger.

Through a heightened play of pronouns and a broader use of synecdoche to evoke the sensation of a perception, Entre la vie et la mort
takes the reader into the universality of tropisms in a way that none of
the earlier novels does. Tropistic perception is recreated, not in the text
of a male narrator masquarading as neutral, nor as the emotional depth
beneath myths. There are no named figures in Entre la vie et la mort,
such that the increased ambiguity of origins of discourse combines
with the movement of figures into all pronominal positions to sustain
the reader's experience of tropisms in a style closer to that of the prose
pieces in Tropismes. Differences between figures are more clearly recognized in this novel as a difference in positions of discourse. The
fluidity of the figures' relationship to discourse gives the reader the
experience of changing positions in relation to the socio-symbolic
structure that it represents. The play of pronouns found in Entre la vie
et la mort dramatizes the exchange between Alain and one of the female figures in Le Planétarium in which the former asserts that "tout
le monde se ressemble" [everyone is like everyone else], and the latter
responds that "je vous garantis que je ne suis pas comme vous" [I assure

you that I am not like you]. Universality in *Entre la vie et la mort* is not represented by either statement, it is rather in the gesture of the exchange itself.

That gesture takes place at the level of relationships between individual subjects and at the level of an individual subject's relationship to language. Language as an invitation to exchange is more clearly seen in this novel to be the "social contract" that Monique Wittig describes, "one where there are neither men nor women, neither races nor oppression, nothing but what can be named progressively, word by word, language. Here we are all free and equal or there would be no possible pact, [. . .] there would be no meaning." The speaking subject initially enters into this "social contract" as a "hero [. . .] to which the world, which it forms and deforms at will, belongs." By entering into exchange with another *je*, however, or even more dangerously, with a plural *ils* or *elles*, the *je* is taken prisoner. "Absolute liberty, the necessary reciprocity" of the contract, Wittig continues, becomes "but a surrender." Wittig notes that this conflict takes place at various levels in all of Sarraute's novels: "[. . .] the strange wrenching, the tension in the movement from particular to general, experienced by any human when from an 'I'—unique in language, shapeless, boundless, infinite—it suddenly becomes nothing or almost nothing, 'you,' 'he,' 'she,' 'a small, rather ugly fellow,' an interlocutor."[8]

In *Entre la vie et la mort* the central figure becomes the site of the conflict, and this figure is given many surfaces, only one of which is male. Both *ils* and *elles* represent "le lieu commun," and once the central male figure's images are juxtaposed with those of other female figures, *elles* is released from the status as Absolute Other that it retained in *Portrait* and *Martereau*, where the narrator as Every Man obscured gender bias. The conflict inherent in the contract in *Entre la vie et la mort* is not represented in terms of gender distinctions. The tension settles instead on the figure of *je* joining or separating from a plural *ils*, *elles*, *vous*, or *nous*, best seen in a passage from Chapter 10. The chapter begins with the words, "Vous voilà donc, parmi nous" [There you are now, here among us], and this *nous* elaborates itself, introducing each paragraph:

Nous aussi, comme vous [. . .]. Nous qui ne sommes pas capables de ne pas nous répéter [. . .]. Nous avons tous appris [. . .]. Nous formons à nous tous un petit bloc homogène, fait de la même substance. [. . .]. Nous sommes là, vous nous entendez? [. . .] Nous. Qui nous? Vos pareils. Chacun enfermé comme vous. [. . .] —Qui nous? —Vous le saurez. —Je ne veux pas le savoir. [. . .] Mais pas moi, je ne veux pas. [. . .] Il est tout pareil à eux, semblable à eux, il le sait bien. [. . .] C'est juste ce nous, quand ils l'emploient en faisant

allusion à quelque chose de si intime, de si unique ... [. . .] Le nous est
dégradant.[9]

[Us too, like you (. . .). We who are incapable of not repeating ourselves (. . .).
We have all learned (. . .). We form unto ourselves a little homogenous block,
made of the same substance. (. . .) We are here, do you hear us? (. . .) Us. Who
us? Your similars. Each one closed up like you. (. . .) —Who us? —You'll
learn. —I don't want to know. (. . .) But not me, I don't want to. (. . .) He is
just like them, similar to them, he knows that. (. . .) It's just this us, when
they use it as a way of alluding to something intimate, something so unique
... (. . .) The us is degrading.]

With little punctuation marking the origin of discourse, the separation,
joining, and objectifying gesture is operated by the pronouns themselves as they appear on the page.

In Le Planétarium the presence of antecedents for the personal pronouns allows for an investigation of the way in which the antecedent is
constructed as character. Sarraute's third novel plays with the illusory
nature of "character," that is, character as social and personal construct
and character as literary convention. As Newman observes, "à l'opposé
du texte historique où 'Napoléon' renvoie à une réalité vécue, dans le
roman 'Alain Guimier' est dépourvu du référent 'réel,' ne renvoyant qu'à
un simulacre doué d'une existence imaginaire dans la seule mesure où
un signe se trouve dans le texte pour postuler cette existence" [as opposed to the historical text in which "Napoléon" refers back to a lived
reality, in the novel "Alain Guimier" is deprived of a "real" referent,
referring simply to a simulacre endowed with an imaginary existence
only insofar as a sign is in the text in order to postulate that existence].[10]
Sarraute's fifth novel also plays with the illusory nature of character,
but the relative absence of antecedents and marked discourse destroys
the surface created by names or name substitutes found in previous
novels, as well as the line between conversation and sous-conversation.
The dichotomy between interior and exterior is less marked in this
novel, and the reader's orientation depends much more on the moment
of discourse.

One of the consequences of this disorientation in all of Sarraute's
novels is that any meaning created by the language is continually ambiguous, especially in relation to what can be read as ironic. As a
convention, irony results from an incongruity between apparent and
intended meaning, but as Newman explains, the "ironie irréductible"
[irreducible irony] of Sarraute's work is that "la signification des mots
est autre" [the meaning of words is other].[11] As seen in the previous
novels discussed, irony reflected back on one or another of the narrative
figures and/or on the reader's perception and response to figures. With

fewer figures on which to project irony in *Entre la vie et la mort*, the
reader's criteria for establishing it becomes a more personal one.

When the figure of *je* returns to the narration as *moi* in the passage
discussed above, the image and the repetition of the pronoun representing this figure move between a certain horrifying reality and one resembling a cartoon: "Il lève la tête, s'il hurlait à la lune . . . Mais moi. Mais
moi, moi, jamais . . . C'est une idée qui ne me vient pas. Une idée
ignoble . . . de petit" [He raises his head, why not howl at the moon
. . . But me. But me, me, never . . . It's an idea that doesn't come from
me. An ignoble idea . . . small] (86). And as if the text expected an
empathetic reader, another presence enters the narration: "Des yeux où
la satisfaction s'étale en une tache huileuse se posent sur les siens . . .
mais moi non plus [. . .]. Moi, en tout cas, je suis comme vous. Je vous
comprends" [Eyes where satisfaction spreads out in an oily spot come
to rest on his own . . . But me neither (. . .). I, in any case, I'm like you.
I understand you] (86). If those same words might have fluttered
through a reader's consciousness, they hesitate to land when *je* takes
control of the play of pronouns: "Il sent la répulsion monter en lui
[. . .]. Vous, le plus chétif de tous, vous que j'ai été surpris de trouver,
même ici parmi eux, vous dont la présence, plus que celle de tout autre,
a éveillé mes craintes, mon dégoût, vous dont la promiscuité me couvre
de honte . . . Vous . . . [. . .] Regardez-vous. Voici votre image reflétée
dans mes yeux. Voyez ce miniscule tas gris" [He feels repulsion rising
to the surface (. . .). You, the most puny of all, you who I was surprised
to find, even here among them, you whose presence, more than any
other, awakened my fears, my disgust, you whose promiscuity covers
me in shame . . . You . . . (. . .) Look at yourself. Here is your image
reflected in my eyes. Look at this miniscule gray spot] (86–87).

The *il* in this passage is the central figure of the novel and its referent
is often designated by critics as "a writer." That designation, however,
like the name "Alain Guimier," can obscure the *imaginary* existence
that this figure represents. *Entre la vie et la mort* does not represent
the existence of a writer, it presents a narrative figure in the *act of
imagining* a writer's existence. The dynamic quality of that act is sustained by this figure's movement between the designations *je* and *il*.
Because of the play of pronouns and the unmarked discourse, these
designations move beyond the discursive paradigm of subject and object and into the more ambiguous territory of "subject for whom" and
"object for whom." The figure of *il* as writer begins the novel in its
most stylized existence.

Discourse in the first person is designated in the opening pages by
quotation marks and is surrounded by a narration resembling stage
directions: "Il hoche le tête, il plisse les paupières, les lèvres . . . 'Non,

décidément, ça ne va pas.' Il étend le bras, il le replie . . . 'J'arrache la page. [. . .] Je jette'" [He shakes his head, he squints his eyes, wrinkles his lips . . . "No, definitely, that's not it." He stretches out his arm, he folds it back . . . "I rip out the page. (. . .) I toss"] (7). This figure as *je* represents a commanding subject because of what it represents as *il* for his audience.

Even so, another subject cannot resist stepping onto the stage: "Et elle maintenant, sa compagne effacée, pose son regard au loin, contemple une image . . . 'Tout le bureau en est jonché.' Elle parle d'une voix très douce" [And her now, his self-effacing companion, looks into the distance, contemplates an image . . . "The whole office is littered with them." She speaks in a very soft voice] (7). The attributes assigned to the figure of *elle* at first construct a traditionally gendered configuration. "Sa compagne effacée" comments in a "wifelike" manner about the mess he leaves in his office. This configuration continues as the narration ignores the intervention of this "compagne effacée" and descends below marked discourse. The split between *je* and *il* remains, but without punctuation, and this *sous-conversation* gives the central figure a certain interiority: "Je reprends une nouvelle feuille. Ses doigts s'agitent. [. . .] Parfois je me réveille la nuit, je m'interroge. A quoi bon tant de luttes, d'efforts? Pourquoi, mon Dieu, pour quoi?" [I take another piece of paper. His fingers move. (. . .) Sometimes I wake up in the night, I ask myself. What's the use of so many battles, so much effort? Why, my God, why and what for?] (8).

Undermining the depth of this interiority, a subject speaks in marked discourse and addresses the question above. "'Oui. Moi aussi'" ["Yes. Me too"] (8). This *moi* (which the reader soon discovers is another/the same *elle*) is not the subject whom *ils* wish to make the object of their regard; this "hero" is taken prisoner: "Tous les yeux se tournent vers elle et se fixent. Que fait-elle? Qu'est-ce qui lui prend?" [All eyes turn around toward her and stare. What's she doing? What's got into her?] (8). Negative and affirmative responses rise up from the "lieu commun": "C'est l'impulsion sacrilège [. . .] . . . Non, c'est un excès de candeur, l'innocence d'une âme très pure . . . Moi aussi—tout simplement. Ne sommes-nous pas tous pareils, tous semblables, des frères?" [It's a sacrilegious impulse (. . .) . . . No, it's an excessive candor, the innocence of a very pure soul . . . Me too—just that. Aren't we all alike, all the same, all brothers?] (8). The *moi* persists, and by his response *il* allows this figure a position in the discourse: "'Moi aussi, parfois, comme vous, la nuit surtout je me demande . . .' [. . .] Il opine de la tête lentement . . . 'Ah, vous aussi . . .'" ["Me too, sometimes, like you, at night especially, I wonder . . ." (. . .) He nods slowly . . . "Ah, you too . . ."] (8). In the end the pressure is too great for *moi*, and the referent for the figure in the narrative returns to *elle*, that is, one of *ils*: "[. . .] elle s'écarte, elle rentre dans le cercle" [(. . .) she withdraws, she returns to the circle] (9).

Now that the "scène" has been interrupted, *ils* continue the "jeu," "le spectacle est trop amusant" [the show's too good]. With this continuation, the configuration of assertive-male-writer and self-effacing-female-wife dissolves because another figure is introduced, another *je*: "'Et vous?' On me tire. [. . .] On me pousse, on me jette devant lui, je tombe à ses pieds . . . Il me prend par le menton, [. .] échauffé, je me dégage, je cours me réfugier parmi eux. Me voici de nouveau l'un d'eux, un chaînon anonyme. Nos yeux sont fixés sur lui" ["And you?" I'm pulled. (. . .) I'm pushed, I'm thrown before him, I fall at his feet . . . He takes me by the chin, (. . .) overheated, I pull myself away, I run to take refuge among them. Here I am again, one of them, an anonymous link. Our eyes are fixed on him] (9–10). The initial order is restored, except that the original object of "leurs yeux," the writer, is now interpreted more intimately through "nos yeux": "[. . .] une moitié de lui-même [. . .] prend place parmi nous dans le cercle [. . .], l'autre moitié restée au milieu du cercle s'efforce comme elle peut de nous aider [à percer le mystère] . . ." [(. . .) one half of him [. . .] takes a place among us in the circle] (. . .), the other half remaining in the middle of the circle makes the best possible effort (to penetrate the mystery). . .](10).

Returned to center stage, *il* assumes the role of *je* for *ils*, now addressed as *vous*: "'Vous savez, j'ai été orphelin de bonne heure . . . un enfant unique, sans père. Pas aimé et trop aimé . . .' Mais nous honchons la tête" ["You know, I was an orphan at an early age . . . an only child, without a father. Not loved and too loved . . ." But we shake our heads] (10). When this central figure refers to "ma machine à écrire" at the end of the first chapter, the gestures from the beginning are repeated, but now through the subtext of "nos yeux": "'Je prends une nouvelle feuille blanche.' [. . .] Comment? Un rythme dans la tête? Une arabesque que les mots dessinent? Sa tête tourne de gauche à droite . . ." ["I take another blank page." (. . .) What? A rhythm in his head? An arabesque drawn by words? His head turns from left to right] (12).

Wittig refers to the opening passage of Chapter 3 in this novel when she calls *I* a "hero," for this chapter is an examplary instance of a subject in the process of forming and deforming the world "at will": "Hérault, héraut, héros, aire, haut, erre haut, R.O., rythmné sur le bruit du train roulant à travers les plates plaines blanches" [Hérault, herald, hero, area, high, roam high, R.O., rhymed in the sound of the train rolling through the flat, white plains] (22). The "hero" in this chapter encounters the conflict that Wittig describes, but without being taken prisoner until the end. The narration moves between unmarked and marked discourse, the child's rumination on the words which open the chapter and the words addressed to the child by another voice: "—Combien d'enfants seraient ravis de pouvoir faire un pareil voyage'" [—How many other children would be thrilled to make such a journey"] (23). Both positions are represented in *sous-conversation*, though neither is clearly the origin. By its content, however, the reader imagines mother and son in a silent and familiar struggle.

When *elle* succeeds in bringing discourse back to the surface, the tropistic reaction of both figures which surrounds this discourse separates them: "'Je t'ai entendu tout à l'heure . . .' il se rétracte légèrement . . . elle se penche, allons, encore un peu de patience et ce sera fini . . . 'Tu répétais un mot . . . —Oh non, ce n'était rien. —Si. Dis-moi. [. . .].' Il faut être raisonnable, c'est pour son bien . . . [. . .] 'Je répétais le nom d'un département. Hérault [. . .]'" ["I heard you a little while ago . . ." he withdraws slightly . . . she leans forward, come on, just a little patience and this will be over . . . "You were repeating a word . . . —Oh no, it wasn't anything. —Yes it was. Tell me. (. . .)." Let's be reasonable, it's for his own good . . . (. . .) "I was repeating the name of a department. Hérault. (. . .)"] (25–26).

The marked exchange about geography which follows characterizes only the surface of this interaction. As seen in Chapter 1, however, a surface which pretends to exist in opposition to a depth is just as quickly opened up to mingle with that depth. In the earlier scene the *sous-conversation* of the central figure reveals that "il se réveille la nuit," and a discursive figure responds in marked discourse, "moi aussi. . . ." When the narration returns to *sous-conversation* after the marked exchange about geography in Chapter 3, an image serves to bring it to the surface of these two figures' discourse: "Qu'est-ce que tu rumines encore? [. . .] regarde ces petites maisons . . . à ton âge, je pouvais rester devant elles pendant des heures, mon coeur fondait . . . ces fenêtres ouvragées . . . comme des dentelles, regarde ces jolies couleurs . . . et tous ces pots de fleurs, ces rideaux blancs . . . c'est comme les maisons des contes de fées . . . celle-ci . . . tu la vois?" [What are you still brooding about? (. . .) look at those pretty houses . . . at your age, I could stand in front of them for hours, my heart melting . . . those carved windows . . . like lace, look at the pretty colors . . . and all those flower pots, those white curtains . . . it's like a house from a fairy tale . . . that one . . . do you see it?] (26).

The will of the parent is marked by the imperatives, softened commands to see the world as she does, as she did, the domestic detail and fairy tales that she saw as a child. Her commands insist but they also invite: "Viens voir les petits lapins, n'aie pas peur, étends ta main, c'est doux, n'est-ce pas? on dirait de la soie . . . caresse-les . . ." [Come see the little rabbits, don't be afraid, put out your hand, it's soft, isn't it? you'd think it was silk . . . pet them] (26). The child responds in *sous-conversation*, "un courant sorti d'elle le traverse, lui fait étendre la main et la promener sur la fourrure des lapins" [a current from her passes through him, makes him put out his hand and pass it over the rabbits' fur], and the passage continues to enumerate what he touches and sees at her invitation (27).

Whereas the mother's expression focuses on sensation and color, that of the son loses any evocative power when he describes the game he has been playing with his own discourse: "'Regarde ce que je fais. D'un seul mot je peux faire surgir des images de toutes sortes. On peut les varier . . . —De quels mots, mon chéri? —Par exemple du mot hérault . . . il en donne plein . . . il suffit de le prononcer, l'image sort. Hérault . . . et je fais venir la maison de Tatie. Héraut . . . un héraut s'avance sur la route, vers le château fort . . . Héros . . . un officier en habit blanc . . . il crie, il s'élance, ses hommes le suivent" ["Look what I'm doing. From one single word I can make all kinds of images. You can vary them . . . —What words, my darling? —For example, the word *hérault* . . . it's full of them . . . just pronounce the word and the image comes out. *Hérault* . . . and I make Tatie's house come out. *Hérault* . . . a herald comes along the road, toward a big fort . . . *Héros* . . . an officer in a white uniform . . . he calls out, rushes forward, his men follow him] (27).

These are not the mother's images, so *elle* joins the game, "'tiens, en voilà d'autres, je vais t'en donner'" ["here, there are others, I'll give them to you"]: "'Tu as Air haut . . . Une belle princesse qui descend fièrement les marches de marbre rose de son palais. Elle se tient tête haute. Les courtisans s'inclinent sur son passage. Elle regarde au loin d'un air pensif . . .'" ["You have lofty Air . . . A beautiful princess who proudly descends the rose marble staircase of her palace. She holds her head high. The courtiers bow as she passes. She looks off in the distance with a pensive air"] (27–28). Other images elaborated by *elle* incorporate an attention to details and color. In addition to enacting the power play that adults often use on children to direct their imagination, the mother's appropriation of the child's word game also reveals that many can play, and the gender bias of his imagery is more obvious when it is juxtaposed with her own. This scene takes place in Chapter 3, which establishes early in the novel the inflection of the central figure's personal and sexual identity on all of his subsequent perceptions.

At the end of this chapter the mother's marked discourse brings the reader out the tropistic interaction between these two figures. The use of the third-person pronoun to refer to the son creates the sense of another presence which then emerges: "'Des mots . . . Il se répète des mots. Il joue avec des mots . . . [. . .].' Il sent leurs regards qui l'effleurent comme en passant [. . .], il connaît des échanges muets entre eux . . . tandis qu'elle le pousse devant elle . . ." ["Words . . . He repeats words. He plays with words . . . (. . .)." He feels their look brush past him (. . .), he knows those silent exchanges between them . . . while she pushes him in front of them] (30). The repetition of the pronoun *ils* as the passage continues enacts a textual claustrophobia associated with any group designated by the third-person plural in the novel, masculine or feminine. That threat is usually created by spatial imagery of physical proximity, as when "ils le cernent de plus près" [they circle round him more closely] (105), or "elles gardent les issues" [they block the exits] (36).

In the scene at the end of Chapter 3, the threat represented by *elles* is given a particular image which recalls those used by the male narrators in *Portrait* and *Martereau*: "[. . .] le bout pointu de leurs doigts grassouillets aux ongles peints se redresse comme la queue d'un scorpion" [(. . .) the pointed end of their fattish fingers with painted nails straightens up like the tail of a scorpion] (37). The potential of this image to represent an Absolute (feminine) other, as similar images did in the first two novels, is unrealized in part because descriptions of a threatening presence in *Entre la vie et la mort* are represented by pronouns of both genders. In addition, the "fattish fingers" in Chapter 1 become the object of irony in Chapter 13 when a figure questions the writer figure about the origin of this very image: "'Allons, ne niez pas. Avouez. [. . .] Ces doigts grassouillets aux bouts pointus qui se redressent. Je sais où vous les avez pris. [. . .] Ce sont les doigts de Mme. Jacquet'" ["Come on, don't deny it. Confess. (. . .) Those fattish fingers with pointed ends that straighten up. I know where you got them. (. . .) They're Madame Jacquet's fingers"] (104). There is a similar image in another scene between the central figure and his mother in Chapter 15, and though the horror is not reduced, it is contextualized: "[. . .] elle lui enfonce dans la chair les longues pointes de ses ongles peints . . ." [(. . .) she sinks into his skin long, pointed, painted nails] (122).

In the process of imagining himself as a "writer," *il* inevitably represents himself through the eyes of Mother and Father. Even though *je* announced in Chapter 1 that he was an "orphelin, sans père," a chapter is devoted to each parent. Both scenes take place after the central figure has had his book accepted for publication. The difference between the representation of each parent highlights the gendered side of the central figure. The distinctions are classic: the Father's chapter is about the Father, the Mother's chapter is about the Son.

The Father's chapter (113–20) opens with a question which takes the writer "entre hommes" [among men], "'combien t'a-t-on pris pour publier ça?'" ["how much did they get from you to publish that?"]; then the narration slips into *sous-conversation:* "Que les faibles femmes crédules pleurent de joie en s'étreignant derrière la porte. Ici, entre hommes, on 'connaît la musique'" [Let the credulous women cry for joy while embracing one another behind the door. Here, among men, we "know the score"] (114). This statement turns *il* into "le garçonette en culotte courte" [the little boy in shorts] and the past is superimposed on the present.

[. . .] la vieille servante qui lui barre le chemin, un doigt sur les lèvres . . . "Où vas-tu? Tu sais bien que ton père travaille [. . .]," mais il la fait pivoter, il l'embrasse sur ses joues ridées . . . "Ne crains rien, [. . .] je vais lui faire une surprise [. . .]," il bondit, il se penche pardessus l'épaule de son père, [. . .] "Tu sais . . . J'ai écrit un livre et il a été pris. [. . .]."
La main tenant le stylo continue à glisser sur la feuille de papier à lettres à en-tête gravé . . . la main s'arrête, se redresse, la plume du stylo levée, le regard entre les paupières rapprochées fixe intensément quelque chose droit devant soi . . . "Combien t'a-t-on pris pour publier ça?" (113–14).

[(. . .) the old servant who stood in his way, a finger to her lips . . . "Where are you going? You know very well that your father is working (. . .)," but he turns her around, he kisses her on her wrinkled cheeks . . . "Don't worry about a thing, (. . .) I am going to give him a surprise" (. . .), he jumps, he leans over his father's shoulder, (. . .) "You know what . . . I wrote a book and it's been accepted." (. . .)
The hand holding the pen continues to slide over the sheet of engraved stationary . . . the hand stops, straightens itself, the tip of the pen raised, the look between the half-closed lids stares at something out in front . . . "How much did they get from you to publish that?"]

The emotional tension created by this passage is replaced by military images. The "garçonnette" becomes "le déserteur" [the deserter] returned to his unit: "[. . .] il veut combattre avec nous dans nos rangs . . ." [(. . .) he wants to fight with us, alongside us . . .] (115). The "déserteur" arrives with his hands up, but "de tous côtés des fusils sont braqués sur lui: 'Combien t'a-t-on pris?'" [on all sides guns are pointed at him: "How much did they take you for?"].

The repetition of the question intensifies the emotion it provokes as the thoughts of the other *il* participates: "Il connaît depuis longtemps les plans de l'ennemi [. . .]. Il sait prévoir quels détours prendra pour s'introduire ici, bien camouflé, tous feux éteints, son énorme besoin de conquêtes, de domination. Il le guette depuis longtemps" [He's known the enemy's plans for a long time (. . .). He knows how to predict what detours its enormous need for conquests, for domination, will take to

slip in here, well camouflaged, all fires extinguished. He has been waiting a long time] (116). Not until the "déserteur" gives a proper response
to the question can he be admitted "entre hommes": "'Mais rien. Je n'ai
rien payé du tout. Au contraire, j'ai reçu une avance'" ["Why nothing. I
didn't pay anything at all. On the contrary, I received an advance"]
(117). Everything changes with the statement, and other lines are
drawn: "'Chez nous, vous savez, dans ma famille, de mon côté, on a
toujours été des travailleurs'" ["In our house, you know, in my family,
the family on my side, we have always been workers"] (118).

The chapter ends with the same voice repeating another phrase, and
the silence of the central figure is contained in *sous-conversation:* "'Ah
il a du talent au moins, celui-là . . .' et il se sent tout à coup saisi
férocement, la main épaisse s'abat sur lui, appuie, le force à se courber,
à s'agenouiller, là, devant n'importe qui [. . .]" ["Ah at least he has talent,
that one . . ." and he feels all at once brutally seized, the thick hand
beats down on him, pushes, forces him to bend, to kneel, there, before
anyone (. . .)] (120).

The chapter devoted to the figure of the Mother follows without a
break after an opening paragraph. *Il* remains at first in an observing
position in relation to *elle:* "[. . .] il faut se soumettre à l'ordre, accepter
de voir enfin les choses comme elles sont . . . voir ce visage levé vers
lui, sillonné par toutes les rides que tracent sur les visages des mères
aimantes les sacrifices, soucis [. . .]" [(. . .) he must submit to the order
of things, accept to see things finally as they are . . . to see this face
raised up toward him, furrowed with all the wrinkles drawn on the
faces of loving mothers by sacrifices, cares (. . .)] (121–22). Whereas the
figure of the Father is introduced by his "discours," that of the Mother
is created by a synecdochical description originating from the son's
consciousness and creating a child's sensual relationship to a parent;
and again the past is superimposed on the present: "[. . .] il passe ses
doigts sur les cheveux encore blonds, si doux, douces plumes d'oiselet
. . . seule la peau de ses joues, de son front a cette douceur [. . .] . . . ses
lèvres d'enfant aspirent son parfum [. . .]" [(. . .) he runs his fingers over
the still blond hair, so soft, soft feathers of a baby bird . . . only the skin
on her cheeks, on her forehead has that softness (. . .) . . . his child's
lips breathe in her perfume (. . .)] (122).

The quality of the mother-son relationship described in the opening
phrase of the paragraph, "les choses comme elles sont," includes in-
flecting the role and discourse of the Mother with religious terms of
devotion: "[. . .] les mères savent pardonner, les mères oublient aussitôt
toutes les offenses" [(. . .) mothers know how to pardon, mothers soon
forget all offenses]: "'Mais mon enfant, [. . .] je te l'ai dit, je n'ai jamais
douté [. . .]. Depuis toujours j'ai su.' Su. Comme elle a dit ça en appuy-

ant. [. . .] Su . . . l'indicible . . . Ce qu'on ne peut nommer [. . .]. Vierges
que l'ange annonciateur a visitées, portant dans leur sein l'enfant prédestiné . . . Mères des Dalaï-lama . . ." ["But my child, (. . .) I've told
you, I never doubted (. . .) I have always *known*." Known. How she said
that with emphasis. (. . .) Known . . . the unsayable . . . What cannot be
named (. . .). Virgins visited by the annunciating angel, carrying in their
breast the preordained child . . . Mothers of Dali-Lamas] (123–24). The
uninterrupted narration continues from the open quotation marks, but
it flows in and out of orientation with *elle* and with *il*.

A moment from the past appears, Mother and Son walking in the
country. The mother is represented by *elle* as if the son were describing
them both with his epic imagery—"quand elle le promenait, le guidait,
jeune prince héritier" [when she took him on walks, guided him, the
young prince]. At another moment, *il* refers to the son and suggests a
reversal of orientation, "il s'arrache brutalement" [he pulls away bru-
tally], or "il pousse des cris sauvages" [he lets out wild cries] (124).
There are also exchanges in which *je* addresses *tu*, acting out the devotion suggested at the beginning of the chapter: [. . .] "mais elle ne le
perd jamais de vue, elle le suit [. . .] . . . Même quand tu avais tes mauvais moments [. . .], je n'ai jamais douté. Je savais" [(. . .) but she never
loses sight of him, she follows him (. . .) . . . Even when you had your
bad moments, (. . .) I never doubted. I knew] (124). The religious imagery also returns, but now from the Mother's orientation: "Mais alors,
quand tu te croyais seul, je te voyais, [. . .] mais je ne m'approchais . . .
c'était si sacré pour toi . . . c'était très étonnant chez un petit enfant
déjà cette pudeur . . . je comprenais ça si bien . . ." [But then, when
you thought you were alone, I would see you, (. . .) but I didn't go
near. . . . it was so sacred to you . . . it was very surprising to see such
modesty already in a small child. . . I understand that so well] (125).

The fluid representation of the interaction between these two figures
creates an affective weight which is threatened at the end of the chapter
by the presence of "la couverture" [the cover of his book] that "elle
caresse [. . .] avec précaution" [that she caresses (. . .) cautiously] (126).
The central figure's attempt to reduce that weight is seen in his words
addressed to *elle*, "'Lis-le sans idée préconçue'" ["Read it without any
preconceived ideas"]; but the impossibility of reducing that weight is
contained in the mother's response: "'Oui, mon chéri, je te promets . . .
la tendresse tremble dans les miroitements liquides de ses yeux . . .
Mais dis-moi . . . son regard le caresse [. . .] A moi tu peux l'avouer: Toi
aussi, n'est-ce pas, *tu sais*'" ["Yes, my dear, I promise you . . . tenderness
trembles in the liquid shimmering of her eyes . . . But tell me . . . her
look caresses him (. . .) You can admit it to me: You too, right? *you
know*"] (127).

The parents remain enclosed in their chapters, memories of different kinds of interaction. In order to come face to face with "les mots," *il* retreats from all voices in Chapter 8: "Pas de mères ici, ni de pères. [. . .] Il n'a, ici, plus besoin de personne" [No mothers here, nor fathers either. (. . .) He has, here, need for no one] (61). Here, "la chose l'aveugle" [the thing blinds him], and a struggle follows, "cela veut s'échapper, mais il le tient, il le serre de toutes ses forces . . ." [it wants to escape but he holds it, he squeezes it with all his might] (61–62). As in reverie or meditation, figures from "outside" rise to consciousness who represent internalized censorship. First *ils* arrive on the scene, applying first aid and offering advice, but *il* turns this plural figure away, "Lâchez-moi" [Leave me alone] (61). Nevertheless, *il* cannot resist internalizing the word *ils* applied to his work, "vulgaire": "Vulgarité. Il faut arracher cela [. . .]: un seul coup bref, et c'est arraché. La vulgarité est en miettes . . . [. . .] des molles voyelles vautrées cela coule . . . je m'ouvre . . . l'absorber . . . aspirer la fade odeur . . ." [Vulgarity. I must rip that out (. . .): one quick blow, and it's out. The vulgarity is in crumbs . . . (. . .) it flows out of the soft, sprawling vowels . . . I open myself up . . . absorb it . . . breathe in the insipid odor] (63).

This seems to be a forbidden pleasure, for it must be contained when another presence interrupts: "Une face plate et lisse se tend par l'entrebâillement de la porte. Vous écrivez?" [A flat, smooth face is stuck through the opening in the door. You're writing?] (63). This figure, identified as "Madame," is a representative of *nous*: "—Dites-nous. Nous attendons, nous sommes impatients" [—Tell us. We're waiting, we're impatient]. Rather than reject the appeal, *il* separates from this plural by manipulating a shared myth: " —Rien que vous n'approuviez. Tout ce que vous souhaitiez. [. . .] Je suis de taille à affronter ses angoisses, son absurdité. Noble. Fort et triste. [. . .] Rien de louche, je vous assure [. . .], avec les mots, je construis ce monument à notre gloire à tous" [—Nothing you would disapprove of. All that you would hope. (. . .) I'm big enough to confront her anguishes, her absurdity. Noble. Strong and sad. (. . .) Nothing shady, I assure you [. . .], with words, I am building this monument to the glory of us all] (63). Satisfied, "Madame" leaves: "L'image qu'elle a plaquée dessus aussitôt a tout recouvert: celle de la cathédrale superbe où déjà elle s'avançait, extatique, se prosternait" [The image that she has stuck on it already covers it totally: the one of a superb cathedral which she is already approaching, ecstatic, prostrating herself] (64).

Another voice takes over the narration in the next section to give a brief description of the "writer": "Seul, replié sur lui-même, il ne fait rien. Vraiment rien. Rien à quoi le mot faire puisse s'appliquer" [Alone, withdrawn into himself, he does nothing. Truly nothing. Nothing to which the word could be applied] (64). Hours pass, years, "la longueur de toute une vie. De plusieurs vies" [the length of a lifetime. Of several lifetimes] (64–65). This is a voyage of the mind, a voyage to no place in no time, a voyage to "l'abandon," where "tant est forte la sensation de solitude, de silence" [it is so strong, the sensation of solitude, of silence] (65). The narrating voice is situated inside the consciousness of *il:* "Par moments, tant l'abandon où il se trouve est grand, [. . .] qu'il en vient à se dire que personne probablement, s'étant laissé déporter si loin, n'en est revenu, puisque personne n'a jamais raconté une telle expérience" [Sometimes, so great is the isolation where he finds himself, (. . .) that he goes on to tell himself that probably no one, having been transported so far, has returned from there, because no one has ever recounted such an experience] (65).

The anonymous origin of these observations about the central figure preserves the quality of interiority usually effected by the use of the first-person pronoun. For the admiring plural in Chapter 1, as well as for the paternal figures in Chapters 3, 14, and 15, the central figure speaks as *je* and is described as *il* through the mediation of these interactions. When this figure is constituted as a subject for *ils* in Chapter 1, *je* represents a "writer." The subject then constituted itself as boy-child for the figures representing "Mother" and "Father." In the voyage of the mind in Chapter 8, however, *il* is not contained *for* an identified or constructed figure. The reader is thus invited into a subjectified objective position in relation to this figure. This is a position in which "les mots" take on a personified presence with which *je* as *il* interacts.

Before this presence enters the narration in a more constituted state which can be represented by "les mots," the reader encounters it through sensual imagery. The separation of the central figure from the interactive and privileged position as *je* allows this imagery an unmediated entrance which places the reader in direct contact with the sensation created. The following passage sits alone as a paragraph: "De la substance molle aux fades relents a filtré comme une vapeur, une buée . . . elle se condense . . . les gouttelettes des mots s'élèvent en un fin jet, se poussant les unes les autres, et retombent. D'autres montent et encore d'autres . . . Maintenant le dernier jet est retombé. Il n'y a plus rien" [A lifeless substance with an insipid stench has filtered like a vapor, a mist . . . it is condensed . . . the drops of words rise up in a fine spray, pushing against one another, and fall. Others rise and still more . . . Now the last spray has fallen. There is no longer anything] (65).

The central figure emerges momentarily as an orientation for perception, but just as quickly the narration returns to the "tumulte" of "les mots": "Là, il lui semble qu'il perçoit . . . on dirait qu'il y a là un

battement, une pulsation . . . [. . .] Cela grandit, se déploie . . . Cela a la
vigueur, la fraîcheur intacte des jeunes pousses, des premières herbes,
cela croît avec la même violence contenue, propulsant devant soi des
mots . . . Ils s'attirent les uns les autres . . . Leur mince jet lentement
s'étire . . . L'impulsion tout à coup devient plus forte, c'est une brève
éruption, les mots irrésistiblement dévalent, et puis tout se calme"
[There, it seems to him that he perceives . . . one would say that there
is there a beating, a pulsation . . . (. . .) It grows larger, spreads out . . .
It has vigor, the intact freshness of young sprouts, of early grass, it
grows with the same contained violence, propulsing before it words
. . . They attract one another . . . Their thin stream slowly moves on . . .
The impulse suddenly becomes stronger, it's a brief eruption, the words
rush down irresistibly, and then everything is calm] (65–66).

The perspective returns momentarily to il, "seul avec eux" [alone
with them], but each time that orientation is established, it is again
overrun by the activity of "cela," "leurs mouvements" [their move-
ments], "leur vibration" [their vibration], "leurs miroitements" [their
shimmerings] (67). The orientation implied by the use of "leurs" in the
passage above is represented by the impersonal on and an ambiguous
vous, both of which bring the reader more directly into the experience
than the use of je would have: "On peut, avec cela qui vous attend,
courir au-dehors, plein d'énergie inemployée, en gaspiller joyeusement
quelques parcelles, s'ébattre . . . sauts, bonds, cabrioles, rires contagieux . . . jeux d'enfant protégé, insouciant" [You can, with that which
awaits you, run outside, full of unused energy, waste happily a few
pieces of it, frolic . . . jumps, bounds, somersaults, contagious laughter
. . . games of a protected child, carefree] (67).

The spell is broken when je resurfaces and, sounding like an interior
decorator, attempts to take control of "les mots": "Mais il faut savoir
s'arrêter, il faut du naturel, un certain air de négligence . . . Se garder
surtout des manies, des excès, si dangereux" [But you have to know
how to stop, it must be natural, a certain look of negligence . . . Above
all, avoid manias, excesses, so dangerous] (68). The pretense to control
is deflated in the next breath by a more affective image in which il,
"derrière les mots" [behind the words], is compared to "la vieille servante au visage gris, aux yeux, aux mains usés qui tapote un pli de la
robe aux lourdes broderies" [the old maidservant with the gray face,
tired eyes and hands, who pulls on a wrinkle in a heavily embroidered
dress] (68). "Les mots sont ses souverains" [the words are his sovereign
masters], and il constitutes itself as "leur humble sujet" [their humble
subject] (68).

The only way "s'arracher à cela" [to pull away from it] and "sortir
dans la clarté du grand jour" [to go out into broad daylight] is "se

dédoubler" [to double himself] (69). The subjective objectivity effected by the anonymous origin of the earlier designation of the central figure as *il* is now internalized as *je:* "Une moitié de moi-même se détache de l'autre: Un témoin. Un juge . . ." [Half of me detaches from the other half: A witness. A judge . . .] (69). The narration rushes from one voice to the other in marked discourse, the "judge" lays out the criteria: " —Vous savez, moi, je suis tout simple. Très primitif. Je ne me sers que de deux mots . . . A quoi bon les autres [. . .] . . . Soyez tranquille, on vous les dira. Mais entre nous deux mots suffisent. Aussi grossiers que ceux-là: c'est mort. C'est vivant" [—You know me, I'm very simple. Very primitive. I only use two words . . . What good are the others (. . .) . . . calm down, we'll tell them to you. But just between us, two words are enough. As crude as these: it's dead. It's alive] (70). The central figure then dismisses "le témoin": "J'ai besoin d'être seul. Je me sens un peu secoué" [I need to be alone. I feel a little shaken] (72).

When interaction between "les mots" and the central figure resumes after this exchange, *il* is constituted by a more concentrated control in relation to this fluid presence: "Il faut capter cela, ce mouvement, l'isoler, chercher . . ." [It must be captured, that movement, isolated, sought . . .] (73). In the end "les images" created are described as "nettes, le mouvement en elles se précise . . ." [clear, the movement in them sharpens . . .] (74). The figure of "le témoin" is called back, "Maintenant vous pouvez revenir" [Now you can come back] (74). The plural *nous,* the doubled *je,* looks at "cette construction érigée" [that set up construction], "mot après mot" [word after word]. The "témoin" recedes when all images stop to center on "une grande complexité" [a great complexity]: "Longtemps il la contemple . . . elle est bien telle qu'il l'avait aperçue quand elle lui était apparue pour la première fois, telle qu'il avait pressentie, et pourtant différente . . . pareille à la divi-nité qui s'éntoure d'une lumière plus vive et parle à celui qu'elle revient visiter plus clairement et à plus haute voix . . ." [He contemplates it/her a long time . . . it/she is the very one that he had seen when it/she appeared to him for the first time, as he had predicted it/her, and yet different . . . similar to the divinity who surrounds it/herself with a more vivid halo and who speaks more clearly to the one it/she returns to visit, and in a louder voice] (75).

This passage marks the constitution of the central figure as *il* the "writer." The object of this figure's contemplation is "la grande com-plexité," represented by *elle.* The juxtaposition of these two pronouns in the passage carries the trace of a conventional configuration in which a feminine element represents "the muse" and that element is attributed by a masculine subject with "une grande complexité." When the central figure as a solitary subjectified objective *il* engaged with "les mots," that presence was described with a variety of images in which "la substance" was not isolated as is "une grande complexité" in the passage above. In the fluid presence represented by the movement between "la substance," "les mots," "leurs vibrations," etc., the figure is the "hero" Wittig describes, engaged in an interaction where "there are neither men nor women, neither race nor oppression, nothing but what can be named progressively, word by word, language" (134–35). Now that the central figure is constituted as a "writer," however, the pronoun *il* embodies the plural *nous, je* and "le témoin," and the presence which was earlier in movement is now taken prisoner as *elle*.

The central figure's feminization of this fluidity is checked in the next chapter, which seems to take place in a publisher's office:

> Il tend le cou, il se soulève . . . est-il possible qu'en eux aussi cette chose, comme en lui, toute tremblante, tâtonnante, se fraie son chemin . . . "C'est musclé. — Musclé? ah, musclé, comme on dit ficelé, comme on dit brossé, torché, enlevé . . .—Ça a de la vigueur. [. . .] "Il y a bien des imperfections, c'est normal [. . .], voire même une certaine vulgarité. Il faudra corriger cela. —Oui, vous avez raison. Je l'aurais déjà fait . . . mais alors, elle disparaît, elle se durcit, se dessèche . . . —Qui elle? —Cette chose, là, qui bouge, se propulse . . . elle s'arrête, elle ne se passe pas . . . Quand on la cherche, on trouve des mots . . . —mais les mots seuls comptent. Oubliez-la [. . .] (77, 79).

> [He stretches his neck, he raises up, is it possible that in them as well that thing, like in him, all trembling, groping, is clearing a way . . . "It's muscular. —Muscular? ah, muscular, as they say, all done up, as they say, spit and polished . . . —It's got vigour (. . .) "There are certainly imperfections, that's normal (. . .), that is to say, a certain vulgarity. You will have to correct that. — Yes, you're right. I would have already done it . . . but then, it/she disappears, it/she hardens, dries up . . . —Who she/What it? —That thing, there, that moves, is propulsed . . . it/she stops, it/she doesn't move on . . . When you look for it/her, you find words . . . —But only the words count. Forget it/her (. . .) .]

The conflict represented in this scene enacts the imprisonment of *je* by other interlocutors. At the same time, the exchange between these figures also serves to personalize and problematize through irony the feminization of the "unsayable."

The novel also allows for a representation of the "thickness" of this motivating force ("cela"), which is as pronounced as the subject's own. That is, in addition to its designation as "ce qui ne se laisser pas nommer, cette petite chose" [that which does not let itself be named, that little thing], a feminine noun replaced in French by the feminine pronoun *elle*, this "thing" is given many designations. That variety is best seen when *il* is not a subject but a subjectified object. Chapter 12 begins with an orientation which is probably that of the central figure, but it is only implied by the reference to *ils:* "Il est impossible qu'ils ne le voient pas" [It's impossible that they don't see it] (91). *Il* does not appear for two pages, and the play of pronouns and metaphors usually reserved for discursive figures enacts the complexity of this "thing":

> Au centre de *cela* il y a quelque chose d'indestructible. *Un noyau* qu'il n'est pas possible de désintégrer, vers lequel *toutes les particules* convergent, autour *duquel elles* gravitent à *une vitesse* si énorme qu'*elle* donne à l'ensemble l'apparence de *l'immobilité*. Autour de *cela* des *ondes* se répandent, *tout* oscille, *tout* vibre autour, si on s'en approche on se met à vibrer.
>
> C'est là, *étalé avec une impudeur innocente, comme une chose naturelle, comme une plante, comme un arbre* (my underlining, 91).

> [In the center of *it* there is something indestructible. A *center* which is impossible to disintegrate, toward which *all particles* converge, around which *they* gravitate with such an enormous *speed* that *it* gives to the whole an appearance of *immobility*. Around *it, waves* spread out, *everything* oscillates, *everything* vibrates around, if you approach it you begin to vibrate.
>
> It's there, *laid out with an innocent immodesty, like a thing in nature,* like *a plant, like a tree.*]

When reference to this quality returns to the pronoun *elle* at the end of the novel, the source and instance of its enunciation identifies the specificity as motivated by the male subject, at the same time that it is superimposed with the reader's unmediated tropistic experience of the fluidity of its referent in passages such as the one above.

Elle is also given voice in the second chapter of the novel as a narrative figure with whom the central figure seeks union: "Avec elle il sent qu'il n'a rien à craindre . . . [. . .] 'Avec vous je peux parler . . . A vous je peux tout dire . . . enfin . . . dire ce qui compte . . . Il y a en vous tant de générosité . . .'" [With her he feels that he has nothing to fear . . . (. . .) "With you I can speak . . . To you I can say everything . . . well . . . say what matters . . . There is in you so much generosity . . ."] (14). This figure of *elle* not only listens but also dissents: "'Mais voyons, il ne s'agit pas de cela entre nous [. . .] . . . —Oui, j'ai eu tort de parler de générosité. [. . .] Pardonnez-moi, je me suis montré mesquin . . .' Elle rit, il sent dans son rire comme de la tendresse . . . 'Non, vous êtes fou . . . Mais c'est vrai, ne me parlez pas de la générosité'" ["Listen, that's not what it's about between us (. . .) . . . —Yes, I was wrong to speak of generosity. (. . .) Excuse me, I showed my petty side . . ." She laughs, he feels in her laughter something like tenderness . . . "No, you're crazy . . . But it's true, don't talk to me about generosity"] (14).

The battle of the sexes from the earlier novels becomes a momentary narrative union in this one. Its "realism" is at first suggested by the punctuation marking the exchange, a familiar touchstone. The origin of the marked discourse, however, becomes ambiguous as the exchange continues: " — [. . .] c'est que nous parlons la même langue —Oui, n'est-ce pas? La même langue'" [— (. . .) it's that we speak the same language —Yes, isn't that so? The same language"] (15). Either figure could have made the observation or the response. It is not until the last voice above continues that a separation takes place: "[. . .] —Mais maintenant je le sais: [. . .] vous êtes d'ici. Elle lève les sourcils pour exprimer l'étonnement" [(. . .) —But now I know it: (. . .) you're from here. She raises her eyebrows to express surprise] (15). The marked discourse of *il* continues as an uninterrupted account of his fascination with words similar to the monologue he pronounced for *ils* in Chapter 1. In that case, *il* was an adored prisoner encased in his own version of a "writer" and the other single subjects who arose returned to the plural. At the beginning of the exchange in Chapter 2 *il* speaks in accord with the contract of reciprocity, "ici entre eux il n'y a pas d'indiscrétion, pas de réserve" [here between them there is no indiscretion, no reserve]. When *elle* speaks as a subject, however, *il* is taken prisoner: "'Ah oui, [. . .] vous faisiez vraiment enfant prédestiné'" ["Ah, yes, (. . .) you really played the predestined child"] (17–18). No chance for union here: "Regardez-le. Je l'ai ramené. Capturé au cours d'une brève razzia" [Look at him. I've brought him about. Captured during a little raid] (18).

As seen in the earlier discussion of the voyage of the mind in Chapter 8, the only Other with whom union is possible is "l'autre moitié de moi-même" [the other half of myself]. This "half" returns in the last chapter, where the narrative figures of *ils, elles, il* and *elle* are present only as the internalization of an idea: "peut-être faut-il encore un peu attendre, retarder encore le moment . . . [. . .] que cela vous force la main . . . Cela. Quoi cela [. . .]: il n'y a pas de 'cela' qui compte. Cela n'est rien. Cela n'existe pas. Les mots seuls" [Perhaps it's necessary to wait still a little longer for the moment . . . (. . .) for that to force your hand . . . That. What that (. . .): there is no "that" that means anything. That is nothing. That does not exist. Only the words] (165). "Les mots" are brought back with all the movement this presence represents, but now *il* knows how to intervene. A union is formed as "les mots" are first the object and *il* the subject and then subject and object appear to mingle: "Il va les prendre, les tailler, les polir, les disposer avec précaution . . . [. . .] Prendre celui-ci pour commencer, ce fragment minuscule . . . [. . .] Tirés, amenés par lui, par cet infime fragment, des mouvements, des formes encore à peine ébauchés apparaissent à perte de vue . . ." [He's going to take them, tailor them, polish them, put them around carefully . . . (. . .) Start by taking this one, this minuscule fragment . . . (. . .) Pulled, led by it/him, by the tiny fragment, the movements, the forms, still barely clear come into view] (168).

It is at this point that the "double" reappears, but "quelque chose a changé entre nous" [something has changed between us]. The *nous* of "autrefois" [before], "vous et moi," is now in opposition to *ils:* "Ils sont tous là, [. . .] j'entends cette rumeur qui monte d'eux et couvre votre voix . . . La couvre? Ou avec elle se confond" [They are all there, (. . .) I hear that noise that rises up from them and covers your voice . . . Covers it/her? Or mixes with it/her] (169). The play between the translation of the pronoun referring to "la voix," *elle,* as *it* or *her* is possible because of the role that this pronoun comes to play in this chapter.

When the double accuses the writer of being "corrompu" [corrupted], silence follows, except for "un petit claquement léger . . . la fine pointe souple d'un fouet . . ." [little, light snapping . . . the fine, supple end of a whip . . .]: "[. . .] les bêtes féroces qui me faisaient trembler, la platitude, la naïveté, la simplicité, [. . .] l'ostentation, la grossièreté docilement se couchent . . . elle est là, vivante, sûre d'elle . . . il suffit qu'elle agite légèrement sa lanière souple, et les fauves domptés reprennent leur place [. . .] Elle n'est jamais plus fière et sûre de sa force que lorsqu'elle se tient ainsi au milieu d'eux" [(. . .) the ferocious beasts that used to make me tremble, the platitude, naiveté, simplicity, (. . .) ostentation, vulgarity lie down, docile . . . it/she's there, alive, sure of it/herself . . . all it takes is for it/her to move her supple whip lightly, and the tamed beasts return to their places (. . .) . It/She is never more proud and sure of its/her power than when it/she is there in the middle of them] (170–71). Although this figure of *elle* controls the "beasts," the central figure needs the "double" as well: "[. . .] il ne m'est pas possible de m'en passer" [(. . .) it's not possible for me to do without him] (171).

Il pulls "le double" closer as they set to work; their exchange presented as one discourse superimposed on the other until the voice which probably belongs to the double brings *ils* back into the exchange: "[. . .] un peu plus de vide encore [. . .] mettrait à l'épreuve notre pouvoir, le crédit qu'ils nous font" [(. . .) a little more emptiness here (. . .) would prove our power, the credit that they give us] (172). Whereas the presence of *ils* in Chapter 1 invited *il* to play the role of "writer," here that presence only poses the threat of imprisonment. This threat is dramatized by the reaction of *il* to the words of "le double": ". . . je le tire, je me crammpone à lui de toutes mes forces . . . restez près de moi, restons *entre nous*, je vous en conjure, *oubliez-les* . . ." [. . . I pull him, I cling to him with all my strength . . . stay near me, let's stay *entre nous*, I beg you, *forget them*] (my underlining, 172).

Like the place where the central figure as a subjectified objective *il*

engages with the fluid presence of "les mots/cela," the place entre nous
is characterized as a sensual interaction. The orientation is at first clear
because of the identification of je and vous in the passage above, and
of a change in speakers which is marked by dashes in the passage
which follows: ". . . rapprochez-vous . . . Sentez-vous ce pouls . . . ce
souffle léger . . . cette vibration . . . vous seul . . . —Bien sûr que ça
vibre. Je vibre. Nous vibrons. On est comme galvanisés . . . Je sens
passer le courant . . . Je sens, oui, je sens . . . oh comme c'est fort . . .
Ils se convulsent, ils tombent en transes, ils se contorsionnent, la sueur
coule sur leurs fronts, vous avez chaud . . . le soleil vous brûle . . .
chaud . . . chaud . . . chaud . . . oh comme vous avez chaud . . . et ils
perdent toute pudeur, ils frémissent, ils arrachent leurs vêtements . . .
[. . .]" [. . . come closer . . . feel this pulse . . . that light breathing . . .
that vibration . . . you alone . . . —Of course it vibrates. I'm vibrating.
We're vibrating. It's as if we're galvanized . . . I feel the current passing
. . . I feel, yes, I feel . . . oh it's strong . . . They convulse, they fall into
a trance, they are contorted, the sweat flows down their foreheads,
you're hot . . . the sun is burning you . . . hot . . . hot . . . hot . . . oh how
hot you are . . . and they lose all modesty, they shiver, they tear off their
clothes . . . (. . .)] (172).

As in the journey in Chapter 8, when the central figure is represented
by an unspecified orientation as il, je and vous in this passage similarly
slip into the designation ils. The sensuality of the images overtakes the
orientation of the designation, bringing the reader into direct contact
with the experience of the union. That contact is most clearly recognized when the passage ends and a more observing orientation separates ils from the reader once again: "Vite . . . ils boutonnent leur veste,
tirent sur leurs manches" [Quick . . . they button their shirts, pull down
their sleeves]. The plural nous separates and a single je speaks, "Je
vibre, je tremble . . ." [I vibrate, I tremble . . .]; and the threatening
presence of ils is interjected indirectly: "Il faut avoir la force de m'arracher à eux [. . .]" [I must have the strength to tear myself away from
them] (172).

It is only after the embrace with "le double" and the return to consciousness of the threat represented by eux that the referent is named
for elle, the figure who tamed the "beasts" two pages earlier: "Elle qui
ne se laisse pas nommer . . . ce que je sens . . . moi seul . . . cette chose
intacte, vivante . . ." [It/she which does not let it/herself be named . . .
which I feel . . . I alone . . . that thing intact, living . . .] (173–74). When
the dreaded presence of ils returns, "Et tout à coup je les vois, ils
apparaissent ici, puis là [. . .]" [And all of the sudden I see them, they
appear here, then there], je is saved by elle: "Quand par moments je
m'arrête [. . .] . . . Je reconnais des mots de là-bas . . . leurs mots . . .

[. . .] Un oeil tourné vers nous toujours [. . .]. Heureusement elle est là, elle le seul garant, le seul guide . . . elle s'impatiente, nous n'avons pas de temps à perdre . . ." [When at certain moments I stop (. . .) . . . I recognize words from down there . . . their words . . . (. . .) An eye turned always toward us (. . .). Fortunately it/she is there, the only guarantee, the only guide . . . it's/she's impatient, we haven't any time to lose . . .] (173–74). The referent to *nous* above is ambiguous enough to include *je*, "le double," and *elle*. Until the referent for *vous* is identified, that ambiguity flows into the paragraph that follows, the last one in the novel, and *elle* becomes "cela":

> Plus près de moi, mais pas trop près . . . un peu à l'écart tout de même . . . mais assez loin de tous les autres . . . juste à la bonne distance . . . vous mon double, mon témoin . . . là, penchez-vous avec moi . . . ensemble regardons . . . est-ce que cela se dégage, se dépose . . . comme sur les miroirs qu'on approche de la bouche des mourants . . . une fine buée? (174).

> [Closer to me, but not too close . . . a little to the side just the same . . . but far enough from the others . . . just the right distance . . . you my double, my witness . . . there, lean over with me . . . let's look together . . . does it disengage, settle . . . like on the mirrors that they place near the mouth of someone dying . . . a fine mist?]

The slippage of *elle* back to "cela" allows the referent of both to refer back to the multiple images the reader has encountered throughout the novel at the same time that the reader is left at the end with the *process of the perception* of "cela" rather than with any specific referent for it. Just as the surface-depth dichotomy was obscured by the tropistic rendering of mythic constructions in *Le Planétarium*, here the split between subject and object remains, "juste à la bonne distance." This is not, however, a gendered split; it is an internal division that allows for a difference within, the distance and integration which invite creation. The range of pronominal positions and the play between them parallel the attention to the process of creation alluded to in the final image. The quest for the creation of an identity in *Portrait d'un inconnu*, *Martereau*, *Le Planétarium*, becomes in *Entre la vie et la mort* the quest for expression.

"Write, let no one hold you back, let nothing stop you," Hélène Cixous proclaims in "The Laugh of the Medusa": "not man; not the imbecilic capitalist machinery [. . .]; and not *yourself*. Smug-faced readers, managing editors, and big bosses don't like the true texts of women— female-sexed texts. That kind scares them. I write woman: woman must write woman. And man, man."[12] This statement is often interpreted as a call to "l'écriture féminine." When Cixous's statement is read through this discussion of *Entre la vie et la mort*, attention turns away from the prescriptive nature of that interpretation and toward the call itself. It is a call which suggests that the quest for expression can reveal the fluidity of identity, not that the identity assigned by culture is the source of expression.

Entre la vie et la mort and the two novels that follow in our discussion, Vous les entendez? and "disent les imbéciles," begin the process of deflating identity which was seen in the earlier novels as an undermining of narrative authority. This deflation is like sticking pins in a balloon which is inflated by constructs of personal, sexual, and professional identity. The puncture inflicted on the identity of the Father by his Children's laughter in Vous les entendez? is so deflating that his identity changes places with theirs. In "disent les imbéciles" identity disappears, or loses form, and becomes a voice that is also a vide [emptiness], an intense impersonality through which the previous novels can be read and from which, perhaps, creative energy can escape, leaving "une fine buée."

6

Identity in Process: I-You-We-They

Vous les entendez?

At certain moments during their quest, tropistic perception placed the narrators of *Portrait d'un inconnu* and *Martereau* in a position of childlike vulnerability. Fairy-tale and epic imagery, as well as tropistic recreation of childhood experience, represented their fears and desires and evoked a Child's innocence when facing the murky, Adult world. These narrators were, however, on a quest for gender identity. The older male figures' interpretation of the narrators' sensitivity as "girlish" or "womanlike" contributed to the self-doubt they internalized, which is represented in their narration.

In *Vous les entendez?*, Child and Adult worlds also begin in opposition. The Adult here is a Father whose aspiration to be a Cultured Gentleman is problematized by his sensitivity to his Children's laughter. A friend of the Father, also a Cultured Gentleman but childless, has stopped in for a visit. As Father, Children, and Friend sit together in the living room, the Friend gets up to admire a statue sitting on the mantel. He takes the statue down and places it on the coffee table. Discussion follows, and the Children excuse themselves and go upstairs to bed. As the novel opens, the two Gentlemen are together in the living room, but the laughter from upstairs continually distracts the Father.

Just as the Young Husband's identity in *Le Planétarium* depends on his Young Wife's pure adoration, the Father's identification of himself and the Friend as Gentlemen depends on the Innocence of the Children's laughter. In the opening scene the two male figures are represented as one, which gives the unmarked discourse in the passage a single origin: "Tous deux la tête levée écoutent . . . Oui, des rires jeunes. Des rires frais. Des rires insouciants. Des rires argentins. Clochettes. Gouttlettes. Jets d'eau. Cascades légères. Gazouillis d'oiselets . . ." [The two of them, head raised, listen . . . Yes, young laughter. Fresh laughter. Carefree laughter. Silvery laughter. Churchbells. Droplets. Fountains. Gentle cascades. The chirping of fledglings].[1]

The description of the laughter is then transformed into an image of the laughter of "les dames," which serves to establish "les deux" as "gentlemen": "Leurs rires innocents, mutins, juste un peu malicieux, fusent . . . Fossettes, roseurs, blondeurs, rondeurs, longues robes de tulle, [. . .] les notes pures de leurs rires cristallins s'égrènent . . . Elles s'amusent . . . Vous les entendez? Les gentlemen assis autour de la table tapotent leurs vieilles pipes culottées, sirotent leur brandy . . ." [Their innocent laughter, impish, just a little malicious, bursts forth . . . Dimples, bows, fairness, plumpness, long tulle dresses, (. . .) pure notes of their crystalline laughter ripple out . . . The women are having fun . . . Do you hear them? The gentlemen seated around the table tap their old, seasoned pipes, sip their brandy] (10). The room itself also begins as a fixed image, washed by the innocence of the laughter, the sign which stabilizes all signifiers: "Amples housses de chintz aux teintes passées. Pois de senteur dans les vieux vases. Des charbons rougeoient, des bûches flambent dans les cheminées . . ." [Rich chintz slipcovers in faded shades. Sweet peas in old vases. Coal glows, logs burn in fireplaces] (10).

The laughter and the room become transparent icons of security, but the irony at the end of the passage rubs off on the reader's own tendency to read "innocently": "Rien qui puisse nous atteindre et nous faire vaciller, nous, si robustes et droits, si bien plantés . . . Nous poussés parmi les pois de senteur, les pots de géraniums et d'impatiences" [Nothing could reach us and make us vacillate, us, so robust and straight, so sturdy . . . Us, coming up among the sweet peas, the pots of geranium and impatiens] (14). When an undesignated voice interrupts this image, the tropistic perception which structures the novel is itself questioned: "Mais non, pas besoin de pois de senteur [. . .] Qu'on prenne n'importe qui, [. . .] qui pourrait . . . qui pourrait ou qui voudrait? . . . [. . .] peu importe . . . qui pourrait ou qui voudrait percevoir dans ces rires [. . .]? Qui, sans être préparé . . . qui sans être entraîné aurait pu . . . quand avec son air d'assurance paisible le vieil ami s'est approché de la cheminée, a tendu la main et caressé . . . qui aurait pu percevoir la menace, le danger [. . .]" [But no, no need for sweet peas (. . .). Take anyone, (. . .) who could . . . who could or who would want to? . . . (. . .) never mind . . . who could or would want to perceive in that laughter (. . .)? Who, without being ready . . . who without being led could have . . . when with his calm, confident air the old friend approached the fireplace, held out his hand and caressed . . . who would have been able to perceive the threat, the danger (. . .)] (14). The narration follows this retreat from the depth below the scene, and the Father's tropistic fear identifies him as the point of the orientation: "Non, pas ça, ne le faites pas, n'y touchez pas . . . pas maintenant, pas devant eux" [No, not that, don't do it, don't touch it, not now, not in front of them] (14). The Father's fear is that the Children are Adolescents in Rebellion against the Cultured World of the Statue. If the Friend took the statue down for inspection, the Children could mock him for his admiration and undermine the security of the Father's Aesthetic Judgment.

The self-doubt represented by various figures in all of Sarraute's previous novels is internalized for the figure of the Father in *Vous les entendez?* in terms of Aesthetic Value. The undermining of his judgment, as represented by the Children's laughter, resonates within Alice Jardine's analysis of the "questioning and turning back upon their own discourse" within the "master narratives in the West over the past century." In her study of modernism Jardine discusses the way in which the self-questioning "intrinsic to the conditions of modernity" is enacted by what she calls "gynesis." Gynesis is the process by which this self-questioning takes place in a "space [which] has been coded as *feminine, as woman.*"[2] The Father's insecurity in *Vous les entendez?* about the meaning of the Children's laughter dramatizes a self-questioning of the master narrative.

The master narrative in this novel is not characterized as "la politique, les affaires" from "le cercle des hommes" found in *Portrait* and *Martereau.* At the same time, however, this narrative could not have been represented by a Mother or a Woman. As seen in the treatment of Germaine Lemaire by her male contemporaries, the Fathers in *Le Planétarium,* the female relationship to culture is too problematic for a female figure to represent the master narrative because She is continually perceived as a Sexed (not Neutral) Subject. The central conflict of *Vous les entendez?* takes place between the Father as representative of the master narrative and his most significant others, his Children. This Gentleman's Culture is challenged by a New Generation, represented as *ils, les enfants. Ils* designates a vague plural which threatens the Father's identity just as *elles* threatened that of the narrators in *Portrait* and *Martereau.* Their treatment in the narration of *elles* (or *elle*) established a distance between the male narrator (self) and the threat of the female figure(s) (other). In *Vous les entendez?* the threat to identity represented by the Children cannot be contained, because the Father cannot maintain distance between himself and these beings who are part of his self; *les enfants* will not be reduced to the status of undifferentiated Other. The Father's difficulty maintaining distance from the Children is represented by the narration itself, which enacts an interchangeability between Father and Children. The title and opening scenes place the Father in the position of subject of perception and the Children in that of object, "Vous les entendez?" As the novel continues, however, the Children's discourse and laughter move between being the object of the Father's perception and assuming an autonomous perception of which the Father is the object.

Thus when the Father's discourse about the Statue creates an opposition in terms of gender, another discourse problematizes or mocks it. At one point, the text says that the "mal caché" [hidden evil] in the children's disrespect for art is "une tare héréditaire de la mère aux enfants" [a defect inherited from the children's mother] (65). The observation is then undermined as the context for the narration becomes a Kafkaesque interview between the Father as Young Husband and a figure resembling a Marriage Counselor: "—Ah, vous n'avez pas de goûts communs?" [—Ah, you don't have the same tastes?] (67). The Counselor looks through his "casier des mariages" [marriage files] to see how to resolve the conflict implied by the Father's statement about the Mother's influence on their Children. A "vieillard à cheveux blancs" [an old man with white hair] at a neighboring table overhears the discussion and calls the Young Husband a "petit tyran" [little tyrant]. In the end the Counselor consults a file called "Dictons/vox populi" [Dictums] where he finds the advice necessary to resolve the conflict: "—Mais vous voyez, nous ne pouvons rien vous donner d'autre que: 'Des goûts et des couleurs'" [—But you see, we cannot give you anything except: "There's no accounting for taste"] (68–69). The stereotyped characterization of "leur mère" is itself subject to classification. The ironic dramatization of the statement about the Mother deflates the gender characterization it represents.

The narration representing the Father's appreciation of the Statue similarly tends to a gendered language which is also undermined. A male subject caressing a female as object is a configuration so widespread in Western civilization that it passes into that culture as "neutral." In the opening pages of Vous les entendez? such a caress is suggested by the sensual language used to describe the Father's admiration of his Statue, "la bête" [the beast]: "Une drôle de bête, n'est-ce pas? Sa main suit ses contours, flatte ses flancs lourds" [A funny beast, isn't it? His hand follows its contours, pats its heavy flanks] (13). Later in the novel, the sensual undertones seen in this passage rise to the status of narrative: the Father's "love of art" is dramatized as his "having a mistress." This amorous liaison is not designated in the text, it is suggested by the imagery, just as sexual topics are often referred to in "polite" conversation. What is not said in this passage is contained by moral terms such as "vice" and thus becomes the underside of the Father's sexual relationship to the Statue.

He is described as leaving the house and pretending to go to work but is "seen" by another eye: "[. . .] courant presque dans son impatience de se livrer à cela, ce vice [. . .] . . . en plein jour, un jour ouvrable, n'est-ce pas honteux?: Pas un mot à nous, bien sûr, quand il rentre enfin, l'air affairé . . . Y a-t-il eu des coups de téléphone?" [(. . .) almost running in his impatience to give himself over to it, that vice (. . .) . . . in the middle of the day, a working day, isn't it shameful? (. . .) Not a word to us, of course, when he comes home, looking tired . . . Were there any calls?] (113). The referent for *nous* is the Children and appears in the context of their imagining what is "permis" [allowed] "quand nous n'étions pas là" [when we weren't there] (113).

In this transformation of the Gentleman's Love of Art into the Gentleman's having a Mistress, the Father and the Friend are described as "vieux jouisseurs" [old sensualists], "vieux noceurs" [old revellers], their "lèvres mouillées" [wet lips] identify them as "vieux gourmets" [old epicures], and their conversation is marked by a language which refers ambiguously to the Statue as Gentlemen might refer in "polite" conversation to a Lady of Dubious Morals. The implication depends upon a conflation of the Statue, "la bête," and a Lady of Dubious Morals, possible because of the ambiguity of the language which joins the feminine pronoun to both an explicit referent and an implicit one: ". . . Oui, je la connais . . . Une perfection. Superbe. Mais vous savez, [. . .] . . . je ne sais si vous l'avez remarquée [. . .] . . . sa main remonte le long de sa cuisse, de sa hanche . . . ici, vous voyez, dans cette jambe droite qui s'avance, là, comme ça . . . ses lèvres font un bruit répugnant, son baiser claque sur le bout de ses doigts . . . Je ne vous dis que ça. Une pure merveille" [. . . Yes, I know it/her . . . A perfection. Superb. But do you know, (. . .) . . . I don't know if you've noticed (. . .) . . . his hand goes up the length of its/her thigh, of its/her hip . . . here, you see, in that right leg that comes forward, there, like that . . . his lips make a repugnant noise, his kiss clicks on the end of his fingers . . . That's all I can tell you. A pure marvel] (114). When the reader follows the children downstairs in the scene that follows, "les uns derrière les autres" [one behind the other], the "spectacle" realizes the implications suggested above: "[. . .] se reboutonnant encore tout échauffé, se redressant, se tournant vers nous, toussotant pour gagner du temps, pour prendre de l'assurance . . . —Alors, vous voilà redescendus? . . . On n'a pas sommeil?" [(. . .) buttoning up still overheated, straightening up, turning around toward us, coughing to gain time, to reassure . . . —Well, you've come back down? . . . Aren't we sleepy?] (115). The demeanor of the male figures as Gentlemen has been completely undermined by the implication of their salacious escapades as "vieux gourmets," just as their Aesthetic relationship to the Statue is undermined by the suggestive language of the dramatization.

The power of the challenge the Children represent lies in the violent and emotional way in which it takes shape in the Father's consciousness. His internalization of this conflict is not a gendered identity quest, and it does not depend on Woman in any way, which frees the female reader to experience the emotional tension created as the male figure's role of Arbiter of Taste overlaps with his affective relationship to these children as their Father. The projection of mythic constructs onto another figure which takes place in *Le Planétarium* becomes a projection of emotional states in *Vous les entendez?* The fluidity of the boundaries between narration, interior monologue, exterior dialogue, imaginings, and narrative real continually undermines orientation. In none of Sarraute's previous novels is the ambiguity of origins of discourse so consistently upheld, such that the reader often identifies with or against a position in relation to the master narrative before identifying with either the Father or the Children. The fluidity of the narration prevents a simple reversal of the hierarchy in which a questioning of the master narrative assumes the position of superiority. The positions *for* and *against* in this novel are re-viewed in terms of their value as positions, and they are experienced as centers around which emotive states congregate.

In addition to perceptions moving between Father and Children, often there is one which rises above, or descends below, the apparent conflict of the novel. In the opening pages the Gentlemen's appreciation of the Statue is represented by sensual imagery which is not gendered and which evokes a parallel to tropisms: "Ce qui sort de là, ce qui émane, [. . .] les pénètre, s'infiltre en eux partout, ce qui les emplit, [. . .] les soulève . . . fait autour d'eux une sorte de vide où ils flottent, [. . .] aucun mot ne peut le décrire . . . [. . .], il savent qu'il faut surtout ne laisser aucun mot s'en approcher, y toucher" [What comes out of there, what emanates, (. . .) penetrates them, infiltrates them everywhere, what fills them, (. . .) raises them up . . . makes a kind of emptiness around them where they float, [. . .] no word can describe it . . . (. . .) they know that, above all, no word must be allowed to approach it, touch it] (11).

Later in the novel, the union between the two Gentlemen is not represented by words but by their physical relationship to one another. The context created is a non-gender specific Parent-Child relationship in which the two male figures are the Parents and the Statue is the Child: "En [cette relique], comme deux tendres parents qui se penchent sur leur enfant, ils se rejoignent, ils se confondent . . . Moments d'entente parfaite . . ." [In (that relic), like two tender parents who lean over their child, they are joined, they are indistinguishable . . . Moments of perfect understanding . . .] (64). The description is then itself elaborated by what seems to be an outside voice: "Si fragile, on le sait bien. Qui ne sait que les fusions les plus complètes ne durent que peu d'instants. Il est imprudent d'engager trop souvent [. . .], une autre ligne ramenée d'ailleurs ne suffit-elle pas pour qu'aussitôt se séparent, s'éloignent l'une de l'autre, encerclées de solitude, les deux âmes soeurs? N'est-ce pas là notre lot à tous, notre inévitable sort commun?" [So fragile, we know it well. Who doesn't know that the most complete fusions only last a few moments. It is foolish to engage too much too often (. . .), another line brought from somewhere else, isn't that enough to separate one from the other just as quickly, to distance one from the other, circled in solitude, the two sister souls? Isn't this our lot, all of us, our inevitable common destiny?] (64–65).

When this passage is read as originating from an outside observer, the pronoun *notre* generalizes the observation and places it in the context of one of Sarraute's recurring themes. Like the earlier interpretation of the laughter, however, the origin and meaning of the observation are superimposed onto another origin and thus another meaning. After a break in the page the text shifts the referent of *nous* to be the Children: "Alors pourquoi quand nous, tout à l'heure [. . .] . . . Pourquoi ce regard de mépris haineux quand nous nous sommes levés, quand nous nous sommes approchés et inclinés poliment pour prendre congé?" [Well why when we, a little while ago (. . .) . . . Why that look of hateful scorn when we got up, when we came and politely bowed to be excused?] (65). The narration here refers to the *feeling* of being observed and thereby judged, and in a sense these shifts in orientation create a text which observes its own reader.

Early in the novel the label "un collectionneur" [an art collector] adheres to the Father. His halting protest to the label is presented in first-person marked discourse to which the Friend responds, and both are surrounded by a third-person narration which enacts an observation of the two male figures: "L'ami se rejette brusquement en arrière, lève les sourcils et fixe sur lui des yeux inquiets . . . Tiens! Au contraire . . . Pourquoi? — Enfin, je ne sais pas . . . Je me suis mal exprimé . . . il bafouille, il rougit . . . Naturellement . . . je comprends . . . mais ce que je veux dire . . . Ils observent amusés, un peu gênés pour lui [. . .]" [The friend jumps back abruptly, raises his eyebrows and stares at him with uneasy eyes . . . Well! On the contrary . . . Why? —Ah, I don't know . . . I didn't explain myself very well . . . he stammers, he blushes . . . Naturally . . . I understand . . . but what I mean is . . . They watch, amused, a little embarrassed for him (. . .)] (24). This "observing" commentary continues until the end of the passage: "Il n'est pas un collectionneur . . . Au contraire" [He's not a collector, on the contrary] (25). The textual silence which follows represented by a break in the page is ominously filled by the sentence beginning the next paragraph: "Leurs rires si clairs, limpides . . ." [Their laughter so clear, so lim-

pid . . .] (25). The image continues to characterize the Laughter as innocent, but the status of that quality has been undermined by the irony
of the preceding passage. To the "entente parfaite" [perfect understand-
ing] of the two Gentlemen in the presence of the Statue is added this
threatening play of perceptions which ultimately separates the two
male figures.

The scene where the Friend takes the Statue down off the mantel is
"re-viewed" several times in the novel, as is the scene in which the
Father goes upstairs to see what the Children are laughing about. In
the first account of his trip upstairs, a narrative identified with the two
Gentlemen has been affirming the "innocence" of the laughter. The
Father's uneasiness about what the laughter means makes him the
"guilty" one in relation to that innocence. The passage begins in the
subjunctive mode and the future tense, as if Father or Children is/are
anticipating the scene, but then shifts to a use of participles which
creates an affective "present" for the reader. The Father is given different "ogre" roles and the Children corresponding ones: "Que le barbon
irascible se lève [. . .] . . . et ils vont s'arrêter, [. . .] tout effrayés, des
nymphes effarouchées qu'un satyre surprend, des petits cochons roses
en train de danser quand entre tout à coup, hurlant, montrant ses grandes dents, le méchant loup noir, des poulets [. . .] du poulailler où vient
de pénétrer le fourbe et cruel renard. Le vilain ogre, le trouble-fête, le
pion . . ." [Let the irascible old fogey get up (. . .) . . . and they are going
to stop, (. . .) all frightened, terrified nymphs who a satyr surprises,
little pink pigs dancing and carrying on, when all of a sudden, shouting
and showing his big teeth, the mean, black wolf comes in, chickens
(. . .) in the henhouse just entered by the treacherous, cruel fox. The
nasty ogre, the kill-joy, the study hall supervisor] (16–17).

For the reader who might be assigning these images a meaning or
the passage an orientation, the text jumps back after an ellipsis to a
position of assessment, "Qu'y a-t-il encore?" [What else is there?], only
to be followed by more unmarked discourse which pulls it further back
to the straightforward language that any group of children giggling after
bedtime might use—"Comment a-t-il entendu? On riait si doucement . . ." [How did he hear? We were laughing so softly . . .] (117). The
scene is given a more sinister context in keeping with the tone set by
the fairy-tale imagery, but the "innocence" assigned to the children is
not as clear when their judgment is given more sophisticated terms:
"Mais il est toujours là à surveiller chaque geste, à réprimer le moindre
élan, le plus léger signe d'insouciance, de liberté, toujours à scruter, à
doser, à juger" [But he's always there watching every move, repressing
the least enthusiasm, the slightest sign of being carefree, of freedom,
always ready to scrutinize, to measure, to judge] (17).

The tension of this scene is raised again and resolved in a later re-counting which begins from the Children's position: "Où est-on? Ils lancent autour d'eux des regards stupéfaits. Nous sommes bien dans la salle du haut, la salle où depuis toujours on se réunit avant d'aller [. . .] se coucher? . . ." [Where are we? They glance around with dumb-founded looks. Are we really in the room upstairs, the room where we've always met before going (. . .) to bed? . . .] (51). The account pre-sents only the Children's side of the exchange with the Father until his marked discourse introduces narrative order. The Children's language is now conventionally "innocent," and the Father's conventionally "comforting and apologetic." It is not until the scene ends that the conventions of their language are given value: "— [. . .] C'était un cauchemar?" [—(. . .) Was it a nightmare?] (53).

The reassuring words that follow replace the Father in the living room with the Friend: "—Mais non. [. . .] Vous n'avez jamais bougé d'ici, vous n'avez pas quitté cette pièce si calme . . . les pois de senteur" [—Why no. (. . .) You never budged from here, you haven't left this room, so calm . . . the sweet peas] (53). The scene is then replayed as it would happen between two Gentlemen. The Father is the Firm Parent who excuses himself, goes upstairs, scolds the Children for locking the door, and the Polite Children ask if they should have stayed downstairs with the Guest. When the scene ends the earlier grounding of the per-spective from the "salle du haut" is completely reversed and the tension contained: "—Pardonnez-moi. Ils disent qu'ils sont fatigués et puis ils restent à bavarder, demain ils auront des mines de papier mâché, ils se plaindront" [—Excuse me. They say they are tired and then they stay up talking, tomorrow they are going to be pale as ghosts and they'll complain about it] (56).

The ambiguity of orientation continues to parallel the ambiguity of the meaning of the laughter as it is perceived by the Father. The laughter is a source of fury when it signifies his exclusion and also represents his corresponding desire to participate in the world of the Children. This neat opposition, however, is also problematized by the text when the Father's desire expressed in tropistic terms rises to a banal surface: "[. . .] il se penche, il se tend vers ce qui est chaud, palpitant, bondis-sant, vers ce qu'il aime comme eux, ce que comme eux il préfère, la bonne grosse vie qu'on saisit à pleines mains, qu'on étreint . . . Ah bon chien, va brave bête . . ." [(. . .) he leans over, he stretches toward what is warm, throbbing, leaping, toward what he loves as they do, what like them he prefers, the good, big life that we/I/one seize(s) with both hands, that we/I/one hug(s) . . . Ah good dog, how are you, good boy] (29). The Father's desire to join the Children is often represented with the vocabulary found in the first part of this passage, but as seen at the end, the meaning and affect of this desire is sometimes undermined by a return to the surface. The use of the ambiguous pronoun *on* in the phrase "on étreint" veils the shift in reference, effected by the Father's address to the dog, from *nous*, Father and Children, to *il*, the Father.

The Father's desire also descends to the depths of the affection it represents to the Children, or the Children as seen through the Father's eyes: "Il tremblait légèrement, il a serré mes genoux entre ses bras, les larmes ruisselaient sur son visage: Si vous m'acceptiez, moi, si vous ne me rejetiez pas . . . [. . .] ne jamais plus vous éloigner comme tout à l'heure, ne jamais plus faire ça . . ." [He was trembling slightly, he hugged my knees in his arms, tears streamed down his face: If you accept me, if you don't reject me . . . (. . .) don't go away like you did a little while ago, don't do that anymore] (137).

The ambiguity of the perception and thus the "affection" it represents are effaced when the next paragraph begins in response to the unmarked discourse above: "Quoi ça? Il n'a pas osé dire quoi, il savait que c'était dangereux, [. . .] il s'est contenté, pour montrer combien il était devenu pareil à nous, [. . .] . . . Tu as vu? . . . Je n'ai pas pu y tenir, je l'ai embrassé . . ." [Don't do what anymore? He didn't dare say what, he knew that it would be dangerous, (. . .) he was happy, to show how much he had become like us, (. . .) . . . Did you see? . . . I couldn't help it, I kissed him] (137). The discourse at the end of the passage is only marked by its address and its content: "Dépêche-toi, redescends, ton visiteur doit se demander ce qui se passe [. . .]" [Hurry up, go back downstairs, your visitor must be wondering what's going on (. . .)] (138). The next paragraph begins with marked discourse between the two Gentlemen, which reestablishes for the reader the novel's original orientation. This orientation, however, cannot remain stable, because the dramatization of the Father's uncertainty about the Children's laughter, about their innocence and his own, is continually mirrored in the narration itself.

This reflection is exemplified by a passage which places their laughter in a more general context, only to return it to the Father's world:

> Leurs rires explosent plus fort . . . ils ne peuvent plus les maîtriser . . . c'est naturel, cela arrive quand on est fatigué, ou quand on vient d'échapper à un danger, dans les moments tragiques [. . .] . . . il y a des gens, c'est bien connnu, qui sont pris subitement de ces sortes de fous rires. Eux en ce moment sont comme des écoliers lâches dans la cour de recréation . . . [. . .] ils ont écouté [. . .] la leçon, qu'après, c'est bien normal, ils se détendent, [. . .] . . . Il était drôle quand il a pris cet air de magister revêtu de sa toge . . . [. . .] Je plains ses étudiants . . . Mais d'histoire de l'art, évidemment, ho, ho . . .
>
> Mais quelle naïveté, quelle sottise de leur prêter de tels propos . . . Rien de pareil n'a été dit [. . .]

Chacun d'eux sait bien, [. . .] que des rires à propos de rien, mais vraiment ce qui s'appelle rien [. . .] . . . sont entre eux et lui les signaux qu'il ne peut manquer de capter [. . .] (31–32).

[Their laughter explodes louder . . . they can't control themselves . . . it's natural, that happens when we're tired, or when we have just escaped a danger, in tragic moments (. . .) . . . there are people, it's well known, who are suddenly seized by these kinds of mad laughter. They are in those moments like school children let out to play . . . (. . .) they have listened (. . .) to the lesson, that afterward, it's very normal, they relax, (. . .) . . . He was funny when he took on that air of a schoolmaster dressed in his toga . . . (. . .) I pity his students . . . But history of art, obviously, ho, ho . . .
But what naiveté, what foolishness to attribute such words to them . . . Nothing like that was said (. . .).
Each one of them knows very well, (. . .) that the laughter about nothing, but really what's called nothing (. . .) . . . are signs between them and him that he cannot avoid capturing (. . .).]

Is this the Father questioning his own general interpretation, or that of the Friend, or the Children offering an interpretation which is refused by the Father? Any one of these readings is possible, and the possibility of each heightens the menace of the confusion.

By extension, the Children remain ambiguous, both to the Father and to the reader. The Children's perception of the Father is at first contained as silent observation, "ils l'observent," or by description, "ils veulent le rassurer," both of which mark the image of the Children more clearly as a projection of the Father's insecurity. As the novel continues, however, their perceptions enter the narration more directly, and his insecurity becomes the object of their scrutiny just as their laughter had been the object of his: "Un peu de décence, que diable, un peu de dignité, un peu de gravité. Qu'est-ce que c'est que ces jeux suspects? De quoi as-tu l'air? Vraiment tu nous fais honte" [A little decency, good lord, a little dignity, a little gravity. What's with these suspicious games? How do you think it looks? Really you make us ashamed]. The Children offer their behavior as an example: "Regardez-nous . . . Ils se pressent autour de la table . . . Qu'est-ce que c'est, croyez-vous? De quelle époque? [. . .] Ils écoutent attentivement, ils hochent la tête avec respect" [Look at us . . . They lean in around the table . . . What do you think it is? From what period? (. . .) They listen attentively, they nod their heads respectfully] (30–31). Signification in this novel is forever compromised—what are "decency," "dignity," or "gravity" but moral precepts, or rather, words, "adult" words parroted by "children?" Their discourse enters the text as *sous-conversation*, or as judgments beneath the children's silent gestures of acquiescence, and it implicates them in the world of tropistic "games" that had been reserved only for the Father.

These games are checked when figures from "outside" are brought in to review the situation. "Monsieur le proviseur" [the principal] arrives at one point to question the "truth" of the Father's classification of the Children as "cancres" [dunces]: "C'est grave d'enfermer dans des catégories rigides, d'étiquer ce qui est encore fluctuant, changeant . . ." [It's a serious matter to contain in rigid categories, to label what is still fluctuating, changing] (45). When the Father assumes responsibility for the Children's "manque de curiosité" [lack of curiosity] and classifies himself, "je suis impardonnable" [I am unpardonable], "le proviseur" classifies him: "Il connaît cela: [. . .] dès qu'on ose y toucher se précipitant pour protéger de leur corps leur cher petit qu'un ennemi commun menace . . . C'en est touchant . . ." [He recognizes this: [. . .] as soon as anyone dares touch them, hurrying to protect their dear little one with their own bodies from a common enemy who threatens . . . It's touching] (46).

The text contains and dismisses "le proviseur" and his categories with the Father's unceremonious words, "—Oui, je vois, oui je vous remercie, oui, je comprends . . ." [—Yes, I see, yes thank you, yes, I understand], and the next paragraph flows into what cannot be contained: "Se levant, prenant congé, prenant la fuite, fuyant à travers les tristes cours couvertes de gravier, [. . .] à l'odeur [. . .] de désinfectants, le long des mornes salles vitrées où des médiocres ingurgitent docilement des bouillies insipides . . ." [Getting up, taking leave, taking flight, fleeing down sad corridors covered with gravel, (. . .) with the odor (. . .) of disinfectants, past sad rooms with windows where the mediocre ones swallow obediantly insipid gruel . . .] (47). What the "proviseur" earlier called "touchant," "la consternation, la résignation humiliée, la fureur" [consternation, humiliated resignation, fury], is now given experiential substance and recasts the Father's desire to join the Children: "Des dociles, des faibles, comme il était, lui, le plus soumis, le plus sage de tous, lui, la joie de ses maîtres, la fierté de ses parents, lui [. . .]. Fuyant hors d'ici, courant vers eux . . . Impatient de se joindre à eux, de rejoindre en eux cette parcelle secrète de lui-même qu'il avait toute sa vie aidé à écraser" [The docile ones, the weak ones, like he was, him, the most submissive, the smartest of all, him, the joy of his teachers, the pride of his parents, him (. . .). Fleeing far from here, running toward them . . . Impatient to get back to them, to get back from them that secret piece of himself that he has all his life helped to crush] (47). The phrase "courant vers eux . . . impatient" resembles one discussed earlier in the passage about the Mistress. The repetition invites the reader to superimpose these two dramas. Where the "Mistress" passage is mocking, however, this one is more emotionally charged.

As in the case of the "ogre" imagery, where several variations of the image multiply it in such a way as to leave more of a sensation than a simple designation, variations on the questioning dramatized in the "proviseur" scene are scattered throughout the novel. One scene takes place in a museum where "des gaillards bien plantés sur leurs jambes écartées, [. . .] leurs bras musclés entourant les épaules des filles" [young toughs, sturdy on legs wide apart, (. . .) their muscled arms around the girls' shoulders] are "juste à côté de nous" [just next to us], "riant" [laughing], making fun of the paintings (78–79). The perspective appears to be that of the Father. It is introduced by the phrase, "Mais le mal est partout" [But evil is everywhere], and punctuated by a similar one—"Dans des organismes prédisposés, sur des terrains propices le moindre germe se développe, prolifère . . . On a beau tout aseptiser" [In predisposed organisms, on favorable ground the slightest germ develops, spreads . . . Antiseptics are in vain] (78–79). Dramatizations such as this one pretend to a certain linearity: discourse is often well delineated, and the "scene" unfolds. Then everything returns to one of the "primary" scenes: the Friend taking the statue down off the mantel, the Children excusing themselves to go to bed, and the Father going up to find out the meaning of their Laughter.

At the end of the scene at the museum, the return to a primary scene is marked by a shift in perspective when what appears above to have been from the Father's perspective is re-viewed from another orientation: "C'est ça qu'ils ont capté avec leur appareil mis au point au cours de tant d'années [. . .], c'est cela qu'ils ont perçu quand il s'est écarté de la table d'un mouvement un peu trop vif [. . .] . . . Ils savent [. . .] qu'il est toujours tourné vers eux [. . .]" [That's what they captured with their camera focused on the passing of years, (. . .) that's what they perceived when he got up from the table with a slightly too quick movement (. . .) . . . They know (. . .) that he is always turned toward them (. . .)] (81). The Father's going upstairs is here described in a more metaphorical language than has been earlier seen in the Children's discourse: "[. . .] ils se sont écartés violemment, ils sont montés, le traînant derrière eux, le faisant se cogner durement, sa tête rebondissant contre les marches . . ." [(. . .) they got up violently, they went upstairs, dragging him behind them, making him bang himself hard, his head bouncing on the stairs. . . .] (82).

In another scene, "l'assistante social" [the social worker] tries to separate "reality" from such metaphorical language. The scene begins with the Children coming shyly downstairs, their stammering voices overlap. One comes forward, others nod or speak, someone tells it one way, it is corrected or affirmed by another, until finally the metaphorical language resurfaces: "Alors il s'est jeté sur moi et il a aboyé" [Then he threw himself on me and barked]. Another voice mis-hears the liaison between *il* and *a* in this phrase, which effects the sound *ila;* the voice asks: "La quoi?" [*La* what?] (89). All misunderstanding stops when someone utters the words, "il m'a mordue, [. . .], ils approuvent de la tête . . . —C'est vrai, il l'a mordue" [he bit me, (. . .) they nod in approval . . . —It's true, he did bite her] (89). When "l'assistante" asks to see where "il l'a mordue," a voice replies that it is "une morsure qui ne se voit pas . . ." [it's a bite that isn't visible] and the father charges the children with using "métaphores vulgaires, cette outrance de mauvais goût . . ." [vulgar metaphors, that outrageous bad taste] (92).

The Children later mock the Father's use of excessive language with their own literalness. "Nous menaçant?" [Us threatening?], they ask, "Dangereux?" Their voice tells "messieurs les agents" to come closer: "Venez donc, approchez, vous pouvez nous fouiller, nous n'avons pas d'armes, nous n'avions aucune mauvaise intention. Ce monsieur s'est fait des idées. Voici nos papiers. Nous sommes de bonne famille" [Come on then, closer, you can frisk us, we don't have any weapons, we didn't mean any harm. This monsieur is imagining things. Here are our papers. We're from a good family] (165).

After "l'assistante sociale" leaves, the Friend agrees with the Father that the Children have "des natures médiocres" [mediocre natures]. The Friend's literal use of the term provokes a subsurface response in the Father which reveals that he does not use the term because of what it *means,* he used it because of the *emotion* it represents to him: "Il se sent tout faible, un léger vertigo" [He feels completely weak, a slight vertigo]. The scene becomes a courtroom drama where language is not so fluid, where everything is "net" [clear], "immuable" [immutable] (99). The interrogation begins and the voice of the judge asks for the "facts." The Father's lack of proof, his metaphorical use of language, and his (mis)reading of the Children's silence all cause him to lose his case: "—Alors il n'y a pas de preuves. Ici, on vous le dit, on ne tient compte que de ce qui se montre" [—Well, there is no proof. Here, you have been told, we only consider what can be shown] (101). The courtroom drama is wonderfully conventional, a soap opera. Transparent gestures draw a recognizable and ironic picture that releases the reader momentarily from the tension created by the novel's more predominant disorientation. When it is over, that release is affirmed by the Father's response: "Il sent une faiblesse délicieuse, comme au réveil, quand la grosse fièvre est tombée [. . .]. Comme la sentence rendue est juste. Comme il est bon de s'y plier . . ." [He feels a delicious weakness, as on awakening, when the high fever has fallen (. . .). How just is the sentence laid down. How good it is to submit to it] (105). The conventional quality of the scene remains, however, to remind the reader of the illusory quality of such a transparent text.

The trial scene restores order and the Father takes on the role of someone from the Older Generation: "Plus de luttes . . . A quoi bon? . . . Il faut enfin comprendre qu'on a fait son temps, que c'est à eux de jouer . . ." [No more fights . . . What's the use? . . . We must finally understand that we've had our time, it's their turn to play] (105). The transition is marked by what appears to be the voice of one of the Children who addresses the Old Father, "[. . . .] je vais vous le porter" [(. . .) I'm going to bring it to you]; then the orientation shifts to describe him, "ah mais c'est qu'il est encore gaillard, c'est qu'il va tous nous enterrer . . ." [ah, but he's still strong, he's going to bury us all]. A voice from the Older Generation follows in the same breath, "il faut les laisser s'abandonner à leur lubies, à leur manies" [they must be left to give themselves over to their fads, to their obsessions]: "Quoi de plus normal? Quoi de plus sain?" [What could be more normal? What could be more healthy?] (106–7).

The text that follows this "orderly" statement, however, focuses on how "unhealthy" these "manies" are, and the pronouns suggest that the description comes from the Children instead of the Father: "Est-ce qu'on vous demande de venir avec nous? Est-ce qu'on se permet de vous forcer à suivre avec nous d'un oeil pareil à s'y méprendre à un oeil de verre les déplacements de la petite boule, tout votre corps secoué par les tressautements des flippers? . . . A écouter dans le tintamarre les airs d'une délectable vulgarité diffusée par les juke-boxes? [. . .] A lire des comics?" [Did we ask you to come with us? Did someone force you, with an eye that looks so much like a glass eye that you can't tell them apart, like us, to follow the movements of the little ball, your whole body shaken by the jolt of the flippers? . . . To listen in the racket to songs of a delectable vulgarity coming out of juke-boxes? (. . .) To read comics?] (107). The roles assigned the Gentlemen and the Children as figures from different generations reduce the threat of the laughter. When again "les rires s'élèvent" [the laughs rise up], they are called "de vrais bons gros rires, dirigés sur rien, pas sur nous, c'est évident [. . .]" [true, good, hearty laughs, aimed at nothing, not at us, that's clear (. . .)] (108). The question which opened the novel is repeated and the tension it represented earlier replaced by the transparency of the discourse: "Vous les entendez? . . . Mon père disait de nous: Ils sont si bêtes . . ." [Do you hear them? . . . My father used to say of us: They're so stupid . . .] (108–9).

The two Gentlemen are left alone with "la bête," but no figure is left alone in this novel. The initial configuration is no longer possible, by which the laughter "là-haut" [up there] was interpreted from "là-bas" [down here]. Perspectives from "là-haut" become more and more prevalent: "[. . .] voyez-vous ça, lui aussi, tout comme l'autre, en sécurité parmi les percales glacées, les pois de senteur [. . .] . . . si loin tous deux de là où nous sommes, des arrière-cours humides et sombres où autrefois il jouait avec nous . . ." [(. . .) do you see that, him too, just like the other one, safe among the glazed percale, the sweet peas (. . .) . . . so far, both of them from where we are, the damp, dark backyards where he used to play with us] (117). Words that earlier characterized the Father's fear that the Friend would take the Statue down from the mantel, "devant eux," also seem to shift their origin: "l'autre étend la main vers la bête . . . va la poser . . . il faut le retenir, l'arrêter, ne pas crier . . . attention, ne touchez pas, c'est dangereux, ne sentez-vous rien? . . ." [The other one stretches out his hand toward the beast . . . is going to place it . . . he must be held back, stop him, don't scream . . . watch out, don't touch, it's dangerous, don't you feel anything? . . .] (118).

Even this reversal fluctuates. The change in the perspective of the narration by which the Children are the observing, discursive subjects is marked by the phrase "la porte en haut s'ouvre lentement, les voilà . . . ils descendent en silence" [the door upstairs opens slowly, here they are . . . they come down in silence] (123). The passage reads like a theatre script as *ils* move silently toward the living room, the floor squeaks, they stop, put a finger to their lips. It becomes clearer that the Father's and not the Children's perception has been framing the scene when the narration is interrupted by the questions, "vers quoi? que font-ils? . . ." [toward what? what are they doing . . .], which are followed by the words, "Il attend . . ." [He waits . . .]. This orientation is then verified in the text: "Mais attention, ils vont se retourner . . . [. . .] qu'ils ne sachent pas qu'il est là à les épier . . ." [But look out, they are going to turn around . . . (. . .) don't let them know that he is there spying on them] (123). The Father's intrusion takes over the narration for the next few pages (123–27).

When the scene of the Children coming downstairs is replayed, they are in more clear control of the perspective; as opposed to the earlier reference, "la porte s'ouvre," this passage begins in the active voice: "Ils ouvrent la porte, ils descendent, ils entrent . . ." [They open the door, they come downstairs, they come in . . .] (129). The Children's earlier silent exploration of the living room, which had been interrupted by the Father's perspective, is now replaced by *their* observation of the Gentlemen: "Les deux vieux hommes sont assis l'un en face de l'autre [. . .]. Regardez celui-ci: il tient encore sa pipe serrée entre ses dents . . . [. . .] Et cette bête de pierre . . . [. . .] Un objet sacré qui servait probablement à quelque culte . . . Quel culte? . . . Comment retrouver ce qu'elle pouvait bien représenter pour eux . . .?" [The two old men are seated facing one another (. . .). Look at this one: he's still holding his pipe in his teeth . . . (. . .) And that stone animal . . . (. . .) A sacred object probably used in some cult . . . What cult? . . . How can we know what it must have represented to them . . .?] (129). Just as the Father's sense that "ils l'observent" in an earlier passage brought on "leurs rires," this image of the two Gentlemen frozen in motion brings up marked discourse which realizes the image: "—Vous n'avez pas par moments l'impression que c'est fini, tout ça . . . Mort. [. . .] Nous sommes les habitants de Pompéi ensevelis sous les cendres" [—Do you have the impression that it's finished, all this . . . Dead. (. . .) We are the inhabitants of Pompeii buried beneath the ashes] (130). A variation on the question which began the novel interrupts this marked discourse: "Tu l'entends? Ce que dit ton frère, ton sosie . . ." [Do you hear it? What your brother says, your double . . .] (130). The grammatical alteration from *vous* to *tu* orients momentarily the reversal of perspective.

When the initial perspective from the beginning of the novel returns, the vertigo of orientation comes to a momentary halt: "Mais tout à coup: Ecoutez . . . [. . .] —C'est quelque chose . . . —Ah c'est encore ça? Ce sont ces rires? . . . —Enfin pas les rires exactement . . . les rires en soi ce n'est rien . . . —Non, rien, en effet . . . Je suis heureux de vous l'entendre dire . . . —Ce n'est rien en soi, mais il y a là . . . Je sais [. . .] que c'est insensé. . . —Oui, insensé, ça l'est. [. . .] Ils s'amusent. Un point c'est tout. Des-gosses-qui-s'amusent. Rien d'autre. Ça ne *peut* être rien d'autre. Ces rires sont ce que vous en faites" [All of a sudden: Listen . . . (. . .) —There's something . . . —Ah, still at it? That laughter? . . . —Well not exactly the laughter . . . the laughter in itself isn't anything . . . —No, it isn't anything . . . I'm happy to hear you say it . . . —It isn't anything in itself, but there's something there . . . I know (. . .) that it's crazy . . . —Yes, crazy, that's what it is (. . .) They are having fun. Period, that's it. Kids-amusing-themselves. That's all. That's all it *could* be. This laughter is whatever you make of it] (139–40). The Father agrees and identifies the laughter as evidence of an "éclipse du goût" [eclipse of taste] (141). There is no way, however, to return to such an "innocent" reading of the laughter. As the two Gentlemen discuss concepts of "goût" and of "art," the narration presenting their exchange is interrupted by remarks from "elsewhere": "Goût? Goût, vraiment? Avons-nous bien entendu? Goût. Oui, goût . . . [. . .] Du vrai? Art? De mieux en mieux. Art. De Charybde en Scylla. Art. Ah, Ah, Ah . . . Art . . ." [Taste? Taste, really? Did we hear that right? Taste. Yes, taste . . . (. . .) True? Art? Better and better. Art. From Scylla to Charybdis. Art. Ah, Ah, Ah . . . Art . . .] (141–42).

Unmarked and mutual attacks follow in *sous-conversation*. One perspective mocks the "l'oeil immobile [. . .] dressé dès son jeune âge au service des Maîtres" [the immovable eye (. . .) turned from a very young age to serve the Masters]; this perspective identifies itself as "nous, appelés à lui succéder" [us, called to succeed him] (142, 143). The other perspective reproaches "ces vilains garnements [. . .] on a beau les éduquer, tout essayer . . . la douceur . . . la force . . ." [those nasty hellions (. . .) it's useless to educate them, tried everything . . . gentleness . . . firmness . . .] (143). The emotion of these attacks rises momentarily to the surface of the narration when the Father addresses the Friend in marked discourse and attempts to explain how the Children have taken the Statue upstairs and dressed it up: "—Ils ont . . . mais c'est atroce [. . .] . . . ils ont fabriqué avec du papier gaufré comme celui qu'on trouve [. . .] au fond des boîtes de biscuits, de chocolats . . . un collier, une fraise [. . .]" [—They've . . . but it's outrageous (. . .) . . . they've made, with that embossed paper like the kind you find (. . .) at the bottom of boxes of cookies, of chocolates . . . a necklace, a ruffle (. . .)] (144).

The realist touchstone provided by the Friend's marked response of concern disappears as *sous-conversation* takes over and the passage ends with an image of "fusion complète" which frightens the Father as Gentleman: "Plus rien que ce qui maintenant en lui, à travers lui, entre eux et lui se propulse, circule, ils ne font qu'un, ils sont comme les anneaux d'un serpent qui se dresse, oscille, rampe, grimpe sur les meubles, [. . .] sur l'escalier, se roule en boule, se laisse tomber [. . .] . . . l'eau coule des vases renversés . . . [. . .]. Retombé tout essoufflé dans son fauteuil il lève la tête et voit penchés sur lui leurs visages souriants . . . Vous voyez ce que vous me faites faire . . ." [Nothing any more except what now in him, through him, between them and him is propulsed, circulates, they are one, they are like the rings on a snake which straightens up, sways, slithers, climbs on the furniture (. . .), on the stairway, rolls itself into a ball, lets itself fall (. . .) . . . water flows from overturned vases . . . (. . .). Fallen all out of breath into his easy chair he raises his head and sees leaning over him their smiling faces . . . You see what you make me do . . .] (151). The Father emerges from this hallucination to find the Friend seated across from him at the coffee table, "aussi insensible que les murailles d'un château fort aux vaguelettees qui clapotent à leur pied [. . .]" [as unaware as the walls of a fortress to the little waves which lap at their feet] (151). In the dialogue between the two Gentlemen that follows, surrounded by the Father's *sous-conversation* and the Children's observation, the two figures of the Older Generation move farther and farther apart.

Their separation rises to the surface of the narration when the Children's mockery of the Gentlemen's language takes on a material form as the play of signification and orientation at all levels throughout the novel becomes a "game":

> La porte s'ouvre et quelque chose comme un de ces poissons d'avril en papier qu'on attache au bout d'une ligne . . . lentement descend [. . .] . . . il voit se balançant au-dessus de sa tête un écriteau sur lequel ils ont tracé en noir sur blanc: Rires innocents . . . Il le saisit, l'arrache, le froisse et le cache hâtivement dans sa poche . . . Non, pas ça, pas innocents . . . pour qui me prenez-vous? [. . .] La ligne remonte [. . .] de nouveau au bout de la ligne un écriteau descend, se balance: Rire moqueurs . . . Sa main avide se tend . . . Oui, c'est ça: moqueurs. Parfait. Vous les entendez: ce sont des rires moqueurs. C'est évident et c'est très bien. Il est bon à leur âge de s'affirmer contre nous, je trouve ça très sain . . . (169–70).

> [The door opens and something like one of those April Fool's jokes made of paper tied to the end of a string . . . slowly comes down (. . .) . . . he sees swaying above his head a sign on which they have written in black and white: Innocent laughter . . . He grabs it, tears, crumples it up and quickly hides it in his pocket . . . No, not that, not innocent . . . who do you take me for? (. . .) The string goes back up again (. . .), a sign comes down, sways: Mocking laughter . . . His eager hand reaches out . . . Yes, that's it: mocking. Perfect. Do you hear them: it's mocking laughter. It's obvious and it's very good at their age to affirm themselves against us, I find that very healthy . . .]

With this "sign" before him, the Friend becomes uncomfortable. Another sign rises in the air, "Rires sournois . . ." [Deceitful laughter]: "L'ami [. . .] lève la main, il le saisit, le regarde . . . Qu'est-ce que c'est? Sournois . . . Oui, il n'y a pas de doute: sournois est le mot qui convient . . ." [The friend (. . .) raises his hand, grabs hold of it, looks at it . . . What's this? Deceitful . . . Yes, no doubt about it: deceitful is the word . . .] (170). The passage continues in the Friend's consciousness as he reviews what this characteristic might mean: "Mais ce qu'il voit devant lui le fait se pencher en avant [. . .]: une tête qui opine, un visage luisant de satisfaction, un sourire béat . . . Oui, vous le voyez, j'avais raison [. . .]" [But what he sees before him makes him lean forward (. . .): a head that nods, a face shining with satisfaction, a blissful smile . . . yes, you see, I was right (. . .)] (171). As in a horror film or murder tale, when the most respectable among you comes forth and admits to having committed the grisly act, this nodding head represents the Indulgent Father who is no longer a Gentleman. His position is that *ils* can be as "sournois" as they like, as long as "ils soient ce qu'ils veulent, qu'ils soient n'importe quoi pourvu qu'ils soient ce qu'ils sont" [they are what they want to be, that they are anything as long as they be what they are] (171).

In an inevitable inversion, the challenge to the Indulgent Father's
role does not come from the Friend: "Les rires s'arrêtent. [. . .] Et eux
descendent, s'approchent de lui . . ." [The laughter stops. (. . .) And
they come downstairs, approach him . . .] (171). How can words from
"elsewhere" contain "ce qui sans cesse entre nous circule, si fluide, si
fluctuant?" [what circulates endlessly between us, so fluid, so fluctuating?] (172). The drama, scenes, tensions, emotions, and ambiguity come
to a halt with this passage, which introduces an exemplary tropistic
image and realizes the Father's earlier desire for union: "C'est vrai, ils
ont raison, comment ces vieux mots sclérosés pourraient-ils retenir,
enserrer ce qui sans cesse entre nous circule, si fluide, fluctuant, [. . .]
il hume l'odeur de lait et de miel de leur peau, la jeune sève qui monte
d'eux coule en lui . . ." [It's true, they're right, how could those old,
ossified words hold back, shut in what endlessly between us circulates,
so fluid, so fluctuating, (. . .) he breathes in the milk and honey odor of
their skin, the young sap that rises from them flows into him . . .] (172).
The neatness of this tropistic union is ripped away from the reader as
violently as the Father pulls away from the Children as the sentence
continues: ". . . il s'arrache à eux, les repousse . . ." [. . . he tears himself
away from them, pushes them back . . .] (172).

Like someone who must return to his own tribe to die but wishes to
leave a token of remembrance, the Father gives the Statue to the Children in the end and their exchange is represented in marked discourse.
The Statue is handed to a figure designated as *elle*, "elle la serre contre
elle . . ." [she hugs it to her]. This Child wags her finger at her Father
and says: "— [. . .] tu monteras peut-être chez nous plus souvent, grand
méchant loup . . ." [— (. . .) perhaps you will come up to our room
more often, big, bad wolf . . .] (174). The mirroring of the pronouns in
the phrase "elle la serre contre elle" parallels the mirroring of Father
and Children: "Il a compris enfin qu'il ne lui reste qu'à se soumettre, à
accepter l'inéluctable . . ." [He finally understood that the only thing
left for him to do is submit, to accept the inescapable . . .] (177). This
mirroring lasts only momentarily, because these figures can only maintain their roles as one *or* the other. A union may not be possible between
the subject and object of the question "Vous les entendez?"; it becomes
increasingly apparent, however, that a reversal of roles is inevitable.

In the passage that follows the Father returns to the Children's room.
There he sees a shell tied to the Statue's back and full of cigarette butts.
He turns around to face the Children, puts his hands in his pockets,
and resumes his role as Father: "Il y a dans son regard une expression
étrange, insolite, d'indifférence, de distance bienveillante . . . —On a
tort, vous savez, de maltraiter ainsi ce pauvre animal . . ." [There is in
his look a strange, unusual expression of indifference, of kindly dis-

tance . . . —It's wrong, you know, to treat that poor animal like that]
(178). The Children assume their role as well, blaming one another for
the disrespect shown to the Statue and suggesting that it would be
better off in a museum, "Pourquoi pas au Louvre?" [Why not in the
Louvre?] This is a role the Children have never played without the
Father being cast as the "ogre."

The Father's response is silence, which is represented by his shift as
subject of narration to object, that is, his silence leaves him open to
interpretation: "Mais parle . . . Tu préfères ça? Tu voudrais qu'on la
mette dans une vitrine, sous clef? . . . Il secoue la tête faiblement . . .
Non, il ne veut pas . . . pas dans une vitrine . . ." [But say something
. . . Do you prefer that? Would you like us to place it in a showcase,
under lock and key . . . He shakes his head weakly . . . No, he doesn't
want that . . . not in a showcase . . .] (180). In a narration that is clearly
not the Father's, the sumptuousness of the museum where the Statue
should be housed is presented in terms like the ones the Father had
used earlier in the novel when he imagined the kind of treatment that
the Statue deserved.

At the end of the passage above, the Father becomes a Childlike Old
Man: "[. . .] il approuve de la tête, sa bouche s'étire en un bon sourire
édenté . . . Je ferai comme vous voudrez. De toute façon bientôt ce sera
à vous de décider . . ." [(. . .) he agrees with a nod of the head, a good,
toothless smile spreads across his mouth . . . I'll do whatever you like.
In any case, soon you will have to decide for yourselves] (181). The
Father's enthusiastic acceptance of the idea of giving up the Statue and
of taking on the perception of the Children as "très gentils avec moi"
[very nice with me] is represented in an over-affirmative *sous-conversation* (181–82). When his discourse returns to the surface of an exchange
with the Children, they address him and he responds in keeping with
the role of Sweet Old Father: "Mais qu'est-ce que tu as? [. . .] tu as l'air
désolé . . . —Non, pas du tout . . . Bien sûr, j'aurais préféré que vous la
gardiez, mais j'ai tort, je le sais bien . . . [. . .] D'autres en profiteront . . .
Ils lui caressent la tête, ils lui sourient . . . Il lève vers eux un regard
humble, un regard craintif, fautif, d'enfant . . ." [But what's the matter
with you? (. . .) you seem sad . . . —No, not at all . . . Of course, I would
have preferred that you keep it, but I'm wrong, I know it's true . . . (. . .)
Others will profit by it . . . They caress his head, they smile at him . . .
He raises toward them a humble look, the frightened look, guilty, of a
child . . .] (183).

The Father disappears from the narration in the last pages of the
novel and the Children act out the attribute he assigned to them, "gentils." They go to the museum to see the Statue and give it its due
respect: "Ils s'approchent et se tiennent devant elle dans un pieux si-

lence. Les amis se penchent et lisent respectueusement l'inscription . . ." [They approach it and stand there in pious silence. The
friends lean over and respectfully read the inscription . . .] (185). The
Children tell the story about the time when one of them dared suggest
that the sculpture was "une sculpture crétoise" [a Cretan statue], and
all earlier tension is effaced by the narrative they tell: "— [. . .] Quel
crime! Mon père avait envie de le tuer . . . hochant la tête . . . Ah, ce
pauvre papa . . ." [— (. . .) What a crime that was! My father felt like
killing him . . . shaking heads . . . Ah, that poor papa . . .] (185). Similarly, all tropistic perception is effaced by the surface discourse of these
"nice children": "—[. . .] Mais vous savez que si nous voulons tout voir
[. . .] . . . Vous voyez, nous avons encore beaucoup de pain sur la plan-
che . . ." [— (. . .) But you know that if we want to see everything (. . .)
. . . Look, we still have a lot to do . . .] (185).

Two short paragraphs following this scene end *Vous les entendez?*
The first refers to "leur rires," but the neatness of the preceding image
of the Children places these figures so far away from the confusion that
these words have evoked throughout the novel that the reference returns to the reader as only a memory of the fluid, disorienting experience of reading: "Leurs rires s'égrènent . . . Des rires insouciants. Des
rires innocents. Des rires pour personne. Des rires dans le vide. Leurs
voix font un bruit confus qui s'affaiblit, s'éloigne . . ." [Their laughter
falls. Carefree laughter. Innocent laughter. Laughter for no one. Laughter
in the emptiness. Their voices make a confusing sound that grows
fainter, fades away . . .] (185). The point of view which might orient
this paragraph appears vaguely in the final one, which consists of one
sentence: "On dirait qu'une porte, là-haut se referme . . . Et puis plus
rien" [You could say that a door, upstairs closes . . . And then nothing]
(185).

This novel begins with an *il* interrupting himself and asking the
question that comprises the title, "Vous les entendez?" The opening
question leads to a play of perception by which the fluid figure of the
Father emerges and merges with the equally fluid figures represented
in the question by *vous* and *les*. The textual elements of the narration
enact that play in the reading such that in the end, all figures converge
on the personal pronoun which orients the final image, *on*. The disorientation created by the play of perceptions continues with the conditional mode of the verb, "dirait." The Father's longed-for union with
his Children has taken place, not within the narrative, where its frozen
form would have effaced its fluidity, but in the evocative power of this
image. The principal figures of the novel have moved from one category
to another: Father as Gentleman is "vieux papa" at the end, and *ils*
as Rebellious Adolescents are "gentils enfants." "Leurs rires," which

represent in multiple images "les enfants" throughout the novel, are reduced in the final sentence to the single "bruit confus qui s'affaiblit et s'éloigne . . ." The ambiguity which marks the play of perception within the structure of *Vous les entendez?* no longer resides in the relationship between the figures; it remains in the mind of the reader.

The master narrative has not been undermined by the Children's Revolt; it has been problematized by the Father's ambiguous relationship to his designation of the laughter as Other—innocent or malevolent—which was necessary for that narrative to remain intact. Sarraute would never identify the Father's aesthetic taste as a "master narrative." Her novel simply opens up the space that an Absolute Value occupies and reveals the complexity of the desire that creates it.

"disent les imbéciles"

Like *Vous les entendez?*, Sarraute's seventh novel, *"disent les imbéciles,"* begins with an invitation to perceive: "Elle est mignonne, n'est-ce pas? Regardez-moi ça . . ." [She's cute, isn't she? Just take a look at that]. The figure of *elle* placed at the center of "le regard," however, is merely a lure to character-ize. The subjective nature of character-izing is clear at the beginning of the novel when the referent to *elle* is designated not simply as "notre grand-mère" [our grandmother], but also as "ce qu'elle représente pour chacun de nous" [what she represents for each of us].[3]

This qualification parallels the Friend's words to the Father in *Vous les entendez?*, "ces rires sont ce que vous en faites" [this laughter is what you make of it]. In *"disent . . ."* that same observation is given a slightly different emphasis, as seen in a phrase which appears toward the end of the novel, "C'est vous que ça juge" [It's you that that judges]. In the intertextuality of Sarraute's *oeuvre* this statement also resonates with a statement from *Les Fruits d'Or*, "Parce que vous savez, si vous n'aimiez pas ça, c'est vous que cela jugerait, pas Les Fruits d'Or, ce chef-d'oeuvre . . ." [Because you know, if you didn't like it, that would say more about you than about "Les Fruits d'Or," that masterpiece. . .]. Whereas *Les Fruits d'Or* dramatizes the threat implied by the use of the imperfect and conditional verbs in this statement, *"disent . . ."* animates the space of the character-ization which the threat enacts, or rather this novel invades that space with voices:

"C'est vous." Vous. Vous. Vous. Plus d'infinis, d'espaces sans bornes. [. . .] Vous: ce que vous désignez déjà, et que vous serez forcé de désigner chaque fois qu'on fera l'appel, par le mot: Moi. Vous. [. . .] "Ça" que vous aviez affublé du nom pompeux de "pensée," du nom prestigieux de "vérité," "ça" que vous aviez dissimulé sous de jolies images poétiques [. . .] . . . "Ça" est votre produit. "Ça" est votre sécrétion. "Ça" qui a permis de vous reconnaître et de vous arrêter au moment où vous alliez porter atteinte . . . "Ça" qui figure désormais à votre dossier et qui permet de vous condemner: "C'est vous que ça juge" (133–34).

["It's you." You. You. You. No more infinities, limitless spaces. (. . .) You: what you already designate, and what you will be forced to designate each time that appeal is made, by the word: Me. You. (. . .) "That" which you had fabricated with the pompous name of "thought," with the prestigious name of "truth," "that" which you had dissimulated under pretty, poetic images (. . .) . . . "That" is your product. "That" is your secretion. "That" which allowed you to recognize yourself and to stop yourself when you were going to attack . . . "That" which, from now on, is part of your dossier and which allows you to be condemned: "It's you that that judges."]

This novel takes up where the preceding one left off because the context of "disent . . ." is so anonymous that the figures move back and forth across the line between naming and being named. In none of Sarraute's other novels is address used more effectively to elude definition and to bring the reader into the affective experience of character-ization.[4] Discourse is rarely marked, imperatives, statements, questions are simply addressed; . . . a pronoun is sometimes but not always there to receive them. There is a figure in the opening scene who resists the character-izing of the "notre grand-mère." In Minogue's analysis this figure "apostrophises the work," but that centering is itself a lure which becomes inconsequential in this most fluid of all Sarraute's novels.[5]

In Portrait d'un inconnu, the surface is a mask made up of the constructs which characterize "le lieu commun" and hide from the narrator the "authentic" tropistic reality of "le vieux" and "sa fille." The narrator saw one or the other. The arrival of Monsieur Dumontet represented the triumph of surface reality. The nephew's experience in Martereau begins breaking apart this surface-depth dichotomy. Not only does the narrator recognize the possibility of superimposing many masks on one figure, but by the end he sees the surface and the depth of Martereau simultaneously. In Le Planétarium every surface of every figure is at once surface and depth. This simultaneity is seen most clearly in the figures of Berthe and Pierre, but it is experienced by the reader because of the sous-conversation which gives a depth to the figures in spite of the surface they create for themselves. The surface represented in "disent . . ." is neither authentic nor inauthentic reality, neither exterior nor interior, because the narrative style is virtually devoid of the punctuation and syntax which usually signal to the reader that the text has entered one or the other reality.

Although the fluidity of the style found in the previous novels continually undermines the limits of their settings, the "verbal tyranny" represented takes place in recognizable contexts which serve as a porous surface and structure the ensuing tropistic battles: a literary quest, a nephew's dilemma, a literary debate, a bourgeois family milieu, a writer's struggle, a father's living room. The tropistic battles in these novels achieve a certain "universality" through the use of fairy-tale or epic imagery and of personal identity constructs, because they address the reader at the level of known and recognizable personal experience. Such imagery and familiar contexts are replaced in *"disent . . ."* by a predominance of references to parts of the body. The body and the physical presence it represents become the context where words separate individuals, and where separation is thus felt more profoundly as a corporeal experience.

As in surrealist painting, body parts and gestures are grotesquely enlarged or tenderly diminished; what is "known" is seen in a completely different way. What is recognized is not an imagery the reader has seen before; these are not constructs usually used to define ourselves or others. A sensation of the imagery is instead evoked by the presence of the corporeal, that which cannot be reduced by intellection, which can only be clumsily covered with adhesives.[6] The opening imperative "Regardez-moi ça . . ." leads not into a simple description of *elle*, that which can be *seen*, but what is *felt*, physically: "Leurs doigts caressent la peau soyeuse un peu fripée de la joue . . . la chair moelleuse cède docilement à la pression des doigts . . . ils descendent le long de l'épaule recouverte d'un duveteux châle blanc, se posent sur les mains légèrement boursouflées" [Their fingers caress the silky, slightly crumpled skin of the cheek . . . the flabby skin gives way obediently to the pressure of the fingers . . . they descend the length of the shoulder covered by a downy, white shawl, come to rest on the somewhat puffy hands] (9).

The reader's role as participant in this "caresse" shifts uncomfortably to that of witness when this performative text is replayed as narrative: "Et nous la cajolions et tu la caressais et nous ne pouvions pas détacher nos yeux de son doux visage fané" [And we were cajoling her and you were caressing her and we could not take our eyes off her soft, withered face] (12). The figure that Minogue feels "apostrophies the work" represents the reader as this scene shifts in orientation to make *him* the object of *their* regard, covering him with the affective weight of the earlier "caress" that "their" regard enacted on *elle*: "[. . .] il a peur, il a honte, regardez-le, il cache son visage dans ses mains" [(. . .) he's afraid, he's ashamed, look at him, he hides his face in his hands] (13). "Their" regard naturally turns into a character-ization of *il*: "[. . .] rien de nouveau sous le soleil, tout est connu, classé, d'une lamentable monotonie,

rien n'est plus clair, mieux étudié que son cas [. . .]: il est jaloux" [(. . .)
nothing new under the sun, everything is known, classified, with a
lamentable monotony, nothing is clearer, better studied than his case
(. . .): he's jealous] (15).

In this "tyranny of words," figures are taken prisoner by the look or
words of others, but just as the self is represented as a corporeal mass
whose parts are dissected for character-ization, so too are words. In this
passage the text opens up the word *ja-loux*, and voices in unmarked
discourse play with the resemblance of its ending to the word used to
describe the "grand-mère," *doux*. Then another voice dissects that play:
"Mais il ne faut pas s'y fier, rien n'est plus traître que ces sonorités"
[But don't trust it, nothing is more treacherous than these resonances].
This voice goes on to note that *loux* of *ja-loux* also sounds like *loup*
[fox] (15–16). The play of signification is mirrored by a subsequent play
of images in which *il* becomes *like* a *loup*: "Le violà qui court sous
leurs rires [. . .]. Regardez-le, je le tiens, [. . .] je vais le dégager pour que
vous puissiez mieux l'examiner [. . .] . . . On ne sait pas où se mettre, on
voudrait être, n'est-ce pas, à mille lieues sous la terre quand on a été pris
sur le fait . . . Quel fait? . . . Vous entendez ses pitoyables couinements?"
[There he is running beneath their laughter (. . .). Look at him, I have
him, (. . .) I'm going to let him go so you can examine him better (. . .)
. . . One doesn't know where to place oneself, one would like to be a
thousand leagues under the sea, right, when one is caught in the act
. . . What act? . . . Do you hear his pitiful whining?] (16–17). *Il* is pinned
down with the names "faux frère" [false friend], "traître," "rapace"
[rapacious], "haineux" [hateful], and although the last attribute is questioned—"haineux?"—it too is taken prisoner, "pas de jalousie sans
haine" [no jealousy without hatred] (17).

A play on the meaning of words is continually started and then
brought to a halt before meaning becomes tyranically frozen. This petri-
fication is not always as serious as it was in the passage where the
phrase, "C'est vous que ça juge," becomes a "product." At the end of
Chapter 1 the opening phrase of the novel, "Elle est mignonne," is
juxtaposed with the phrase "un bonbon fondant [. . .], délicieux [. . .] à
amollir dans *sa* bouche" [a fondant (. . .), delicious (. . .) to soften in
her/his mouth]. The parallel implied by the juxtaposition gets stuck,
however, as the passage continues: ". . . mais qu'est-ce que c'est? ce
n'est pas un bonbon, pas une pâte fruitée, *je* ne peux pas le mâcher, *je*
le retire de ma bouche tout mouillé et luisant . . ." [. . . but what's this?
it's not a bonbon, not a fruit flavored toffy, *I* can't chew it, *I* take it out
of my mouth all wet and shiny . . .] (my underlining, 27). The fluctua-
tion of the pronouns from third person to first person in relation to the

image also serves to re-place for the reader an intellectual comprehension of the implied comparison with a more sensual experience.[7]

At another moment in Chapter 1 the character-ization which opens the novel is turned like a coin to represent a threat. "Les cheveux si fins" of "notre grand-mère" are now called "ces mèches grises en désordre de vieille mégère, de vieille sorcière" [those grey, untidy locks of an old shrew, an old witch] (22). The coin is reversed again by the subsequent description of a different kind of physical interaction which resituates the earlier "caresse" of "their" regard in a more familiar semantic register: "[. . .] elle lui sourit de son doux sourire innocent, elle lui pose la main sur sa tête qu'il enfouit dans le creux de sa jupe duveteuse, elle lui caresse les cheveux" [(. . .) she smiles at him with her sweet, innocent smile, she puts her hand on his head that he buries in the folds of her downy skirt, she caresses his hair]. In this reversal, "their" character-ization of the figure of *il*, "jaloux," is tamed by unmarked discourse, and its implied origin is *elle:* "un peu jaloux, c'est vrai, mais un coeur d'or" [a little jealous, it's true, but with a heart of gold] (24).

A thickening of the word "jaloux," as in the case of the description of the grandmother's hair, takes place as a word or an image is juxtaposed in the reader's mind with an earlier reference. Such a play of signification is familiar to the reader. In Sarraute's previous novels the play of pronouns establishes a variety of positions in relation to discourse and to the constructs placed by one figure on another. The reader is implicated in that play by the constant shift in orientation. A certain affectivity on the part of the reader necessarily occurs in that shift, as seen when various subjects speak of being "taken prisoner," but in "*disent les imbéciles*" another dimension of affectivity is added by the play between positions of affectivity itself. The word play enacts not simply a thickening of meaning, but also a thickening of affective experience for the reader which is subtly created not by the many possible meanings for words, but by the sensual effect they may have on a narrative figure. Word play thus goes beyond creating meaning from different points of view, and it sometimes serves inversely to orient the reader by allowing a momentary recognition of one of the impersonal narrative figures, most often in relation to a figure designated as *il*. The figures thus assume a subjective affectivity while retaining an impersonality.

Chapter 1 begins with the sensual construction of *elle*, "ce qu'elle représente pour chacun de nous." Chapter 2 offers a variation on the first, opening with questions *about* an *il:* "Qui? Qu'est-ce? Qui est-il?" [Who? What? Who is he?] (29). Where traits of "grandmotherliness" were attributed to parts of the body of "notre grand-mère," traits of "maniless" are attributed to this figure's body parts: "C'est un menton qui va, en se développant, montrer de la volonté, de la virilité, car pour être viril, ah, il n'y a pas à dire, c'est un vrai garçon, et avec ça, voyez ces longs cils, c'est même dommage, quel gâchis, quand tant de filles . . . et ces mains . . ." [It's a chin that, as it develops, is going to demonstrate will, virility, for in order to be virile, ah, it goes without saying, he's a real boy, and with that, look at those long eyelashes, it's too bad all the same, what a waste, when so many girls . . . and those hands] (29).

As in the case of the "grand-mère" whose look betrayed nothing "pénétrant," this figure of il is described as "aveugle" [blind], "sourd" [deaf], and "inconscient" [unconscious] that the character-izing is taking place. The quality of unconsciousness is itself dramatized through a subtle linearity that prolongs the reader's comprehension of the comparison: "Et lui aveugle, [. . .] tout comme ce jour-là, quand ils le laveront, l'habilleront, le coucheront sur le dos, lui croiseront les mains sur la poitrine, l'entoureront de fleurs, contempleront son haut front [. . .] . . . Regardez comme il a l'air jeune [. . .] Vraiment il n'a jamais été plus beau" [And him, blind (. . .) exactly like on that day when they will wash him, dress him, lay him on his back, cross his hands on his chest, put flowers around him, contemplate his high forehead (. . .) . . . Look how young he looks (. . .). Truly, he has never been so handsome] (29–30). The final sentence gives an ironic twist to the recurring theme of all Sarraute's novels, character-ization freezes and petrifies: here it kills, and the dead figure has "never been so handsome," the irony itself checked by some orderly voice who asks, "pourquoi se porter à de telles extremités?" [why take it to such extremes?] (30).

Each of the narrative figures in Vous les entendez? acts as a representative self for the other; these representative selves then begin to change places. The reversal creates an affective experience which is juxtaposed at the end of the novel with the reader's intellectual experience such that an ambiguity remains like "une fine buée" sought by the two voices at the end of Entre la vie et la mort. In "disent . . ." the narrative figures who emerge become immediately the site of an affective experience. A reversal, exchange, or transferal of that experience serves not to delimit a representative self but to enlarge the possible effects of that experience.

The sensation of refuge is created by a phrase in Chapter 1, after ils have judged il to be "jaloux": "[. . .] il s'enfouit dans le creux de sa jupe duveteuse, elle lui caresse les cheveux . . ." [(. . .) he buries himself in the fold of her downy skirt, she caresses his hair . . .] (23). The giver of that refuge, represented by the synecdoche "sa jupe," then becomes the recipient of a "regard" which similarly effects a sensation of refuge. When the sensation is given an image, however, its connotation enlarges: "[. . .] il tient posé sur elle son regard qu'elle aime [. . .]. Dans ce havre où elle est entrée, où, sans jamais tenter de fuir, [. . .] elle est allée prudemment, sagement se ranger auprès [. . .] de ces beaux vieux voiliers qu'on visite avec émotion, avec respect" [(. . .) he holds the look on her that she loves (. . .). In that haven she has entered, where, without ever trying to escape, (. . .) she has gone to take her place sensibly next to (. . .) those beautiful, old boats that are visited with emotion, with respect] (25).

To the sensation of "refuge" is added "emotion" and "respect," but the words attached to the sensation are not allowed to enter the text transparently. After a break in the page, questions gather around the sensation, which is given a contrasting image: "Que veut-il? Où veut-il l'entraîner, les entraîner tous les deux, son petit fou, son gros bêta? [. . .] Vers quels asiles d'aliénés, où l'on enferme les vieilles agitées aux mèches grises en désordre, les vieilles lubriques aux regards allumés [. . .]" [What does he want? Where is he leading her, leading them, both of them, her little madman, her silly goose? (. . .) Toward what lunatic asylums where old troublemakers with untidy gray strands are kept, lecherous old ladies with burning eyes (. . .)] (25). Contrasting images often effect a change in perspective in Sarraute's novels, but by enforcing the anonymity of the figures in interaction this novel gives a fuller affective weight to the images and the contrast.

Just as the opening call to look materializes into a physical performance in Chapter 1, "leurs doigts caressent," words pass in and out of intellectual play and material effect, as seen in Chapter 2:

—Son menton s'allonge, oui, j'en ai peur qu'il aura un menton en galoche . . . "Son" . . . Ils regardent [. . .], il est enfermé, enserré, circonscrit, délimité, séparé, désigné par ce mot qu'ils appliquent sur lui: son. [. . . Sous] tous les yeux, ça s'avance, un menton auquel le mot "galoche" est venu se coller . . . galoche, valoche, oche . . . la terminaison répugnante, molle, vautrée, adhère, leste, pèse, gonfle, étire, tire toujours plus bas, et à l'aide du g . . . galoche . . . relève hideusement le bout enflé . . . Impossible de l'arrêter, [. . .] ça va grossir toujours plus fort . . . (32, 33).

[—His chin is extended, yes, I'm afraid that he will have a jutting chin . . . "His" . . . They look (. . .), he is enclosed, hugged too tightly, circumscribed, determined, separated, designated by that word they apply to him: his.
(. . . Beneath) their gaze, it moves forward, a chin where the word jutting has been stuck . . . jutting, butting, gutting, gut . . . the repugnant prefix, flabby, sprawled, adheres, weighted down, weighs, distends, stretches, pulls always lower, and with the help of the j . . . jutting . . . raises hideously the swollen end . . . Impossible to stop it, (. . .) it's going to grow even bigger.]

The affective response of *il* to this "naming" allows the reader to conflate this figure with the earlier *il* who was called "jaloux." A caress like the one in Chapter 1 is repeated, "les doigts [. . .] caressent sa joue, son cou . . ." [fingers (. . .) caress his cheek, his neck . . .] (34), and "il cache son visage dans les plis de sa jupe" [he hides his face in the folds of her skirt] (34). The image represents a refuge and reenforces its earlier meaning by recreating a threatening situation in which *il* has only this response.

The novel thus plays not only with words and images, but also with its own linearity. The linearity created is not one in which narrative time passes; it is instead suggested by the repetition of an earlier image which is linked to a later moment or reading by the sensation evoked. A similar kind of linking takes place in the works of Proust. There, however, a sensation in the narrative present collapses the temporal distance between childhood and adulthood, the child self merges with the adult self. The conflation of two narrative moments in *"disent . . ."* takes place beyond the confines of a *self*. Whereas the sarrautien figure as *self* struggles to construct a "true self" by imposing a construction of others in *Portrait* and *Martereau*, or in spite of the constructions imposed by others in *Le Planétarium* and *Entre la vie et la mort*, the narration in *"disent . . ."* goes back and forth across the line between the intellectual and the sensual effects of constructions of the self.

The figure of *il* in Chapter 2 is shocked to hear "son nom" followed by an exchange between two voices: "'Pas intelligent? Vraiment? Tu crois? . . . —J'en suis sûr. Doué, c'est certain, mais pas intelligent'" ["Not intelligent? Really? You think so? . . . —I'm sure of it. Talented, that's certain, but not intelligent"] (35). What is called a "dédoublement" [doubling] takes place within the figure of *il*. One part has "une sensation inconnue" [an unknown sensation] that is compared to someone who has "des jambes paralysées" [paralyzed legs], and the other part tries "de se hisser à leur hauteur" [to raise himself to their height] by claiming that "vous avez raison" [you're right], which then becomes "une petite idée, juste à sa mesure" [a little idea, made just for him] (36–38). This "doubling" could introduce a dichotomy between intellect ("une idée") and sensation, here heightened because the sensation is described as "inconnue." Even intellection, however, is turned into an affective experience when "une idée," "une pensée" [a thought], "une opinion," become, as Minogue writes, "uniforms and weapons of warring selves demanding or denying recognition, asserting or refusing categorisation."[8]

The exchange overheard by *il* is then recounted to another figure: "—[. . .] C'était réel. J'ai entendu de mes oreilles" [—(. . .) It's real. I heard it with my own ears] (41). The context surrounding the account of the exchange is that of a child speaking to an adult. The phrase "il cache son visage dans les plis de sa jupe" precedes the account, identifying one of the grandchildren as the *il* who overheard the exchange and who is now telling his grandmother (34). The account is followed by the words that corroborate this reading: "Allons, allons, mon petit, ce sont des choses qui arrivent à ton âge" [Now, now, my little one, these are things that happen at your age] (41). The gentleness of this remark is somewhat undercut by the speaker's final judgment of the situation: "—[. . .] C'est tout de même insensé de se laisser impressionner à ce point par des petits imbéciles" [—(. . .) All the same, it's crazy to let oneself be impressed to such a degree by little fools] (42).

Between these two points, however, the character-ization the reader attempts to identify the two voices with these secure roles is slightly displaced by the tone of their exchange. It especially does not correspond to the figure of *il* who, like a child, "se cache dans les plis de sa jupe." Although a childhood image is used to describe the effect of the statement on *il*, that image is one of several commonplace experiences more characteristic of an adult's language: "'Des petits imbéciles' . . . du tac au tac, répondre du tac au tac. [. . .] Rendre quelqu'un la monnaie de sa pièce. [. . .] C'est ainsi qu'on nomme ça. [. . .] Bien d'autres expressions pourraient sans doute convenir à cette opération pratiquée avec succès dès l'école maternelle: 'Puisque tu l'as dit, c'est toi-même'" . . . ["Little fools" . . . tit for tat, always have a quick reply. (. . .) Pay them back in kind. (. . .) That's what they call that. (. . .) Many other expressions would surely fit that operation practiced successfully since first grade: "Takes one to know one" . . .] (42). The voices thus represent and do not represent the grandmother and her grandson; they become merely two voices in a barely marked dialogue, almost as if the "dédoublement" between sensation and intellect referred to above has taken on voices.

This is where Chapter 3 begins, not with the identification of the voices, but with the difficulty a figure designated as *je* has in pronouncing the words that the "grandmother" voice used so easily in the preceding chapter, "des imbéciles." Before the words themselves appear, that difficulty is performed through metaphorical language, dramatic effect, and comparison, and in the context of a dialogue: "[. . .] je le saisis, je le tiens, j'appuie [. . .]. Petit à petit le durcissement gagne [. . .]. C'est un lieu clos, [. . .] je me cogne contre elles, je tourne en rond . . . Des voix [. . .] répètent les mêmes . . . —Les mêmes quoi? Les mêmes stupidités? —Non, je ne le dirai pas . . . [. . .]. Il crie . . . sa voix comme contaminée [. . .]: 'C'est faux. Ce que vous dites est faux. Faux. Faux. [. . .] Ce que vous dites est une stupidité. [. . .] C'est ce que disent

les imbéciles'" [(. . .) I grab hold of it, I hold it, I push (. . .). Little by
little the hardening takes over (. . .). It's a tight place, (. . .) I bang against
them, I turn in circles . . . The voices (. . .) repeat the same . . . —The
same what? The same inanities? —No, I will not say it . . . (. . .) He
cries out . . . his voice like one contaminated (. . .): "It's false. What you
say is false. False. False. (. . .) What you say is an inanity. (. . .) That's
what fools say"] (44–46). Because of this attack against "les imbéciles,"
the speaker is aligned with "un de nos maîtres" [one of our masters],
one who knows how to isolate an idea and pronounce it as spoken by
"les imbéciles," even though il does not want to pay "ce prix" [this
price] of being character-ized himself (46–47). The price is confine-
ment in an idea, and the image of imprisonment is dramatized in the
following pages where the world divides between "us" and "them"
"eux les imbéciles" [them the imbeciles] and "nous exclus par notre
faute, nous ignorants, bernés, menés à notre insu par le bout du nez"
[us, excluded through our own fault, us the ignorant ones, tricked, lead
on our own by the end of our noses] (52).

Abstractions become realized, words pronounced in the text call
forth the "reality" of their referent, as if a president declared war with
the phrase, "I declare war," and just as quickly finds herself beamed to
a battlefield in the middle of gunfire where a soldier next to her falls
dead. Seeming and being fold in upon themselves: "Mais petit à petit,
à les observer de si près . . . vous ne trouvez pas qu'on éprouve une
sensation . . . vous ne la reconnaissez pas? [. . .] . . . c'est comme un
début d'asphyxie dans un air confiné, dans un lieu hermétiquement
close . . . Nous avons été enfermés avec eux . . . avec ces momies . . .
c'est un tombeau, un sarcophage . . ." [But little by little, to look at
them this closely . . . don't you feel something . . . don't you recognize
it? (. . .) . . . it's like the beginning of asphyxiation in a confined place,
in a place that's hermetically sealed . . . We have been closed up with
them . . . with those mummies, it's a tomb, a sarcophagus . . .] (53).
This performative text also acts out its own reflection, a voice repeats
a variation of the earlier phrase, "it takes one to know one": "—Quoi?
[. . .] Vous poussez l'audace jusqu'à essayer de nous faire admettre que
ceux qui disent des autres: [. . .] deviennent eux-mêmes . . . c'est bien
ça?" [—What? (. . .) You would carry audacity so far as to try and make
us admit that those who speak of others: (. . .) become that themselves
. . . is that it?] (53).

There are "des idées," "des pensées," "des opinions" in this novel:
distinguishing between self and other is the only way to survive; "je
vous les désigne—eux les imbéciles" [I point them out to you—them
the fools] versus "les imbéciles n'existent pas," "c'est un produit de
votre imagination" [fools do not exist, (. . .) it's a product of your imagi-

nation]. These ideas, however, are juxtaposed with a voice asking desperately, "—Quelle idée?" [—What idea?], and another answering, "—Oh je ne sais plus . . ." [—Oh, I don't know any more . . .] (47). "Une idée" is at one point dismissed as a "stupidité," that is, not as important as the one who offers it. "Lui" [him], for example, who himself is an idea, "il est l'intelligence faite homme" [he's intelligence made flesh]. Another voice offers a contrasting philosophy: "Il n'y a pas de moi ici . . . pas de vous . . . Il ne faut à aucun prix se laisser distraire par ces futilités [. . .] . . . il faut se concentrer juste là-dessus . . ." [There is no self here . . . no you . . . One mustn't at any price let oneself be distracted by these futilities (. . .) . . . one must concentrate just there . . .] (59). "—Sur l'idée?" [—On the idea?], another asks. If you insist on naming it, yes, is the answer. Minogue concludes that "Nathalie Sarraute raises a voice that insists that any idea, however comforting, or however disconcerting it may be, must be treated as an idea, not as an appurtenance of a personality, group, class, nation, or race."[9] The voice that claims to be "un vide" [an emptiness] does suggest that conclusion, but this novel also continually pulls an idea out of a safe, subjective context to make it part of an emotional struggle, privileging again and again the process by which intellection is detached from and re-attached to emotions, sensations and egos.

Just as words or abstractions take on a physical reality, so too do figures when they are described by others. This is seen in the opening passages of the novel when the signification given to the phrase "ce qu'elle représente pour nous" is "son doux visage fané" and other body parts. A figure at the end of Chapter 3 is described with the phrase "vous êtes à plaindre" [you're to be pitied], and the phrase materializes at the beginning of Chapter 4 with the image of "ce pauvre bougre" [this poor bloke]: "Voyez-le tendant aux passants . . ." [Look at him leaning out to passers-by] (58).

Such transformations are also enacted textually by a change in personal pronouns to refer to the figure transformed. In an exchange of marked discourse which follows in Chapter 4, the figure who relinquishes "selfhood" in order to let the "idée" live, "il n'y a pas de moi ici," gives "l'idée" to the interlocuteur vous, and the pair make up a plural ils: "Ils se taisent. Des petites flammes s'allument dans leurs yeux" [They grow quiet. Little flames light up their eyes] (59–60). In the beginning of Chapter 5 a figure il identifies "l'idée," not by its content, but by the "physical" change it has made: "C'est à peine s'il la reconnaît [. . .] . . . Mais c'est bien elle . . . et on voit qu'elle a fait son chemin . . ." [He hardly recognizes it (. . .) . . . But that's it . . . it's clear that it has gained ground] (66).

This same figure assumes subjectivity in discourse with a plural (68), but the individual's subjectivity is subsequently refused: "Ils se regardent . . . Que dit-il? [. . .] —Le Maître est dans un de ses bons jours" [They look at one another . . . what's he saying? (. . .) —The Master is having one of his good days] (67). The transformation from *je* to *il* in this scene has been made without the subject knowing about it: "Qui?" [Who?], the figure asks, "Mais vous, bien sûr . . ." [Why you, of course . . .] (67). The figure then settles comfortably into the "caress" of the designation: "C'est leurs regards réunis sur lui qui lui donnent cette aisance, [. . .] tout en le contenant à l'abri d'une forme . . . la sienne . . . qu'ils modèlent, qu'ils caressent" [It's their look focused on him that gives him this ease, (. . .) all the while sheltering him in a form . . . his . . . that they sculpt, that they caress] (71). The materiality of the image emphasizes the rigidity of character-ization, at the same time that the play of pronouns and the movement between marked and unmarked discourse recreates the subtle means by which character-ization takes place.

Once the character-ization has been enacted, a narrative can begin. The exchange above materializes into a scene that takes place "dans le palais du roi" [in the king's palace]. Even though unmarked discourse which seems to originate from the subject (now the "Maître") remarks that this transformation is "un rêve" [dream], the text continues to create a "narrative real." The transformation of the figure of *je* into *il* that the reader has experienced above at the level of syntax is now experienced more directly as in a dream when the body of the dreamer seems to take off on its own: "Le voici transporté de l'autre côté, derrière les hautes fenêtres éclairées qu'il contemplait mêlé à la foule massée contre les grilles [. . .]. Il est aussi devant une table somptueusement garnie [. . .], devant lui une coupe d'argent . . . dans un instant il va . . . au lieu de tremper le bout de ses doigts . . . il va la prendre dans ses mains, la soulever jusqu'à ses lèvres et boire . . ." [There he is transported to the other side, behind the high, lit windows that he was contemplating, mixed in with the crowd gathered at the gate (. . .). He is also seated at a sumptuously laid table (. . .), in front of him a silver bowl . . . in an instant he is going . . . instead of rinsing the ends of his fingers . . . he is going to take it in his hands, raise it to his lips and drink . . .] (67–68). "Chassez-moi," the Maître says at the end, "Je suis un imposteur. Je suis un usurpeur" [Chase me out. I'm an imposter. I'm a usurper] (69). Even such self-designation, however, is not respected: "Ils sont aux anges . . . Décidément aujourd'hui il est à son meilleur, dans sa très grande forme" [They are in seventh heaven . . . Decidedly, today he is at his best, in very great form] (69).

Dialogic exchange takes place throughout this novel, but it is more between voices than between narrative figures. The only setting is the page itself, and the absence of markers of discourse such as "dit-il" and "dit-elle" creates an intimacy between text and reader. Dashes appear momentarily to separate voices, but as a passage continues they disappear, and the reader is left with only an interiority created. In Chapter 6 intimacy and union are enacted by a conversation which frames and is then framed by *sous-conversation* as one figure offers another "une idée qui m'est venue" [an idea that came to me]. The offer is made from a metaphorical position in which *nous* are united, and the union, as in so many cases, is given a material image and a syntactical presence: "*Je* suis pareil à *vous*, impossible de *nous* distinguer, de *nous* séparer l'un de l'autre, *nous* sommes liés, [. . .] des frères siamois, ne tirez pas, *vous me* déchirez" [I am like *you*, impossible to tell *us* apart, to separate *us* one from the other, *we* are connected, (. . .) siamese twins, don't pull, *you'll* tear *me*] (my underlining, 81).

Separation then takes place in a more metaphorical space by means of an image that joins the fear of "tearing" evoked above to a more sinister fear—"[. . .] là où se place l'empoisonneur quand il regarde sa victime lever vers lui des yeux reconnaissants" [(. . .) there where the poisoner is when he sees his victim raise knowing eyes toward him]. The affective reality of "distance" finally rises to the surface of the narration when the other figure "se rassoit d'un air lassé, contraint, il s'appuie au dossier de son fauteuil et m'observe. Immobile. Silencieux" [takes his seat again, looking tired, constrained, he leans on the back of the armchair and watches me. Immobile. Silent] (84).

It is not until the end of this chapter, however, that the "leçon" [lesson] of the journey from depth to surface is drawn. The figure who had offered the "idée" recounts the experience to another: "— [. . .] J'ai reçu ma leçon. [. . .] Il est lui. Je suis moi. Nous sommes nous? Ah oui, je comprends: Nous séparés l'un de l'autre, nous tenant juste par le petit doigt . . . Vous êtes vous. Ils sont eux" [— (. . .) I learned my lesson. (. . .) He's him. I'm me. We're us? Ah, yes, I understand: Us separated one from the other, holding us together with just a little finger . . . You're you. They're them] (88). Separation leads to and/or extends from character-ization and narrative. The "lesson" of the inevitability of subjects being separated one from another by language is told again and again in Sarraute's novels, and the reader experiences the affective weight of separation through the poetic language of the images. The dreamlike style of "*disent* . . .", however, re-creates the "reality" of that lesson somewhere beyond images. Without characters with whom to identify, the reader is forced to follow a subject of discourse into the place where that subject becomes an object, into the chaos or comfort that objectification creates.

At the same time that the "lesson of separation" seems to give cohesion to the novel, there also is a fluidity created in the reading of the middle chapters. This fluidity is created by the repetition of a phrase or the continuation of an image that serves to extend the reader's affective experience from one chapter to another and suggests a similar continuation of theme. By the end of each chapter, however, the "theme" suggested at the beginning is subtly displaced by another, which in turn leads to the next, in much the same way that a figure moves from one discursive position to another.

Chapter 3 ends with the words, "Vous êtes à plaindre" [You're to be pitied], and Chapter 4 begins, "Oui, à plaindre. Regardez-moi ce pauvre bougre" [Yes, to be pitied. Take a look at that poor bloke]. This chapter ends with a subject's liberation of "une idée": "Elle a besoin de se montrer, de se répandre . . . et il le comprend" [It needs to show itself, to spread out . . . and he understands this]. Chapter 5 opens without the referent "une idée"; instead the referent assumes presence with a pronoun: "C'est à peine qu'il la reconnaît [. . .]. Je lui trouve quelque chose de mal grossi" [He hardly recognizes it (. . .). I find in it something badly enlarged]. In spite of the changed perception this figure experiences in relation to "cette idée," association with it elevates *il* to the status of "le Maître." Another transformation takes place by the end of Chapter 5. "L'idée" has disappeared, and the figure designated as "Maître" declares, "c'est ce que je suis: un monstre d'orgueil" [that's what I am: a monster of pride]. This phrase is the object of an exchange between two figures as the Chapter 6 opens: "—Un monstre d'orgueil, vous croyez? Oui, peut-être . . . puisque vous me dites que le grand homme lui-même le reconnaît . . ." [—A monster of pride, do you think so? Yes, perhaps . . . since you tell me that the great man recognizes it himself] (78). The statement loses its status as thematic organizer when it is quickly replaced by discussion between the two figures about "une idée qui m'est venue." This "idée" looks like it could be the one that was lost at the end of Chapter 5, but it is lost again in Chapter 6, which ends with the lesson of separation discussed above: "Il est lui [. . .]."

The word "cela" in the opening passage of Chapter 7 seems to refer to the lesson of separation: "C'est cela qu'on sent quand le gardien qui surveille la sortie, [. . .] vous ouvre la grille, vous donne une poignée de main . . ." [That's what you feel when the guard who watches the exit, (. . .) opens the gate for you, shakes your hand . . .] (89). The theme of separation continues when the implied subject of this phrase becomes the observing and character-izing "eye": "Sous les éclairages crus des cafés le patron, la patronne joviale plaisantent, discutent le coup avec ceux qui devant le comptoir sirotent leur verre de rouge [. . .]" [Beneath the harsh light of cafés the owners, the man and the jovial woman, exchange pleasantries, chat with those on the other side of the counter who sip their glass of red wine (. . .)] (89). These character-ized figures are described as "apaisants comme le doux ronflement du poêle" [calming like the soft roaring of the stove], and the subject's experience of the lesson from Chapter 5 is represented: "Eux. Lui. Moi. [. . .] Ils savent chaque fois qui est là devant eux, levant son verre, [. . .] . . . Bon petit gars [. . .] . . . Beau brin de fille" [Them. Him. Me. (. . .) They know every time who is there in front of them, raising a glass, (. . .) . . . Good lad (. . .) . . . A fine-looking girl] (91).

The security of this separation by character-ization is destabilized for the reader when the figure of *elle*, described as "la vraie mère poule" [the real mother hen], turns out to have "des mains potelées reposant sur ges genoux entre lesquels sa jupe moelleuse fait un creux . . ." [chubby hands resting on her knees where her soft skirt makes a fold] (91). "Notre grand-mère" from Chapter 1 was described similarly: "[. . .] ses mains tranquilles qui reposent sur ses genoux écartés entre lesquels sa jupe de lainage moelleux fait un creux . . ." [(. . .) her calm hands that rest on her spread knees where her soft, wool skirt makes a fold] (12). The vague connection between these two figures opens up the character-ization of *elle* as "une mère poule," or perhaps it "thickens" it, because it conflicts with other images the reader has thus far associated with "notre grand-mère."

The figures in this passage then play out the very sensation of destabilization that the reader has experienced. A young voice addresses a "petit vieux au dos coubé" [a bent-over, little old man] in a characteristically deferential manner in keeping with the character-ization the reader has just read about the figures "sous les éclairages crus des cafés" [beneath the harsh light of cafés]: "'On se sent bien? Vous ne trouvez pas?'" ["We're feeling all right? Don't you think?"] (93). This time however, the character-ization does not stick: "—Est-ce que tu te moques de moi? [. . .] Je me sens bien, tu oses me dire ça?" [—Are you making fun of me? (. . .) I feel well, how dare you say that to me?] (93). These questions not only undermine the character-ization ("le petit vieux au dos courbé"), but when the orientation of address changes from the younger voice to that of the "petit vieux," the object of character-ization reverses as well: "Qu'est-ce qu'ils ont dans le ventre, ces petits gars-là? [. . .] Tu vas voir, [. . .] ce ne sera pas long avant que tu sois comme moi. Logé dans la même enseigne" [What's in that head of theirs, those little lads? (. . .) You'll see, (. . .) it won't be long before you're like me, in the same boat] (93).

Once the "surface" of "le petit vieux au dos courbé" has been pierced, the surface of his language also gives way. The repetition of the phrase at the beginning of the next paragraph, "tous logés à la même enseigne," suggests that the passage continues from the same perspective, but that orientation does not hold: "Oui, logés à la même enseigne. Avançant courbés, regardant les touffes d'herbe, [. . .] adhérant à cela . . . Juste pour ça, accepter . . . mais n'importe quoi . . . accepter d'être plié en deux [. . .] . . . Non? Même pas ça?" [Yes, in the same boat. Moving forward, bent over, looking at the tufts of grass, (. . .) adhering to that . . . Just to accept being bent in two (. . .) . . . No? Not even that?] (94). Even when the reader establishes the origin of this unmarked discourse as one of "ces petits gars-là," the doubling of voices seen above oscillates between that of an internal dialogue within that figure and an external one between that figure and another "lad." The very impulse to bring to the surface what lies beneath a cliché is mocked: "Essaie donc de lui dire ça, de le lui présenter, si tu l'oses . . . vas-y, offre-le lui, enrobé dans tes mots, un joli petit joyau [. . .] . . . Ah tu n'oses pas . . . On se tient tout de même à sa place, à distance respectueuse" [Try then, try to tell him that, to present it to him, if you dare . . . go ahead, offer it to him, wrapped up in your words, a pretty little gem (. . .) . . . Ah you don't dare . . . All the same we stay in our places, at a respectable distance] (94).

This "respectable distance" is the one described at the beginning of the chapter between *Lui-Eux-Moi*. At the same time, however, the narration destroys that distance by a lack of punctuation distinguishing inside from outside. Marked discourse emerges in the next paragraph, separating "le vieux courbé en deux" from "ces petits gars-là," and a look is given voice in the following passage where character-ization is not made on the exterior, one figure of another, but from the inside: "L'oeil [. . .] regarde avec l'expression d'un réalisateur satisfait le film qui est en train de se dérouler . . . Tous autour de lui, [. . .] le contemplant dans un respectueux silence" [The eye (. . .) looks with the expression of a director, satisfied by the film that is rolling . . . All around him, (. . .) contemplating him in respectful silence] (95).

The character-ization that follows is not the same as the one seen above in the café conversation; it goes deeper than discourse: "[. . .] chacun pareil à chacun des autres éprouve les mêmes sentiments graves, profonds. Chacun les reconnaît dans les yeux qui un instant se posent distraitement sur les siens" [(. . .) each one like each of the others feels the same serious, profound sentiments. Each one recognizes them in the eyes which meet one's own for an instant] (95). This is "le lieu commun" at its most intimate place, and it is not by accident that this "recognition" takes place "dans ce geste de la main qui prend le goupillon et trace dans l'air . . . qui prend à la main qui la tend la pelle, la plonge, la lève, l'incline . . . bruit granuleux de la terre qui tombe . . ." [in this gesture made by the hand which takes the container of holy water and traces in the air . . . which takes from the hand which holds it the shovel, plunges it, raises it, tilts it . . . granular noise of earth falling](95). The earlier metaphorical "death" enacted by charac-ter-ization is released from its referent to a static object in Chapter 2, "washed, laid out and surrounded by flowers"; here the affective experience of death is created by body parts, the hand with the shovel and the fleeting eyes which carry "les mêmes sentiments."

As if this intimacy cannot be endured, or the opportunity for charac-ter-ization cannot be avoided, the looks turn away from one another, and "chacun voit, plus noble et plus grave que tous les autres, la jeune mère sous ses longs voiles noirs, ils retombent sur son ventre arrondi . . ." [each one sees, more noble and more serious than all the others, the young mother beneath her long, black veils, they fall on her rounded stomach] (95). One voice asks who would dare "observer ces sortes de choses" [look at these sorts of things], and within the reprimand for such character-ization, names it: "Qui ose manquer de respect à celle qui garde lové en elle ce dépôt sacré, notre avenir, notre espoir, nos chances?" [Who would dare to show such disrespect to her, the one who keeps coiled inside her in sacred trust, our future, our hope, our dreams?] (96). "Eh bien" [Ah well], another answers, "j'ose" [I dare], proclaiming that this is "une délicieuse sensation" [a delicious sensa-tion]. The theme of the individual separating or joining the group is demonstrated in a variety of ways in Sarraute's novels; here it goes beyond a mere play of pronouns, "je vais me réfugier parmi eux," be-yond the image of "victime" and "bourreau" [executioner], or even the "héros" facing "le lieu commun," to the "délicieuse sensation" of being "enfermé" [enclosed], that is, separated and venerated.

As always, however, that sensation is not left to lie alone; it is super-imposed with another, also represented by a *je*, a figure which refuses the distance created by being "enfermé dans une forme" [enclosed in a form]: "Moi seul, oui, moi je n'en veux pas, passez-la à d'autres, je romps le cercle, je sors du rang, je m'approche par-derrière de la jeune mère, je la saisis par les épaules et je la force à se pencher . . . seule . . . [. . .] ne demandant qu'à suivre, qu'à se confondre . . . toute pare-ille . . ." [I alone, yes, me, I don't want any of that, pass it on to the others, I break the circle, I leave the ranks, I come up behind the young mother, I grab her by the shoulders and I force her to bend over . . . alone . . . (. . .) asking only to follow, to mix in . . . all the same . . .] (96–97).

The desire to "se confondre" which is repressed earlier in this chap-ter by a neat succession of pronouns—"Eux. Lui. Moi"—here gives way to an elaborate play of pronouns, as hands are placed together: "[. . .] tu vois nos mains posées . . . [. . .] tu vois, chacun de mes doigts tout contre chacun des tiens a exactement la même forme . . . Tu soulèves tour à tour et serres entre ton pouce et ton index le bout de chacun de mes doigts, [. . .] ta voix se fait plus aiguë pour ressembler à ma voix d'enfant . . . la corneille, la pie [. . .] . . . Oh encore, fais-le encore papa . . ." [(. . .) you see our hands posed . . . (. . .) you see, each of my fingers right up against yours has exactly the same form . . . You raise one by one and squeeze between your thumb and your forefinger the end of each of my fingers, (. . .) your voice is made more high to be like my child's voice . . . this little pig went to market, this little pig (. . .) . . . Oh, again, do it again, papa . . .] (96–97). The initial referent for *tu* is "la jeune mère," when it is part of the address made by the figure of the rebellious *je* in the phrase introducing this passage, "je la saisis." *Tu* remains "la jeune mère" when *je* then appears to be identified by "ma voix d'enfant." The address to "papa" at the end of the passage changes all that went before, the "jeune mère" is at the grave of her father and must (?) therefore be the referent for the "enfant" who addresses "papa."

Just as the figure of "papa" is represented by the synecdoche "ses mains," this figure is also contained by epithets in the unmarked discourse as this passage continues: "un petit garnement, casse-cou, boute en train, jeune père" [a little hellion, daredevil, live-wire, young father] (97). Added to this identification is that of his "regard," which is recalled in an address to what is now a truly ambiguous *tu:* ". . . quand il vous regardait avec ce regard, tu t'en souviens? ce regard chargé d'attention tendre qu'il pouvait avoir . . ." [. . . when he would look at you with that look, you remember? that look full of tender attention that he could have] (98). Marked discourse enters the narration and adds yet another dimension to the portrait of "papa": "—C'est vrai . . ., mais aussi, n'est-ce pas? il y avait des moments . . . sa fureur, cette rage, rappelle-toi . . ." [—That's true, but also, no? he had his moments . . . his fury, that anger, you remember] (98). Marked dialogue recommences, and with it a response that resumes the variety of ways in which "papa" has been represented: "—[. . .] Bien sûr, qui ne le sait? il n'était pas tout d'une seule pièce. Il était, comme chacun de nous, fait de morceaux disparates" [—(. . .) Of course, who doesn't know that? he wasn't all of a piece. He was, like all of us, made of disparate pieces] (98). This is the place where Sarraute's novels lead her readers, not into a simple dichotomy of surface and depth, but into the tropistic fluidity of assigning attributes and character-izing. This complexity can be described critically as the impossible and problematic relationship of a subject to language, but the text enacts a reading experience beyond the confines of a critical one.

Both the limits and the necessity of character-ization are shown to be indispensible for a discursive exchange; first person speaks to second

person about the third, and each is the third for another. The play of
pronouns in the passage about "les mains" enacts that experience, felt
personally by the reader through the use of an address made to the
second person (*tu* or *vous*). The figure of *il* that is originally designated
as "le vieux courbé en deux" is not represented by one term but by
several which pass through time. *Il* is at one and the same time the one
surrounded by those who stood "le contemplant" [contemplating him]
at his deathbed, the one who signifies "noblesse, dignité, pureté," "le
jeune papa," the one with "ce regard chargé d'attention tendre," the
one with "sa fureur." The "vieux courbé en deux," as signifier, floats,
and he is finally described as "fait de morceaux disparates." Through
a narrative in which disparate discourses and perspectives are juxtaposed on a page, the reader's experience of the simultaneity of the
variety of character-izations seems to take place outside discourse in
the affective reality created by multiple and different images. Chapter
7 ends with an image of individual and shared complexity: "— [. . .] Il
était, comme chacun de nous, fait de morceaux disparates, pareil à ces
courte-pointes bariolées . . . non, laisse-le, n'y touchons pas. Laissez
reposer en paix" [— (. . .) He was, like all of us, made up of disparate
pieces, like those multicolored quilts . . . no, leave him alone, don't
touch. Let rest in peace] (98).

Chapter 8 continues from that imperative—"Soyez tranquille, je n'y
toucherai pas" [Calm down, I won't touch him]—and certain details
identify the origin of the unmarked discourse as "la grand-mère." Here
she is called "la mère l'Oye" [Mother Goose], and voices address her
in unison: "Raconte-nous, tu racontes si bien. Dis-nous, toi qui l'as si
bien connu, toi qui a eu cette chance . . ." [Tell us, you tell such good
stories. Tell us, you who knew him so well, you who had that luck]
(99).

The main "character" of the story "la mère l'Oye" tells is said to be
unique: "Vous avez raison, j'ai eu de la chance. Il n'avait vraiment pas
son pareil. Je n'ai jamais vu quelqu'un de si changeant" [You're right, I
was lucky. He really didn't have an equal; I have never seen anyone so
changeable]. Some of the details about the physical traits attached to
il, gestures and words reported, recall various figures the reader has
encountered throughout the novel. Now each of these "morceaux disparates" comes to rest on this one figure, and they are joined by other
attributes (100–102). This complexity can be reduced by taking a certain distance, which in the passage is given the physical image of looking at the countryside from the air: "[. . .] nous planons, comme en
hélicoptère, comme en avion, et là en bas, je vois moi aussi se dessiner
avec une extrême netteté cette forme" [(. . .) we glide, like in a helicop-
ter, like in an airplane, and down there, I myself also see that form

drawn with an extreme clarity] (103–4). Just as the theme of separation
was recreated in Chapter 6 through a fluid style which conflicted with
that theme, here the quality of "netteté" [clarity] is composed of a variety of adjectives which compromise its meaning: "compassé" [stuffy],
"pleutre avec parfois des élans de bravoure" [cowardly, sometimes with
bursts of bravery], "vaniteaux comme pas un" [conceited like no one],
"velléitaire" [indecisive,] "très paresseux" [very lazy], "mesquin jusqu'à
la manie" [obsessively stingy] (104). The form seen by the figure of *je*
may be "clearly" recognizable, but the variety of the attributes undermines its "netteté."

The semantic undermining represented by the juxtaposition of this
term with the variety of qualities attributed to the same figure is paralleled by an undermining of the "distance" from which the "forme" is
seen. The terms of the passage as it continues create a space of contact
which elicits comparison and provokes emotion, both of which create
proximity: "Le voici devant nous aussi vivants que nos plus intimes
amis, que nos plus proches parents [. . .], il éveille une ignoble pitié
[. . .] . . . il est si démuni, il est si seul, le pauvre bougre . . ." [Here he
is before us as lifelike as our most intimate friends, as our closest
relatives [. . .], he awakens a vile pity [. . .] . . . he is so destitute, he is
so alone, poor devil] (104). The separation represented by the "netteté"
of the form seen from "on high" is destabilized by the comparison (*he*
is *like* those *we* know) and by the emotion reaching across the distance
of that separation.

The elements of emotion and comparison prefigure what happens
in the next paragraph, when "notre construction [. . .] se défait" [our
construction (. . .) comes apart]: "Soudain des mots, une strophe, une
seule, elle flotte, se déploie, elle m'enveloppe, me pénètre . . . une
chaude buée. . ." [Suddenly words, a verse of poetry, just one, it floats,
unfurls, it envelops me, penetrates me . . . a warm mist] (104). Once
again, what the reader has experienced in the process of reading, the
emotion which effaced the separation implied by "netteté," is now
articulated in the text itself: "[. . .] des mots qu'il suffira de murmurer
à mon oreille pour me faire dans la béatitude passer là-bas d'où ils
viennent [. . .]. Mais qui moi? Il n'y a plus de moi, plus de lui, plus de
séparations, plus de fusion, il n'y a que leur balancement, leur vibration, leur respiration, leur battement . . ." [(. . .) words that when merely
whispered in my ear make me pass blissfully over there where they
come from (. . .). But who me? There is no more me, no more him,
no more separations, no more fusion, only their rocking motion, their
vibration, their breathing, their beating] (105).

The narrative figure recovers from this "self-less" position by means
of the distance created in discourse: "Non. Je suis . . . [. . .] je me retro-

uve ... grâce à lui ... Je ne suis pas lui" [No. I am ... [. . .] I find myself again ... thanks to him ... I'm not him] (105). The passage moves through repeated statements which represent an effort to affirm the separation and to efface the earlier effect of "des mots, une strophe": "Il me suffit de me rappeler qu'ils sont à lui: ce qui se nomme 'son oeuvre'" [All I have to do is to remember that they are his: what's called "his work"] (106). The figure of *je* uses a synecdoche to create a sinister image of *lui*, but as in a nightmare, the image suddenly becomes benign: "[. . .] ses yeux guettaient sur les visages l'effet produit ... par quoi? Eh bien, figurez-vous, par ses bottes . . ." [his eyes would lie in wait to see on the faces the effect produced ... by what? Well, imagine, by his boots . . .] (106). Reader and speaker rise up ironically out of the emotion and the comparison by which *we* are *like* the *other*. The sinister intention attributed to *lui* is nothing more than silent stone: "Qu'on fasse le vide autour de sa personne. Qu'on fasse silence. Qu'il ne soit désormais permis que de s'approcher de sa statue [. . .], lire sur le socle son nom ... lever les yeux et le contempler, [. . .] ses bras croisés sur sa poitrine, sa mèche au vent, posant au loin son regard de marbre" [Let the emptiness be made around his person. Let there be silence. Let it only be permitted to approach his statue [. . .], read his name on the base, raise eyes to contemplate him, [. . .] his arms crossed on his chest, his tufts of hair in the wind, directing his marble gaze into the distance] (107).

In Chapter 9 the "vide autour de sa personne" is filled in by a style that begins with as much certainty as the "statue" above is concrete: "Tous ce qu'ils sont. Adhérant complètement à eux-mêmes" [All that they are. Adhering completely to themselves] (108). The preceding experience of the complexity of intersubjective relationships, represented by a multiplicity of designation, by union, separation and concretization now extends to other figures: "mignonnes petites vieilles" [sweet, little old ladies], "exquis vieillards" [delightful old men], "amoureux enlacés sur les bancs" [lovers entwined on benches], "attendrissants vieux couples déambulant la main dans la main" [touching old couples strolling hand in hand], "jeunes mères comblées et fiers jeunes pères" [overjoyed young mothers and proud young fathers], "enfants" [children], "oiseaux s'ébattant et pépiant" [chirping, frolicking birds], "chats . . ." [cats] (108). The figure of the "chats" brings the certainty to a halt; the ellipsis marks a resistance to such character-ization, or rather, the problematic line it pretends to efface between "seeming" and "being." In the case of "les chats," "il faut les avoir surpris cent fois, au moment où il n'est pas possible qu'ils sachent qu'on les regarde, pour être certain qu'ils ne font pas les chats, mais qu'ils sont, tout bonnement, des chats" [you have to have surprised them a hundred times, just when it is possible for them not to know that you are looking, in order to be sure that they are not pretending to be cats, but that they are, quite simply, cats] (108).[10]

The example which follows from this "idée" presents a myriad of character-izations imposed from inside and outside, blurring, redrawing, and therefore calling attention to the line between "font" and "sont," until the "idée" is completely overtaken by the multiplicity of examples, of interpretations of examples, of possibilities of conscious or unconscious dissimulation. Children are described as usually not awakening "aucun soupçon" [any suspicion], but then the text corrects itself, suggesting that perhaps they possess such "dons" [talents]: "[. . .] une si admirable technique qu'on peut les observer à longueur de journée sans penser un seul instant qu'ils ne 'sont' pas, mais qu'ils 'font'" [(. . .) such an admirable technique that one can watch them all day long without thinking for a single instant that they 'are' not, but that they are 'pretending' to be] (108–9). There are those, however who "forcent leur ligne . . . plus enfants que la nature" [force their line . . . more children than is natural], while others "s'obstinent à rester des bébés . . . ou au contraire se vieillissent, s'emparent de mots qu'ils ne connaissent pas" [persist in remaining babies . . . or inversely grow old, seize upon words that they don't know] (109).

The "idea" of "forcing the line" between seeming and being is dramatized in the next passage where "une main" does not remain a synecdoche representing a figure, but becomes instead the origin of a gesture which then resumes an individual's character. The entire, complex character-izing process that takes place throughout the novel is dramatized by the gesture of "la main" in this chapter. To introduce the drama, the narration presents the image of "des amoureux enlacés sur les bancs des quais" [lovers entwined on benches along the quais] (111). The picture, however, does not remain static: ". . . une main [. . .] comme un petit animal rétif se dégage de la main qui l'enserre, puis, apeurée, s'immobilise, attend [. . .] . . . recommence . . . parfois s'enhardit jusqu'à aller se poser sur le genou et là, prudemment, [. . .] essuyer sur la jupe ou sur le pantalon sa paume moite . . ." [. . . a hand (. . .) like a little, rebellious animal frees itself from the hand that holds it, then, scared, stops, waits (. . .) . . . begins again . . . sometimes is bold enough to go place itself on a knee and there, cautiously (. . .) to wipe on the skirt or the pants its damp palm] (111). Attribution of gender, age, or social, familial status of the figure connected to "la main" is never made; all attention is directed to *its* "story."

In the next example given, investigation goes beyond "la main" itself and onto the significance of its gesture, "un autre geste, le geste de cette main" [another gesture, the gesture of this hand], "plongeant dans le gousset, en sortant une poignée de pièces de monnaie, puis s'ouvrant et les tenant étalées sur sa paume . . . longtemps . . ." [digging into the vest pocket, taking out a fistful of change, then opening up and holding it out in its palm . . . for a long time . . .] (111–12). The reader's gaze is first directed to the outstretched hand with the fistful of change, then to the hand that receives it, such that when the first narrative figure appears, the reader is dramatically implicated in the response: "[. . .] un cocher . . . qui à son tour abaisse les yeux sur le maigre pourboire au creux de sa paume, puis lève son regard et l'appuie longuement sur le dos qui s'éloigne" [(. . .) a cabby . . . who in turn lowers his eyes to the skimpy tip in the hollow of his hand, then raises his look and presses it on the back that walks away] (112).

Just as the figure who gave the tip is resumed by "sa main," so too are those who watch resumed by their "sourires méprisants, petits ricanement, hochements de tête, haussement d'épaules, 'réflexions' échangées à voix basse . . ." [scornful laughter, faint sniggerings, heads nodding, shoulders shrugging, "thoughts" quietly exchanged . . .] (112). Finally a figure arises out of this affective murmuring, and the "story" begins: "Comment peuvent-ils savoir que ce geste est un signal sinistre . . . qu'il sonne le glas du Bonheur, le tocsin annonçant les Malheurs qui vont s'abattre sur "Une Vie." Sa vie . . . En elle quelque chose s'arrache, elle sent une faiblesse [. . .] tandis qu'elle continue à avancer auprès de lui avec ce regard braqué sur leur dos [. . .]" [How could they know that this gesture is a sinister signal . . . that it tolls the death knell of Happiness, the alarm announcing the Unhappiness that is going to beat down "A Life." Her life . . . Something tears inside her, she feels weak [. . .] as she continues to walk next to him with that look aimed at their back (. . .)] (112).

"La main" is transformed by this gesture into "cette main étrangère" [that foreign hand], and the metaphor of tearing enlarges to become "une plaie qui va s'élargir" [a wound that is going to get bigger]. This wound requires certain "onguents" [ointments], "la tendresse, l'indulgence, l'admiration," "un peu d'humilité" [a little humility] (113). But it is too late, the gesture has turned "le Prince charmant" into "ce grigou" [skinflint]: "[. . .] il est dangereux, il peut être contagieux . . . et elle est seule avec lui, séparée à jamais des siens, ils ne peuvent rien pour elle" [(. . .) he's dangerous, he can be contagious . . . and she is alone with him, separated forever from her people, there's nothing they can do for her] (113–14).

The figure of *ils* does arrive, bearing a maxim which denies any complexity to the gesture: "Ab ungue leonem. A la trace laissée par sa griffe, on connaît le lion . . . mais le traduire ainsi, c'est le diluer [. . .]. D'après la griffe le lion. Rien ne vient séparer les deux termes, [. . .] un

seul geste et tout l'homme est là" [*Ab-ungue-leonem*. In the trace left
by its claw, the lion is known . . . but translating it like that dilutes it
(. . .). As goes the claw so goes the lion. Nothing separates the two
terms, (. . .) a single gesture and the whole man is there] (117–18). The
"onguents" applied by *elle* have no effect on these wounds: "Sordide.
Sans coeur. Profiteur. Il est ainsi. Contre cela il n'y a pas de recours"
[Base. Heartless. Profiteer. Thus he is. There is no recourse against that]
(119). The idea that an individual had many sides, already seen in the
case of "le vieux courbé en deux," here offers some salvation when *elle*
says, "Mais il est mon amour aussi" [But he's my love as well] (119).

Where a "gray" area is sometimes evidence of another's uniqueness,
here it is a breach of order, here one must choose, stay or leave, "aime
ou n'aime pas" [love or not love] (120). The only solution is to accept
that "il est ainsi fait" [he's just like that]: "Je l'aimerai toujours? Tel
qu'il est? —C'est vrai. Tel qu'il est" [I'll love him always? Just as he is? —
That's right. Just as he is] (121). Character-ization makes our narratives
possible, narratives about others, about ourselves, and always at the
risk of appropriation.

The same phrase opens Chapter 10. Outside the context of the "story"
of *elle*, it is repeated with an obstinately certain tone which is then
undermined when a play of pronouns takes over: "Tous tels qu'ils sont.
Tels que Dieu les a faits. Que voulez-vous, il est ce qu'il est, vous ne le
changerez pas. Je le connais. Si vous le connaissiez comme moi. Si vous
saviez comment il est. Comment est-il? Racontez-le-moi. Oh toi je te
connais. Il me connaît. Je me connais. Connais-toi toi-même. Je sais
comment je suis. Moi, voyez-vous, je suis ainsi fait. Fait. Ainsi. Faites-
en le tour" [Just as they are. Just as God made them. What do you want,
he is what he is, you'll never change him. I know him. If you knew him
like I do. If you knew how he is. How is he? Tell me. Oh you I know
you. He knows me. I know myself. Know yourself. I know how I am.
Me, see, that's how I am. Am. That. Let's take turns] (123).

The statements and attributes which follow this play of pronouns all
begin with the first person *je*, but the repetition of the pronoun creates
a sense of the plural *jes*. In his study of the "Nouveau Roman," Stephen
Heath summarizes Benveniste's discussion of the "false plural" represented by *nous*: "'Nous' is 'je' plus 'non-je,' whether 'toi,' 'lui,' 'elle,'
'vous,' or 'eux'; as such, it is a 'false' plural, a fact rendered by the
change in sign found in most languages, je/nous, as opposed to a normal
pluralization, je/jes: "'nous" est, non pas une multiplication d'objets
identiques, mais une *jonction* entre "je" et le "non-je," quelque soit le
contenu de ce "non-je"'" ["'nous' is, not a multiplication of identical
objects, but a *junction* between 'I' and the 'not-I,' no matter what is
contained in this 'non-I'"].[11]

One voice threatens this plural when it announces that "aucun de ces mots ne me convient" [none of these words fits me]: "Je ne suis rien . . . un vide . . . un trou d'air . . . Infini" [I'm nothing . . . emptiness . . . an airhole . . . Infinity]. If everyone is something and this figure is nothing . . . another speaker assesses the statement, and a plural *nous* that effaces difference is created out of this *rien:* "Il n'est rien. C'est-à-dire, n'est-ce pas? qu'il est tout. Tout avec un grand T, et que nous tous, que chacun de nous . . . comme lui . . . alors voyez l'effet sur certains . . . [. . .] quelle aubaine, ils ne se tiennent plus, il n'y a plus moyen de les tenir . . ." [He's nothing. That is to say, right? that he's everything. Everything with a big E, and that we all, that each one of us . . . like him . . . well look at the effect it has on certain ones . . . (. . .) what a godsend, they do not hold together, there is no longer any way to hold them . . .] (127).

Chapter 10 flows into Chapter 11 with the same fluidity seen earlier: "Oui, c'est un bon, c'est un doux, bienveillant visage . . ." [Yes, it's a good, it's a sweet, welcoming face . . .] (128). For a brief moment, the sense of the *rien* from the preceding chapter remains. "Les yeux" are described as "ces petites fenêtres derrières lesquelles des espaces sans bornes . . . à travers lesquelles une âme infinie répand sa lumière . . ." [those litte windows, and behind them limitless space . . . through them an infinite soul gives off its light . . .] (128). In the next paragraph an effect is represented before its cause, "le doux visage se durcit" [the soft face hardens], then marked discourse is revealed to be the cause, "'Ah, vous trouvez?'" ["Ah, you think so?"] (128). The voice that utters this statement continues to structure in marked discourse "des espaces sans bornes" and the voice attached to them. This passage enacts what Monique Wittig calls the "fundamental flaw in the contract, the worm in the fruit, [. . .] the fact that the contract in its very structure is an impossibility."[12]

From within the interior discourse of the *je* who declared, "je ne suis rien," this other voice emerges to say, "C'est vous que ça juge . . ." (131). This voice speaks, even though the figure's identification is with *rien,* even though the words attributed to this figure in unmarked discourse repeat that identification at the beginning of Chapter 11: "[. . .] une chaude lumière qui fait [. . .] sortir de mes lèvres que je ne vois pas, que je ne sens pas remuer, portés par ma voix que je n'entends pas, des mots que produit en moi . . . mais pourquoi en moi? Il n'y a pas de moi . . . c'était dans l'air, c'est venu de partout [. . .]" [(. . .) a warm light which makes (. . .) come out of my lips which I do not see, which I do not feel move, carried by my voice which I don't hear, words that produce in me . . . but why in me? There is no me . . . it was in the air, it came from everywhere (. . .)] (128). Marked or unmarked, discourse marks its subject.

The only "espoir du salut" [hope of salvation] is found in what is called the "vice de forme" [defect in the form], that is: "[. . .] le 'vous' n'est pas seul, le 'vous' a un envers, un complément . . . une autre face . . . Sous le 'C'est vous' il y a . . . ça saute aux yeux . . . il y a 'Ce n'est pas lui' . . . Vous. Pas lui. Lui et moi. Impossible de nous séparer. Nous sommes les deux points d'une comparaison. Nous sommes les deux termes d'une équation. Nous sommes les deux pôles d'une opposition. Lui que rien ne permet de juger, moi qu'un rien juge. Nous avons été mis en balance. Placés à chaque bout de la bascule. Nous nous faisons face, lui et moi" [(. . .) the "you" is not alone, the "you" has a reverse side, a complement . . . an other side . . . Beneath the "It's you" there is . . . it jumps out at you . . . there is "It's not him" . . . You. Not him. Him and me. Impossible to separate us. We are two points of a comparison. We are two terms of an equation. We are two poles of an opposition. Him who nothing is allowed to judge, me who a nothing judges. We have been weighed. Placed at either end of the scale. We face one another, him and me] (135).

By means of various textual strategies "disent . . ." amplifies "l'épaisseur subjective" to a degree not found in the previous novels. Sarraute uses the term le même fond commun [the same common ground] to describe it, and the generality that phrase represents leads to its characterization as part of "une tradition moraliste." Germaine Lemaire's closing phrase at the end of Le Planétarium is often quoted to resume the universality of Sarraute's novels, "nous sommes bien tous un peu comme ça" [we are all very much a little like that]. The critical character-izations which identify Sarraute's novels as creating a "universal reality" presume a plural nous which effaces the different "morceaux disparates" of that plural by placing all its elements in an unequal union. It is only in the reading that the fluidity remains, and the experience of the reading as a simultaneous juxtaposition of disparate pieces, if retained at that visceral level, reveals the process of character-ization to be a plane of interaction. Because of the experience of reading that Sarraute's style creates in "disent . . .", the reader is left with an intimate experience of the fluidity and the complexity of this process, that is, of its limits and of its absolute necessity: "Nous nous faisons face, lui et moi."

An emotional and intimate dynamic takes place in both Vous les entendez? and "disent les imbéciles" in a more fluid narration than that of the previous novels. The power of Sarraute's sixth and seventh novels is similar to Sarraute's first work, in which the affective experience of tropisms dominates the narration. The reader who moves inside and outside the text of an anonymous observer in Tropismes, however, is moved in these later novels inside and outside the tropistic perception of various figures, similarly anonymous but not as unified, a plural jes.

7

A Space Beyond?

The evolution in the seven novels discussed in this study has been described by critics as a movement from a descriptive to a more performative style, that is, toward conversation and dialogue. Rather than identify an evolution in the style of the novels themselves, this study proposes that the differences in style from one novel to another invite the feminist reader to investigate her evolution in reading as it interacts with that of literary criticism in the United States and France. This evolution is possible because of the "lesson" learned from these novels, a lesson which is at first obscured by the proposed "neutrality" of Sarraute's male narrators.

Sabine Raffy offers a model for one of the lessons to be found in Sarraute's novels when she speaks of "the constitutive journey" of the sarrautien subject from "the crystalization of the unconscious" to the construction of an "imaginary base" by which the subject establishes relations with the world and an ideology which gives meaning to the subject's existence. This construction makes it possible for the subject to enter "a social milieu which confers it a representative character."[1] The descriptive style of Portrait d'un inconnu and Martereau allows the feminist reader to reconstruct representative gendered characters out of the narrators of these novels. If that reader identifies herself in relation to these "characters" she risks remaining stuck in Kristeva's first two generations, that is, identifying herself as "like" or as "not like" a male subject. In Le Planétarium, however, the reader is both witness to and actor in the process by which figures construct "imaginary" bases in order to interact. The tropistic representation of these constructions shakes loose the fixity of identity they imply. In Entre la vie et la mort, the central figure moves toward and away from the "representative character" conferred on him by his milieu. The reader's simultaneous role as witness and actor in this novel is itself brought under scrutiny by a style in which the recognizably gendered identity of the central figure which could exclude the reader is continually thrown into a nongendered space of creation.

The family milieu created in Le Planétarium appears to be re-created by the figures of Father and Children in *Vous les entendez?* When this novel opens, the Father is seeking to establish a "representative character" in relation to the Children, but the process of conferring such a character is then magnified to such a degree by the style of this novel that the figures of Father and Children change places. In the end the reader is left with an affective experience of the ambiguous juxtaposition of "leurs rires," the act by which the Father and the Children had been assigning one another "characters," and "le silence."

The "third attitude," or "third generation of feminism," implies for Kristeva "an apparent de-dramatization of the 'fight to the death' between rival groups and thus between the sexes."[2] The figures in *"disent les imbéciles"* are engaged in a *dramatization* of the "fight to the death" between rival groups, but that fight takes place beyond "character" and thus beyond gender because of the virtual anonymity of these figures and of the continually changing referents for pronouns. The end of the novel succeeds in "de-dramatizing" the fight when the words "disent les imbéciles" are separated from the emotional weight they have carried throughout the novel. The words are part of the process of exchange between figures whereby each receives and confers "representative characters." This process is at the same time framed by the image of "des morceaux disparates" and the words "il n'est pas tout d'une pièce."

The dislocation of syntax and displacement of narrative positions which create the "constitutive journey" of the sarrautien subject invite the reader to glimpse at what Kristeva might mean by the attitude of the "third generation." In this third attitude, Kristeva advocates that "the very dichotomy man/woman as an opposition between two rival entities may be understood as belonging to *metaphysics*." This attitude is not simply "a very hypothetical bisexuality," because that could aspire "toward the totality of one of the sexes and thus an effacement of differences." The "de-dramatization" of the fight between rival groups "consists," she concludes, "in trying to explore the constitution and function of [the socio-symbolic] contract, starting [. . .] from the very personal affect experienced when facing it as subject and as a woman." Kristeva finds this exploration in the "hesitant but always dissident" research of women in the social sciences, as well as in the work of male avant-garde artists. These works attempt "to find a specific discourse closer to the body and emotions, to the unnameable repressed by the social contract." Kristeva emphasizes that she is not speaking of a specific "women's language," but of a specificity that is the "product of a social marginality [more] than of a sexual-symbolic difference."[3]

Sarraute's novels also represent an investigation of the contract, and in this sense her work joins that of Virginia Woolf, a writer whose work is often discussed when anglophone feminists investigate the "overlap" between women's writing and avant-garde or (post)modernist writing. As a way of concluding my study of Sarraute, I would like to continue this discussion by looking briefly at the works of Nathalie Sarraute in their "parallel existence" with those of Virginia Woolf, so that, as Kristeva says of the three generations of feminisms, "they be interwoven one with the other." Woolf and Sarraute were born almost a generation apart, the former in 1882 and the latter in 1902. Each is read as similar to and different from modernist and postmodernist male writers, and each has a different relationship to feminism as it is defined by their contemporaries. An investigation of that difference helps to clarify what Sarraute's works offer the feminist reader.

Virginia Woolf is a more quotable subject for the second generation feminist than Nathalie Sarraute. Woolf has written specifically about women's relationship to economic, political, and social issues, and to writing in a post-Victorian world in which she says men are the "arbiters of convention." In light of the fact that the "man's sentence," as Woolf specifies literary tradition in *A Room of One's Own*, is "unsuited for a woman's use," she herself pursues what has been called a "woman's sentence," one that "takes the natural shape of her thought without crushing or distorting it." At the same time, however, Woolf calls for the writer, and the woman writer in particular, to strive for an "impersonal" voice, that is, one which is not conscious of its sex. "It is fatal," Woolf says, "for anyone who writes to be conscious of their sex," for writing founded on such positions "is doomed to death," "it ceases to be fertilised."[4]

The Woolfian critic Makiko Minow-Pinkney argues that it is Woolf's concept of androgyny which "mediates" these two positions. The logic behind their apparent contradiction is, Minow-Pinkney writes, "the principle of *difference* as opposed to the logic of identity. The forgetting of one's sex does not erase difference [. . .]."[5] Unlike Sarraute or postmodernist writers a generation later, Woolf refuses to give up characters, and Minow-Pinkney shows how these characters embody a play of difference to act out a Woolfian androgyny which is Woolf's own model for sexuality. Minow-Pinkney interprets Woolf's concept of androgyny as a Kristevan play between the semiotic and the symbolic that calls into question "the very identities which support [a] pattern of binary opposition. The concept of androgyny," Minow-Pinkney concludes, "then becomes radical, opening up the fixed unity into a multiplicity, joy, play of heterogeneity, a fertile difference."[6]

Patricia Waugh takes Woolf's contradiction in a similar direction as Minow-Pinkney, away from the "logic of identity" and toward the "principle of difference," though Waugh puts it in different terms: away from the question "Who am I?" and toward the question "What represents me?" "This question," Waugh writes, "carries an implicitly and necessary recognition of alienation, the phenomenological perception that 'I' am never at one with myself because always and ever already constituted by others according to whom, and yet outside of what, I take myself to be." Waugh concludes that unlike her male contemporaries, Woolf accepts "the recognition that differentiation is not necessarily separateness, distance, and alienation from others, but a form of *connection* to others," and Woolf embodies that recognition in her characters.[7]

Virginia Woolf's pursuit of a woman's sentence and second generation feminism's search for female identity are compelling when we seek to constitute a sense of autonomy and agency within a discourse which poses "woman" as psychologically, metaphysically, linguistically, and socially *other*. Both Minow-Pinkney and Waugh are sensitive to the second generation desire to privilege the female subject's critical position in relation to the socio-symbolic; each of these critics thus seeks "alternative modes and models of subjectivity" in the works discussed. Patricia Waugh identifies such a model in Woolf's works, that is, "a subject constructed historically through relations with other subjects rather than a subject positioned through discourse in terms of 'alienation' [. . .]"[8] And Minow-Pinkney wonders if woman's "precarious, double position" might not make her "in a sense privileged, in touch with the possibility of a utopian existence which lives at once desire and repression, summons *jouissance* and yet has voice in the socio-symbolic order."[9]

Woolf's creation of female characters who embody her notion of androgyny and who enact differentiation as a form of connection thus keep leading us back to the questions, "Is androgyny a woman's privileged position," and "is connection found only in women's writing," questions which resonate with the other question that has plagued feminist critics for more than a decade—"Is there a woman's writing?" The work of Nathalie Sarraute can help to check this privileging by placing both the reader and her "characters" at the very center of the struggle and the violence of differentiation, and by refusing either access to a privileged position.

Unlike Woolf, Sarraute refuses to join in the feminist debate around the question "Is there a woman's writing." She has stated that "Any good writer is androgynous, he or she has to be, so as to be able to write equally about men and women." As it is embedded in her characters, Woolf's androgyny represents a play between male and female, and it mediates the dual position she finds herself in as a woman writing. Sarraute's call for androgyny operates in another signifying space and represents a move toward what she feels to be the universal subtext of tropistic movement. In Sarraute's works, personal and sexual identity is constructed and deconstructed as diverse subjects interact to align themselves with or distance themselves from the socio-symbolic contract. That contract is most overtly represented by language and the subjects' use of language. Whereas Woolf's use of character enacts what Waugh calls "the deconstruction of the myth of woman as absolute Other," and exposes this myth to be "a position within masculinist discourse," Sarraute's work exposes all identity and character as positions within discourse.[10]

This is a postmodern position, a *nouveau romancier* position, but with two differences that are important for our discussion. The first, obviously and simply, is that Nathalie Sarraute is the only woman who figures as an early member of this group; the second is her adamant assertion that her works present her *personal* vision of a psychological reality which is invisible until the artist makes it visible. It is this assertion that isolates Sarraute from the male group of writers with whom she is identified as they seek in their works to dispel the notion of a surface-depth dichotomy.

Sarraute's insistence on re-presenting *her* view of reality cannot help but be read by the feminist critic in the context of Sarraute who is a *woman* writing, and in this discussion, in light of Woolf's search for "a woman's sentence" "that takes the natural shape of my thoughts." From a second generation feminist position, we could privilege the reality *Sarraute* sees as one that only a woman, positioned both inside and outside the socio-symbolic order *could* see, but Sarraute cautions us against that. If that position is privileged, it is not because it is assigned a gender; it is because that is the position in which she puts us as readers, male and female.

What critics have called Woolf's contradiction between her search for a woman's sentence and her call for the woman writer to be impersonal does not exist for Sarraute as a writer, but for us as her readers; for what Sarraute's work privileges above all is the act of reading. Thus at the narrative level, Sarraute's "characters" become emblematic subjects and objects, positions of discourse, continually putting themselves and being put by others in the subject or object position. Running parallel to this narrative level, the textual strategies at work in Sarraute's novels force the reader to oscillate between two positions of perception traditionally assigned to gender, intellect, and intuition. Tropistic movement becomes an activity that is both observed from outside the text and experienced from within.

Sarraute uses what might be called an impersonal form to present her personal vision. Masculine and feminine pronouns and characters eventually become virtually interchangeable in the fluid world of tropisms her works represent. This is not Woolf's play between masculine and feminine as "real" qualities. It is rather two activities at work simultaneously: a movement between the hard masks of sexual and personal identity and the universal tropistic world beneath these masks; and a play between the reader's lingering desire to construct sexual identity and the text's constant deconstruction of all identity.

In a chronological reading of Sarraute's work, the reader becomes aware that the position of the narrating subject or the narrative point of view that maintains the line between inside and outside, intuitive and analytical becomes more fluid, and with it the line is less easily discernible. The changing nature of the narrative voice and of the interaction between reader and text represents an exploration of the relationship between the polarities of intuition and intellect, and by extension, between the gender constructs of female and male. Sarraute not only succeeds in re-presenting her vision of reality, her works call upon the personal, sexual identity of the reader such that she shifts the question from a concern with the gender of her writing to an exploration of our identity, and by extension, of the gender of our reading.

The works of Virginia Woolf and Nathalie Sarraute offer women writing and reading today access to another "signifying space," another generation. Woolf's female characters, and the androgyny that they embody, enact a notion of differentiation as a form of connection which may help us to fill the "corporeal space" Kristeva envisions. Sarraute leaves the gendered corporeal space alone and addresses her readers in their "desiring mental space." She offers us a more frightening space than Woolf because we are forced to face the socio-symbolic contract alone as readers, deciding for ourselves to what extent differentiation can be a form of connection. Although Sarraute is less quotable for feminist critics, and some of the time less pleasurable to read than Woolf, her works leave us nothing but ourselves, desiring subjects facing a reality which we perceive with varying degrees of familiarity depending upon our experience. We cannot be tempted to a counter-ideology, and this may be potentially a very productive place to situate ourselves if we are to envision a third generation.

*   *   *   *

In his article on Le Planétarium, A. S. Newman underlines Sarraute's irony, noting that "judgements on the psychology of the characters and on the issues raised based on explicit expression are therefore suspect."[11] Similarly, in the conclusion to his study, Valerie Minogue addresses various "misreadings" of Sarraute's novels by which critics have neglected her "fundamental irony" and "are apt to ignore the form of the novels, as if it were an optional extra rather than the creator, shaper, and communicator of their content."[12] The reading of Sarraute's critics reviewed in Chapter 1 addresses my own version of those "misreadings," which is also founded on critics taking the language of these novels at face value and ignoring the examination of language essential there. The investigation of these issues made by both Minogue and Newman has been invaluable to my interpretation, keeping me continually aware of my own tendency to take Sarraute too "seriously" when every possible conclusion one can draw from her novels must be laced with irony and self-reflection. It is the "essential irony" that Newman describes in his phrase "la signification est *autre*" that invites Sarraute's readers to reveal *themselves* in their criticism. The experience of ambiguity provoked by her irony takes place at the most basic level of a subject—*me* as subject, *you* as subject, *us*, *them*, *her*, *him* as subjects—alone and not alone in a meaning-making process, or rather *the* meaning-making process because it is the only one *we* have.

The studies by Minogue and Newman are particularly appealing because they reflect a personal encounter with Sarraute's novel which is both *intellectual* and *intimate*. Their encounters can be described as "intimate" because Sarraute's work seems to have addressed each of these critics at the very juncture of his identification as a reader and a critic. In the preface to her study, Rous-Besser demonstrates a similar attraction to Sarraute on an intimate level when she, a female critic, hails Sarraute as a "pathfinder" and "explorer of *women's* equality," even though her study departs from *that* intimacy to conclude as Minogue does that Sarraute contributes to the "moraliste" tradition, that is, "a far more general concern with *human* truth."[13]

My study of Sarraute's novels veers at times into psychological categories and often takes expressions made by Sarraute's "characters" literally, not in an effort to reduce the irony, but rather as a way of charting what the irony reveals to this woman reader who is also a feminist critic. As Minogue writes, Sarraute "insists on exploring language not in and for itself, but in its profound attachments to human beings striving to express and create themselves."[14] I join all Sarraute's critics who celebrate her exploration into this "même fond commun" which human beings share by virtue of language; but the term itself, as well as the use of the term *universal*, seem to me to obscure the narrative and narrating process which in these novels is enacted by a *variety* of subjects. What may be termed "universal" is the process of exchange and encounter between subjects who have very different reservoirs from which to draw a myriad of constructs as they engage in the fluid and continual process of constituting identity. Thus my encounter with Sarraute's novels, for example, is necessarily different from that made by Newman and Minogue for reasons of gender; our explicit contracts are not the same, and the breaking of that contract thus creates a different conflict.

If the Feminist Reader is tempted (as are Others for different reasons) to read the anonymous observer of the first work as Nathalie Sarraute herself—"Aha! this is a woman's point of view, minute details of silence set in a domestic milieu"—the first two novels serve to problematize that conclusion because sensitivity to tropisms is given to male narrators whose authority is undermined. If this Reader persists—"This woman writer is hiding behind male narrators who are obviously *feminized* by practicing *her* (female) perspective in the world of patriarchy"—*Le Planétarium* introduces female narrators, a mother-daughter conflict, and a Woman Writer who has the last word. But when Germaine Lemaire says, "Je crois que nous sommes bien tous un peu comme ça," the Reader also recalls another *elle* in that novel who interrupts *il* and says, "Ah, je vous garantis que je ne suis pas comme vous." "Well, which is it?" "Continue the chronology," words deformed by linear thinking—yes, continue . . . There it it, *Les Fruits d'Or*, all the female figures are disciples to pontificating males . . . "A critique of Patriarchy. . . ! But . . . Why is the Writer Male in *Entre la vie et la mort?*" "You're naively ignoring the Form of this novel . . . remember the Ambiguity. . . ? . . . And that last image of doubling . . . *il* becomes *nous*. . ." I have been the Hysterical Woman, adhered to Those Images "sur l'écran," been the Young Wife, even defended D. H. Lawrence, "Je crois que nous sommes bien tous un peu comme ça," hated Norman Mailer, "Ah, je vous garantis que je ne suis pas comme vous," and leaned over a piece of writing with a mirror, looking for "une fine buée." But go even further, through the mirror which becomes a window, as Sarraute's statement to Simone Benmussa suggests, "Il y a en nous toutes les virtualités" [There is in us all virtualities]. "Tu m'as souvent dit que tu te sentais neutre, ni homme ni femme" [You've often told me that you felt neutral, neither man nor woman], Benmussa remarks in this interview. "Rien, ni vieux, ni jeune," Sarraute responds, "Cela vous donne une grande liberté" [Nothing, neither old nor young. That gives you a lot of freedom].[15]

"Je la connais. Si vous la connaissiez comme moi. Si vous saviez comment elle est. Comment est-elle? Racontez-la-moi. Oh toi, je te connais. Elle me connaît. Je me connais. Connais-toi toi-même. Je sais comment je suis. Moi, voyez-vous, je suis ainsi fait" [I know her. If you knew her like I do. If you knew how she was. How is she? Tell me about her. Oh you, I know you. She knows me. I know myself. Know yourself. I know how I am. As for me, you see, I'm like that]. Because of the proposed "neutrality" of the narrators in *Portrait d'un inconnu* and

Martereau, the feminist reader's history intervenes in the reading of these novels. By the end of *Vous les entendez?*, however, the exterior world of gender has been eliminated, and the reader is left with what Sarraute says she seeks to create in all her works, "deux consciences d'où est éliminé tout l'extérieur, deux consciences presque à l'état nu, à l'état d'égalité" [two consciousness in which all exterior has been eliminated, two consciousness at an almost nude state, at the state of equality].[16] It is thus that *elle* can replace *il* in the passage above from "*disent les imbéciles.*"

Although certain resonances in Sarraute's novels tempt the feminist reader away from what Sarraute wishes to create, "les réactions entre des consciences, peu importe lesquelles" [reactions between consciousness, it matters little which ones], the experience of finding those resonances delineates the surface, the mirror, of the reader's reading, of her history. In the works that follow, *L'Usage de la parole*, *Enfance*, and *Tu ne t'aimes pas*, words take over and become a kind of window or frame for exchange, much as they did in "*disent...*"; for as Sarraute explains to Benmussa, "C'est le mot [. . .] qui est intéressant ici, ce ne sont pas les consciences elles-mêmes" [It's the word (. . .) that is interesting here, not the consciousnesses themselves].[17] For the feminist reader who is interested in a "de-dramatization of the 'fight to the death' between rival groups and thus between the sexes," the words are interesting as well. It is in the reading and writing of words that she encounters her own desire as she faces the socio-symbolic contract alone, able to look with irony at the constructs she carries within her, with recognition of the history she represents, and with compassion for any Other she may find out there.

Notes

Introduction

1. Sabine Raffy, *Sarraute Romancière: Espaces Intimes* (New York: Peter Lang, 1988).
2. In an interview with Mark Saporata, "Introduction à la connaissance de Nathalie Sarraute," *L'Arc* 95 (1984): 8. Unless otherwise indicated, all English translations are my own.
3. Sarraute, *L'Ere du soupçon* (Paris: Gallimard, 1956), p. 8.
4. Sarraute in an interview with Germaine Brée, trans. Cyril Doherty, *Contemporary Literature* 14, no. 2 (Spring 1973): 140, 141.
5. Ibid., p. 142.
6. Sartre, "Préface," *Portrait d'un inconnu* (Paris: Gallimard, 1956), p. 9. See Sarraute.
7. Mimica Cranaki and Yvon Belaval, *Nathalie Sarraute* (Paris: Gallimard, 1965).
8. Micheline Tison Braun, *Nathalie Sarraute ou la recherche de l'authenticité* (Paris: Gallimard, 1971), p. 9.
9. Toril Moi, ed., *The Kristeva Reader* (New York: Columbia University Press, 1986), p. 187.
10. *The American Heritage Dictionary*, 4th ed. s.v., "evolution."
11. Sarraute, *L'Ere*, p. 147.
12. Alain Robbe-Grillet, *Pour un Nouveau Roman* (Paris: Les Editions de Minuit, 1963), p. 10.
13. *Contemporary Literature* (Spring 1973): 138.
14. In an interview with Jean-Louis Ezine, "Nathalie Sarraute. Sartre s'est trompé à mon sujet," *Nouvelles Littéraires* 2552 (30 September–October 1976): 5.
15. A. S. Newman, "For a New Writing—A New Criticism: Nathalie Sarraute, *Le Planétarium*, *Australian Journal of French Studies* 11, no. 1 (January–April 1974): 118.
16. This is especially true for the following studies: Cranaki and Belaval, *Sarraute*; Christine B. Wunderli-Muller, *Le Thème du masque et des banalités dans l'oeuvre de Nathalie Sarraute* (Zurich: Juris, 1970); Stephen Heath, *The Nouveau Roman: A Study in the Practice of Writing* (Philadelphia: Temple University Press, 1972); A. S. Newman, *Une Poésie des discours* (Geneva: Librairie Droz, 1976); Gretchen Rous-Besser, *Nathalie Sarraute* (Boston: Twayne Publishers, 1979); and André Allemand, *L'Oeuvre romanesque de Nathalie Sarraute* (Neuchâtel: Baconnière, 1980).
17. Newman, *Une Poésie des discours*, p. 13.
18. Raffy, *Sarraute Romancière*, p. 2.
19. For an overview of these discussions, see the following: Toril Moi, *Sexual/Textual Politics* (London: Methuen, 1985); Alice Jardine, *Gynesis* (Ithaca,

N.Y.: Cornell University Press, 1985); Domna C. Stanton, "Language and Revolution: The Franco-American Dis-Connection," in Hester Eisenstein and Alice Jardine, eds., *The Future of Difference* (New Brunswick, N.J.: Rutgers University Press, 1988); and Rita Felski, *Beyond Feminist Aesthetics. Feminist Literature and Social Change* (Cambridge, Mass.: Harvard University Press, 1989).

20. Kristeva, "Women's Time," trans. Alice Jardine and Harry Blake, in *The Kristeva Reader*, p. 209. See Moi. "Le Temps des femmes" was first published in France in *33/44: Cahiers de recherche de sciences des textes et documents* 5 (Winter 1979): 5–19; its first English translation appeared in *Signs* 7, no. 1 (Autumn 1981): 13–35.

21. Moi, *The Kristeva Reader*, p. 187.

22. Kristeva, "Women's Time," ibid., p. 209.

23. For Sarraute's most recent discussion of her "feminism," see the following interview: "The Art of Fiction CXV. Nathalie Sarraute," trans. Jason Weiss and Shusa Guppy, *The Paris Review* 114 (Spring 1990): 150–84. Xavière Gauthier suggests that Sarraute "might be moving" toward "l'écriture féminine" but also implies that others (Marguerite Duras, for example) are moving more specifically in that direction. "Is There Such a Thing as Women's Writing?" trans. Marilyn A. August, in *New French Feminisms* (New York: Shocken Books, 1981), p. 163. See Elaine Marks and Isabelle de Courtivron, eds. Gauthier's essay was originally published in French as "Existe-t-il une écriture de femme?" *Tel Quel* 58 (Summer 1974): 95–104.

24. Rous-Besser, *Sarraute*, p. 8.

25. Helen Watson-Williams, *The Novels of Nathalie Sarraute: Toward an Aesthetic* (Amsterdam: Rodolpi, 1981), pp. 123–24.

26. Valerie Minogue, *Nathalie Sarraute and The War of the Words: A Study of Five Novels* (Edinburgh, U.K.: University of Edinburgh Press, 1981), pp. 171–72.

27. Kristeva, "Women's Time," in *The Kristeva Reader*, p. 209. See Moi.

28. For one interpretation and critique of "l'écriture féminine," see the following: Anne Rosalind Jones, "Writing the Body: Toward an Understanding of l'Ecriture féminine," in Elaine Showalter, ed., *The New Feminist Criticism. Essays on Women, Literature and Theory* (New York: Pantheon Books, 1985), pp. 361–78; also, Jones's article, "Inscribing femininity: French theories of the feminine," in Gayle Greene and Coppélia Kahn, eds., *Making a Difference. Feminist Literary Criticism* (London: Methuen: 1985), pp. 80–112.

29. See, for example, Jonathan Culler's overview of what has come to be called Reader Response Criticism, especially the essay entitled "Reading as a Woman," in *On Deconstruction* (Ithaca, N.Y.: Cornell University Press, 1982), pp. 43–64. For another view, see Patrocinio P. Schweickart's work, "Reading Ourselves: Toward a Feminist Theory of Reading," in Showalter, ed., *Speaking of Gender* (New York: Routledge, Chapman & Hall, 1989), pp. 17–44; and Nancy K. Miller's work, esp. "Changing the Subject: Authorship, Writing, and the Reader," in Teresa de Lauretis, ed., *Feminist Studies. Critical Studies* (Bloomington: Indiana University Press, 1986), pp. 102–20.

30. Newman, "For a New Writing," p. 124.

Chapter 1. Critics Read Sarraute

1. *Contemporary Literature* (Spring 1973): 141. "De Dostoïevski à Kafka" is reprinted in *L'Ere du soupçon*.

2. Nathalie Sarraute, "La Littérature Aujourd'hui," *Tel Quel*, no. 9 (Spring 1962): 50.

3. Nathalie Sarraute, "Les Deux Réalités," *Esprit*, no. 329 (July 1964): 72.

4. In his review article of *L'Ere du soupçon*, Robbe-Grillet describes Sarraute's work as written "à la gloire de la psychologie, non d'une psychologie classique, peut-être, néanmoins d'une psychologie des *profondeurs*" [to the glory of psychology, not a classical psychology perhaps, but nevertheless, to a psychology of *depths*]. "Le Réalisme, la Psychologie et l'Avenir du Roman," *Critique*, nos. 111–12 (December 1956): 695.

5. Sarraute, "Les Deux Réalités," p. 72.

6. Robbe-Grillet continues: "Or tout cela n'a plus guère de sens à partir du moment où l'on s'aperçoit, non seulement chacun voit dans le monde sa propre réalité, mais que le roman est justement ce qui la crée" [None of this makes any sense from the moment when one perceives that not only does one see one's own reality in the world, but that the novel is precisely what creates that reality]. *Pour un Nouveau Roman*, p. 138.

7. Sarraute, "La Littérature Aujourd'hui," p. 49.

8. Stephen Heath, *The Nouveau Roman: A Study in the Practice of Writing* (Philadelphia: Temple University Press, 1972), pp. 18, 65.

9. Newman, *Une Poésie des discours*, p. 5.

10. Cranaki and Belaval, *Sarraute*, p. 9.

11. Heath, *The Nouveau Roman*, p. 24.

12. Ibid., p. 22.

13. Cranaki and Belaval, *Sarraute*, p. 42.

14. Raffy, *Sarraute Romancière*, p. 3.

15. Cranaki and Belaval, *Sarraute*, p. 21.

16. Ibid., p. 26.

17. Ibid., pp. 41–42.

18. Ibid., p. 135.

19. René Micha, *Nathalie Sarraute* (Paris: Editions Universitaires, 1966), pp. 8, 68–69.

20. Ibid., pp. 70, 65.

21. Ibid., p. 66.

22. Rous-Besser, *Sarraute*, p. 13.

23. Ibid., p. 8.

24. Ibid.

25. Ibid., p. 17.

26. For a revealing discussion of this question, see Robert Kanters, "Livres de Femmes ou Littérature Féminine," *Revue de Paris* 75 (August–September 1968): 119–27.

27. Ruth Temple, *Nathalie Sarraute* (New York: Columbia University Press, 1968), p. 3.

28. Ibid., pp. 6–7.

29. Ibid., p. 29.

30. Ibid., pp. 16–17.

31. Ibid., pp. 43–44.

32. Ibid., p. 9.

33. As seen earlier in her comments on Ivy Compton Burnett in *L'Ere du soupçon*, Sarraute not only aspires to participate in a literary evolution but also hopes it will continue beyond her work. Temple's search for analogies is guided by a desire to fix Sarraute in a tradition rather than to reflect upon her stated

relationship to that tradition in much the same way that a categorical approach to Sarraute as a distinctly "woman" writer reveals a second-generation feminist desire to fix a female literary tradition. The difference between these two desires, however, is that Temple is imposing an established tradition on Sarraute's work, while some feminist scholars in the United States have felt and continue to feel that attempts must be made at certain moments to establish a female literary tradition before an investigation of its value can take place. See Elaine Showalter, *A Literature of Their Own: British Women Novelists from Brontë to Lessing* (Princeton, N.J.: Princeton University Press, 1977); and Moi, *Sexual/Textual Politics*, esp. pp. 75–80.

34. Ruth Levinsky, *Nathalie Sarraute and Fedor Dostoevsky* (Lubbock: Texas Tech Press, 1973), p. 3.

35. Ibid., pp. 8, 10.

36. Ibid., p. 5.

37. Ibid., p. 40.

38. Ibid., pp. 6–7. Levinsky lists these shared myths: "repressed desire, such as incest and homosexuality, and the wish to destroy the father; moral constructs, such as good versus evil, the angel as opposed to the devil, good fairies and bad fairies; and thoughts and dreams projected through myth, as in the expression of doubt and in various quests" (40). Fifteen years later, Sabine Raffy also identifies the myths at work in Sarraute's novels, not as static categories, but as signifying systems which Sarraute's characters share with the reader in an effort to establish an identity.

39. Ibid., p. 15.

40. Sarraute, *L'Ere du soupçon*, pp. 41–42.

41. Ibid., pp. 92–93.

42. Cranaki and Belaval, *Sarraute*, p. 131.

43. Rous-Besser, *Sarraute*, pp. 20, 22.

44. Ibid., pp. 140–42.

45. Ibid., p. 164.

46. Ibid., p. 113.

47. Minogue, *The War of the Words*, p. 216, note 10.

48. In an interview, "The Art of Fiction CXV. Nathalie Sarraute," *The Paris Review* 114 (Spring 1990): 160.

49. Jean-Luc Jaccard, *Nathalie Sarraute* (Zurich: Juris, 1967).

50. *Le Thème du masque*, see note 16 above; *La Conscience d'autrui* (Bern: Lang, 1972).

51. Sartre, "Préface," *Portrait d'un inconnu*, pp. 10–11. See Sarraute.

52. Ibid., pp. 12–14.

53. Jaccard, *Sarraute*, p. 6; Wunderli-Muller, *Le Thème du masque*, p. 31; Eliez-Ruegg, *La Conscience d'autrui*, p. 66.

54. Jaccard, *Sarraute*, p. 23; Wunderli-Muller, *Le Thème du masque*, p. 26; Eliez-Ruegg, *La Conscience d'autrui*, pp. 66, 85.

55. Jaccard, *Sarraute*, p. 60; also see pp. 45, 51.

56. Wunderli-Muller, *Le Thème du masque*, p. 62.

57. Ibid., pp. 108–9.

58. Eliez-Ruegg, *La Conscience d'autrui*, p. 126.

59. Ibid., pp. 23–24.

60. Wunderli-Muller, *Le Thème du masque*, p. 109.

61. Eliez-Ruegg, *La Conscience d'autrui*, p. 129.

62. Jaccard, *Sarraute*, p. 91.

63. Cranaki and Belaval, *Sarraute*, p. 87.

64. Ibid., p. 55.

65. Rous-Besser also notes this interaction: "The narrator's creative imagining is not one-sided activity, but part of the inter-creativity implicit in every relationship." *Sarraute*, p. 38.

66. Cranaki and Belaval further observe that Sarraute has two techniques to reveal us to ourselves: "soit que partant des profondeurs du cela, elle nous montre comment il prend forme dans des clichés, soit que, partant de ces clichés eux-mêmes, tels qu'on les emploie chaque jour, elle en fasse sonner le creux et nous dévoile à quelles profondeurs ils se rattachent" [either by beginning with the depth of it all, she shows us how it takes shape in clichés, or by beginning with the clichés themselves, the ones we use every day, she makes them sound false in such a way as to reveal the depths that they are latched on to]. *Sarraute*, p. 115.

67. Ibid., pp. 93–95.

68. Ibid., pp. 118–19.

69. Ibid., p. 109; also see p. 125.

70. Ibid., p. 79.

71. Rous-Besser, *Sarraute*, p. 105.

72. Cranaki and Belaval, *Sarraute*, pp. 44–45; also see pp. 41–42.

73. At the beginning of her study, Tison Braun writes: "Sur le plan esthétique, elle cherche la 'substance romanesque.' Ce mot dangereux, ambigu, semble désigner deux choses. D'abord, la matière première du roman, c'est-à-dire ce qui subsiste sous les débris des sentiments cohérents et des personnalités constituées, et après élimination de tout ce que d'autres arts peuvent rendre aussi bien, ou mieux [. . .]. La substance du roman, c'est son aptitude à exprimer la réalité psychique qui se cache sous les paroles et les actions et dont d'autres arts, comme le théâtre et le cinéma ou l'art du portrait, ne peuvent que suggérer l'existence" [In terms of aesthetics, she searches for the 'novel's substance.' This dangerous, ambiguous word seems to mean two things. First, the primary material of the novel, that is, what remains beneath the debris of coherent sentiments and unified personalities and after the elimination of all that the other arts can render well, or better (. . .). The novel's substance is its ability to express the psychic reality which is hidden beneath the words and actions, whose existence the other arts, like theater and cinema or the art of portraiture, can only suggest]. *La Recherche de l'authenticité*, p. 16. Also see pp. 14, 24–25.

74. Ibid., p. 22.

75. Ibid., p. 24.

76. Cranaki and Belaval, *Sarraute*, p. 75.

77. Temple, *Sarraute*, pp. 16–17.

78. Rous-Besser, *Sarraute*, p. 37.

79. Tison Braun, *La Recherche de l'authenticité*, pp. 13–14.

80. Ibid., p. 15.

81. Ibid., p. 248.

82. Ibid., p. 245.

83. Ibid., p. 57.

84. Ibid., pp. 241–42.

85. Ibid., p. 241.

86. Ibid., p. 250.

87. Watson-Williams, *Toward an Aesthetic*, pp. iii–iv.

88. See, for example, Watson-Williams's statement: "The consistent point of view from which the family incidents are presented through the narrator's consciousness makes him an outstanding example of Sarraute's declared intention to introduce a reader to the world known by the narrator at the same distance from the events as that narrator, and hence the author, adopts" (57–58).

89. Ibid., pp. 71–72.

90. Ibid., p. 115.

91. Ibid., p. 63; also see pp. 116, 122–23, 136–37.

92. Ibid., p. 64.

93. Ibid., p. 155.

94. Ibid., pp. 123–25.

95. In an interview, "The Art of Fiction CXV," p. 161.

96. Monique Wittig, "The Mark of Gender," in Nancy K. Miller, ed., *The Poetics of Gender* (New York: Columbia University, 1986), p. 64.

97. Françoise Calin, *La Vie retrouvée: l'étude sur l'oeuvre romanesque de Nathalie Sarraute* (Paris: Lettres Modernes, 1976), p. 106.

98. Ibid., pp. 10–11. Calin bases her method of presenting both thematic and technical analyses of "le psychologique" on Sarraute's own description of her works as a "recherche dans le domaine de la psychologie" [search in the domain of psychology]: "et j'entends par là, l'exploration et la création, au moyen d'une forme qui lui est propre, d'un nouvel aspect de l'univers mental" [and I mean by that, the exploration and the creation, by means of a form which is its own, of a new aspect of the mental universe] (9).

99. Ibid., pp. 15–16.

100. Ibid., pp. 39–40.

101. Ibid., pp. 126–30.

102. Ibid., pp. 142–43.

103. Ibid., p. 88.

104. Newman, *Une Poésie des discours*, p. 5.

105. Ibid., pp. 1–2, 6.

106. Ibid., p. 7.

107. Ibid., pp. 196–97.

108. Ibid., pp. 154–56.

109. Newman relies on M. J. Lefebvre's distinction of three kinds of referent in terms of the relationship each has to "le réel" [the real]: that of "langage quotidien" [everyday language] in which the words have a referent which exists in the world, for example, the name Napoléon has a historical referent; that of "langage poétique" [poetic language] in which "le téléscopage du mot et du référent est totale" [the telescoping of the word and the referent is total], that is, the intention of poetry to create a third term by the interpenetration of the word and the thing as it may exist in the world; that of the "récit" [story], in which the intention is to disguise the lack of a "référent réel" [real referent], that is, to create the illusion of one. In the works of the *nouveaux romanciers* there is a play on this characteristic of the novel because the process of the creation of the "illusion réaliste" becomes the material of the novel. Newman finds that Sarraute's work destabilizes the principal element on which this characteristic depends, "l'optique" [perspective]: "la signification [. . .] est fonction de l'optique, c'est-à-dire, la source sous-entendue de l'énonciation" [meaning (. . .) is a function of the perspective, that is, the implied source of enunciation]. Ibid., p. 16.

110. Ibid., p. 107.
111. Cranaki and Belaval, *Sarraute*, p. 42.
112. Minogue, *The War of the Words*, p. 1.
113. Ibid., p. 164.
114. Minogue continues: "She teaches implicitly that the humble pursuit of truth is always worthwhile, whatever we are doing, creating, or saying; that authority is no substitute for argument, and words, no matter how loaded, no substitute for thought. She persuades that superiorities are transitory, for 'nous sommes bien tous un peu comme ça (we are all very much a little like that),' and have more in common than we are usually prepared to recognize, whatever our class, sex, race, creed, or colour. All these works testify to the conviction that reality is always on the underside of language, and humility the natural and only mode of pursuing truth" (191–92).
115. Ibid., pp. 172–74.
116. Ibid., p. 172.
117. Ibid., p. 50.
118. Valerie Minogue, "Childhood Imagery in Nathalie Sarraute's *Portrait d'un inconnu*," *French Studies* 27, no. 2 (April 1972): 177–78, 186.
119. Minogue, *The War of the Words*, p. 26. In his conclusion, Minogue gives this psychological process more universal dimensions: "It is arguably somewhere in the war of the words and the struggle to define the self that the real wars originate, and it is from the arsenal of words that politics derives its powerful rhetoric. The movements of the cell may be as revealing as the march of armies" (172).
120. Ibid., pp. 1–2.
121. Allemand, *L'Oeuvre romanesque de Nathalie Sarraute*, p. 116.
122. Ibid., p. 119.
123. Ibid., p. 302.
124. Ibid., p. 295.
125. Ibid., pp. 307–421.
126. Ibid., pp. 460–61.
127. Ibid., p. 299.
128. Raffy, *Sarraute Romancière*, pp. 2–5.
129. Ibid., pp. 250–51.

Chapter 2. A Feminist Reading *Tropismes*

1. See Elaine Showalter, *The New Feminist Criticism*, esp. the Introduction.
2. One of the many instances in which Sarraute has emphasized the personal intention motivating her renovation of the novel form is found in an interview cited by Valerie Minogue: "As far as the rejection of tradition and the necessity to escape from the conventions of the novel are concerned, I had felt the need for that long before the *nouveau roman*. As for the latter's emphasis on objective description of the external and on formalistic language experimentation, I do not agree with it at all." *The War of the Words*, p. 16.
3. Sarraute, *L'Ere du soupçon*, p. 8.
4. Moi, *Sexual/Textual Politics*, p. 108.
5. Verena A. Conley, *Hélène Cixous: Writing the Feminine* (Lincoln: University of Nebraska Press, 1984), p. 129.

6. Kristeva, "Women's Time," in *The Kristeva Reader*, p. 194. See Moi.

7. Patrocinio Schweickart, "Reading Ourselves," in *Speaking of Gender*, p. 31. See Showalter.

8. Minogue, *The War of the Words*, p. 216, note 10.

9. Sandra Gilbert and Susan Gubar, *The Madwoman in the Attic: The Woman Writer and the Nineteenth-Century Literary Imagination* (New Haven: Yale University Press, 1979), p. 46.

10. Ibid., p. 49.

11. Ibid., p. 73.

12. One of the earlier versions of this criticism is found in Annie LeClerc, *Parole de femme* (Paris: Grasset, 1974).

13. Cranaki and Belaval, *Sarraute*, p. 1.

14. Elaine Showalter, "Feminism in the Wilderness," in *The New Feminist Criticism*, p. 248. See Showalter.

15. Gauthier, "Is There Such a Thing as Women's Writing?" in *New French Feminisms*, p. 95. See Marks and Courtivron.

16. These categories have been somewhat simplified for this discussion. For a more indepth study, see Moi, *Sexual/Textual Politics*, esp. part 1; and Jardine, *Gynesis*, esp. "The Woman-in-Effect."

17. Newman, *Une Poésie des discours*, p. 2.

18. I am able to formulate my response in this way because of an essay by Nelly Furman, "Textual Feminism," in Sally McConnell-Ginet, Ruth Borker, and Nelly Furman, eds., *Women and Language in Literature and Society* (New York: Praeger, 1980), pp. 45–55.

19. Lynn Sukenick, "Women in Fiction," in A. Diamond and L. Edwards, eds., *The Authority of Experience: Essays in Feminist Criticism* (Amherst: University of Massachusetts Press, 1977), pp. 34–36.

20. Susan Griffin, *Woman and Nature: The Roaring Inside Her* (New York: Harper & Row, 1978); Hélène Cixous and Catherine Clément, *La Jeune Née* (Paris: Union Général d'Editions, 1975); translated under the title *The Newly Born Woman* by Betsy Wing, introduction by Sandra M. Gilbert (Minneapolis: University of Minnesota Press, 1986).

21. Emil Benveniste, *Problems in General Linguistics*, trans. Mary Elizabeth Meek (Coral Gables, Fla.: University of Miami Press, 1971), pp. 197–98. Also see pp. 200–201. Originally published in French as *Problèmes de linguistique générale* (Paris: Gallimard, 1966).

22. Nathalie Sarraute, *Tropismes* (Paris: Les Editions de Minuit, 1957), pp. 21–23. "Tropismes III" has been reproduced with the permission of Les Editions de Minuit.

23. Benveniste, *Problems of General Linguistics*, pp. 218–19.

24. *Le Petit Robert*, s.v. "sombre."

25. *Le Petit Robert*, s.v. "modeste."

26. Sarraute, *L'Ere du soupçon*, p. 8.

Chapter 3. Readers Talking: *Les Fruits d'Or*

1. In an interview with Genviève Serreau, "Nathalie Sarraute et les secrets de la création," *La Quinzaine Littérature*, no. 50 (1–15 May 1968).

2. Minogue, *The War of the Words*, p. 138.

3. Minogue describes these chapters as offering "a structure, which illumi-

nates the multiple situations of similar structure that occur in the course of the novel: "[. . . The] *dramatis personae* in these first pages are limited to three. They are a man and woman, who form a somewhat uneasy couple, and their host. The action is of the simplest: it centers on the host's production of a print of a Courbet painting for the admiration of the couple. We are introduced to the feelings and movements of all three in relation to this single action. The Courbet print here plays the part later played by 'Les Fruits d'Or.'" Ibid., p. 114.

4. Nathalie Sarraute, *Les Fruits d'Or* (Paris: Gallimard, 1963), pp. 8, 10. Further page references to citations from this novel appear in parentheses within the text.

5. Kristeva, "Women's Time," in *The Kristeva Reader*, p. 200. See Moi.

6. For different accounts of the effect of this "totalitarian" view, see Showalter, *A Literature of Their Own*; Ellen Moers, *Literary Women: The Great Writers* (New York: Doubleday, 1976; reprint London: The Women's Press, 1977); Gilbert and Gubar, *The Madwoman in the Attic*; and Tillie Olsen, *Silences* (London: Virago, 1980).

7. The text tells us that "elle voudrait être une de ces petites rides autour de ses yeux fatigués d'avoir fixé avec quelle concentration, quelle acuité, tant de toiles, de statues [. . .] signées de noms inconnus, où elle, (à qui oserait-elle jamais l'avouer?) elle, ignorante, insensible, n'aurait vu qu'un magma hideux) [. . .]" [she would like to be one of those little wrinkles around his eyes, worn out from having studied with such concentration, such acuity, so many paintings, statues (. . .) signed by unknowns, where she (to whom could she ever dare admit such a thing?), she, ignorant, insensitive, would only have seen a hideous muddle (. . .)] (36).

8. This "truth" is given some elaboration in the text: "C'est là. Ce qu'elles cherchent toujours, fouillant avidement dans tout ce qui passe à leur portée, dans tout ce qui leur est offert, préparé, pour elles spécialement . . . films, romans, biographies, mémoires, confidences de leurs petites soeurs souffrantes, compatissantes, conseils, exemples de leurs grandes soeurs plus heureuses et fortes, triomphantes . . . bribes qu'elles arrachent et emportent pour les examiner à l'écart, craintives, un peu honteuses, jamais très sûres . . . Mais cette fois . . . elles tendent le cou [. . .], elles peuvent tout prendre, encouragées par tous, admirées pour leur bon goût, tout ce qui leur convient" [It's there. What they always look for, digging madly in everything that passes within their reach, in everything that is offered to them, prepared, especially for them . . . films, novels, biographies, mémoires, confidences from their little suffering sisters, sympathetic, advice, examples of their happier, stronger big sisters, triumphant . . . scraps they attach and carry around to look at in secret, fearful, a little ashamed, never very sure of themselves . . . But this time . . . they crane their necks (. . .), they can take anything, admired as they are for their good taste, everything suits them] (44).

9. Minogue, *The War of the Words*, p. 125.

10. See Part 1, Gilbert and Gubar, *The Madwoman in the Attic*; and Showalter, *The New Feminist Criticism*.

11. See Nancy K. Miller, "Women's Autobiography in France: For a Dialectics of Identification," in McConnell-Ginet, Borker and Furman, *Women and Language*, pp. 258–73; Jonathan Culler, *On Deconstruction* (Ithaca, New York: Cornell University Press, 1982); and Felsky, *Beyond Feminist Aesthetics*.

12. Minogue, *The War of the Words*, p. 122.

13. Ibid., p. 138. Minogue interprets the narrator's words, "people like me"

and "people like you" as referring to Bréhier, even though such a reference takes the narrator out of "direct contact" with the work itself. He recognizes that the object of the narrator's "apostrophe" is ambiguous, citing Ann Jefferson's article in which she says that "address resolves the impossible problems of definition" (137).

14. Judith Gardiner, "Mind Mother: Psychoanalysis and Feminism," in *Making a Difference: Feminist Literary Criticism*, p. 121. See Greene.

Chapter 4. Identity Quests: Male

1. Nathalie Sarraute, "Ce que je cherche à faire," in Jean Ricardou and Françoise Rossum-Guyom, eds., *Pratiques, Nouveau Roman: Hier, Aujourd'hui*, vol. 2 (Paris: Union Générale d'Editions, 1972), p. 29.

2. Nathalie Sarraute, *Portrait d'un inconnu* (Paris: Gallimard, 1956), p. 68. Further references to citations from this novel appear in parentheses within the text.

3. *Contemporary Literature* (Spring 1973): 140.

4. Minogue, *The War of the Words*, p. 31. Minogue has a particularly interesting discussion of this narrator's tentative authority: "While the narrative thus weakens [the reader's] resistances based on convention and 'normality,' it does not seek to raise its own versions to an authoritative level. On the contrary, the narrative remains resolutely tentative, despite N's inevitable longings for approval and assent" (39–40).

5. See especially, Robbe-Grillet, "Nature, humanisme, tragédie," and "Nouveau Roman, homme nouveau," *Pour un nouveau roman*; Roland Barthes, *Essais critique* (Paris: Editions du Seuil, 1964); and *S/Z* (Paris: Editions du Seuil, 1970); Rosalind Coward and John Ellis, *Language and Materialism: Developments in Semiology and the Theory of the Subject* (London: Routledge & Kegan Paul, 1977); Moers, *Literary Women*; Showalter, *A Literature of Their Own*; Gilbert and Gubar, *The Madwoman in the Attic*; Marks and de Courtivron, *New French Feminisms*.

6. Moi, *Sexual-Textual Politics*, p. 132.

7. See Laura Mulvey, "Visual Pleasure and Narrative Cinema," *Visual and Other Pleasures* (Bloomington: Indiana University Press, 1989); Teresa De Lauretis, "Desire in Narrative," *Alice Doesn't. Feminism, Semiotics, Cinema* (Bloomington: Indiana University Press, 1984); Constance Penley, *Feminism and Film Theory* (New York: Routledge, Chapman & Hall, 1988).

8. In one interview, for example, Sarraute says, "Je prends [les personnages] toujours dans des conditions où ils pourraient être aussi bien des femmes que des hommes, où ils sont 'neutres'" [I always take (the characters) where they could just as easily be women and men, where they are "neutered/neutral"]. Simone Benmussa, *Nathalie Sarraute: Qui êtes-vous? Conversations avec Simone Benmussa* (Paris: La Manufacture, 1987), p. 144.

9. *Contemporary Literature* (Spring 1973): 141.

10. Minogue, *The War of the Words*, pp. 58–59, 61.

11. Nathalie Sarraute, *Martereau* (Paris: Gallimard, 1953), p. 7. Further references to citations from this novel appear in parentheses within the text.

12. See Georges Matoré, *Le Vocabulaire et la société sous Louis-Philippe*, (Genève: Libraire Droz, 1951). Matoré describes the feminization of dandies and artists in nineteenth-century France. He writes: "Comme ceux des femmes

leurs sentiments atteignent facilement le paroxysme" (49). Kari Weil also discusses the romantic artist as *androgyne*, one who must negotiate both masculine (public) and feminine (private) domains, that is, both the values of a bourgeois, industrialized society upheld by males and the interiority of feelings associated with females. See *Androgyny and the Denial of Difference* (Charlottesville, Va.: University of Virginia Press, forthcoming).

13. Minogue, *War of the Words*, p. 82.

Chapter 5. Identity at Play: Male-Female

1. Nathalie Sarraute, *Le Planétarium* (Paris: Gallimard, 1959), p. 13. All further references to citations from this novel appear in parentheses within the text.

2. Minogue, *The War of the Words*, p. 109.

3. In Sarraute's novels identity is constructed through narration. Minogue comments that *Le Planétarium* shows narration to be a "bid for possession of the world, an attempt by the narrator to make the world support for his own identity." All the characters "are guilty of trying to make the world over into a property with the function of reflecting a desired image," and all these attempts fail, enacting "a systematic questioning of the narrator, the act of narration." Minogue traces how Sarraute reduces Alain from individually mastering his role as narrator, to "Alain as simply part of 'nous tous.'" Ibid., pp. 92–93.

4. Newman, *Une Poésie des discours*, pp. 47, 54–56, 60–61.

5. Kristeva, "Women's Time," in *The Kristeva Reader*, p. 209. See Moi.

6. Newman cites this passage as exemplary of the "typically Sarrautien device of repetition with changed narrative perspective." "For a New Writing— A New Criticism," pp. 123–24.

7. After a scene in Chapter 13 in which Germaine Lemaire and her coterie pay an unexpected call on Alain, the next chapter begins with an image drawn from tales of cowboys and Indians which recreates the sensation of having been invaded. This passage could easily describe Gisèle's sensation on returning home after "strangers" have visited her little "nest": "Sur la poussière d'une des pistes menant au ranch on a vu des traces insolites de grands pieds nus" [In the dust of one of the paths leading to the ranch, discomfiting prints of big, bare feet were seen] (176). A page later, the speaker is identified as "ma petite Berthe."

8. Monique Wittig, "The Place of Action," in *Three Decades of the French Novel*, pp. 134–37. See Oppenheim.

9. Nathalie Sarraute, *Entre la vie et la mort* (Paris: Gallimard, 1968), pp. 82–85. All further references to citations from this novel appear in parentheses within the text.

10. Newman, *Une Poèsie des discours*, pp. 13–14.

11. Ibid., p. 2.

12. Hélène Cixous, "The Laugh of the Medusa," trans. Keith Cohen and Paula Cohen, in *New French Feminisms*, p. 247. See Marks and de Courtivron. This translation first appeared in *Signs* (Summer 1976), and it is a revised version of "Le Rire de la méduse," *L'Arc* (1975): 39–54.

Chapter 6. Identity in Process: I-You-We-They

1. Nathalie Sarraute, *Vous les entendez?* (Paris: Gallimard, 1970), p. 9. All further references to citations from this novel appear in parentheses within the text.

2. Jardine, *Gynesis*, p. 25.

3. Nathalie Sarraute, *"disent les imbéciles"* (Paris: Gallimard, 1970), pp. 9–10. All further references to citations from this novel appear in parentheses within the text.

4. For a discussion of the use of address in Sarraute's novels, see Ann Jefferson, "What's in a name? . . .? From surname to pronoun in the novels of Nathalie Sarraute," *PTL: A Journal for Descriptive Poetics and Theory of Literature*, no. 2 (1977): 205–20. "Address resolves the impossible problem of definition" (217).

5. Minogue, *The War of the Words*, p. 109.

6. Minogue speaks of the "wax-modeling" that goes on among the figures of *"disent les imbéciles"*, "this is an area where adjectives congeal into a mask." Ibid., p. 188.

7. Newman uses the term "retarded intellection" to refer to this replacement of intellectual by sensual experience. "For a New Writing—A New Criticism," p. 123.

8. Minogue, *War of the Words*, p. 189.

9. Ibid.

10. Minogue also calls attention to this passage and connects it to Sarraute's other novels: "If *Les Fruits d'or* already showed the spurious self-definitions underpinning the expression of literary judgements, *'disent les imbéciles'* takes the reader into the very heart of that self-defining movement, into that crucial area where, as in *Entre la vie et la mort*, 'faire' and 'être' dangerously and often comically intermingle." Ibid., p. 188.

11. Heath, *The Nouveau Roman*, p. 62.

12. Wittig, "The Place of Action," p. 138. See Oppenheim.

Chapter 7. A Space Beyond?

1. Raffy, *Sarraute Romancière*, pp. 250–51. This citation is quoted in its entirety in Chapter 1 of this study.

2. Kristeva, "Women's Time," in *The Kristeva Reader*, p. 209. See Moi.

3. Ibid., p. 200.

4. These quotes from Woolf come from *Collected Essays* and *A Room of One's Own*; cited in Minow-Pinkney, *Virginia Woolf and The Problem of the Subject* (New Brunswick, N.J.: Rutgers University Press, 1977), pp. 4–8.

5. Ibid., p. 8.

6. Ibid., pp. 10, 12.

7. Patricia Waugh, *Feminine Fictions: Revisiting the Post-Modern* (New York: Routledge, 1989), p. 11.

8. Ibid., pp. 20–21.

9. Minow-Pinkney, *Virginia Woolf*, p. 22.

10. Waugh, *Feminine Fictions*, pp. 8–9.

11. Newman, "For a New Writing—A New Criticism," p. 125.

12. Minogue, *The War of the Words*, p. 166.
13. Ibid., p. 172.
14. Ibid., p. 176.
15. Benmussa, *Nathalie Sarraute. Qui êtes vous?*, pp. 81, 76.
16. Ibid., p. 121.
17. Ibid.

Works Consulted

Allemand, André. *L'Oeuvre romanesque de Nathalie Sarraute*. Neuchâtel, Suisse: Baconnière, 1980.

Barthes, Roland. *Essais critiques*. Paris: Editions du Seuil, 1964.

——. *S/Z*. Paris: Editions du Seuil, 1970.

Benmussa, Simone. *Nathalie Sarraute. Qui êtes vous? Conversations avec Simone Benmussa*. Paris: La Manufacture, 1987.

Benveniste, Emil. *Problems of General Linguistics*. Translated by Mary Elizabeth Meek. Coral Gables, Fla.: University of Miami Press, 1971. Originally published in French, *Problèmes de linguistique générale*. Paris: Editions Gallimard, 1966.

Brée, Germaine. "Experimental Novels? Yes, But Perhaps 'Otherwise': Nathalie Sarraute, Monique Wittig." In *Breaking the Sequence: Women's Experimental Fiction*, edited by Friedman and Fuchs.

Calin, Françoise. *La Vie retrouvée: l'étude sur l'oeuvre romanesque de Nathalie Sarraute*. Paris: Lettres Modernes, 1976.

Cixous, Hélène. "The Laugh of the Medusa." Translated by Keith Cohen and Paula Cohen. In *New French Feminisms*, edited by Marks and deCourtivron. Originally published in French, "Le Rire de la méduse." *L'arc* (1975): 39–54.

——., and Catherine Clément. *La Jeune Née*. Paris: Union Générale d'Editions, 1975.

Cohn, Ruby. "Sisters Under the Skin: Virginia Woolf and Nathalie Sarraute." In *Un nouveau roman?*, edited by John H. Matthews. Paris: La Revue des Lettres Modernes, 1964.

Conley, Verena A. *Hélène Cixous: Writing the Feminine*. Lincoln: University of Nebraska Press, 1984.

Coward, Rosalind and John Ellis. *Language and Materialism: Developments in Semiology and the Theory of the Subject*. London: Routledge & Kegan Paul, 1977.

Cranaki, Mimica and Yvon Belaval. *Nathalie Sarraute*. Paris: Gallimard, 1965.

Culler, Jonathan. *On Deconstruction*. Ithaca, N.Y.: Cornell University Press, 1982.

de Beauvoir, Simone. *La Force des choses*. Paris: Gallimard, 1963.

de Lauretis, Teresa. *Alice Doesn't. Feminism, Semiotics, Cinema*. Bloomington: Indiana University Press, 1984.

——, ed. *Feminist Studies. Critical Studies*. Bloomington: Indiana University Press, 1986.

Diamond, A., and L. Edwards, eds. *The Authority of Experience: Essays in Feminist Criticism*. Amherst: University of Massachusetts Press, 1977.

Eisenstein, Hester, and Alice Jardine, eds. *The Future of Difference*. New Brunswick, N.J.: Rutgers University Press, 1988.

Eliez-Ruegg, Elisabeth. *La Conscience d'autrui et la conscience des objects dans l'oeuvre de Nathalie Sarraute*. Berne, Suisse: Lang, 1972.

Felski, Rita. *Beyond Feminist Aesthetics. Feminist Literature and Social Change*. Cambridge, Mass.: Harvard University Press, 1989.

Freund, Elisabeth. *Return to the Reader*. London: Methuen, 1987.

Friedman, Ellen G. and Miriam Fuchs, eds. *Breaking the Sequence. Women's Experimental Fiction*. Princeton: Princeton University Press, 1989.

Furman, Nelly. "Textual Feminism." In *Women and Language in Literature and Society*, edited by McConnell-Ginet, Borker, and Furman.

Gardiner, Judith Kegan. "Mind mother: psychoanalysis and feminism." In *Making a Difference. Feminist Literary Criticism*, edited by Greene and Kahn.

Gauthier, Xavière. "Is There Such a Thing as Women's Writing?" Translated by Marilyn A. August. In *New French Feminisms*, edited by Marks and de Courtivron. Originally published in French, "Existe-t-elle une écriture féminine?" *Tel Quel*, no. 58 (Summer 1974): 95–104.

Gilbert, Sandra, and Susan Gubar, eds. *The Female Imagination and the Modernist Aesthetic*. New York: Gordon & Breach Science Publishers, 1986.

———. *Madwoman in the Attic*. New Haven: Yale University Press, 1979.

Greene, Gayle, and Coppélia Kahn, eds. *Making a Difference. Feminist Literary Criticism*. London: Methuen, 1985.

Griffin, Susan. *Woman and Nature: The Roaring Inside Her*. New York: Harper & Row, 1978.

Heath, Stephen. *The Nouveau Roman: A Study in the Practice of Writing*. Philadelphia: Temple University Press, 1972.

Irving, Katrina. "Still Hesitating on the Threshold: Feminist Theory and the Question of the Subject." *NWSA Journal* 1, no. 4 (Summer 1989): 630–43.

Jaccard, Jean-Luc. *Nathalie Sarraute*. Zurich, Suisse: Juris, 1967.

Jardine, Alice. *Gynesis. Configurations of Women and Modernity*. Ithaca, New York: Cornell University Press, 1985.

Jefferson, Anne. "What's in a name? From surname to pronoun in the novels of Nathalie Sarraute." *PTL: A Journal for descriptive Poetics and Theory of Literature*, no. 2 (1977): 205–20.

———. "Imagery versus Description: The Problematics of Representation in the Novels of Nathalie Sarraute." *Modern Language Review* 73, no. 3 (July 1978): 513–24.

Jones, Anne Rosalind. "Inscribing Femininity: French theories of the feminine." In *Making a Difference: Feminist Literary Criticism*, edited by Greene and Kahn. London: Methuen, 1985.

———. "Writing the Body: Toward an Understanding of *l'Ecriture féminine*." In *The New Feminist Criticism. Essays on Women, Literature and Theory*, edited by Elaine Showalter. New York: Pantheon Books, 1985.

Kanters, Robert. "Livres de Femmes ou Littérature Féminine." *Revue de Paris* 75 (August–September 1968): 119–27.

Kristeva, Julia. "Women's Time." Translated by Alice Jardine and Harry Blake. In *The Kristeva Reader*, edited by Toril Moi. New York: Columbia University Press, 1986.

LeClerc, Annie. *Parole de femme*. Paris: Grasset, 1974.

Levinsky, Ruth. *Nathalie Sarraute and Fedor Dostoevsky*. Lubbock: Texas Tech Press, 1973.

Matoré, Georges. *Le Vocabulaire et la société sous Louis-Philippe*. Geneva (Switzerland): Librairie Droz, 1951.

Marini, Marcelle. *Territoire du féminin avec Marguerite Duras*. Paris: Minuit, 1977.

Marks, Elaine, and Isabelle de Courtivron, eds. *New French Feminisms*. New York: Shocken Books, 1981; reprinted, 1988.

Matthews, John H., ed. *Un nouveau roman?* Paris: La Revue des Lettres Modernes, 1964.

McConnell-Ginet, Sally, Ruth Borker, Nelly Furman, eds. *Women and Language in Literature and Society*. New York: Praeger, 1980.

Meese, Elizabeth, and Alice Parker, eds. *The Difference Within: Feminism and Critical Theory*. Philadelphia, Penna.: John Benjamin, 1989.

Micha, René. *Nathalie Sarraute*. Paris: Editions Universitaires, 1966.

Miller, Nancy K. "Changing the Subject: Authorship, Writing, and the Reader." In *Feminist Studies. Critical Studies*, edited by de Lauretis. Bloomington: Indiana University Press, 1986.

———, ed. *The Poetics of Gender*. New York: Columbia University Press, 1986.

———. "Women's Autobiography in France: For a Dialectics of Identification." In *Women and Language in Literature and Society*, edited by McConnell-Ginet, Borker, and Furman. New York: Praeger, 1980.

Minogue, Valerie. "Childhood Imagery in Nathalie Sarraute's *Portrait d'un inconnu*." *French Studies* 27, no. 2 (April 1972): 177–86.

———. *Nathalie Sarraute and the War of the Words: A Study of Five Novels*. Edinburgh, UK: Edinburgh University Press, 1981.

Minow-Pinkney, Mikako. *Virginia Woolf and the Problem of the Subject*. New Brunswick, N.J.: Rutgers University Press, 1987.

Moers, Ellen. *Literary Women: The Great Writers*. New York: Doubleday, 1976; reprinted, London: The Women's Press, 1977.

Moi, Toril, ed. *The Kristeva Reader*. New York: Columbia University Press, 1986.

———. *Sexual/Textual Politics*. London: Methuen, 1985.

Mulvey, Laura. *Visual and Other Pleasures*. Bloomington: Indiana University, 1989.

Newman, A. S. "For A New Writing—A New Criticism: Nathalie Sarraute, *Le Planétarium*." *Australian Journal of French Studies* 11, no. 1 (January–April 1974): 118–28.

———. *Une Poèsie des discours*. Geneva (Switzerland): Librairie Droz, 1976.

Olsen, Tillie. *Silences*. London: Virago, 1980.

Oppenheim, Lois, ed. *Three Decades of the New Novel*. Translated by Lois Oppenheim and Evelyne Costa de Beauregard. Urbana: University of Illinois Press, 1986.

Penley, Constance. *Feminism and Film Theory*. New York: Routledge, Chapman & Hall, 1988.

Pierrot, Jean. *Nathalie Sarraute*. Paris: Librairie José Corti, 1990.

Raffy, Sabine. *Sarraute Romancière: Espaces Intimes*. New York: Peter Lang, 1988.

Ricardou, Jean, and Françoise Rossum-Guyom, eds. *Nouveau roman: hier, aujourd'hui*. 2 vols. Paris: Union Générale d'Editions, 1972.

Robbe-Grillet, Alain. "Le Réalisme, la Psychologie et l'Avenir du Roman." *Critique*, nos. 111–112 (December 1956): 695–701.

——. *Pour un Nouveau Roman*. Paris: Les Editions de Minuit, 1963.

Rous-Besser, Gretchen. *Nathalie Sarraute*. Boston: Twayne Publishers, 1979.

Sarraute, Nathalie. "Ce que je cherche à faire." Contribution to the Colloque at Cérisy-la-Salle, July 1971. In *Nouveau roman: hier, aujourd'hui*, vol. 2 *Pratiques*, edited by Ricardou and Rossum-Guyon. Paris: Union Générale d'Editions, 1972.

——. *"disent les imbéciles"*. Paris: Gallimard, 1969.

——. "Les Deux Réalités." *Esprit* (July 1964): 72–75.

——. *Enfance*. Paris: Gallimard, 1983.

——. *Entre la vie et la mort*. Paris: Gallimard, 1968.

——. *L'Ere du soupçon*. Paris: Gallimard, 1956.

——. *Les Fruits d'Or*. Paris: Gallimard, 1963.

——. "Inside Stories." Interview with John Ardagh. *Guardian* (London) 31 August 1977.

——. Interview with Germaine Brée. Translated by Cyril Doherty. *Contemporary Literature* 14, no. 2 (Spring 1973): 138–46.

——. Interview with Jean-Louis Ezine. "Nathalie Sarraute. Sartre s'est trompé à mon sujet." *Nouvelles Littéraires*, no. 2552 (30 September–6 October 1976): 5.

——. Interview with Marc Saporata. "Introduction à la connaissance de Nathalie Sarraute." *Arc 95* (1984).

——. "La Littérature Aujourd'hui." *Tel Quel*, no. 9 (Spring 1962): 48–53.

——. *Martereau*. Paris: Gallimard, 1953.

——. "Nathalie Sarraute et les secrets de la création." Propos recueillis par Geneviève Serreau. *La Quinzaine Littéraire*, no. 50 (1–15 May 1968).

——. *Le Planétarium*. Paris: Gallimard, 1959.

——. *Portrait d'un inconnu*. Paris: Gallimard, 1956.

——. "The Art of Fiction CXV. Nathalie Sarraute." Translated by Jason Weiss and Shusa Guppy. *The Paris Review*, no. 114 (Spring 1990): 150–84.

——. *Tropismes*. Paris: Les Editions de Minuit, 1957.

——. *Tu ne t'aimes pas*. Paris: Gallimard, 1989.

——. *L'Usage de la parole*. Paris: Gallimard, 1980.

——. "Virginia Woolf ou la Visionnaire du 'Maintenant.'" *Lettres Françaises*, 29 June–5 July 1961.

——. *Vous les entendez?* Paris: Gallimard, 1970.

Sartre, Jean-Paul. "Préface." In *Portrait d'un inconnu*, Nathalie Sarraute. Paris: Gallimard, 1956.

Schweickart, Patrocinio. "Reading Ourselves: Toward a Feminist Theory of Reading." In *Speaking of Gender*, edited by Elaine Showalter. New York: Routledge, Chapman & Hall, 1989.

Showalter, Elaine. "Feminist Criticism in the Wilderness." In *The New Feminist Criticism. Essays on Women, Literature and Theory.* New York: Pantheon Books, 1985.

———. *A Literature of Their Own: British Women Novelists from Brontë to Lessing.* Princeton: Princeton University Press, 1977.

———, ed. *The New Feminist Criticism. Essays on Women, Literature and Theory.* New York: Pantheon Books, 1985.

———, ed. *Speaking of Gender.* New York: Routledge, Chapman & Hall, 1989.

Stanton, Domna C. "Language and Revolution: The Franco-American Dis-Connection." In *The Future of Difference,* edited by Eisenstein and Jardine. New Brunswick, N.J.: Rutgers University Press, 1988.

Sukenick, Lynn. "Women in Fiction." In *The Authority of Experience: Essays in Feminist Criticism,* edited by Diamond and Edwards. Amherst: University of Massachusetts Press, 1977.

Temple, Ruth A. *Nathalie Sarraute.* New York: Columbia University Press, 1968.

Tison Braun, Micheline. *Nathalie Sarraute ou la recherche de l'authenticité.* Paris: Gallimard, 1971.

Watson-Williams, Helen. *The Novels of Nathalie Sarraute: Toward an Aesthetic.* Amsterdam: Rodolpi, 1981.

Waugh, Patricia. *Feminine Fictions: Revisiting the Post-modern.* New York: Routledge, 1989.

Weil, Kari. *Androgyny and the Denial of Difference.* Charlottesville: University of Virginia Press, forthcoming.

Wittig, Monique. "The Mark of Gender." In *The Poetics of Gender,* edited by Nancy K. Miller. Bloomington: Indiana University Press, 1986.

———. "The Place of Action." In *Three Decades of the New Novel,* edited by Louis Oppenheim. Urbana: University of Illinois Press, 1986.

Wunderli-Muller, Christine B. *Le Thème du masque et des banalités dans l'oeuvre de Nathalie Sarraute.* Zurich, Suisse: Juris, 1970.

Index